Media Entertainment
The Psychology of Its Appeal

LEA's Communication Series

Jennings Bryant and Dolf Zillmann, General Editors

Selected titles in Mass Communication (Alan Rubin, Advisory Editor) include:

Alexander/Owers/Carveth • Media Economics: Theory and Practice, Second Edition

Harris • A Cognitive Psychology of Mass Communication, Third Edition

Moore • Mass Communication Law and Ethics, Second Edition

Moore/Farrar/Collins • Advertising and Public Relations Law

Sohn/Wicks/Lacy/Sylvie • Media Management: A Casebook Approach, Second Edition

Van Evra • Television and Child Development, Second Edition

For a complete list of titles in LEA's Communication Series
please contact Lawrence Erlbaum Associates, Publishers

Media Entertainment
The Psychology of Its Appeal

Edited by

Dolf Zillmann
University of Alabama

Peter Vorderer
University of Music and Theater, Hannover, Germany

 LAWRENCE ERLBAUM ASSOCIATES, PUBLISHERS

2000   Mahwah, New Jersey   London

Lawrence Erlbaum Associates, Inc., Publishers
10 Industrial Avenue
Mahwah, NJ 07430

Cover design by Kathryn Houghtaling Lacey

Library of Congress Cataloging-in-Publication Data

   Media entertainment : the psychology of its appeal / edited by
Dolf Zillmann, Peter Vorderer.
      p. cm.
   Includes bibliographical references and index.
   ISBN 0-8058-3324-2 (cloth : alk. paper) —
   ISBN 0-8058-3325-0 (pbk. : alk. paper)
   1. Mass media—Psychological aspects. I. Zillmann, Dolf.
II. Vorderer, Peter.
   P96.P75 M34   2000
   302.23'01'9—dc21   99-059306
                                                          CIP

Books published by Lawrence Erlbaum Associates are printed on
acid-free paper, and their bindings are chosen for strength and dura-
bility.

Printed in the United States of America
10 9 8 7 6 5 4 3 2 1

Contents

Preface

The period since the late 1980s is often considered the beginning of the "information age." The proliferation of digital technology, with its immense capacity for compression, transmission, and exhibition of massive amounts of information via computers and similar devices, and the associated enormous growth in the conveyance of informational displays to vast numbers of recipients, has invited the characterization of present times as such an age. What has been mostly overlooked is that the indicated technological development toward increasingly rich media environments carries with it a previously unimaginable wealth of entertainment choices. In fact, entertainment offerings obtrusively dominate media content and are bound to do so in the foreseeable future. This circumstance, together with the apparent growing public demand on entertainment provisions, lend equal justification to characterizing the present times as the "entertainment age." Never before in human history has so much entertainment been so readily accessible, to so many, for so much of their leisure time as is now, primarily because of the media of communication. All conceivable forms of media entertainment avail themselves at all times, competing with alternative forms for the attention of those seeking diversion, relaxation, excitement, amusement, bewilderment, or other alterations of prevailing experiential states. Potentially serving such ends, a great variety of music seems ever-present. Storytelling, the undisputed "main course" of media entertainment, is similarly omnipresent, mostly as fictional narrative but also in nonfictional formats. Athletic displays and competitions apparently also hold a universal appeal.

Western media consumers have apparently adjusted quickly to the abundance of entertainment offerings. In prosperous industrial societies, the citizens' pursuit of happiness seems to entail an entitlement to being well-entertained, especially by the media. More and better entertainment is expected, if not demanded. And as more societies become prosperous, this call is likely to be heard around the world. Thus, a formidable challenge is issued to makers of media entertainment. Business as usual might not suffice in meeting the challenge. Specifically, it might not suffice to follow intuition in creating additional formula programs and to discern, essentially by trial-and-error, which productions work and which do not. More systematic inquiry is necessary to determine what it is that people deem gratifying and that brings about desired experiential states. The entertainment needs of vastly diverse audiences with vastly diverse intellectual, aesthetic, and emotional interests will have to be explored with increasing care and rigor. Most importantly, however, more attention, in terms of both theory and research, must be directed at understanding the basic mechanisms of enlightenment from, and emotional involvement with, the various forms of entertainment. As yet to be comprehended fully are, for instance, the means of making people laugh and cry, feel the sadness and happiness of others, share their terror and triumph, or simply, of generating calming or thrilling sensations and experiences of serenity or elation. It is astounding, in fact, how little genuine scholarship and basic research has addressed questions as fundamental as exactly what it is that gives comedy the power to make people laugh and tragedy the power to make them cry. It is also far from clear how it can be possible that mere spectators feel triumphant or depressed when seeing athletic competition between others go one way or the other, or, what empowers music to make listeners shudder or feel glorious. All too often, commercial prerogatives limit research to staking out consumer interest in particular formats without concern for the more fundamental issues of entertainment. These issues must be addressed if media entertainment is to serve the global population better and more successfully in the forthcoming millennium and beyond.

Fortunately, a more systematic exploration of media entertainment is beginning. Psychologists, sociologists, and communication scholars, in particular, have begun to replace speculations with meticulous assessments of the content and usage of many forms of entertainment and their effects on different types of people, ultimately, of their consequences for society. For the first time, the primary function of media entertainment—namely, attainment of gratification—takes center stage in this exploration. Specific theories have been proposed to elucidate issues of emotionality and enjoyment, and numerous research demonstrations have been published to clarify the appeal of all conceivable genres and subgenres of media offerings. Unfortunately, however, the findings of many of these investigations are scattered about in the journals of various disciplines, and much needed integration has been lacking.

In this volume, a collection of independently authored chapters, we intend to correct this situation. Each chapter addresses a vital aspect of media entertainment and summarizes pertinent findings concerning it. An overview of what is currently known about the appeal and function of the essential forms of media entertainment is provided, and some degree of integration is offered.

The editors of this volume, Dolf Zillmann and Peter Vorderer, began to solicit and assemble contributions in 1998, during Zillmann's tenure as a visiting professor at the Hochschule für Musik und Theater in Hannover, Germany. Vorderer obtained funding for an international conference entitled "Only Entertainment." Scholars from various countries, among them the United States, Canada, Germany, and Denmark, were invited to Hannover to share their knowledge and exchange their ideas for future work. The presentations of many of these contributors were eventually condensed or expanded to some of the chapters in this volume. In the wake of the conference, other scholars were invited to contribute chapters, this in an effort to cover all major aspects of the media–entertainment cornucopia.

The anthology opens with introductions to the entertainment phenomenon in historical and contemporary terms, features approaches to the appeal of content-defined groupings of media entertainments, addresses technical aspects of nonmanipulable delivery as well as interactivity, considers individual differences among consumers of media entertainment, and concludes with an exploration of modes of aesthetic information-processing.

More specifically, in chapter 1, Zillmann traces the entertainment phenomenon through the ages, from antiquity to the present time. His focus is on the universality of the cultural preoccupation with various basic forms of entertainment in the pursuit of merriment, gaiety, enlightenment, and ultimately, happiness.

In chapter 2, Vorderer examines principal shifts in contemporary media entertainment as a function of technological developments. In particular, he analyzes the transition from the delivery of invariable entertaining messages by the so-called mass media, to interactive media entertainment that allows the occasional, to continual, alteration of information flow. This transition converts a mere witness of unfolding events to a participant, player, or actor who can, to a degree, control events and modify outcomes. Vorderer also considers the implications of this technological breakthrough for the future of entertainment.

Chapter 3 tackles humor and comedy. Zillmann presents the major theories that ancient and contemporary scholars have advanced to explain the human fondness for laughing at and about people, things, and circumstances. Pertinent research demonstrations are described to discern which theories have explanatory value and which do not. Focus is on the appeal and enjoyment of humor and comedy, but the question of consequences of merriment in regard to health benefits is also addressed.

In chapter 4, Vorderer and Knobloch scrutinize enjoyment derived from conflict-laden and suspenseful drama. Pertinent theories and research findings are presented in efforts to explain what seems a paradox to many scholars, namely, how repeated, prolonged, empathic distress from witnessing liked others in imminent danger—clearly an aversive emotion—can enhance the enjoyment of drama at the resolution of the threat. Explanations of the enjoyment of dramatic narratives that do not rely on this suspense paradigm are considered as well.

Sparks and Sparks, in chapter 5, examine the conditions under which displays of violence hold appeal and have the power of evoking joyous reactions. They probe to what extent the appeal of scary, shocking, and terrifying entertainments may be biologically determined. The authors search for perceptual properties intrinsic to displays of destruction that would provide such displays appeal. They also examine physiological mechanisms that might foster enjoyment, or at least, enhance alternatively evoked responses of this kind. Sparks and Sparks also address issues such as adolescents' desensitization to violence and the associated joy from the mastery of entertainment-elicited distress, especially when socially exhibited.

In chapter 6, Greenberg and Hofshire provide a meticulous account of sexual behaviors that are featured in media entertainment. Bypassing pornography, they focus on erotic displays in television soap operas and talk shows. Also considered are primetime programs and MTV. Among other curious findings, their analysis reveals young adults' disproportionately great enjoyment of seeing intercourse with prostitutes. By comparison, seeing the same behavior among unmarried couples was deemed highly erotic, whereas the same action among married couples proved erotically deficient and the least entertaining.

Bente and Feist, in chapter 7, examine what it is that lends talk shows their extraordinary appeal. They elaborate on the various content classes that give these shows their shock value. A psychophysiological analysis is provided that focuses on embarrassing revelations about persons in the programs and spectators' peculiar affective reactions of engrossment to such embarrassment and humiliation.

In chapter 8, Valkenburg and Cantor provide an overview of what children like and dislike within media entertainment. The analysis details the overcoming of initial difficulties with the distinction between fantasy and reality, and the comprehension of bodily transformations with its consequences for enjoyment. Attention is also given to maturation in perspective-taking as a function of cognitive development.

Bryant and Raney, chapter 9, address spectators' fascination with sports and reflect on the pervasiveness of athletic competition as a form of media entertainment. They provide an account of various theories that explain emotions sport exhibitions are capable of liberating and enumerate salient research demonstrations. The focus is on the conditions that ensure sports spectators' enjoyment.

In chapter 10, Hansen and Hansen summarize what is known about the contents, uses, and effects of popular music. They concentrate on the appeal that the recent art form "music television" holds for adolescents and young adults. The authors elaborate on the vital aspects of this appeal and discern which kind of person is, and for what reasons, attracted to which subgenre of popular music. Much attention is given to factors mediating favorable emotional reactions to music.

Grodal, in chapter 11, ponders the pleasures that playing video or computer games provides. He offers a conceptual account of the differences between responding to a given, invariable narrative, on one hand, and the exercise of control over the flow of information in the narrative on the other. His analysis focuses on the pleasures that are derived from the playful, or strategic, manipulation of mediated events as a creative process. Complementary sources of enjoyment, such as the mastery of challenges provided by games with strategic objectives, are considered in contrasting active game engagement with the comparatively passive absorption of unmanipulable narrative.

Oliver addresses gender differences in chapter 12. The author traces such differences in the enjoyment of the various forms of media entertainment. The analysis reveals stark differences for such genres as tragedy, horror, erotica, and sports, but also for displays of violence in any context. Oliver considers biological and cultural influences in providing an integrated perspective on the determination of obtrusive gender differences.

In chapter 13, Weaver looks for connections between personality traits and media entertainment preferences. He shows that both the enjoyment and the seeking-out of particular genres of entertainment are consistently linked with basic dimensions of personality, and elaborates on the advantages of stratifying audiences along these dimensions in the exploration of media entertainment.

Finally, in chapter 14, Cupchick and Kemp examine aesthetic orientations in dealing with popular media culture as compared to other forms of artistic expression. Using concepts such as modulation and matching, they examine the conditions under which artistic artifacts provided in media entertainment are used to alter moods and emotions in desired, potentially beneficial ways, versus conditions under which these artifacts are sought out for intellectual challenge with the possible result of enlightened experiences. As a cultural artifact itself, this final chapter may constitute such a challenge, and provoke much-needed further contemplation of the functions and merits of entertainment as a central cultural phenomenon.

ACKNOWLEDGMENTS

Beyond the contributions in writing, numerous agencies and persons provided invaluable support and assistance in making this volume possible. The editors are greatly indebted to the Deutsche Forschungsgemeinschaft (German Research Foundation) for their support of Dolf Zillmann in Germany. The conference subsidies from the Niedersächsische Landesmedienanstalt für privaten Rundfunk (Commercial Broadcasting Agency of Lower Saxony, Germany), the Kommunikations Kulture V., Förderverein des IJK Hannover (Alumni Association of the Hannover Institute for Journalism and Communication Research), and the Hochschule für Musik und Theater in Hannover are also gratefully acknowledged. So are the untiring efforts on the part of numerous students who made the conference a great success by serving as perfect hosts. Last but not least, the editors are deeply thankful for the grand cooperation by all contributors in refining their manuscripts and in meeting deadlines. We hope our joint efforts bear results in helping to put media entertainment research on the academic map and to instigate new generations of scholars to elucidate the issues further than we have been able to do.

—*Dolf Zillmann*
—*Peter Vorderer*

1

▼▼▼▼▼▼▼▼

The Coming of
Media Entertainment

Dolf Zillmann
University of Alabama

> *Commercial entertainment in the 21st century will in its way be as petroleum has been in the 20th century. . . . By imperceptible degrees, the United States Declaration of Independence's inalienable right to the "pursuit of happiness" has in many quarters developed into an entitlement that Thomas Jefferson could not have foreseen: a right to be entertained.*
> —Anonymous (from a hotel and restaurant administration journal, 1997)

This chapter provides a brief overview of the emergence of leisure in human life, along with the activities chosen during such "labor-free" periods. Various entertainments are traced through the ages. Those of elites are contrasted with those of commoners. Entertainments with universal appeal are noted. The ascendance of the performing arts is given special consideration, because these arts have come to define much of media entertainment. Efforts at squelching entertainments deemed undesirable by some are inspected, and the rationales behind the convictions that drive such efforts are considered. The irrepressibility of some basic forms of leisure and entertainment activities is highlighted. But projections of the ideal usage of leisure are also discussed. Finally, the status quo of media entertainment is sketched, with hints at things to come.

BUSY BODIES

Watching ants or bees at work should convince anybody that these insects do not live a life of leisure. Driven by innate programs, such insects toil unselfishly in never-ending efforts at securing the welfare of the colony. Watching birds in the

1

wild gives a similar impression. They continually search for food. In addition, these birds have to find mates, build nests, and feed their progeny. While doing all of that, they are on perpetual alert for predators. Even when they rest for a moment to preen their feathers, it is not for fun, but for survival—by keeping the feathers in working condition for flight and thermal regulation. If leisure is based on time left after survival needs have been satisfied (Shivers, 1979), these animals seem to be condemned to a life of hard labor devoid of recreational opportunities.

The situation is somewhat different for predators such as lions and tigers, but also snakes and otters, because of highly nutritional food intake. These animals, unlike most others whose endlessly growling stomachs stir them to keep on searching and fighting for another edible morsel, have ample leisure time between gluttonous meals. For the most part, they snooze this time away, or they use it for playful interaction. Noncarnivorous species find themselves in a similar situation only when food is aplenty; for example, during particular fruiting seasons.

Social organization, especially something akin to a division of labor, also can generate leisure time. Many species of nonhuman primates employ guards and sentinels, for instance, to provide carefree time for all others of their troops. The main beneficiaries are the troops' progeny. Infants and adolescents can engage in rough-and-tumble play and practice vital behaviors, such as tree climbing (Poirier, 1972).

This assessment applies to the early hominids as well. These primates had abandoned life in the trees and, owing to evolving bipedalism, were remarkably capable of moving about in the world's savannas and forests (Pfeiffer, 1969). The genus *Ramapithecus* is thought to have roamed large portions of India, Kenya, China, Germany, and Spain, among other territories. But *Ramapithecus* lacked powerful teeth, and despite some tool usage, they were quite limited in aggressively defending themselves. Not only were they vulnerable to predation, they also were inept predators. All indications are that *Ramapithecus* wandered from morsel to morsel, taking fruit, berries, roots, grubs, and whatever food predators were unable to ingest in one sitting and scavengers had left behind. With the exception of an occasional fortuitous encounter of a great supply of food, *Ramapithecus* was completely occupied by working for subsistence. Life was exhausting and without frills. If we accept Shivers' (1979) definition of leisure, which stipulates that it be "a time of opportunity wherein the individual has the freedom to perceive and select experiences which are either worthwhile or simply gratifying without any other redeeming quality" (p. 15), *Ramapithecus* probably had no such "quality time."

The genus *Australopithecus* did not fare much better. Social organization and tool use improved somewhat. But for the most part, these hominids were still low-order scavengers (Blumenschine, 1987; O'Connell, Hawkes, & Blurton Jones, 1988; Shipman, 1986). Along with other primates, such as baboons and chimpanzees, they had to wait their turn for the scraps left on carcasses after the predators had had their fill (Hasegawa, Hiraiwa, Nishida, & Takasaki, 1983; Strum, 1983). A momentous discovery was to crack bones for the marrow by smashing them against one another or against rock. Extraction of the potent nutrient, which quickly became an essential food source, is believed to have been practiced for millennia. Hunting with sticks and stones as well as bones (Dart, 1971) was still comparatively ineffective and largely failed to satisfy subsistence needs, but these tools may have offered a most effective means of chasing hyenas and vultures off carcasses. Nonetheless, *Australopithecus* is thought to have started hunting in organized parties of males. The females cared for and guarded the offspring. Despite such division of labor and the likely rough-and-tumble play characteristic of primate–family interactions, life was still without appreciable choices in doing things for sheer pleasure and without ulterior motives.

TIME ON THEIR HANDS

Leisure originated alongside the genus *Homo.* Specifically, during a period spanning more than 600,000 years (from the Pleistocene to about 200,000 years ago), *Homo erectus* brought a host of innovations that made it easier to satisfy subsistence needs and to relax defense vigilance. First, hunting became a highly organized venture, depending largely on stealth mixed with action-coordinating signals (Lee & DeVore, 1968). Hunting consisted mainly of trapping or cornering animals and, as killing tools were still quite primitive, of clubbing them to death. Initially, then, hunting became more efficient because of advances in communication skills (Holloway, 1966; Zillmann, 1979). Second, *Homo erectus* "domesticated" fire (Pfeiffer, 1971). Fire provided safety by keeping predators at bay. It gave comfort during inclement weather, and it lit up the immediate vicinity. Fire instantly became the centerpiece of family life. Probably first in China, but then also in Europe, fire was employed to cook meat. In Europe, controlled burns were additionally used in trapping and killing animals.

Because of these advances in the provision of nutritious food and home security, along with having light at night, *Homo erectus* had ample time between meals and forays. It is speculated that the gained leisure time fostered the first cultic and ritualistic ceremonies, some in reverence of elephants as the most powerful and dangerous game of the time. It also has been suggested that this period initiated the family dinner around the hearth, with the slurping of marrow from bones carried to the homestead as a pleasurable, not entirely necessary dessertlike treat (Shivers, 1979). But whether such comparatively minor leisure-time usage amounts to more than joyous gorging, whether it invited contemplation and fostered creative thinking, ultimately spawning deliberate play and culture (Huizinga, 1955), remains a matter of conjecture and interpretational preference.

The Neanderthals had about the same degree of spare time after meeting subsistence needs. Their rituals extended to burying the dead (Howell, 1965). As they preferred to live in caves, they had to displace the great cave bear of their days. They ended up worshipping this powerful animal, creating rituals that have been likened to religious ceremonies (Cornwall, 1968).

The Cro-Magnards of the late Paleolithic had substantially more to offer. They manufactured blade tools for hunting, thereby making killing and food processing more efficient. They effectively hunted big game, such as mammoth, bison, reindeer, and aurochs. But more importantly, they exhibited the yields of much leisure in their artistry. They furnished images of the animals they hunted, tamed, and ate. They painted them in side view onto cave walls, and they carved their statuary in ivory, bone, and clay. They appear to have painted their own bodies as well as those of their dead, and there is evidence that their women were well coiffured (Marshack, 1975).

It appears, however, that much of Cro-Magnon imagery was created not to satisfy aesthetic impulses, but to serve practical objectives. It has been suggested that these artistic efforts were made to gain control over natural forces by a process referred to as sympathetic magic (Clark, 1967). Depictions of game in paint or clay were stabbed with spears and daggers, as if to kill the depicted animals. Speculations about ritual accompaniments of such actions abound. But whether the Cro-Magnards danced in front of their animal representations and called anybody's spirits for assistance and protection, and whether they believed they could kill their prey in voodoo fashion by poking a knife into these images, remains intriguing speculation. It would be more conservative to assume that the depiction of hunted animals was a way for hunters to relive the experience and practice for future hunting success, and also served to indoctrinate novice hunters.

It may be considered well established, however, that the Cro-Magnards had more leisure time on their hands than any other genus before them, and that this leisure time allowed specializations in which individuals could develop and hone personal skills and talents. Training in apprenticeships seems to have existed, ensuring the passing on of elaborate procedures among craftsmen. These were, no doubt, the leisure conditions under which arts and crafts could evolve and flourish.

During the Mesolithic era, hunting became more proficient when the spear was supplemented with bow and arrow. It became so proficient, in fact, that the hunters' animal supply was critically depleted and the world's first food crisis came into being (Pfeiffer, 1975). The need to supplement diets eventually spawned the agricultural revolution. People started to grow wild barley and wheat and somewhat later vegetables and fruit. The nomadic lifestyle of hunters changed into farming in settled communities. Some 9,000 years ago, the first permanent community settled in Jericho (in what is now Israel). Grain was harvested in large quantities and sheltered for leaner times. Cooperation and coordination were essential and led to time schedules for working assignments. The other side of this time regimentation was a large surplus of leisure time. However, the storage of large food supplies motivated those less committed to working for a living to attain the food by violent means. Jericho saw the making of organized agricultural theft and its escalation to the world's first wars (Zillmann, 1979). Walls had to be erected and armies maintained to protect against plunder and usurpation. Such necessities undoubtedly took a bite out of the newly found leisure.

The Neolithic era saw more of the same. Communities generating appreciable food supplies had to be walled and protected by hunters-turned-soldiers. But inside the walls there was sufficient leisure to foster uncounted innovations. Animals were domesticated and bred. The larger ones were used to carry loads and pull plows. The smelting of copper and alloys such as bronze and brass was perfected. Metal tools, especially the handaxe, were refined. The wheel and sails were invented and revolutionized travel and the transportation of goods. Pottery flourished and weaving was practiced. Artistic expression was greatly elaborated. Speech was converted to basic forms of writing.

Most of these innovations served practical ends, essentially diminishing the drudgery of much physical labor but also enhancing comfort. There are suggestions, in fact, that the people of the Neolithic enjoyed leisure that had little or no connection with labor. Percussion instruments (animal skins over hollow tree trunks or pottery bases) have been found, along with flute-like whistles carved from bone. Given that they had the bow, stringed instruments were probably used as well. Music-making must have been practiced. Songs must have been sung. But in the absence of records, it can only be speculated whether music was tied to somber ceremonies—religious ceremonies in particular—or used in festivities, especially in connection with dancing, whose sole purpose was the expression of joy. Regardless of the degree to which the use of leisure time was linked to rituals, however, humans managed to generate a good deal of it, and they initially seem to have put it to good use. Leisure, it appears, was indeed a necessary condition for human culture to evolve (Huizinga, 1955; Pieper, 1952).

ANCIENT PARTYING

There has never been such a thing as egalitarianism in leisure entitlement. Much as in nonhuman primate groups, in the primordial human groupings there have been leaders and followers, with the leaders invariably enjoying more privileges than the followers. This inequality escalated to social stratification in any more complex society. Those with greater power reserved more privileges, leisure privileges included, for themselves than they granted those with lesser power. Leisure classes emerged, coincidental with the inception of private ownership (Veblen, 1931).

Ancient Egypt produced the first complex cultures that exemplify the indicated stratification. Pharaohs, nobles, and priests constituted the ruling class. They employed craftsmen, quarriers, masons, carpenters, bricklayers, sculptors, and painters to build their palaces, temples, and tombs; and there were chariot makers, boat builders, armorers, and leather workers to supply their standing armies (Ibrahim, 1979). Wages were paid in produce (bread, beans, dried meat, beer, salt) and graded by labor skill. Needless to say, those who did the digging, lifting, and hauling, mostly slaves, filled the ranks of the least privileged class.

Little is known about leisure behavior among the underprivileged. This is in contrast to the leisure habits of the upper crust. We happen to know, for instance, about a banquet of the seventh dynasty. At Sakkara, near Zoser's step pyramid, the world's oldest papyrus was found. It details, among other things, the invitation to a noble dinner party. According to this party announcement, barley porridge, quail, kidneys, pigeon stew, fish, ribs of beef, honey cake, and siddar cherries were served. Prior to dining, the guests were bathed, rubbed with scented oils, and decorated with flowers. They were welcomed with wine and music. Hired dwarfs, wrestlers, and storytellers performed during the first course. Dancing girls followed, offering sensuous, erotic gyrations as well as acrobatic stunts—the latter in elaborately choreographed splits, pirouettes, cartwheels, and somersaults. No doubt, leisure for sheer pleasure had arrived, and lavish banquets defined a major forum for its expression (Ibrahim, 1978).

But ancient Egypt provided some entertainments for its "middle classes," too. Most towns had theaters in which acrobats, gymnasts, and dancers performed (Kraus, 1971). For the so-called masses, beer houses existed for communal tale-telling. Various sports were practiced as well. Swimming, rowing, running, jumping, wrestling, and archery were popular. Some ball games appear to have been played. Oddly, however, none of these athletic endeavors were practiced competitively (Ibrahim, 1979).

Developments in ancient China were surprisingly parallel. Banquets were lavish and exotic. Among other things, marinated snails, dog meat, raw turtle in ginger, and ant eggs were served. And as in Egypt, hired troupes performed to enhance the culinary experience. The opulent banquets eventually got out of hand, and dinner parties were limited to three guests by government decree. In connection with entertaining guests, ancient China pioneered luxury in the homes of the mighty. Their large houses were equipped with baths, heaters, mechanical fans, artificial fountains, and most surprisingly, air conditioning by way of the ice-cooling of rooms (Schafer, 1967).

More than ever before, leisure served the attainment of sheer pleasure—and where the means allowed it, of excessive and outrageous pleasure. Leisure was no longer confined to serving cultic, ritualistic, and religious objectives. This is not to say that these rituals vanished. On the contrary, they persisted and can be seen as having unified the populace across its strata, as even the most powerful shared with those of lesser fortune the desire to be on good terms with the forces believed to govern the earth and all life on it.

LEISURE ELITISM

Ancient Greece produced further fruits of leisure. On Crete, the Minoans dwelled in luxury. On the mainland, the Mycenaeans did likewise. The leisure classes' utensils were in bronze, silver, and gold; artistic decor in houses, often with plumbing, reached new stages of lavishness; and elaborate strategic games were played. Acrobatic spectacles, some involving larger animals, were performed before large audiences (Bowra, 1965). During a period in which dictators and military governments ruled the communities, preparation for war had priority over artistic expression. Nonetheless, even during these "dark ages" advances were made in poetry, song, and dance. Sparta, for instance, is said to have celebrated festivals in which these accomplishments were featured (Ibrahim, 1979).

But Greece eventually overcame its intercommunal feuding, and culture ascended to new heights during the two centuries between 500 B.C. and 300 B.C. The mostly geometric styles of earlier times were abandoned and replaced by grand naturalistic designs. Painting and sculpting projected idealistic grandeur. In poetry, the glorification of past heroics and accomplishments gave way to addressing personal, more common experience. Lyrical song was presented with flute or lyre accompaniment by individuals or groups. Music and poetry were combined with dance and presented at civic festivities. Impressive progress was also made in the "intellectual arts," mainly geometry and arithmetic. Poetry, music, and dance, all in ambitious and refined form, were popular in the privileged classes.

But Greek culture also had its less refined moments. Eating and drinking at banquets were as excessive as ever. The dinner proper was followed by the symposium, plainly a drinking session. Dancing girls, acrobats, and magicians then entertained the intoxicated dinner party.

Most communities in ancient Greece staged athletic games. Some of these games were intercommunal. The Olympic Games, for instance, were Panhellenic, bringing all of Greece together. Such games were attended by commoners and socialites alike. The Olympic Games' opening spectacle was a four-horse, 9-mile chariot race on a straight track with sharp turns on each side. Up to 40 chariots started, but few finished the race. Collisions, spills, and upendings were no doubt the principal attraction. The race was followed by competition between individual athletes, mostly in the nude but some in armor. There were various foot races, distance jumping and throwing, and wrestling. Also, there was pankration, a mixture of wrestling, boxing, kicking, and strangling. Somewhat peripheral to the games, there was much street entertainment, trading, and politicizing (Harris, 1972).

The main alternative pastime to the games was the theater. The ancient Greeks built outdoor amphitheaters to accommodate sizable audiences. A sequence of about three tragedies followed by a satire play or a comedy defined a typical theatrical outing. Tragedies tended to feature the struggle of bringing desires into accordance with precepts and regulations, and they also focused on the fortunes of the less-than-perfect mortals whose destiny was mapped by higher powers. Satire, an admixture of residues from fertility rituals and the Dionysian wine cult, featured music and dance intertwined with derision or ridicule of public figures and deities. Comedy, deriving from "*komos,* the nocturnal revels in which the gentlemen of Attic society for a few days shed all their dignity in the name of Dionysus and indulged their proclivities to drink, dance, and love" (Berthold, 1972, p. 148), was similarly coarse, lacking neither demeaning punch nor sexual rawness. Put-down humor flourished in between the emerging stock characters of boasters and flatterers, parasites and procurers, and drunkards and cuckolds.

With such unrefined fare, the Greek theater held broad appeal. Drama and comedy competitions attracted the populace at large (Smith, 1831). During such festivals, Athens suspended all business. Prisoners were granted temporary release in order to see the plays; and even women, who were usually barred from public meetings, were permitted to attend.

Greek culture thus offered entertainments within a well-defined dichotomy: those for the privileged versus those for the commoners (or the masses). More importantly, however, the Greeks distinguished themselves by being the first to ponder leisure and its implications. They contemplated what entertainment is, what effects it might have, and who should practice or consume which form of it.

Aristotle (trans. 1984), for instance, examined leisure in connection with happiness and concluded that it "is better than occupation and is its end; and [that] therefore the question must be asked, what ought we to do when at leisure?" (p. 2122). In other words, we labor to have leisure; and once we have it, we should use it to good end. The question is profound in that it implies that leisure may serve different functions and seeks to discern the most beneficial ones.

Aristotle's own answer to the question is rather disappointing, however. Trapped in the confines of his culture, he suggested that leisure time be used to do something that was desirable for its own sake, which was to practice or enjoy noble music and noble poetry in the company of noble friends (de Grazia, 1962). In addition, the speculative faculties were to be exercised. Aristotle thus endorsed the finest of the fine arts and philosophy; that is, the leisure activities that were practiced by the elite of the time.

The application of this leisure formula to the populace highlights the formula's partiality. In Aristotle's day, Athens provided the leisure under consideration to only a small minority of its men (13%). Women (17%), aliens (50%), and slaves (20%) were not eligible for these elitist benefits (Ibrahim, 1979). It appears that Aristotle accepted leisure as a lifestyle that is necessarily limited to a fortunate few.

However, Aristotle proposed elsewhere (trans. 1951) that drama, tragedy in particular, would affect everybody by eliciting the emotions of pity and fear that, in turn, would bring about "the proper purgation of these emotions" (p. 23). This notion, known as the catharsis doctrine, projects an apparent benefit to all consumers of drama, members of the elite and commoners alike. Although Aristotle never elaborated the social implications of his proposal, the catharsis doctrine eventually became a cornerstone of drama theory. It did so despite the fact that social scientists never managed to show that the proposed cathartic effect actually exists (Geen & Quanty, 1977).

A few years earlier, Plato (trans. 1946) had expressed similar views on leisure. Music, dance, and gymnastics were the activities of virtue; and in an enormously stratified societal schema, they were prescribed for the elites because of presumed beneficial effects on character formation (Hunnicutt, 1990).

Neither Plato nor Aristotle seems to have recognized the more prurient leisure interests. Or they must have elected to ignore these interests. Be this as it may, their proposals suggested that the aristocracy be granted leisure for refined entertainments, while excluding those needed to serve. Additionally, these proposals show little, if any, sympathy for the amusement needs of the lesser classes. This is leisure snobbery, indeed.

THE LEISURE STATE

During the period from the onset of the first century A.D. to the beginning of the fourth century, the Roman Empire enjoyed enormous prosperity. Mostly as a result of this unprecedented wealth, leisure became an entitlement across all strata of Roman society. This is not to say that the poor enjoyed the lifestyles of the rich and famous, but rather that they became an integral part of what could rightly be called mass entertainment.

The democratization of leisure is apparent in the number of holidays during which entertainments were offered, often from dawn to dusk and free of charge. During the reign of Claudius, 93 holidays were devoted to games, and that at public expense. By the middle of the fourth century, there were 200 holidays. Almost every other day (175 days a year) was dedicated to state-supported entertainments (Kraus, 1971).

The Romans adopted essentially all Greek leisure activities, refining some of them, but for the most part modifying and extending them for greater mass appeal. Greek poetry became more practical and the theater less ritualistic (de Grazia, 1962). More importantly, the Olympic chariot races were made into ever more sensational spectacles.

The Circus Maximus, built under Julius Caesar, accommodated 250,000 spectators. In this greatest mass-entertainment forum of its time, brass bands played, and acrobats and clowns performed as backdrops to the main event: the chariot races in team competition. Their pageantry, recklessness, and sheer violence put the Greek races to shame.

The enormous audiences of the amphitheaters, particularly the Colosseum with a seating capacity in excess of 50,000, were treated to similarly sensational happenings. Gladiators fought wild beasts, mostly lions, and each other. Contemptuous Christians were thrown to the lions. Animal fighting was also popular. Bears wrestled buffaloes and bulls battled rhinos. Curiosities, such as tamed panthers pulling chariots and elephants spelling words with their trunks, were crowd-pleasers, too.

The gladiators were "expendables," such as prisoners of war, slaves, or criminals. Audiences were roused to intense involvement, in large measure because they were waging money on the combative outcome (Ibrahim, 1979). In many contests, when a defeated gladiator had failed to convince the spectators of genuine effort, the crowd called for his head. The emperor usually accommodated their wishes by signaling impromptu execution.

Not all Roman entertainments had this sensational character, however. The public baths, accommodating as many as 60,000 citizens simultaneously, became centers of leisure. Swimming, running, and similar forms of "working out," along with relaxing in hot or cold rooms, were popular in various social classes. Bathers were massaged, oiled, manicured, depilated, and otherwise pampered for hours on end.

The banquet may have been the foremost institution perpetuating elitism. The wealthy continued to celebrate much as their Egyptian and Greek counterparts had done earlier. Three-course meals, preceded by the lavish washing and decorating of all participants, were typical. Entertainments were offered during the main course. Performances involved dancing girls, gymnasts, mimes, clowns, and on occasion gladiatorial combat.

Roman philosophers, as far as leisure goes, very much followed the Greek lead. Seneca adopted Aristotle's position of leisure as enlightenment and an end in itself. He provided a minimalistic conception, however, arguing that, as a perfect state of life is unattainable, a life of leisure constitutes the next best thing. Cicero, primarily a politician, took a slightly different stand. He essentially accepted the idea that leisure activities may be useful in serving a preparatory or regenerational function (de Grazia, 1962). He thus embraced the recreational value of leisure in the endless cycle of work, leisure, and work.

It is usually assumed that the Romans were forced into providing as much free entertainment as they did in order to control the restless masses of unemployed and partially employed people in their communities (Ibrahim, 1979; Kraus, 1971). The leaders, in all probability, used entertainment as a means of pacification. But they also used it to ingratiate themselves to the masses, which led to the choice of spectacles with popular appeal. It is usually overlooked that the masses had their share of influence on the development of entertainment. The applause of audiences, and equally their shouts of disapproval, must have functioned as a guide for the modification and perfection of enjoyable spectacles. The audiences essentially "rated" what they liked and, by inference, wanted to see. As much as their behavior may have been controlled by entertainments, their behavior also controlled entertainment. And for better or worse, it did so in an anti-elitist, democratic fashion.

SOMBER SPIRITS

It was Christianity that started to dismantle the leisure state. Increasing numbers of the new converts objected to the brutality of chariot races, gladiatorial combat, and hunting spectacles. They were similarly offended by the theater, with its performances that were deemed vulgar and immoral. Refusal to attend was also inspired by the required worship of Roman heroes and deities upon entering the theaters. The leisure state's fate was sealed in 313 A.D. when Emperor Constantine converted and pronounced Christianity the official religion of Rome (Bishop, 1968).

In their glory days, the Romans, uninclined to do their own fighting, started to employ barbarian mercenaries to do it for them. Their dependence on such assistance grew and eventually emptied the coffers of the regime. Moreover, the mercenaries came to power and plundered the empire. Massive tribal migrations of Slavs and Huns were highly destructive and put Europe back into agricultural subsistence conditions. During these times, essentially the second half of the first millennium, various cultures fused and created their own limited entertainments in the process.

The Church regulated leisure time. Sunday became the established day of rest, with a few saint's days added. Despite the Church's efforts at curbing excessive celebration, these days were times of singing, dancing, and partying. As a legacy of pagan festivities, there was excessive drinking and much sexual promiscuity. Singing and storytelling were ribald, sometimes sacrilegious, and mostly vulgar (McCollum, 1979).

Fairs became the forum of entertainment. Often planned as religious festivals, and certainly meant to promote bartering and other commercial activities, eating, drinking, and merriment were usually the main attractions. At the beginning of the sixth century, Justinian had to close the Roman theaters, and the so-called histriones (i.e., actors) abandoned town. They became nomadic street entertainers, performing at fairs, local alehouses, town squares, and street corners across much of Europe. But they also performed in the castles of nobility and kings (Cohen & Greenwood, 1981).

The histriones had been trained in speech, dance, mime, music making, and acrobatics. They were sword swallowers and fire eaters. And there were always animal trainers with their menagerie, as well as dancing girls (Bucknell, 1979). These wandering entertainers were to be found wherever men gathered to drink, gamble, sing along with others, and cohabit with any willing maiden (McCollum, 1979). The entertainers assured a good time with taking the lead in telling raunchy tales and in music making. They also were famed as impromptu comedians who incorporated local gossip into their routines and derided anybody not in attendance (Bucknell, 1979).

Folk entertainments were mocking Christian values enough to prompt further restrictive action from religiously inspired leaders. Charlemagne, for instance, tried to curtail the entertainments at fairs, although with little success. His son, Louis the Pious, was more austere than his father. He tossed the minstrels out of his court and, by decree, prohibited all dancing, singing, and tale-telling in public places and at crossroads on Sundays. He also deprived the histriones of civil rights, making them outlaws and fugitives. Tolerated were only those entertainers who promoted, or at least in no way undermined, Christian faith and values (Cohen & Greenwood, 1981).

THE REBIRTH OF MERRIMENT

Merriment went underground in a most peculiar way. Christianity usurped its artistry and put it to use in preaching the gospel—as well as entertaining the parishioners with morality plays and allegories, but also with clownery and sottish play (Berthold, 1972). The theater moved into the church.

The progressive theatrical dramatization of Christian social values was soon transformed and transferred back into the mundane world, however. Allegories fell into the service of political indoctrination, and morality plays became melodrama without being didactic in religious terms. Disenchanted clergy were active in this transition. As a new breed of histriones, they became the wandering goliards, troubadours, and minstrels of their time. These buskers not only revived street entertainment, but increased its variety. Much like the Teutonic gleemen, they sang the praises of war heroes of the past, on occasion including Biblical figures and saints. The jongleurs, a type of minstrel, addressed the baser tastes of both commoners and the nobility. The troubadours sang about life in general. Their main attraction, however, was to sing of the beauty and charm of lady-love. The ballad of the brokenhearted knight or nobleman, seeking true love outside the stifling confines of married life, was the troubadours' hit song. Tournamental mock-fighting often expressed the same romantic theme (Cohen & Greenwood, 1981).

The fairs became ever more popular and provided the forum for theatrical performances. Makeshift stages were erected in marketplaces, usually adjoining the churches. The need to move the stages from fair to fair led to stages on wheels (see Fig. 1.1). Eventually such stages were arranged in a circle. Short routines were offered, allowing the crowds to mill along and absorb numerous performances. On occasion, the mobile stages or "pageant wagons" moved from street corner to street corner, bringing their entertainments as close to home as possible (McKechnie, 1969).

FIG. 1.1   Theatrical performances on mobile stages were grand attractions at medieval markets in Europe.

The fact that the fair theaters staged religious plays did not prevent them from offering lesser fare. By the middle of the second millennium these theaters also featured, with some regularity, "low comedy" laden with gross obscenities. Such comedies were exceedingly popular with the crowds, to the dismay of puritans who sought to prohibit the performances on grounds of immorality (McCollum, 1979).

Notwithstanding occasional challenges, the theater eventually strengthened its position as a vital communal institution of entertainment. Permanent theaters were built and enjoyed popularity. The first public playhouse in London, The Theatre, opened its doors in 1576. It did not so much serve an elite as cater to an unruly, uncultured mob with plays featuring brawling witches and other incredulous mayhem. Advances in the professionalism of actors and writers, such as in the *Commedia dell'arte* in Italy, eventually elevated the artistry of playmaking. Operatic performances, in particular, quickly became grand displays of pageantry and extraordinary musical talent (Berthold, 1972). These displays tailored more to nobility and the well-to-do than to common folks.

The well-to-do formed what has been labeled the manorial system. Wealth was aggregated and retained by elites who had distinguished themselves, for the most part, in battle for their appreciative and apparently generous rulers. Landownership and its financial benefits created gentlemen who, along with their families, lived a life of consummate leisure. The boredom associated with these circumstances fostered an entertainment culture all its own, especially in England. Many activities became pompous rituals and spectacles. The hunt tended to be deprived of its original objective, turning into pageantry and an exhibition of equestrian skills. Social dancing was excessively choreographed. Self-presentation was stylish and extravagant. Board and card games within the family and with friends were enormously popular. But there also existed numerous parlor games of the physical variety, such as blindman's bluff, leap frog, or squeak piggy squeak (Bucknell, 1979). These games could become wild and rowdy, giving players a chance to break with restrictive etiquette and get "in touch" with one another. Moreover, just as in Roman times, "blood sports" were popular, apparently across class boundaries. Cockfighting was common, and animal baiting enjoyed a semi-secretive following of commoners, nobility, and kings (see Fig. 1.2). Bulls, bears, and occasionally horses were tethered to a post, and hounds were let loose in relay to fight them. The spectators were often betting on the number of casualties and on the specifics of mauling and mutilation (Moss, 1963).

The settling of America is of interest in that history had to repeat itself. Initially, the life of settlers was demanding, and there was little time for leisure. The conditions of subsistence by hunting and agriculture were soon overcome, however, and Americans turned to entertainments (Dulles, 1965). New England, in the early part of the 18th century, featured taverns with a British-style pub culture. Patrons could enjoy the bottle and play billiards, cards, shuffleboard, and similar games. Shooting contests were popular. Communal work such as barn raising or cornhusking invariably prompted much drinking, singing, dancing, and games.

FIG. 1.2   In medieval Europe, animal baiting was popular among commoners, the
nobility, and kings.

Country fairs became popular recreational spots with plenty of merry making. Finally, the theater arrived as well, in both traveling and stationary form. America's
first theater was erected in Williamsburg in 1716, and drama quickly became a
favorite pastime from New York to Savannah (McCollum, 1979). It then followed
the people—wherever they went.

ANTILUST LEGISLATION

Entertainment has been outlawed on occasion. The efforts of Louis the Pious were
repeated, for instance, under Oliver Cromwell's rule in England (Firth, 1900).
Public houses and theaters were closed, and all sorts of celebrations were curbed
as the Puritans thought them sinful. Somewhat later, owing to puritan influence,
the American colonies prohibited all public extravagance and expensive diversions, among them horse racing, cockfighting, gaming, and various plays. During
such times, things as innocent as the wearing of colorful dresses were deemed
heretic and frowned upon (McCollum, 1979).

Such curtailment of merriment never lasted very long. People always found
ways to amuse themselves, even if they had to topple governments or, more char-

acteristically, force them to liberalize legislation. In contrast, the debate over what is "good" entertainment and what, therefore, should be promoted, if not prescribed, has never lost intensity. And the debate over "bad" entertainment—the sort that, in the judgment of some, calls for the public's protection—has become even more intense, at times furious and utterly devoid of reason (Zillmann, 1992).

Lowenthal (1961), and also Mendelsohn (1966), framed the debate between religiosity, Christianity in particular, and unmitigated hedonism in terms of arguments advanced by the French intellectuals Pascal and Montaigne during the 16th and 17th centuries. Pascal (1887), as the spokesperson for Christian values, argued for salvation seeking, a total commitment to God that does not allow diversions into merriment by dubious, if not devilish, causes. All entertainments were considered "pleasures of the flesh" and were to be resisted. Montaigne (1958), on the other hand, is viewed as the writer who anticipated Freud's (1933/1964) conception of basically unsatisfactory conditions of life in general, conditions in need of correction. Thus, Montaigne is said to have made palatable the notion that people, in the interest of their mental welfare, must "escape from reality." The idea of entertainment as therapy was born—although only within the limiting conception of escapism.

It should be noticed that both stances concerning the merits of entertainment, though they seem diametrically opposed, are actually based on the same gloomy premise of inadequate existence. In the one case, efforts are made to overcome this inadequacy for the promise of a better life hereafter. In the other, entertainments are seen as instant relief-providers. The logic here is that entertainments diminish aversions, possibly removing them. Missing from the debate is the view that entertainments may provide genuine pleasure, pleasure capable of enriching life that is good and gratifying already.

The point to be made is that much of the ethical debate of the merits of leisure and entertainment is unnecessarily narrow in principal terms. Moreover, presumptions of corrupting effects are usually based on limited personal observation by the claimants. The same holds true for presumed positive effects, such as health benefits from gaiety. It constitutes a formidable challenge to the social sciences, in fact, to discern exactly what consequences various forms of entertainment have. As long as these consequences are in doubt, the merit debate will continue to be uninformed (i.e., opinion-bound), and thus, unproductive.

THE MEDIA AVALANCHE

Notwithstanding minor curtailments, during the second half of the second millennium, the entertainment arts enjoyed considerable freedom and support, and they flourished and matured as a result. Theater, opera, concerts, and sports became primary institutions of leisure. Recreation, rather than escape, was the concept that guided the creation of public parks (Sapora & Mitchell, 1961; Welton, 1979) and exercise movements (Leonard, 1923; Rice, 1926). At home, the board and parlor games of earlier days continued to be popular, and reading for pleasure became an essential pastime. Reading provided entertainment for the individual in privacy. Ambitious and "trashy" books alike were read and defined focal points of social discourse. So did the serial writings of magazines and newspapers (Hughes & Lund, 1991; Tebbel, 1972, 1975). Comic strips accommodated the not-so-literate. But theatrical and musical performances continued to be consumed by audiences whose size was limited by the distance the human voice or the sound of instruments could travel.

All this changed dramatically with the invention of the technology for sound recording and transmission, soon to be followed by that for the transmission and recording of imagery. The movies made attending live theatrical performances unnecessary, and records did the same for live concerts. Radio and television, finally, converted every home to a concert hall, a movie theater, and a sports arena. It was no longer necessary "to go where the action is."

In the industrial world, the invasion of the home by machines capable of delivering entertainments by sound and image representations was fast and comprehensive. Radio conquered America in approximately 25 years. Begun in 1922, receiver penetration of households was practically complete (above 95%) at midcentury. Television, that began in 1946, took merely two decades to reach this saturation level (Smith, Wright, & Ostroff, 1998). At present, three fourths of American households are multi-set, and almost half of them have three or more units (Nielsen Media Research, 1998). Many children, especially teens, have their own reception and replay devices (Andreasen, 1994). The computer, with Internet access to entertainments, among other things, has quickly reached 50% of all households (Nielsen Media Research, 1998).

The number of channels has grown from a handful to seemingly unmanageable numbers, almost all offering programming around the clock (Zillmann & Bryant, 1998). The diversity of programming is massive. All conceivable genres of entertainment are represented. Any form of drama is there for the choosing. Comedy abounds. So does suspense, horror, tragedy, science fiction, and erotic fare. Numerous types of sport are represented. All of this and more avails itself day and night. Choice is the issue, if not the problem, because there is so much that must be passed up.

News programs, often an extension of ancient gossiping, are adding to these entertainments. The distinction between news and entertainment is often blurred by the fact that news programs, in competition for viewers' attention, draw on sensational occurrences that are of no practical consequence to the viewers— other than to have them hold their breath for a moment or be in shock about things that happened to faraway strangers. Variety and "reality" programs offer further entertaining nonfiction.

Entertaining happenings that used to be difficult to attend, if they were not out of reach altogether, now are, literally, at the consumer's fingertips. Convenience is altogether a salient component of media use. Each and every viewer now has the front seat that used to be reserved for nobility and a few illustrious citizens. And viewers get to see and hear not backyard stagings but performances by the world's greatest actors, singers, athletes, magicians, scholars, cooks, and assorted others. If there is a democratization of entertainment, it has manifested itself, first and foremost, on the flickering screen.

Media entertainment, because it avails itself to everyone, may be considered entertainment for the masses, but it is not mass entertainment. The media users' freedom to choose their heart's content from among the wealth of offerings ensures that democratization does not lead to massification, as some have feared (Adorno, 1950, 1962; Rosenberg, 1957). Viewers can and will follow their own needs, tastes, and preferences (Zillmann, 1999) and, in view of the diversity of offerings, form fan and taste cultures that perpetuate and possibly even increase the complexity of social stratification (Epstein, 1994; Gans, 1966; Zillmann & Gan, 1997; Zillmann & Paulus, 1993).

CYBERTOPIA

The Entertainment Age cometh! The never-ending talk of present times as the Information Age is not necessarily misleading. However, what is usually overlooked is that the monumental capacity to generate, manipulate, and transmit information is likely to serve leisure as much as labor, if not more so. Clearly, the information age will significantly advance automation and robotics. The manufacture of products and the rendering of services will successively require fewer human hands and brains and be shifted over to ever more intelligent machines. The process has actually been underway for some time, although with machines that future generations are likely to brand as primitive.

But these "primitive" devices already have about halved the time of labor, this in just one century. Between 1850 and 1950, the average workweek shrank from 70 to 40 hours (de Grazia, 1962). In various industrial countries, people are able to dedicate about one third (30%) of their waking hours to leisure activities. The same portion goes to labor, and the rest to necessary work around the house— such as cooking, cleaning, shopping, grooming, and childcare (Szalai, 1972). In the United States, the leisure share is even higher (35%), with labor taking a lesser chunk (28%), and the rest going to maintenance (Robinson, 1977, 1989). Needless to say, much of the leisure time is spent watching television as the primary source of entertainment (Robinson, 1981).

The trend toward more leisure time, and conversely, toward fewer working hours, is bound to continue. Where will it end? Will the Roman leisure state repeat itself, with an entertainment extravaganza every other day? Might we outdo the Romans, working only one day a week or three years before retirement? One thing is certain: We shall have plenty of time on our hands with which to do something (Neulinger, 1981). Aristotle's question about ideal leisure use will come to haunt us. What shall we do with all that spare time?

Media entertainment will be there and will beckon for our attention. And there will be much entertainment outside of the media. Will entertainment evolve to new forms? Or shall we merely modify the basic pleasure-generating displays and activities that have provided humanity with merriment through the ages? It all remains to be seen. But whatever form the future of pleasure-seeking will take, there can be little doubt that entertainment will define, more than ever before, the civilizations to come.

REFERENCES

Adorno, T. W. (1950). A social critique of radio music. In B. Berelson & M. Jarowitz (Eds.), *Reader in public opinion and communication* (pp. 309–316). Glencoe, IL: Free Press.

Adorno, T. (1962). *Einleitung in die Musiksoziologie* [Introduction to the sociology of music]. Frankfurt-am-Main: Suhrkamp Verlag.

Andreasen, M. S. (1994). Patterns of family life and television consumption from 1945 to the 1990s. In D. Zillmann, J. Bryant, & A. C. Huston (Eds.), *Media, children, and the family: Social scientific, psychodynamic, and clinical perspectives* (pp. 19–36). Hillsdale, NJ: Lawrence Erlbaum Associates.

Aristotle. (1951). The poetics. In S. H. Butcher (Trans.), *Aristotle's theory of poetry and fine art* (pp. 7–111). New York: Dover Publications.

Aristotle. (1984). Politics (B. Jowett, Trans.). In J. Barnes (Ed.), *The complete works of Aristotle: The revised Oxford translation* (Vol. 2, pp. 1986–2129). Princeton, NJ: Princeton University Press.

Berthold, M. (1972). *A history of world theater.* New York: Frederick Ungar.

Bishop, M. (1968). *The Horizon book of the middle ages.* Boston: Houghton Mifflin.

Blumenschine, R. J. (1987). Characteristics of an early hominid scavenging niche. *Current Anthropology, 28,* 383–407.

Bowra, C. M. (1965). *Classical Greece.* New York: Time-Life Books.

Bucknell, P. A. (1979). *Entertainment and ritual: 600 to 1600.* London: Stainer & Bell.

Clark, G. (1967). *The stone age hunters.* New York: McGraw-Hill.

Cohen, D., & Greenwood, B. (1981). *The buskers: A history of street entertainment.* Newton Abbot, England: David & Charles.

Cornwall, I. (1968). *Prehistoric animals and their hunters.* New York: Praeger.

Dart, R. (1971). On the Osteodontokeratic culture of the Australopithecine. *Current Anthropology, 12*(2), 233–235.

de Grazia, S. (1962). *Of time, work, and leisure.* New York: Doubleday.

Dulles, F. R. (1965). *A history of recreation: America learns to play.* New York: Appleton-Century-Crofts.

Epstein, J. S. (1994). Misplaced childhood: An introduction to the sociology of youth and their music. In J. S. Epstein (Ed.), *Adolescents and their music: If it's too loud, you're too old* (pp. xiii–xxxiv). New York: Garland.

Firth, C. (1900). *Oliver Cromwell and the rule of the Puritans in England.* New York: G. P. Putnam's Sons.

Freud, S. (1964). New introductory lectures on psycho-analysis. In J. Strachey (Ed. and Trans.), *The standard edition of the complete psychological works of Sigmund Freud* (Vol. 22, pp. 7–182). London: Hogarth Press. (Original work published 1933)

Gans, H. J. (1966). Popular culture in America: Social problem in a mass society or asset in a pluralistic society. In H. S. Becker (Ed.), *Social problems: A modern approach* (pp. 549–620). New York: Wiley.

Geen, R. G., & Quanty, M. B. (1977). The catharsis of aggression: An evaluation of a hypothesis. In L. Berkowitz (Ed.), *Advances in experimental social psychology* (Vol. 10, pp. 1–37). New York: Academic Press.

Harris, H. A. (1972). *Sport in Greece and Rome.* Ithaca, NY: Cornell University Press.

Hasegawa, T., Hiraiwa, M., Nishida, T., & Takasaki, H. (1983). New evidence on scavenging behavior in wild chimpanzees. *Current Anthropology, 24*, 231–232.

Holloway, R. L. (1966). Cranial capacity, neural reorganization and hominid evolution. *American Anthropologist, 68*(1), 103–117.

Howell, F. C. (1965). *Early man*. New York: Time-Life Books.

Hughes, L. K., & Lund, M. (1991). *The Victorian serial*. Charlottesville: University Press of Virginia.

Huizinga, J. (1955). *Homo ludens: A study of the play-element in culture*. Boston: Beacon Press.

Hunnicutt, B. K. (1990). Leisure and play in Plato's teaching and philosophy of learning. *Leisure Sciences, 12*, 211–227.

Ibrahim, H. (1978, October). Gastronomy: The new American pastime. *Journal of Physical Education and Recreation, 53*–54.

Ibrahim, H. (1979). Leisure in the ancient world. In H. Ibrahim & J. S. Shivers (Eds.), *Leisure: Emergence and expansion* (pp. 45–77). Los Alamitos, CA: Hwong Publishing.

Kraus, R. (1971). *Recreation and leisure in modern society*. New York: Appleton-Century-Crofts.

Lee, R., & DeVore, I. (Eds.). (1968). *Man the hunter*. Chicago: Aldine.

Leonard, F. E. (1923). *A guide to the history of physical education*. Philadelphia: Lea & Febiger.

Lowenthal, L. (1961). *Literature, popular culture, and society*. Englewood Cliffs, NJ: Prentice-Hall.

Marshack, A. (1975, January). Exploring the mind of ice age man. *National Geographic*, pp. 74–81.

McCollum, R. H. (1979). Leisure from medieval times to colonial America. In H. Ibrahim & J. S. Shivers (Eds.), *Leisure: Emergence and expansion* (pp. 79–110). Los Alamitos, CA: Hwong Publishing.

McKechnie, S. (1969). *Popular entertainment through the ages*. New York: Benjamin Blom.

Mendelsohn, H. (1966). *Mass entertainment*. New Haven, CT: College & University Press.

Montaigne, M. de. (1958). *The complete works of Montaigne: Essays, travel journal, letters* (D. M. Frame, Trans.). Stanford, CA: Stanford University Press.

Moss, P. (1963). *Sports and pastimes through the ages*. New York: Arco Publishing.

Neulinger, J. (1981). *The psychology of leisure* (2nd ed.). Springfield, IL: Charles C. Thomas.

Nielsen Media Research. (1998). *1998 report on television* [Brochure]. New York: Author.

O'Connell, J. F., Hawkes, K., & Blurton Jones, N. (1988). Hadza scavenging: Implications for Plio/Pleistocene hominid subsistence. *Current Anthropology, 29*, 356–363.

Pascal, B. (1887). *The thoughts, letters, and opuscules of Blaise Pascal* (O. W. Wight, Trans.). Boston: Houghton, Mifflin.

Pfeiffer, J. (1969). *The emergence of man*. New York: Harper & Row.

Pfeiffer, J. (1971). When *Homo erectus* tamed fire he tamed himself. In H. Bleibtreu & J. Downs (Eds.), *Human variations* (pp. 193–203). Beverly Hills, CA: Glencoe Press.

Pfeiffer, J. (1975). The first food crisis. *Horizon, 17*(4), 33–39.

Pieper, J. (1952). *Leisure: The basis of culture*. New York: Pantheon Books.

Plato. (1946). *The republic* (B. Jowett, Trans.). Cleveland, OH: World Publishing.

Poirier, F. (Ed.). (1972). *Primate socialization*. New York: Random House.

Rice, E. A. (1926). *A brief history of physical education*. New York: A. S. Barnes.

Robinson, J. P. (1977). *How Americans use time: A social-psychological analysis of everyday behavior*. New York: Praeger.

Robinson, J. P. (1981). Television and leisure time: A new scenario. *Journal of Communication, 31*, 120–130.

Robinson, J. P. (1989, April). Time for work. *American Demographics*, 68.

Rosenberg, B. (1957). Mass culture in America. In B. Rosenberg & D. M. White (Eds.), *Mass culture: The popular arts in America* (pp. 3–12). Glencoe, IL: Free Press.

Sapora, A. V., & Mitchell, E. D. (1961). *The theory of play and recreation* (3rd ed.). New York: Ronald Press.

Schafer, E. H. (1967). *Ancient China*. New York: Time-Life Books.

Shipman, P. (1986). Scavenging or hunting in early hominids: Theoretical framework and tests. *American Anthropologist, 88*, 27–43.

Shivers, J. S. (1979). The origin of man, culture, and leisure. In H. Ibrahim & J. S. Shivers (Eds.), *Leisure: Emergence and expansion* (pp. 3–44). Los Alamitos, CA: Hwong Publishing.

Smith, F. L., Wright, J. W., II, & Ostroff, D. H. (1998). *Perspectives on radio and television: Telecommunication in the United States* (4th ed.). Mahwah, NJ: Lawrence Erlbaum Associates.

Smith, H. (1831). *Festivals, games, and amusements: Ancient and modern.* London: Henry Colburn & Richard Bentley.

Strum, S. C. (1983). Baboon cues for eating meat. *Journal of Human Evolution, 12*, 327–336.

Szalai, A. (Ed.). (1972). *The use of time: Daily activities of urban and suburban populations in twelve countries.* The Hague: Mouton.

Tebbel, J. (1972). *A history of book publishing in the United States: Vol. 1. The creation of an industry 1630–1865.* New York: R. R. Bowker.

Tebbel, J. (1975). *A history of book publishing in the United States: Vol. 2. The expansion of an industry 1865–1919.* New York: R. R. Bowker.

Veblen, T. (1931). *The theory of the leisure class: An economic study of institutions.* New York: Viking Press.

Welton, G. (1979). Leisure in the formative years. In H. Ibrahim & J. S. Shivers (Eds.), *Leisure: Emergence and expansion* (pp. 111–155). Los Alamitos, CA: Hwong Publishing.

Zillmann, D. (1979). *Hostility and aggression.* Hillsdale, NJ: Lawrence Erlbaum Associates.

Zillmann, D. (1992). Pornography research, social advocacy, and public policy. In P. Suedfeld & P. E. Tetlock (Eds.), *Psychology and social policy* (pp. 165–178). New York: Hemisphere.

Zillmann, D. (1999). Mood management in the context of selective exposure theory. In M. E. Roloff (Ed.), *Communication Yearbook 23* (pp. 123–145). Thousand Oaks, CA: Sage.

Zillmann, D., & Bryant, J. (1998). Fernsehen. [Watching television.] In B. Strauss (Ed.), *Zuschauer* (pp. 175–212). Göttingen, Germany: Hogrefe.

Zillmann, D., & Gan, S. (1997). Musical taste in adolescence. In D. J. Hargreaves and A. C. North (Eds.), *The social psychology of music* (pp. 161–187). Oxford, England: Oxford University Press.

Zillmann, D., & Paulus, P. B. (1993). Spectators: Reactions to sports events and effects on athletic performance. In R. N. Singer, M. Murphey, & L. K. Tennant (Eds.), *Handbook of research on sport psychology* (pp. 600–619). New York: Macmillan.

2

▼▼▼▼▼▼▼▼

Interactive Entertainment and Beyond

Peter Vorderer
University of Music and Theater, Hannover

If *leisure* means "a time of opportunity wherein the individual has the freedom to perceive and select experiences which are either worthwhile or simply gratifying" (Shivers, 1979, p. 15), we certainly have seen a tremendous increase of leisure over the past few decades (cf. Zillmann, chap. 1, this volume). Most leisure time is spent with entertainment, both with the media and without them. The focus of this chapter is, of course, on media-related entertainment, but the scope of its consideration is not restricted to television viewing. Although television is still the most important source of entertainment, other forms are also readily accessible. Books, movies, newspapers and magazines, radio programs, computer and video games, and more recently, the Internet, provide what most people are looking for: activities "designed to delight and, to a smaller degree, enlighten through the exhibition of the fortunes or misfortunes of others, but also through the display of special skills by others/or self" (Zillmann & Bryant, 1994, p. 438).

In addition to an increase in leisure time, we have recently observed a technological development that is of importance here: the possibility of digitizing and compressing data and, as a consequence of this, a growing capacity to generate and transmit information. Much of this capacity is used to proliferate the distribution of media programs. In fact, there are at least two different effects that stem from this technological development. First, particularly with regard to television, there is more content in more programs on more channels today than ever before. The scope and diversity of television entertainment has grown in a manner that was inconceivable a few decades ago. Entertainment programs are now accessible almost everywhere at almost any time. This process is accompanied by the programs' specialization and diversification, that is, the emergence of special-interest contents for more homogeneous audience segments, or, in other words, for smaller groups of viewers with specific interests (Schulz, 1997).

Second, the way that media users are exposed to programs has changed and is about to change further. In the past, the media typically presented text and pictures in books and magazines and on radio and TV stations in a way that allowed audience members to attend to a presentation or not (i.e., to start, interrupt, continue, or complete a reception). But new information and communication technologies have been developed that have led to a merging of broadcasting, entertainment, and telecommunications; in short, "new media" have developed. They consist primarily of combinations of computers, CD players, telephones and fax machines, TV sets, and radios. Some of them, like interactive TV, computer games, and the Internet, offer their users an opportunity not only to select specific content and respond to it, but also to modify the content that is presented to them. Taken together with the increase in special-interest content, this development leads to a "demassification" of media use, that is, "the control of mass communication systems ... moves from the message producer to the media consumer" (Rogers, 1986, p. 4). And it is even more than that: The mass audience seems to disappear, apparently being replaced by individual media users. Less than ever before, can the audience's use of the media be described as *reception*. It is rather an interaction between participants on one side and offerings of the multimedia on the other.

The term *interactive media* appeared to describe this state of affairs and has already been used synonymously with the terms *new media* and *digital media*, causing some confusion as to its meaning. The meaning of *interactivity* is even more multilayered; not surprisingly, it has been referred to as a "widely used term with intuitive appeal, but it is an underdefined concept" (Rafaeli, 1988, p. 110). Interactivity is often used to describe a technological feature of the media as much as it is used to characterize a way of using the media. The second position is taken here, based on the assumption that there is no such thing as interactive media but rather interactive ways of using these media. As such, I will investigate the psychological differences between interacting with the media and using the media in the more traditional way. This investigation is of special interest within the context of entertainment, which has been described as "killer application" for the new media (Biocca & Levy, 1995; Bryant & Love, 1996; Mundorf & Westin, 1996). It is indeed often expected that the audience will accept and even seek out new forms of media use if they can receive entertainment in the process. More than anything else, this expectation is based on the observation that it is entertainment that has grown and diversified as a result of the aforementioned recent media developments (Schulz, 1997). Today, there are certainly more and better ways to be entertained than ever before. The question that remains to be answered, however, is whether entertainment will ultimately evolve to new forms or whether there will be only peripheral modification of the enjoyment-generating display activities that we have known for such a long time already (cf. Zillmann, chap. 1, this volume). To date, the growth and diversification of entertainment programs has been particularly beneficial to those audience members who in the past have been underprivileged in this regard (i.e., older people, children, and adolescents; Schulz, 1997). But, whether this process has already reached its peak, or whether interactive entertainment offerings in the future will be structurally different from entertainment offerings in the past, remains to be discussed. Such a discussion leads further to two groups of questions that are considered here. First and most importantly for those who develop, finance, and provide interactivity: Does the audience desire interactivity at all? What do TV viewers gain and what do they lose when television goes interactive? Is the interactive user of video games or the Internet entertained, and are the experiences thereby made worthwhile or simply gratifying? Does interactivity overwhelm those who in the past have become accustomed to being passive in front of a screen or a mediated text?

The second group of questions relates to theorizing. Research on entertainment, as presented in this volume, dwells primarily on noninteractive media use. What is known about entertainment—be it in the area of sports, music, comedy, horror, or erotica (see the various chapters dealing with these genres in this volume) or any other type—is based on a model that describes the media user as a witness to depicted events; an onlooker, listener and, in general, an observer of what is presented on a screen, a page, or by a speaker. Existing theoretical models do not yet entail the potential of somebody interacting with the content (i.e., participating in what is presented). And since hypotheses and research that seek to explain what make the media entertaining are also based on such models, the question arises: Are researchers capable of explaining interactive entertainment? Are new hypotheses, theories, and models needed to first conceptualize what interactive media use is? Is it necessary to describe and explain why some forms of interactive exposure are considered to be enjoyable but not others? Is it necessary to answer the question of why some users enjoy interacting with the media while others strive to avoid doing so?

To begin, I first provide a brief overview of various attempts at defining interactivity. Next, I turn to the question of whether the audience seems to want interactivity, followed by a discussion of the potential of existing theories to explain the gratifying experiences. Finally, I consider media forms that one can expect to encounter in the future and that, from a current perspective, appear to be beyond the domain of interactivity.

INTERACTIVITY

In the context of emerging new technologies, no feature or characteristic of potential applications has been discussed as extensively as interactivity. Many theorists have used the terms *interactive media* and *new media* synonymously, or they have defined what is new in media with reference to interactivity: "The new technologies are characterized by the interactivity, by the ability to interact with others through communication channels created by the technological devices involved" (Brody, 1990, p. 103). Thus, interactivity is used to describe specific capacities of the media or of media users that are related to what in sociology has been called interaction. In sociology, interaction refers to the mutual orientation of different individuals in a social context, that is, to relationships between individuals or groups. Interactions differ from simple actions mainly in that an agent, while interacting, is always oriented toward others. In other words, the interacting individual keeps in mind that there is (at least) one other person who can be perceived or who perceives oneself. As such, interaction is a specific form of social action, a form that is guided by the presence of others, even if this presence is only imagined (Esser, 1993; Jaeckel, 1995; Krappmann, 1989; Weber, 1984). Within computer science, however, the term interaction has been extended and applied to processes that take place between humans and machines, primarily computers. Interestingly, these processes have been conceptualized analogously to those between individuals. More than anything else, it was the responsiveness of the machines that enabled computer specialists to talk about *interactive machines*. Within communications, finally, discussions of terminology have described what in the late 1980s and early 1990s appeared to be new media and the ways they could be used: "We generally define new media as those communication technologies, typically involving computer capabilities (microprocessor or mainframe), that allow or facilitate interactivity among users or between users and information" (Rice et al., 1984, p. 35). Keeping the definitions from other disciplines in mind, theorists have emphasized the new machines' potential to respond to the users: "Interactivity is the capability of new communication systems (usually containing a computer as one component) to 'talk' to the user, almost like an individual participating in a conversation" (Rogers, 1986, p. 34). It is obviously the reciprocity of the media that has been of central relevance to the understanding of interactivity within communications. And despite the fact that for man–machine interactions, particularly in comparison with human interactions, the reciprocity of orientations is always limited (cf. Jaeckel, 1995, p. 471), this is what interactivity most often means: that a machine may respond to a user and a user may respond to a machine. In other words, that the individual is no longer only a recipient, but rather a receiver sometimes and a sender at other times (Mast, 1986; Rogers, 1986).

When new media developments emerged and the ways in which the old devices (such as the television set) could be used changed, the term interactive media was at hand, because it was assumed that the extended capacities of these media foster the opportunity to interact with them. Early steps in the direction of interactivity have been identified with the development and use of remote controls and VCRs. Both have enhanced television users' capacity to select specific contents more easily and, in the case of the VCR, to influence the time of reception. Some media researchers have even argued that the acceptance and wide use of these applications signal the audiences' wish to shape their own TV programs (cf., e.g., Hickethier, 1994). It is in this context that the TV viewer has even been described as a TV director (Hasebrink & Krotz, 1996), that is, as someone who is able to and likes to create his or her own personalized program mix.

At the same time, the actual processes between the users and the media were labeled interactive to contrast them with "classical" forms of media use, which again were seen as being limited to turning the media content on and off. Clearly, interactivity is not something that either exists or does not exist. Instead, there is a continuum that acknowledges different degrees of interactivity: continuous interaction with the media being at one extreme and having the potential only to start or stop a reception at the other extreme. Establishing the criteria by which to determine intermediate degrees of interaction, however, has proven to be tricky. When communication researchers attempted to do so, much of the confusion and ambiguity surrounding the term *interactivity* surfaced, stemming primarily from the fact that within communications both the sociological understanding of the term as well as the one deriving from computer science were simultaneously employed. From a communications point of view, media that seems to be the most interactive allow a form of communication that most closely resembles a natural communication between individuals.

> Face-to-face communication is held up as the model because the sender and receiver use all of their senses, the reply is immediate, the communication is generally closed circuit, and the content is primarily informal or "ad lib." (Durlak, 1987, p. 744)

Similarly, Heeter (1989) considered the media to be most interactive when they are responsive to the needs and characteristics of the user. In his view, "human-like responsiveness is the highest level of sophistication" (p. 223). Others have attempted to establish criteria more explicitly. Steuer (1995), for example, used "vividness" and "interactivity" as two orthogonal dimensions to place the different media into a two-dimensional space. In this context, for instance, 3-D films are considered to be highly vivid although low on interactivity, whereas Multi User Dungeons are highly interactive although low on vividness. Interactivity hereby is understood as the extent to which the user is capable of influencing his or her media use. Schrape (1995) distinguished between five levels of interactivity, ranging from sheer potential to turn the device on and off (level 0), to the retrieval of additional information from the TV program (level 2), up to the highest level of interactivity (level 4), which is characterized by two-way interaction with the machine, as in the case of using a videophone.

Based on these conceptualizations, Goertz (1995) attempted to systematize the definitions and suggested the use of the following five criteria to define levels of interactivity:

1. Degree of selectivity;
2. Degree to which a given content may be modified by the user;
3. Quantity of different content that can be selected and modified;
4. Degree of linearity/nonlinearity; and
5. Number of different senses that are activated when using the media.

According to Goertz's proposal, a high degree/amount of these criteria should correspond to a higher degree of interactivity in general. As for the *degree of selectivity*, the range extends from deciding when exposure starts and ends, to selecting between simultaneously presented offerings, to selecting different dimensions. An example of a highly interactive offering, according to this criterion, is provided by video games, at least when the user is able to select the level of difficulty, the presentation, and the outcome of the game. The *degree of modification* is low when possibilities exist only to store or delete messages, and it is high when it is possible to add more information along the users' intention and interest. While the criterion that refers to the *quantity of different content* that may be selected and/or modified is differentiated by the sheer number, the *linearity* dimension is one that takes into account that the user may have to accept the order of the given presentation (as is the case with movies), or may alternately be able to compose the plot by him- or herself (as is the case with hypertext functions). Goertz wished to take vividness into account again when considering the *number of different senses* that are activated while using the media.

Nevertheless, Goertz had to admit that his scale does not measure the actual participation of the interactive user but rather the interactive *potential* that various media provide. Certainly, this is the biggest shortcoming of his proposal. For just as we know that there are no literary texts per se, but rather those that are read in a literary way (Meutsch, 1987), and that there are no entertainment programs per se, but rather programs that entertain viewers or readers (Vorderer, 1996), we also must acknowledge that there is no interactivity independent of the user but rather interactive ways of using the media. Surely some media allow or even enhance interactive use while other media impede it. But it is not that the media or specific programs themselves determine interactivity. Instead, it is the user who makes a program interactive, given that the media "allow" for interactive use. Thus, it is the participant who decides how much interactivity he or she wishes to employ in a specific situation. Without a doubt, the level of interactivity is limited by the potential of the media but is not determined by it.

DO USERS WANT INTERACTIVITY?

Based on the thesis that interactivity can be defined by the extent to which a user selects from and modifies a variety of different offerings and the variety of senses involved, the question arises as to whether such an activity is even gratifying at all (cf. Vorderer, 1995). Discussions about interactive media typically contain the assumption that audience members want nothing less than this kind of activity. Within audience research, however, there has been a controversial discussion as to how this media development should be assessed and what the needs and interests of the audience look like. Those who favor the general development of more interactive media use often refer to the changing role of the audience, noting that whereas the viewers, readers, and listeners of the past were forced to be comparatively passive and had few alternatives regarding the content to which they were exposed, the interactive user is regarded as being "empowered," not only by a far greater variety of offerings but also by a new capacity to deal with them. It is interesting to note that this position has a long tradition. It was Brecht (1967) who in his famous radio theory claimed a new form of media that were capable not only of sending but also of receiving, in order to establish the radio listeners in a position from where they could also speak. The same concern can be identified in most of the critical approaches within the social sciences that apply to media use. The Frankfurt School, for example, criticized the press and the broadcasting companies for placing their focus on sending (cf. Adorno, 1963), and the critical approach of the 1970s claimed to overcome the distinction between sender and receiver (cf., e.g., Prokop, 1972). All of these analyses point to the role of the media user—to the old, passive one that must be overcome, and to the new one that is intended to be empowering.

Today, this perspective is supported by another process, that sociologists have described as individualization. Part of this process involves individuals' tendency not to refer to orientations, values, and goals that are provided for a social segment of a society as much as they did in the past, but rather, to choose their orientations individually. In addition, this process applies to the audience's patterns of media use; audience segmentation and fragmentation are the effects that already can be observed. It is not that individualization causes segmentation and fragmentation or vice versa, but rather that both processes coexist and mutually influence (and likely even foster) one another. One aspect of this general picture is the expectancy—if not already the need and the desire—of the individual to be addressed individually. It has been found that in very different areas of life, people tend to prefer those alternatives that fit them personally. This refers not only to their behaviors, but also to their general preferences and tastes. As a result, it is plausible to predict that most individuals would be eager to use the media interactively, because such a use individualizes the program even more (cf. Rötzer, 1996; Schulz, 1997).

The central counterargument to such a view, raised in the context of audience research, refers to our knowledge about the viewing behavior of television audience members, not only with regard to descriptions and explanations of viewers' loyalty to specific channels (Schwarz, 1995), but also from empirical data of observational studies that reveal how little attention is often paid to the TV. It seems as though watching TV is primarily an act of relaxation, often accompanied by other activities, like household tasks, that have nothing to do with following a program (Hallenberger, 1995). Most researchers suggest that the television audience does not wish to follow instructions or conform to demands and expectations. Onlookers have been described as "couch potatoes," a term intended to reflect the audience's passive role while watching TV. Given that viewers do so little physically while viewing, it has been assumed that they also do not want to be mentally challenged. In fact, research has shown that reading is regarded as being challenging while watching TV is considered to be easy, at least from the recipient's point of view

(Salomon, 1984; Weidenmann, 1989). Furthermore, one of the most attractive features of television viewing appears to be that it requires so little from viewers. Watching TV affords very few prerequisites, comes almost without commitment, and implies hardly any personal consequences. In summary, watching television has been portrayed as a modern form of idleness (Vorderer, 1992).

On considering such beliefs, Schönbach (1997) has called the vision of a "hyperactive audience" an illusion; he believes that TV viewers do not really care about being active as much as communication researchers may think. According to his perspective, everybody has a right and a need to be lazy, and TV viewers in particular tend to behave accordingly (see also Stipp, 1995; Vorderer, 1995). Schönbach's argument is particularly convincing if one takes into account that the high level of selectivity that accompanies interactive media use is, from a psychological point of view, as much of a problem as it is a blessing. If TV viewers are confronted with 30 or 50, or even 100 to 500 channels, how will they know which program will suit them best (Vorderer, 1995)? The process of investigating the different options and the effort required to make a decision, which again would only be of temporal assistance, might reduce what most people expect to receive from entertaining media: gratifying experiences. Hence, there is considerable doubt that such gratifying experiences can be achieved when the users need to continually make up their minds about what they want to select or how they would like to modify what is presented.

Does the audience want to be active, that is, interactively using the media by selecting from a great variety of programs and by modifying what has been presented? Or, do media users instead want to be lazy, voluntarily and with merriment accepting what is offered to them, not being occupied with, but rather being relieved of, figuring out "What could I possibly like even better?"? Unfortunately, no empirical evidence is yet available to resolve this matter. Questionnaires that simply ask respondents what they would like to do with the media (and how much they are willing to pay for specific applications) are of little value when it comes to questions such as this one. Speculation based on social scientific research in this area, however, is possible. Two levels of argumentation—a sociological perspective and a more psychological perspective—may be used as a starting point.

From a sociological point of view, it may be asked whether interactive media suggest the end of mass communication. One of the central functions of mass communications has been to provide participation in a common reality to potentially every member in the same society. In this sense, mass media produce what has been called *collective awareness* by focusing attention on selected issues. Every individual has the potential to feel part of a virtual community to which he or she belongs by referring to these same issues. This feeling of belonging, however, depends on the illusion that the media veridically reflect and depict reality. Given the chance to communicate and/or interact with the media, individuals realize the social construction of this depicted reality, and the illusion of accurately reflecting reality can no longer be upheld. The integration function offered by the mass media is therefore challenged by the understanding of media users that the content is made up. According to this perspective, the integration of a society requires a renouncement of direct interaction and communication by the user with the media (Wehner, 1997a, p. 103). The question is, which is dominant: the users' need to feel part of a community and their interest in the preselection function of the media, or the need to be addressed individually? The problem is that both functions are in conflict with one another. The more individually someone can be addressed by the media, the less the media are able to provide a virtual community for him or her. The more reliable the information from the media is, that is, the more it can be expected that others will also receive the same kind of information, the less individually the user will be addressed.

But it is not only on the social level that a gain in interactivity is accompanied by a loss. Wehner (1997a) argued that it is primarily the "distance" between the media and the users, that is, the nonreciprocity, that allows the recipients to be irritated by perspectives that are provided by the media. It is the lack of obligation to respond to the media that sets the user free to come to his or her own autonomous, critical position about what has been perceived on the screen (Wehner, 1997a, p. 106). What Wehner (see also 1997b) primarily had in mind is information provided by the media in offerings such as news shows. But his argument can easily be applied to media entertainment as well. Of interest in this instance are not so much the positions and attitudes that are presented and responded to by the user's own position; instead, it is more the predictability of story lines, plots, narrative structures, and the like which is of greatest interest. And from what we know about the gratifying effects of drama, comedy, tragedy, sports, and offerings of other genres (see the respective chapters in this volume), the limited predictability of what will happen next is of crucial importance to the enjoyment of the user. For example, a story can be suspenseful only when the viewer or reader has anticipations of what will happen and preferences for what should happen. If the audience knows for sure what will happen, their preferences cannot be in conflict with expectancies and, therefore, suspense will not emerge (cf. Vorderer & Knobloch, chap. 4, this volume). Does this imply that an interactive movie can never be suspenseful? Or that an interactive video game cannot be as involving as a noninteractive one? Obviously not. Research in this area shows how fascinating these games are, particularly to adolescents (Fritz, 1995). The users' involvement seems to be so strong that these experiences have even been described as "immersive," to indicate the psychological pulleffect which is typical for computer games (cf. Grodal, chap. 11, this volume):

> Immersive is a term that refers to the degree to which a virtual environment submerges the perceptual system of the user in computer-generated stimuli. The more the system captivates the senses and blocks out stimuli from the physical world, the more the system is considered immersive (Biocca & Delaney, 1995, p. 57).

Hence, immersion is used to describe what in noninteractive contexts has been described as involvement (Vorderer, 1992). It only depicts this phenomenon as stronger and more absorbing because interactivity adds to the experience (Bullinger, Bauer, & Braun, 1997).

IN NEED OF NEW THEORIES?

But how can this contradiction be explained? How is it possible that interactivity does not prevent involvement, suspense, and enjoyment, while noninteractivity, that is, the fact that a passive viewer is surrendered to what happens on the screen, seems to be an important prerequisite for the emotional participation of the viewer? The solution lies in the more complex structure within which interactive media use takes place. Imagine a scene in a film in which a protagonist has to cut a wire in order to avoid the explosion of a bomb. If he or she cuts the wrong one, they and many others will die. Given that the audience feels sympathy for the protagonist (and the innocent others), they will also feel suspense if the chance to fail is rather high. This is a classic suspense situation in which all conditions are given: The audience cares about the protagonist, the chance to fail is likely and the audience cannot do anything but observe what will happen next. Now, imagine that this scene is contained in an interactive movie. In this case, it is the viewer who may decide what wire will be cut by the protagonist. Will that lead to more or to less suspense? Well, if the user knows the correct choice, there will be no suspense. But if he or she must in fact decide which wire to cut and does not know whether this decision will lead to an explosion, there should be even more suspense. The reason for this enhanced level of suspense may be seen in the following discussion. Onlookers are witnesses of depicted events and feel suspense as a consequence of what is happening on the screen (Carroll, 1990), given that the already mentioned prerequisites such as sympathy for the protagonist are present (Zillmann, 1996). But if, in addition, they are participating in a story where they are not only asked to make decisions as to how this story is to continue, but also to interfere with the ongoing developments, they start being personally responsible for the consequences of their decisions. Of course, they are not really responsible for what will happen, but it may feel as if they were. Watching traditional TV remains an activity with few obligations and few consequences (see previous discussion). But with interactive TV, video games, or online entertainment, the situation changes. Now, when it is not only a matter of preference which wire is to be cut but a question of life and death for a person (at least this is how it looks and feels), the users should care more. The outcome is now dependent on the users, not the director. In this sense, the viewer has really become the director (Hasebrink & Krotz, 1996).

In addition, whatever the users do and however they deal with the media, if they can use them interactively, that is, if they can select and modify, their abilities are put to the test. Again: Watching traditional TV was easy; being interactive with TV, a video game, or the Internet, affords knowledge, skills, and competencies. Whereas a traditional TV viewer can hardly fail, an interactive user may fail easily (Vorderer, 1999). This can best be seen with video games, which may even be adjusted to the player's skills. And the users are well aware of their own potentials to cope with interactivity.

What does that mean for users within the interactive situation? They must concentrate on what to do; their attention for what can be observed and their decisions about how to influence the ongoing developments have to be coordinated. They are monitoring their success and failure and may internally attribute these outcomes to their own potentials. All of these factors are of personal relevance to the user. They provide him or her with personal information on which self-esteem, well-being, and so forth may be grounded. As Grodal (cf., chap. 11, this volume) put it, the users' control is not absolute, but relative to their skills. The more using the media gets to the users' optimal mental level and motor capacity, the higher their experience of involvement, immersion, or flow (Csikszentmihalyi, 1995; Turkle, 1984). Whatever users do has an impact on the story or game, and also on one's picture of oneself. Users of interactive media seem to be captivated by two roles at the same time: the role of a witness and the role of a participant or player. At times, the two roles may function as separate psychological processes.

In this respect, new theorizing is indeed necessary. What researchers need are models and theories that help to describe and explain the ways these two processes influence each other. We certainly do know what influences the witnesses of depicted events, what makes them feel and why (Zillmann, 1996). And we also know how people feel in achievement situations, where they can potentially succeed or fail. What we cannot account for yet, however, are situations such as those of interacting with new media, where these two situations merge (Vorderer, 1999). In my view, media research has just begun to face this challenge.

Still, the question remains as to whether the users actually enjoy experiences like these. One should keep in mind that in an interactive situation users have to continuously make decisions and act accordingly, for example by pressing a button, expressing a preference, and so on. This fact leads to the general question of how active an individual usually wants to be in front of a screen. This question has been the subject of much controversy in audience research (for an overview, see Hasebrink & Krotz, 1991) and is of new interest in this context. From a psychological point of view, this question can hardly be answered generally. Surely, TV is known to provide a rather lazy form of entertainment, and TV users usually show little interest in much activity. At the same time, younger persons particularly are very much attracted by computers, computer games, and the Internet, and it has often been assumed that it is particularly the younger generation, having grown up with new media, who will therefore see the old media as boring. This perception of a generation gap, as it were, has led to different apprehensions that reached their peak in the prediction of "cultural fragmentation" (Schulz, 1997) or, to use an often mentioned catchword, in the fear of a "two-class society": a society that is divided between the younger, better-educated individuals who know how to use new media to their full advantage and older, less-educated individuals who are overwhelmed by such developments (Maletzke, 1987). This fear applies to the possibility that these two groups will sooner or later be unable to communicate with each other anymore, and that the strained and overwhelmed part of the society will withdraw further from the public arena and political participation (Barnett, 1997). In fact, empirical data support this concern. Data have not only confirmed many times that the younger people who are well educated and have a higher income are particularly attracted to interactive media (Mundorf & Westin, 1996), but also that this segment of society deals with these media more easily and assesses their use more positively. Older people who are less trained do not only avoid the new media; as soon as they are confronted with new media, they seem to object to them (Dohlakia, Mundorf, & Dohlakia, 1996).

In an experiment on interactive TV (Vorderer, in press; Vorderer & Knobloch, 1998), 427 subjects between the ages of 14 and 49, representing different education levels, sexes, and previous experiences with interactive media, were asked to watch a 30-minute movie. The movie was shown to one-third of the sample in the traditional (noninteractive) way. Another third could intervene with the movie by choosing how it should end (three possible outcomes were offered to the subjects on the same screen on which they viewed the movie, and they were asked which of the three they would like to see). Still another third was "empowered" to influence the ongoing developments three times during exposure. The dependent measures were obtained after exposure, using a computer-aided questionnaire, as well as online data. Suspense experienced; empathy with the protagonist; the subjects' feeling well; their assessments of the movie, of the protagonists, and of the reception situation; and physiological parameters were the most important variables.

Rather surprisingly, the differences in feeling empathic with the protagonist, feeling suspense, and assessing the movie between the three experimental groups were small and negligible. If, however, the sample was divided into those who had and had not graduated, the picture changed: The "information elite," as indicated in this study by the graduation of the subjects or by their cognitive capacities, for example, by their response times when answering the questions on the screen, were eager to interactively watch the movie. In contrast, those who had not graduated or were slow in their decision making disliked the opportunity to interact. They clearly preferred and felt better about the non-interactive way of watching the movie. The fear that the audience may divide into two parts and that their division implies a differential attachment to interactivity is clearly supported by these findings.

BEYOND INTERACTIVITY

So far, it has been assumed that there is a contradiction between the media users' need to belong to a virtual community and their tendency to individualize. Their affiliation motive may best be served by mass communication, because knowledge about the fact that everybody in a society has access to the same kind of information (and entertainment) supports a common background for everybody and thereby enhances a collective awareness. Their tendency to individualize in what they do, what they feel, and what they prefer, however, is apparently in conflict with their passive role of recipients who are not addressed individually by the media. A greater variety of options that can be exercised by an interactive audience is more of what should appeal to a highly individualized media user. It has been argued that the strength of these two conflicting tendencies or needs may depend on different personal characteristics, which apparently leads to different preferences in different subaudiences. However, another way of combining the two needs could be seen in the experience of "social interactivity" or "multifaceted interactivity," that is, a form of using the media in which the individual interacts with the media and with other users at the same time. Computer games and video games sometimes provide this possibility for social interaction. On a broader scope, companies such as Immersion Studios in Toronto offer this type of social interactivity in a more public sphere. Other such experiences are in a planning stage, for example, for the year 2000 World Exhibition in Hannover, Germany.

In the case of Immersion Studios, theaters invite about 100 visitors at a time to follow an interactive movie ("Monsters of the Deep"), a so-called *voomie*, on three large screens of about 6 by 8 meters each. The story depicted in the voomie can be influenced by 25 touchscreen control panels, called consoles, that are provided for two or three persons each. Prior to the start of the voomie, participants are instructed by a "captain" that they will be the "staff" of the submarine. Naturally, it is the adventures of this submarine that are depicted in the voomie. Every single user, therefore, plays (or at least may play) a role in the story by navigating the submarine in terms of its pace and direction, activating weapons to defend it, employing sensory devices to track down video signals, and using a virtual library for additional information about what can be seen in the sea world. The submarine does what the majority of the participants wants it to do; that is, everybody has an impact on it to the extent that every single order results from the decision of the majority. The main challenge for the participants is that they have to not only control the actions of the submarine, but they also have to coordinate with those who at the same time use the other 24 panels. Even one's own panel is used by three people, which again requires coordination. Multifaceted processes of interactivity with the other users, with the protagonist (who is controlled by oneself), and with the other protagonists or antagonists take place at the same time. This interactive experience surely goes beyond what has been discussed so far, but it seems to be realistic to expect this kind of interactive entertainment in the near future. Again, the question arises of whether people are attracted to this kind of interactivity. The question may be that raised more specifically now: Do individual differences between users account for their assessment of entertainment value?

With Immersion Studios, a study has been conducted to investigate whether sociodemographic and/or psychological parameters influence the users' evaluation of such an environment. Hanisch (1999) presented a computerized, self-administered questionnaire (Beckenbach, 1995) to 1,245 respondents immediately following exposure to the voomie. Although he found a few influences on the participants' assessment by personality traits, most consistent were those that derive from gender and cognitive capacities. As in the aforementioned study on interactive TV (Vorderer, in press), these results show that more cognitive capacities and higher education lead to a more positive evaluation of this offering, while fewer capacities and a lack of an advanced education lead to more distress and thereby to a more negative evaluation. The latter type of respondent clearly seems to be overwhelmed and strained.

In this sense, some entertainment will indeed evolve to new forms. However, these new forms may not be attractive to mass audiences, rather, to specific groups with specific interests and preferences.

REFERENCES

Adorno, T. W. (1963). *Eingriffe: neun kritische Modelle*. Frankfurt a. M.: Suhrkamp.

Barnett, S. (1997). New media, old problems: New technology and political process. *European Journal of Communication, 12*, 193–218.

Beckenbach, A. (1995). Computer-assisted questioning: The new survey methods in the perception of the respondents. *Bulletin de Méthodologie-Sociologique, 48*, 82–100.

Biocca, F., & Delaney, B. (1995). Immersive virtual reality technology. In F. Biocca & M. R. Levy (Eds.), *Communication in the age of virtual reality* (pp. 57–124). Hillsdale, NJ: Lawrence Erlbaum Associates.

Biocca, F., & Levy, M. R. (1995). Virtual reality as a communication system. In F. Biocca & M. R. Levy (Eds.), *Communication in the age of virtual reality* (pp. 15–31). Hillsdale, NJ: Lawrence Erlbaum Associates.

Brecht, B. (1967). Radiotheorie. In B. Brecht (Ed.), *Schriften zur Literatur und Kunst Gesammelte Werke* (Vol. 18, pp. 114–134). Frankfurt a. M.: Suhrkamp.

Brody, E. W. (1990). *Communication tomorrow: New audiences, new technologies, new media*. New York: Praeger.

Bryant, J., & Love, C. (1996). Entertainment as the driver of new information technology. In R. R. Dohlakia, N. Mundorf, & N. Dohlakia (Eds.), *New infotainment technologies in the home* (pp. 91–114). Mahwah, NJ: Lawrence Erlbaum Associates.

Bullinger, H. J., Bauer, W., & Braun, M. (1997). Virtual environments. In G. Salvendy (Ed.), *Handbook of human factors and ergonomics* (2nd ed., pp. 1725–1759). New York: Wiley.

Carroll, N. (1990). *The philosophy of horror or paradoxes of the heart*. New York: Routledge.

Csikszentmihalyi, M. (1995). Das Flow-Erlebnis und seine Bedeutung für die Psychologie des Menschen. In M. Csikszentmihalyi & I. S. Csikszentmihalyi (Eds.), *Die aussergewöhnliche Erfahrung im Alltag: Die Psychologie des Flow-Erlebnisses* (pp. 28–49). Stuttgart: Klett-Cotta.

Dohlakia, R. R., Mundorf, N., & Dohlakia, N. (1996). Bringing infotainment home: Challenge and choices. In R. R. Dohlakia, N. Mundorf & N. Dohlakia, (Eds.), *New infotainment technologies in the home* (pp. 1–20). Mahwah, NJ: Lawrence Erlbaum Associates.

Durlak, J. T. (1987). A typology for interactive media. In M. L. McLaughlin (Ed.), *Communication Yearbook 10* (pp. 743–757). Newbury Park, CA: Sage.

Esser, H. (1993). *Soziologie: Allgemeine Grundlagen*. Frankfurt a. M.: Campus.

Fritz, J. (Ed.). (1995). *Warum Computerspiele faszinieren: Empirische Annäherungen an Nutzen und Wirkung von Bildschirmspielen*. Weinheim: Juventa.

Goertz, L. (1995). Wie interaktiv sind neue Medien? Auf dem Weg zu einer Definition von Interaktivität. *Rundfunk und Fernsehen, 43*, 477–493.

Hallenberger, G. (1995). Fernsehen 2000. Von Utopien und Anti-Utopien. *Aesthetik und Kommunikation, 24*(1), 22–27.

Hanisch, S. (1999). *Let's go to the voomies: Der Einfluss von Persönlichkeitsmerkmalen auf die Affinität zu Neuen Medien.* Unpublished diploma thesis, University of Music and Theater, Hannover, Germany.

Hasebrink, U., & Krotz, F. (1991). Das Konzept der Publikumsaktivität in der Kommunikationswissenschaft. *Siegener Periodicum zur Internationalen Empirischen Literaturwissenschaft, 10*(1), 115–139.

Hasebrink, U., & Krotz, F. (Eds.). (1996). *Die Zuschauer als Fernsehregisseure? Zum Verständnis individueller Nutzungs- und Rezeptionsmuster.* Baden-Baden: Nomos.

Heeter, C. (1989). Implications of new interactive technologies for conceptualizing communication. In J. L. Salvaggio & J. Bryant (Eds.), *Media use in the information age: Emerging patterns of adoption and consumer use* (pp. 217–235). Hillsdale, NJ: Lawrence Erlbaum Associates.

Hickethier, K. (1994). Zwischen Einschalten und Ausschalten. Fernsehgeschichte als Geschichte des Zuschauens. In K. Hickethier (Ed.), *Institution, Technik und Programm: Rahmenaspekte der Programmgeschichte des Fernsehens* (pp. 237–306). München: Fink.

Jaeckel, M. (1995). Interaktion: Soziologische Anmerkungen zu einem Begriff. *Rundfunk und Fernsehen, 43,* 463–476.

Krappmann, L. (1989). Interaktion. In G. Endruweit & G. Trommsdorff (Eds.), *Wörterbuch der Soziologie* (Vol. 2, p. 310). München: Deutscher Taschenbuchverlag.

Maletzke, G. (1987). Aspekte der Medienzukunft: Wertewandel, Nutzungstrends, Veränderungen im Angebot. In M. Grewe-Partsch & J. Groebel (Eds.), *Mensch und Medien: Zum Stand von Wissenschaft und Praxis in nationaler und internationaler Perspektive.* München: Saur.

Mast, C. (1986). *Was leisten die Medien? Funktionaler Strukturwandel in den Kommunikationssystemen.* Osnabrück: Fromm, Germany.

Meutsch, D. (1987). *Literatur verstehen: Eine empirische Studie.* Braunschweig: Vieweg.

Mundorf, N., & Westin, S. (1996). Adoption of information technology: Contributing factors. In R. R. Dohlakia, N. Mundorf, & N. Dohlakia (Eds.), *New infotainment technologies in the home* (pp. 157–172). Mahwah, NJ: Lawrence Erlbaum Associates.

Prokop, D. (1972). Zum Problem von Produktion und Kommunikation im Bereich der Massenmedien. In D. Prokop (Ed.), *Massenkommunikationsforschung* (Vol. 1, pp. 9–27). Frankfurt a. M.: Fischer.

Rafaeli, S. (1988). Interactivity: From new media to communication. In R. P. Hawkins, J. M. Wiemann, & S. Pingree (Eds.), *Advancing communication science: Merging mass and interpersonal processes* (pp. 110–134). Newbury Park, CA: Sage.

Rice, R. E., Bair, J. H., Chen, M., Dimmick, J., Jotier, D. M., Jacob, M. E., McDaniel Johnson, B., Penniman, W. D., Svenning, L. L., Rogers, E. M., Rothenbutiler, E. W., Ruchinskas, J. E., & Williams, F. (1984). *The new media: Communication, research, and technology.* Newbury Park, CA: Sage.

Rötzer, F. (1996). Interaktion - das Ende herkömmlicher Massenmedien. In R. Maresch (Ed.), *Medien und Öffentlichkeit: Positionierungen, Symptome, Simulationsbrüche.* München: Boer.

Rogers, E. M. (1986). *Communication technology: The new media in society.* New York: The Free Press.

Salomon, G. (1984). Television is "easy" and print is "tough": The differential investment of mental effort in learning as a function of perceptions and attributions. *Journal of Educational Psychology, 76,* 647–658.

Schönbach, K. (1997). Das hyperaktive Publikum - Essay über eine Illusion. *Publizistik, 42,* 279–286.

Schrape, K. (1995). *Digitales Fernsehen: Marktchancen und ordnungspolitischer Regelungsbedarf* [Bericht der Prognos AG im Auftrag der Bayrischen Landeszentrale für neue Medien (BLM), München, und der Landesanstalt für Rundfunk Nordrhein-Westfalen (LFR), Düsseldorf]. München: Fischer.

Schulz, W. (1997). Neue Medien - Chancen und Risiken: Tendenzen der Medienentwicklung und ihre Folgen. *Aus Politik und Zeitgeschichte, 42,* 3–12.

Schwarz, A. (1995). Utopie und Realität interaktiven Fernsehens. Ein Bericht aus der Praxis. *montage/av, 4*(2), 144–160.

Shivers, J. S. (1979). The origin of man, culture, and leisure. In H. Ibrahim & J. S. Shivers (Eds.), *Leisure: Emergence and expansion* (pp. 3–44). Los Alamitos, CA: Hwong Publishing.

Steuer, J. (1995). Virtual reality: Dimensions determining telepresence. In F. Biocca & M. R. Levy (Eds.), *Communication in the age of virtual reality* (pp. 33–56). Hillsdale, NJ: Lawrence Erlbaum Associates.

Stipp, H. (1995). Will the digital technologies revolutionize television viewing? In K. Boehme-Duerr & G. Graf (Eds.), *Auf der Suche nach dem Publikum. Medienforschung für die Praxis. Medien und Märkte* (Vol. 6, pp. 273–294). Konstanz: Universitätsverlag, Germany.

Turkle, S. (1984). *The second self: Computers and the human spirit.* New York: Simon & Schuster.

Vorderer, P. (1992). *Fernsehen als Handlung: Fernsehfilmrezeption aus motivationspsychologischer Perspektive.* Berlin: Edition Sigma.

Vorderer, P. (1995). Will das Publikum neue Medien(angebote)? Medienpsychologische Thesen über die Motivation zur Nutzung neuer Medien. *Rundfunk und Fernsehen, 43,* 494–505.

Vorderer, P. (1996). Rezeptionsmotivation: Warum nutzen Rezipienten mediale Unterhaltungsangebote? *Publizistik, 41,* 310–326.

Vorderer, P. (1999). Psychologie der Medienrezeption. In G. Roters, W. Klingler, & M. Gerhards (Eds.), *Mediensozialisation und Medienverantwortung* (pp. 37–46). Baden-Baden: Nomos.

Vorderer, P. (in press). Entertainment, suspense, and interactivity. In I. Bondebjerg (Ed.), *Visual media, culture, and the mind.*

Vorderer, P., & Knobloch, S. (1998). Ist interaktive Fernsehunterhaltung spannend? *Siegener Periodicum zur Internationalen Empirischen Literaturwissenschaft, 17*(1). 58–80.

Weber, M. (1984). *Soziologische Grundbegriffe* (6th ed.). Tübingen: Mohr.

Wehner, J. (1997a). Interaktive Medien - Ende der Massenkommunikation? *Zeitschrift für Soziologie, 26,* 96–114.

Wehner, J. (1997b). *Das Ende der Massenkultur? Visionen und Wirklichkeit der neuen Medien.* Frankfurt a. M.,: Campus.

Weidenmann, B. (1989). Der mentale Aufwand beim Fernsehen. In J. Groebel & P. Winterhoff-Spurk (Eds.), *Empirische Medienpsychologie* (pp. 134–149). München: Psychologie Verlags Union.

Zillmann, D. (1996). The psychology of suspense in dramatic exposition. In P. Vorderer, H. J. Wulff, & M. Friedrichsen (Eds.), *Suspense: Conceptualizations, theoretical analyses, and empirical explorations* (pp. 199–231). Mahwah, NJ: Lawrence Erlbaum Associates.

Zillmann, D., & Bryant, D. (1994). Entertainment as media effect. In J. Bryant & D. Zillmann (Eds.), *Media effects: Advances in theory and research* (pp. 437–461). Hillsdale, NJ: Lawrence Erlbaum Associates.

Humor and Comedy

Dolf Zillmann
University of Alabama

And frame your mind to mirth and merriment, which bars a thousand harms and lengthens life.
—Shakespeare (prologue to "The Taming of the Shrew")

This chapter breaks with tradition. Expositions on humor and comedy usually trace the wisdom of great scholars from antiquity to modern times. In defiance of such chronology of efforts at explaining what it is that makes people smile, giggle, chuckle, or burst out in seemingly uncontrollable laughter, this chapter begins with the conceptualization of humorous formats and contexts, and it then presents the major theories of the enjoyment of humor and comedy. The focus is on theories, as well as on somewhat unorthodox theory combinations, that have withstood the rigor of experimental examination. Representative investigations are noted, and implicated mechanisms of amusement are exemplified by tidbits of humor. Needless to say, in discussing the principal ideas that make up the theories, homage is paid to the innovative thinking of the scholars of earlier and later times. Additionally, the appeal of humor is examined in the context of competition with alternative genres of entertainment, and pertinent research findings are indicated. The chapter concludes with a discussion of the merits of humor as therapy for emotional and physical ailments.

THE DRAMA IN COMEDY

Comedy is, of course, a form of drama. This is so not only because it also dwells on conflict and its resolution, but mostly because it entails the essential plots for enlightenment that characterize drama.

Aristotle (trans. 1966) pondered the conditions that make for enjoyable drama and found fault with two principal narrative transitions. First, he posited, "a good man must not be seen passing from happiness to misery"; and second, "a bad man from misery to happiness." He thought it self-evident that such transitions are incapable of fostering joy and simply asserted that audiences would deem them "odious." In discussing tragic plots, however, Aristotle articulated a moral rationale for the expected reactions of displeasure and vexation. Put simply, he suggested that transitions that violate precepts of what is fair and just not only cannot be enjoyed, but also are irritating and distressing because they amount to miscarriages of justice.

Drama theorists have heeded Aristotle's advice. Accordingly, the indicated failing plots still are to be avoided, and their inversions are accepted as the basic plots that ensure the enjoyment of drama. Now, as ever, the gospel of enjoyable drama is that, first, good persons must improve their lot in life and gain incentives; and second, bad persons must experience a deterioration of their fortunes and suffer due punishment.

These dramatic plots are exactly those of comedy. Olson's (1968) categorization of plots of folly and plots of cleverness, for instance, specifies that for comedy to be enjoyable both the ill-intentioned fool and the ill-intentioned wit must come to harm, and both the well-intentioned fool and the well-intentioned wit must come to glory. Whether fool or wit, then, both well-intentioned and ill-intentioned characters must be seen getting their just deserts: reward or punishment, respectively.

In this scheme of things, it is essential that the actions of characters can be observed, or at least that these characters' intentions can be inferred or guessed. Only if such character development is provided can the characters be deemed evil and deserving of misfortune or good and deserving of rewards.

A MATTER OF DISPOSITION

These expectations have been elaborated in the disposition theory of drama and comedy (Zillmann, 1980, 1983, 1996; Zillmann & Cantor, 1976). This theory focuses on the dispositional consequences of moral assessments and then projects enjoyment or dejection on the basis of the formed dispositions. Specifically, the recipient of drama or comedy is viewed as a moral monitor who applauds or condemns the intentions and actions of characters. Approval fosters dispositions of liking and caring, condemnation promotes dispositions of disliking and resenting. A friendlike hero or protagonist emerges in the former condition, an enemylike villain or antagonist in the latter. Less obvious are the further consequences of such character development, as affective dispositions are seen as the principal determinants of hopes and fears (i.e., of Pollyannish anticipations and gloomy apprehensions) concerning the characters' fate. In the case of liked characters, good fortunes are hoped for and misfortunes are feared. In the case of resented, despised, and hated characters, it is their misfortune and demise that is hoped for, and their not coming to harm—not to mention their coming to glory—is feared. When the anticipated fate finally materializes, resolutions that feature the hoped-for events can be enjoyed, whereas resolutions featuring the feared events are bound to be deplored.

Finally, disposition theory goes beyond the dichotomy of heroes and villains in considering all conceivable gradations of affect. Dispositions toward characters are mapped onto a continuum from extreme hate, through affective indifference, to extreme love. The enjoyment of hoped-for dramatic happenings thus is expected to increase with affective intensity. The enjoyment of feared outcomes, in contrast, is expected to decrease with such intensity, with disappointment and dejection increasing alongside. Additionally, affective indifference toward characters is expected not to engage hopes and fears in any appreciable way, and therefore, to fail to yield sizable reactions of enjoyment or dejection.

Disposition theory is well supported by research on the enjoyment of dramatic fiction (Zillmann, 1996) and related phenomena outside of drama proper, such as the enjoyment of sports (Zillmann & Paulus, 1993) and the news (Zillmann, Taylor, & Lewis, 1998). For humor and comedy, some modification of the theory was necessary, however. Apparently there is little comic value in displays of the benefaction of characters, no matter how deserving of it they may be. Humor and comedy seem exceedingly partial to dishing out put-downs, mishaps, insults, and outright humiliations. Philosophers (Aristotle, trans. 1966; Hobbes, 1651/1968) and uncounted cynics recognized the indicated partiality some time ago. Hazlitt (1826/1926) expressed it most succinctly: "We grow tired of everything but turning others into ridicule, and congratulating ourselves on their defects" (p. 239).

NEGATIVE PARTIALITY

In early psychological research, Wolff, Smith, and Murray (1934) echoed this sentiment by focusing, one-sidedly, on disparagement as the major theme of humor and comedy. Their formula for what is funny, namely, seeing "an unaffiliated object in a disparaging situation" (p. 344), became the keystone of what is now called *superiority theory* (Keith-Spiegel, 1972) or *disparagement theory* of humor (Zillmann, 1983).

The formula presented by Wolff et al. (1934) stipulates two necessary, though not necessarily sufficient, conditions for the evocation of mirth. First, the disposition toward the disparaged entity may not be positive. It is implied that favorable dispositions would prevent or squelch mirth. Second, mirth is made contingent on disparagement in one form or another. It was apparently self-evident that the formula was asymmetrical and could not be supplemented by inversion to read that mirth results from seeing an affiliated object in a gratifying situation.

The premise that liked characters' benefaction is not a viable theme for humor and comedy has been carried into disposition theory. Its formal propositions read as follows:

Disposition Toward Victim

1. The more intense the negative affective disposition toward the disparaged agent or entity, the greater the magnitude of mirth.
2. The more intense the positive affective disposition toward the disparaged agent or entity, the smaller the magnitude of mirth.

Disposition Toward Victor

3. The more intense the negative affective disposition toward the disparaging agent or entity, the smaller the magnitude of mirth.
4. The more intense the positive affective disposition toward the disparaging agent or entity, the greater the magnitude of mirth.

The strongest reaction of amusement is obviously expected for displays that feature the disparagement of an extremely disliked victim by an extremely liked victor. Least amusing should be seeing the reverse happen, with other dispositional victor–victim combinations yielding intermediate results.

Plato's observations are of interest in this connection. In his theory of the ludicrous, Plato (trans. 1871) focused on the display of vain conceit and self-aggrandizement, along with its corrective punishment, as a primary source for amusement. Comedy seems laden, indeed, with situations where characters who exhibit arrogance, snobbishness, vanity, and vainglory—but also ignorance, bigotry, egotism, insensitivity, contemptuousness, and rudeness, as well as other generally frowned-on and detested traits—are humbled by a cutting punch line (Charney, 1978; Feibleman, 1962). In terms of disposition theory, these characters are disliked enough, if only momentarily, to inspire amusement on seeing them "put in their place."

The disposition theory of humor and comedy has been supported by a large number of investigations (cf. Zillmann, 1983). Most have employed jokes and funny stories as a presentational format that is readily manipulated, and some were conducted prior to the theory's formulation. For instance, Wolff et al. (1934) explored ethnic humor by varying the ethnicity of characters delivering the punch line and of those being victimized by it. Their comic material presented, essentially, members of ethnic group A being triumphant (in a humorous fashion, certainly) over members of ethnic group B, with some degree of friction existing between the two groups. In a counter-version, A and B would trade places, other things remaining equal. Wolff et al. used Jews versus gentiles in their humor, and they had Jews and gentiles respond to it. They hypothesized that it would be funnier to see one's own ethnic group triumphant over a rival group than to see one's own group suffer humiliation at the hands of the rival group, and their findings were indeed supportive of their hypothesis.

The experimental paradigm devised by Wolff et al. became standard in ethnic humor research (La Fave, 1972). It was used to explore the ethnic humor of Blacks and Whites (Middleton, 1959) and the development of reactions to ethnic humor by White, Black, and Hispanic children (McGhee & Duffey, 1983a, 1983b; McGhee & Lloyd, 1981), but also to investigate gender differences in humor appreciation (Cantor, 1976; Losco & Epstein, 1975; Love & Deckers, 1989; Mundorf, Bhatia, Zillmann, Lester, & Robertson, 1988; Wicker, Barron, & Willis, 1980). Eventually, the paradigm was expanded to examine the amusement consequences for humor featuring the humiliation of one party by another, with dispositions toward both parties being measured. Of course, if humiliation is brought on incidentally, as "poetic justice," dispositions can be assessed toward the victim only.

Zillmann and Cantor (1972), for instance, exploited the existence of animosity and resentment between employers and their employees and professors and their students. They were able to show that resentment toward the other party in these dichotomies fuels amusement in response to seeing the resented party humiliated. In a more recent study, Zillmann et al. (1998) measured the magnitude of resentment felt toward leading politicians and found that this resentment intensifies amusement reactions in proportion to its magnitude. Specifically, these investigators concocted press releases asserting that either President Bill Clinton or Speaker of the House Newt Gingrich had contracted a venereal disease, a fact that would have been covered up for some time. Not only did those who despised the president or Gingrich find the revelation of these gentlemen's dilemma highly amusing, the magnitude of amusement reactions was also found to vary proportionally with that of the resentful disposition. That is, the more strongly a particular politician was resented, the more amusing and hilarious it was to learn of his victimization. This result is, of course, exactly what the disposition theory of humor and comedy predicts.

Not all witnessed misfortunes of resented persons can be expected to foster amusement, however. Aristotle (trans. 1966) was probably first in setting limits by suggesting that the display of grievous harm, especially death, would evoke pity that overpowers any inclination to laugh. On the other hand, macabre humor exists; and given favorable dispositional circumstances, death apparently can be a laughing matter. Also, catching a venereal disease would seem to qualify as grievous harm. Yet sufficient resentment toward those afflicted did foster considerable amusement in response to the misfortune's revelation—despite its supposed nonfictional status.

THE COMIC FRAME OF MIND

But more generally, it seems to be necessary that humorous presentations be approached with a lighthearted attitude. The very expectation of comedy, according to Olson (1968), signals "contrariety to the serious" (p. 13). The audience must be free from acute needs and "inclined to take nothing seriously and to be gay about everything" (p. 25). The very format of joke-telling (i.e., the recipients' cognizance of the nonseriousness of whatever is labeled a joke or a funny story) may similarly indicate that fun-hampering empathic restraints are to be relaxed or abandoned. Others, however, have stipulated that such indications must be part of the humorous message itself. Freud (1905/1958) elaborated a system of features (under the heading *Witzarbeit*) that, when added to the display of otherwise non-humorous hostile or sexual happenings, would signal the humorous nature of the exposition. McGhee (1972) adopted this view, suggesting that "humor cues" need to be present to ensure that expectations appropriate for drama reception would be converted to expectations appropriate for the reception of humor and comedy. Berlyne (1969) and Flugel (1954) have expressed similar convictions.

At this point, then, humor and comedy part company with drama proper. Comedy, as we have seen, shares all essential plots with drama. Yet, whereas drama invites emotional involvement, and because of its pretense to exhibit "reality," does not absolve empathic sensitivities (Zillmann, 1994), the humor and comedy format encourages lightheartedness, if not outright trivialization, of addressed issues.

COMIC MINIATURES

There are time conventions for comedy. A full-blown exemplar of this genre spans a loosely defined unit of time in which it tends to feature an overarching plot of conflict and resolution. Almost always, however, it features a chain of minor, brief plots also composed of conflict and resolution. Television sitcoms, for instance, aggregate a considerable number of humorous encounters, one following another in rapid succession. These encounters amount to miniature plots in which, among other amusing friction reductions, obnoxiousness is punished and arrogance ridiculed. Usually there are characters whose role it is to "step out of line," thereby targeting themselves for put-downs (Zillmann & Stocking, 1976).

Joke-telling may, of course, be construed as merely another form of miniature-plot presentation. In fact, any kind of humorous expression can be thought of as a miniaturized comic plot—if need be, as a miniaturized miniature plot. All humor, no matter how condensed or reduced, must make a statement or amount to a comment about circumstances. It must have propositional form, although not in linguistic specifics. The use of nonlinguistic propositional form should be clear from inspecting and interpreting Fig. 3.1. The initial statement is that a father criticizes his son for dressing inappropriately. The follow-up statement is that he himself is inappropriately dressed. It is implied, finally, that the father's condemnation is stupid because he fails to recognize that, with his criticism, he shoots himself in the foot. Is this what Plato had in mind when he lectured us on the ridiculous in vain conceit?

The point to be made is that, irrespective of presentational format, any humorous expression, because it entails all essential characteristics of comedy, can profitably be analyzed as miniature comedy. The dispositional elements are usually present to fuel amusement. The same holds true for negative partiality. There obviously is no humor in complimenting and praising good people for impecca-

FIG. 3.1   A case of backfire ridicule.

ble appearance and conduct—unless, of course, the flattery is exaggerated to the point where irony is recognized and compliments turn to cutting criticism.

TRANSIENT BENEFITS OF LAUGHTER

The British philosopher Hobbes (1651/1968) had little sympathy for humor. He thought that "those grimaces called laughter" would express a passion that is "incident most to them, that are conscious of the fewest abilities in themselves" (p. 125). Such passion was not to be pursued by the educated and noble. At the same time, however, Hobbes showed a better understanding of why people laugh, especially about others, than anyone previous to him. Although he dealt with humor in just a few asides, he is rightly credited with the creation of the superiority theory of humor because it was he who provided a rationale for psychological benefits that accrue to laughing about others. He recognized that those who laugh about others place themselves, whether knowingly or not, above the objects of their derision. He suggested that recognition of "some deformed thing in another" would prompt a comparison that renders the comparers superior, which in turn would prompt laughter conveying that "they suddenly applaud themselves" (p. 125). But, as already indicated, he showed little compassion for those celebrating the absence of the deficiencies spotted in others and thereby enhancing themselves, their self-esteem in particular. He spoke derogatorily of those poor souls "who are forced to keep themselves in their own favor, by observing the imperfections of other men" (p. 125).

Some of Hobbes' suggestions have become an integral part of contemporary psychological theorizing about the affective implications of comparing oneself with less (or more) fortunate others. Festinger's (1954) social-comparison theory addresses these implications. For so-called downward comparisons (i.e., the Hobbes variety) it predicts a set of ego-enhancements, such as intensified feelings of superiority and strengthened self-confidence (Suls & Miller, 1977). Most pertinent here are expectations concerning affect-regulation (Taylor, Wayment, & Collins, 1993). Put simply, if the monitoring of the fortunes of others reveals that these others are less well-off than those doing the monitoring (by way of abilities, skills, appeal, health, wealth, and perhaps even plain luck), pleasurable reactions are expected. In regard to mood-management theory (Zillmann, 1988), good moods should be enhanced and bad moods should be diminished and repaired.

The problem for the analysis of humor and comedy is that the social-comparison reasoning projects roundabout reactions of pleasure. It projects enjoyment in general terms, not amusement, merriment, and gaiety specifically. Not surprisingly, then, the theory has been used to explain affective reactions to drama, the enjoyment of tragedy in particular (Zillmann, 1999). The analysis of tragedy poses a challenge to Hobbes, in fact, in that his contentions fail to explain why nobody is laughing when witnessing others' infirmities and misfortunes during tragic play. Irrespective of tragedy, however, it would appear that a comic frame of mind must be provided by dramatic or circumstantial means, if amusement and gaiety are to be extracted from downward social comparisons.

DECONSTRUCTING DEPRESSION

The fact that others' tragic misfortunes can touch our emotions and move us to tears shows that conditions exist in which downward comparisons fail to yield joyous reactions. Moreover, this fact suggests that joyous reactions to others' misfortunes, especially the evocation of amusement, must be limited to particular circumstances. McDougall (1908, 1922) thought he discovered these circumstances and developed an intriguing but much neglected theory around it. Starting with the premise that humans are endowed with an instinct to empathize with the emotions of their fellow beings, he argued that, as mishaps are aplenty and misery abounds, people would continually commiserate with others—to the point of becoming depressed. McDougall then posited that other-directed negative affective dispositions would prevent that outcome. Specifically, he argued that animosity, resentment, and hatred would motivate people to rid themselves of any inclination to empathetically co-suffer the misfortunes of the targets of their sentiment. Laughter, he suggested, is the expressive component of the dissolution of empathic distress.

McDougall's reasoning may seem contrived but accords well with recent theory and research on empathy. Negative affective dispositions define, in fact, the pivotal point at which empathy is abandoned and counteremotions may find expression (Zillmann, 1991). However, it again appears that laughter is only one of many forms of such expression, and that a lighthearted, comic frame of mind must exist for genuine merriment to materialize. On the other hand, hostile comedy can be exceedingly raw and brutal, but the victimization of the most obnoxious characters of such comedy will foster merciless laughter nonetheless—even in situations devoid of embellishments with humorous cues. McDougall would, of course, have predicted this heartless behavior by pointing to the laughers' unwillingness to share the sting of humiliation and pain with those deserving no better.

THE UNFAIRNESS DOCTRINE

The enjoyment of drama is greatly influenced by considerations of justice (Zillmann, 1996). A mostly unarticulated but implied principle is that gratifications have to be earned by drama's characters, just as we all must earn them by our own efforts. Moreover, none of drama's characters may be exempt from the punitive contingencies that govern our own lives. Violations of these conceptions of justice distress us. They inspire vengeful motives which, in turn, let us rejoice when we see violators duly punished, even when this happens in the cruelest of ways.

Humor and comedy are, no doubt, also under this influence of moral assessment. Nothing seems more distressing than seeing someone with dubious credentials and deceitful maneuvering come to glory. Seeing the recipients of such unearned, and thus, undeserved, good fortune take a tumble restores justice. Given the presence of humor cues or a comic mind frame, such restoration certainly should evoke amusement.

The point here is that comparison-based humor is not limited to downward comparisons with others who are less attractive, intelligent, coordinated, or who drive a less impressive automobile. Humor, on the contrary, may entail upward comparisons. As characters are seen attaining gratifications that are unattainable to the onlookers, or at least unattainable without extraordinary effort, their sense of fair play is disturbed and retaliatory correctives are accepted and in fact, applauded. The logic of such reactions is not that people want to feel superior to others, but that, once others' foul play has been detected, people respond with envy that lets them enjoy the restoration of fairness by seeing the foul players put back in their place. Comedies tend to be laden with short-plotted, put-down humor that follows this formula. Nobody is to get something for nothing (i.e., something good for no effort). But when they do, the comic put-down comes to the rescue.

THE HUMOR IN PROBLEM DISSOLUTION

In contrast to those who could see no good in humor—Hobbes first and foremost—the German philosopher Kant (1788/1922) did not engage in castigation and offered a morally neutral explanation for the enjoyment of humor. He proposed that laughter is "an affective reaction that is evoked by the sudden transformation of a strained expectation into nothing" (p. 409, author's translation). He thought that people would respond in a joyful fashion when what seemed to be problematic suddenly resolved itself, proving negligible or trivial. The British philosopher Spencer (1864/1888) rephrased this formula, suggesting that laughter results when an effort suddenly encounters a void. He termed the transition from problematic to laughable "descending incongruity." Spencer is also known for proposing a related physiological theory of humor. He theorized that laughter, because of its semiconvulsive concomitants, depletes nervous energy and thus provides relief from any initial apprehension.

What Kant and Spencer must have had in mind are the numerous stressful and potentially threatening situations in everyday life that turn out to be less than anticipated. Imagine a lady at poolside stepping on a snake and screaming in anguish, who suddenly realizes that it was a rubber snake that her beloved but mischievous husband had planted. Or imagine a good student who, handed a paper with a failing grade, recognizes on closer inspection that it goes to the other Smith in class. Or imagine yourself looking for your car in a dark and reputedly dangerous parking lot with someone following you and grabbing your shoulder, and this someone turning out to be your best friend. Surely, situations such as these meet the stipulated conditions of strained expectations that dissolve into "nothingness." Somewhat more technically expressed, the apprehension of something noxious or dangerous in encounters of the indicated sort fosters response preparation associated with excitedness, and this preparation is suddenly deprived of its cause. The effort was for naught, and excited persons are now sitting atop a charge of energy that no longer has a purpose. Following Spencer, this energy should be depleted by laughing, amusement being manifest in the experience of relief during depletion. Berlyne (1960) took a similar stand with his arousal–jag model, arguing that the experience of relief incorporates amusement in proportion with the amount of arousal that has become superfluous. Kant, however, appears to have favored a purely cognitive interpretation. He thought the recognition of the sudden transformation of a problem into a nonproblem sufficient for the evocation of amusement.

The focus on relief from seeing anticipated trouble evaporate before one's eyes points to explanations of basic, if not archaic, forms of gaiety and humor. The conditions for such experiences obviously predate the evolution of linguistic abilities. Moreover, they exist for nonhuman species, for nonhuman primates in particular. Many of those who have observed monkeys and apes in the implicated situations tend to believe, in fact, that these creatures should not be denied a sense of humor. Baboons, for instance, are known to cackle laughterlike after resolving skirmishes with rivaling troops by sending them off running (DeVore, 1965). They are also known to hop around in synchronized fashion, as if dancing in an effort to use up energy that is now devoid of a cause.

Relief from the confrontation with apparent problems can be conceptualized quite differently, however. Strained expectations can be construed as minimal, even trivial, apprehensions. Such "problems" of the smallest of magnitudes are routinely created by using language—sometimes without intent, but purposely in the creation of humor. Shifting between incompatible contexts, for instance, is a technique that is liberally exploited (Koestler, 1964; Raskin, 1985). The joke "Doctor, doctor. I broke my arm in three places." "Well, stay away from them in the future!" makes this point. So does the children's joke "Why was the bee sad?" "Because he couldn't find his honey!" Or the adult story of the farmer who, when calling his son at college and learning from his roommate that he is in bed with angina, uttered something like "Damn the oversexed bastard!" Such planned derailments of a train of thought can be arranged by nonverbal visual presentations as well, or at least by displays that combine verbal and nonverbal elements. Imagine, for instance, a cartoon depicting a totally dehydrated Martian creature on its knees in the middle of the desert, whispering the words "Ammonia, ammonia!" In all these illustrations, the initial interpretation of a central concept is eventually rendered inappropriate. At times, recognition of the puzzling ambiguity resolves the issue; at other times, this recognition is the only resolution there is (Rothbart & Pien, 1977). In either case, however, a bit of mental effort makes a miniature strain vanish into laughable nothingness.

The fact that incongruity-based humor requires the deciphering of ambiguities, a process that can be likened to problem solving, suggests that amusement in response to such humor is not merely the result of a problem having gone away. The process of making it go away, of getting the point of it all (illogical as this point may be), can be considered an achievement—not one that calls for bringing out the champagne, but one that can contribute to the amusement reaction. Kant (1788/1922) acknowledged as much in that he admired those with the ability to put themselves at will "into a frame of mind in which everything is judged in unusual (even opposite) ways, yet in accordance with particular principles of reason that characterize this frame of mind" (p. 412, author's translation). The indicated principles, plays on words and contortions of issues, have been elaborated by Freud (1905/1958) and many others who explored aspects of incongruity in humor (e.g., Berlyne, 1969; Nerhardt, 1976; Rothbart, 1976; Shultz, 1976; Suls, 1972).

A QUESTION OF FREEDOM OF EXPRESSION

Oddly, it was Freud (1905/1958) who laid the groundwork for the integration of theoretical developments that matured in divergent directions mostly after his time. His distinction between tendentious and nontendentious humor—that is, between humor in which someone or something is victimized (i.e., ridiculed, debased, or humiliated) and humor that is victimless—parallels the themes of hostile humor addressed in superiority theories versus the themes of innocuous, nonhostile humor addressed in incongruity theories. In contrast to the preference of many psychologists, he thought the independent analysis of these humor categories unproductive. Freud recognized that innocuous humor that limits itself to wordplay and the like would not make anybody roll on the floor. He thought such humor to have rather modest powers of evoking amusement. He credited exceedingly hostile tendentious humor, instead, with the capacity to trigger outbursts of laughter and gaiety. However, although Freud thought humor's tendentious elements to be those that fuel the belly laughter variety of amusement, he considered the incorporation of innocuous elements essential, even necessary. This is because he believed that the display of blunt, demeaning hostility cannot be enjoyed, for reasons of social censure, unless it is playfully embellished with innocent jokework. Freud argued that this jokework would bribe our senses by camouflaging the associated hostile component of humor. It is the presence of innocent features, then, that makes unacceptable derision acceptable. It sets us free to enjoy what we otherwise could not.

Freud had even more to say on this subject. He daringly declared people incapable of knowing exactly what it is they find amusing. "We do not know what it is that gives us pleasure and what we laugh about" (Freud, 1905/1958, p. 107, author's translation), he insisted, and he went on to suggest that we routinely misascribe and misapportion our merriment to the innocuous parts of humor when, in fact, we respond primarily to its socially unacceptable parts. He explained, for instance, that "in the case of dirty jokes generally, we commit glaring errors of judgment about the 'quality' of these jokes as far as it depends on formal features; the technique of dirty jokes is mostly rather poor, but their effect on laughter is enormous" (p. 82). Take demeaning sexual humor, for instance. Imagine a cartoon showing a middle-aged, nude woman kneeling before a middle-aged, nude man. He looks down on her, apparently expecting to be fellated. The caption has him say "No, I don't think Richard Simmons would be upset if you took in a few extra calories." Why is anybody laughing? Now imagine if the punchline had been "Yes, that's what I want you to do." Would anybody have laughed? The reference to diet guru Simmons, which invites an inference about the woman's concern with obesity, appears to be necessary because it allows respondents to perceive their reaction as resulting from this "embellishment." The respondents may well enjoy the reluctant woman's humiliation. But they are, thanks to the embellishment, absolved from ever thinking that they did.

Freud's two-factor proposal, then, not only projects that the innocuous element of humor camouflages its tendentious component, but also asserts that people commonly misconstrue what it is they laugh about. Not only are we free to laugh by avoiding social censure, we also are free to take pleasure from something on the inappropriate side by avoiding self-censure—as we do not entirely understand why we do what we do.

Freud's suggestions were eventually formalized in a misattribution theory of humor and put to the test under comedylike circumstances (Zillmann & Bryant, 1980). Specifically, a situation was created and modified, such that tendentious and nontendentious elements could be combined or separated. An unfortunate mishap, a person spilling piping hot coffee over herself, served as the tendentious, potentially demeaning happening. A jack-in-the-box popping up defined the innocuous jokework. The context of the "play" was a laboratory in which a research participant was to judge the display quality of various toys for television advertisements. A female experimenter explained the procedure either in polite or offensive fashion, the latter by questioning the participant's intelligence for the assignment. This variation was used to test the implications of affective disposition for amusement. The experimenter then poured herself a cup of hot coffee and went to the adjoining room, appearing on a monitor to display toys. After displaying a few toys, she presented the jack-in-the-box. In one condition the jack simply popped out, not doing any damage. In the other the jack popped out, causing her to jerk and, in the process, to knock over the cup of coffee. The coffee spilled over her arms, apparently scalding her. Throughout the display of the jack-in-the-box, whether or not associated with the mishap, the research participant's facial expressions were unobtrusively recorded. The records were later coded for expressions of amusement by coders blind to the experimental conditions.

What is to be expected here? Just seeing the jack pop out should be amusing, but only modestly so. Seeing the liked experimenter have the plain mishap should, at best, be minimally amusing; and seeing her have the mishap because of the popping jack also cannot be expected to evoke great hilarity. On the other hand, seeing the obnoxious, disliked experimenter have the accident, even when not embellished with humor cues, should trigger a notable degree of amusement. However, seeing her have the accident as the result of the popping jack should, so to speak, bring the house down.

The findings confirmed all these expectations. Amusement was exceedingly high when all the ingredients of good comedy were present: despised protagonists, their victimization, and humor cues that set the audience free to enjoy these characters' demise. The most telling data point of the described investigation is that the mere presence of an exceedingly innocuous humor cue, a popping jack-in-the-box in this case, more than doubled amusement in response to the observed misfortune. It allowed the onlookers to be *malicious with dignity*, indeed.

THE GRAND ATTRACTION

When queried about their entertainment preferences, people are quick to list all sorts of serious programs. Records of their actual choices tell us otherwise, however. These records leave no doubt about the fact that humor is "King of the Mountain," and has been for some time.

A glance at Fig. 3.2 should convince anyone that comedy is the primary genre of media entertainment. It dominates film and television alike (Zillmann & Bryant, 1991, 1998). And this is no fluke. Over the last three decades, for instance, comedy consumption, as measured in the percentage of top 25 programs, had a whopping share of the genre market: about half of it (55%, 46%, and 49% in the 1960s, 1970s, and 1980s, respectively). In the nineties, marketers had to pay more for placing commercials in comedies than in any other kind of pro-

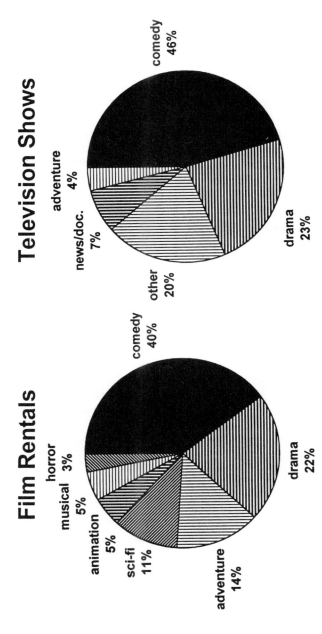

FIG. 3.2   The percentages of the top 100 film rentals of all time, by genre, are displayed at left; those of the top 100 television shows, by genre, at right. Film genres were classified according to Wiener (1989), television genres according to Brooks and Marsh (1988). Adapted from Zillmann and Bryant (1991).

gramming. In 1993, for example, four sitcoms topped *Monday Night Football*, and eight topped *60 Minutes* (Mandese, 1993). Serious drama, in particular, proved to be poor competition. There can be little doubt, then, about comedy as a winning formula for media entertainment. More often than not, people do look for merriment by picking comedy with all its foolishness over serious, problem-laden program alternatives, whether or not they admit to this partiality.

It has been suspected all along that people, after a long day in the office or tiring hours in factory halls, may be drawn to lighthearted diversions rather than to dramatic displays of others' coping with danger and misery in fiction and in the news. Some critics have been cruel enough to brand this inclination as an "escape from reality." Others have focused on the potential recreational value of entertaining diversions and have embraced them, regardless of aesthetic and moral considerations (Repetti, 1989). Still others have simply ascertained what people do when they are "stressed out."

In a massive assessment of daily television viewing in the family context, Anderson, Collins, Schmitt, and Jacobvitz (1996), for instance, measured variations in stress levels and related them to television program choices. They found that high stress levels were associated with increased comedy viewing and diminished interest in the news. Did these people have a tacit understanding of what is good for them?

Mood-management theory (Zillmann, 1988) addresses this very issue of tacit knowledge about how to improve one's affective state. The theory projects that people learn, essentially by trial and error, what works for them; that is, which kind of media entertainment helps them best to repair and improve their emotional condition. When distressed or in a rotten mood, they simply return to programming that has helped them in the past to snap out of such undesirable states. However, not all genres of media entertainment have the same capacity for distress or mood repair. Lighthearted comedy, with its belittlement of everyday problems, is thought to have more of this capacity than, say, crime drama and tragedy. Researchers expected, therefore, that many would have developed a tendency to call on comedy for the repair of their gloom.

Mood-management research shows that this is in fact the case. It has been observed, for instance, that frustrated men and angry women, when given a choice between comedy and drama, tended to pick comedy. They chose comedy more frequently than did men and women in a neutral state (Medoff, 1979). Humorous game shows proved to be similarly over-attractive to disgruntled men and women (Zillmann, Hezel, & Medoff, 1980). The point that people are not necessarily aware of the reasons for their choices is perhaps best made by studies relating media preferences to stages of the menstrual cycle or pregnancy. Premenstrual and menstrual women were found to select comedy programs more frequently than women in any other phase of the cycle (Meadowcroft & Zillmann, 1987). The appeal of comedy also was observed to vary with hormonally mediated depressive moods during pregnancy (Helregel & Weaver, 1989).

Comedy, needless to say, is not for everybody (Weaver, 1991). It is not for all occasions, either. Some research actually suggests that comedy is avoided when negative emotions are to be kept alive for some reason (O'Neal & Taylor, 1989) or when such emotions are particularly strong (Christ & Medoff, 1984). This should be good news for those who fear undue escapism. Apparently, when people have genuine problems that need attention, comedy fails to offer a way to run away from them. But when the daily humdrum with all its little aggravations takes hold of people, comedy appears to offer pleasant distraction with a high potential for mood repair.

AND IT DOES GOOD LIKE A MEDICINE

An old proverb asserts that "a merry heart doeth good like a medicine, but a broken spirit drieth the bones." Does such folk wisdom have merit? Recent developments in humor research suggest that much. On the premise that humor, because it often trivializes the lesser problems in life and converts them to laughing matters, diminishes anguish, it is treated as a potential antidote to stress, both in cognitive and endocrinological terms (Dixon, 1980; Goldstein, 1987; Haig, 1988; Robinson, 1983). Prolonged aversive experiences are known to instigate increased release of stress hormones, mostly cortisol in some form, and also to impair immunological function and ultimately health. Humor, or a humorous disposition that ensures frequent lighthearted responses to problems, can thus be expected to curb and prevent many pathogenic effects suffered by the "deadly serious." Irrespective of potential health benefits, however, humor appears to hold promise as a mood repairer that enhances the so-called quality of life by carrying with it a more positive outlook, increased initiative, and greater tolerance of adversity.

In considering these possibilities it is essential to separate two conditions. First, there is lightheartedness as a personality trait. Such a trait amounts to a persisting disposition to see humor where others do not; or more importantly, to deem many adverse conditions ridiculous and laughable whereas others find them distressing. Second, there is amusement and laughter as a state induced by exposure to humorous situations or materials, including materials presented via the entertainment media.

Research on humor as an individual difference variable has flourished and produced promising results (Lefcourt & Martin, 1986). For instance, individuals' sense of humor was observed to function as a stress buffer for depressive experiences (Nezu, Nezu, & Blissett, 1988). Those who frequently use humor to cope with genuine problems were found to suffer less impairment of their immune function when reacting to imagined daily hassles (measured by the concentration of immunoglobulin A in saliva) than those less capable of humorous coping (Martin & Dobbin, 1988). Jocularity prior to dental surgery was found to relate to both humorous coping as a trait and greater tolerance of the pains of the procedure (Trice & Price-Greathouse, 1986). Humorous coping also was found to be linked to the general morale of older adults (Simon, 1990). Although findings such as these cannot rule out that those reporting better morale than others are generally healthier and thus find it easier to approach some of their problems lightheartedly, the evidence at large shows consistently that people who, for whatever reason, manage to use humor in their coping with adversity, are better off than their less humorously inclined peers.

The effects of humor-induced transitory merriment are less clear. Unless humor is deemed to be in poor taste or offends in dispositional terms (which may happen, of course; see Zillmann et al., 1998), it invariably induces and enhances positive affective states accompanied by feelings of relaxation (Prerost & Ruma, 1987). The implications of such states for morale and toughness were tested in the degree to which persons tolerate pain (measured by fewer requests for analgesics, excessive pressure to limbs, or submersion of a hand in ice water). Exposure to comedy was found to increase pain tolerance more than exposure to a variety of nonhumorous stimuli (Cogan, Cogan, Waltz, & McCue, 1987; Nevo, Keinan, & Teshimovsky-Arditi, 1993; Weaver & Zillmann, 1994; Zillmann, Rockwell, Schweitzer, & Sundar, 1993). Moreover, compared with the effects of serious drama, comedy was found to reduce the number of requests for analgesics at bedtime for older adults (Adams & McGuire, 1986). These observations seem compromised, however, by more recent findings on postsurgical self-medication (Rotton & Shats, 1996). Exposure to comedy, also as compared to serious drama, reduced the number of requests for minor medication, but increased those for stronger analgesics.

Increases in salivary immunoglobulin A were also observed after exposure to comedy as compared to alternatives (Dillon, Minchoff, & Baker, 1985–86; Labott, Ahleman, Wolever, & Martin, 1990). Mirthful laughter per se was found to decrease levels of stress-linked hormones, such as cortisol and dopac (Berk, Tan, Fry, et al., 1989). Laughter also appeared to elevate natural killer cell activity (Berk, Tan, Napier, et al., 1989). Other research suggests, however, that the elevation of killer cell activity is partial to decidedly negative emotions, not to merriment (Knapp et al., 1992). In this connection it should be mentioned that increased pain tolerance, although associated with merriment, is not specific to that state. Increased pain tolerance has also been observed after exposure to tragedy and crying (Weaver & Zillmann, 1994; Zillmann et al., 1993). As these effects were ascertained after tragic resolution, some form of euphoric feelings cannot be ruled out, however. Assuming that exposure to tragedy ultimately induced a degree of enjoyment would bring these discrepant findings in line with those of other recent investigations that implicate positive emotions generally (not merriment specifically) with elevated pain tolerance (Zelman, Howland, Nichols, & Cleeland, 1991; Zillmann, de Wied, King Jablonski, & Jenzowsky, 1996).

The findings concerning transitory health-related effects of comedy exposure thus are marred by inconsistencies. They also should not be interpreted as proof that humor and nothing else has certain effects. It would seem highly informative to compare the effects of humor with those of other media entertainments, such as music and athletic performances of various forms. Comparative research of this kind remains to be conducted, however.

Also, given the state of knowledge provided by humor research, it would seem prudent not to over-promise what humor can do by way of healing. Humor will neither make the blind see nor resurrect the dead. But humor does have the capacity to provide plenty of gaiety in life. It can help potentially everybody to elude the humdrum of daily experience and the anguish of frustrations and setbacks. Humor can serve as an antidote to gloom. In fact, all indications are that its embrace will yield much-needed merriment in displacement of less desirable emotions, thereby furthering happiness and health in the long run.

REFERENCES

Adams, E. R., & McGuire, F. A. (1986). Is laughter the best medicine? A study of the effects of humor on perceived pain and affect. *Activities, Adaptation, and Aging, 8,* 157–175.

Anderson, D. R., Collins, P. A., Schmitt, K. L., & Jacobvitz, R. S. (1996). Stressful life events and television viewing. *Communication Research, 23,* 243–260.

Aristotle. (1966). De poetica (I. Bywater, Trans.). In *The works of Aristotle* (Vol. 11, Chapter 2). Oxford, England: Clarendon.

Berk, L. S., Tan, S. A., Fry, W. F., Napier, B. J., Lee, J. W., Hubbard, R. W., Lewis, J. E., & Eby, W. C. (1989). Neuroendocrine and stress hormone changes during mirthful laughter. *American Journal of the Medical Sciences, 298*(6), 390–396.

Berk, L. S., Tan, S. A., Napier, B. J., & Eby, W. C. (1989) Eustress of mirthful laughter modifies natural killer cell activity. *Clinical Research, 37,* 115A.

Berlyne, D. E. (1960). *Conflict, arousal and curiosity.* New York: McGraw-Hill.

Berlyne, D. E. (1969). Laughter, humor, and play. In G. Lindzey & E. Aronson (Eds.), *The handbook of social psychology: Vol. 3. The individual in a social context* (2nd ed., pp. 795–852). Reading, MA: Addison-Wesley.

Brooks, T., & Marsh, E. (1988). *The complete directory to prime time network TV shows, 1946–Present.* New York: Ballantine.

Cantor, J. R. (1976). What is funny to whom? The role of gender. *Journal of Communication, 26*(3), 164–172.

Charney, M. (1978). *Comedy high and low: An introduction to the experience of comedy.* New York: Oxford University Press.

Christ, W. G., & Medoff, N. J. (1984). Affective state and selective exposure to and use of television. *Journal of Broadcasting, 28*(1), 51–63.

Cogan, R., Cogan, D., Waltz, W., & McCue, M. (1987). Effects of laughter and relaxation on discomfort thresholds. *Journal of Behavioral Medicine, 10*(2), 139–144.

DeVore, I. (Ed.). (1965). *Primate behavior: Field studies of monkeys and apes.* New York: Holt, Rinehart & Winston.

Dillon, K. M., Minchoff, B., & Baker, K. H. (1985–86). Positive emotional states and enhancement of the immune system. *International Journal of Psychiatry in Medicine, 15*(1), 13–18.

Dixon, N. F. (1980). Humor: A cognitive alternative to stress? In I. G. Sarason & C. D. Spielberger (Eds.), *Stress and anxiety* (Vol. 7, pp. 281–289). Washington, DC: Hemisphere.

Feibleman, J. (1962). *In praise of comedy: A study in its theory and practice.* New York: Russell & Russell.

Festinger, L. (1954). A theory of social comparison processes. *Human Relations, 7,* 117–140.

Flugel, J. C. (1954). Humor and laughter. In G. Lindzey (Ed.), *Handbook of social psychology: Vol. 2. Special fields and applications* (pp. 709–734). Reading, MA: Addison-Wesley.

Freud, S. (1958). *Der Witz und seine Beziehung zum Unbewussten* [Wit and its relation to the unconscious]. Frankfurt: Fischer Bücherei. (Original work published 1905)

Goldstein, J. H. (1987). Therapeutic effects of laughter. In W. F. Fry & W. A. Salameth (Eds.), *Handbook of humor and psychotherapy: Advances in the clinical use of humor* (pp. 1–19). Sarasota, FL: Professional Resource Exchange.

Haig, R. A. (1988). *The anatomy of humor: Biopsychosocial and therapeutic perspectives.* Springfield, IL: Thomas.

Hazlitt, W. (1926). On the pleasure of hating. In *Essays* (pp. 235–247). New York: Macmillan. (Original work published 1826)

Helregel, B. K., & Weaver, J. B. (1989). Mood-management during pregnancy through selective exposure to television. *Journal of Broadcasting & Electronic Media, 33*(1), 15–33.

Hobbes, T. (1968). *Leviathan.* Harmondsworth, England: Penguin. (Original work published 1651)

Kant, I. (1922). Kritik der praktischen Vernunft: Zweites Buch. Analytik des Erhabenen [Critique of practical reason: Second book. Analysis of the revered.]. In E. Cassirer (Ed.), *Immanuel Kants Werke* (Vol. 5, pp. 315–412). Berlin: B. Cassirer. (Original work published 1788)

Keith-Spiegel, P. (1972). Early conceptions of humor: Varieties and issues. In F. H. Goldstein & P. E. McGhee (Eds.), *The psychology of humor: Theoretical perspectives and empirical issues* (pp. 3–39). New York: Academic Press.

Knapp, P. H., Levy, E. M., Giorgi, R. G., Black, P. H., Fox, B. H., & Heeren, T. C. (1992). Short-term immunological effects of induced emotion. *Psychosomatic Medicine, 54,* 133–148.

Koestler, A. (1964). *The act of creation.* London: Hutchinson.

Labott, S. M., Ahleman, S., Wolever, M. E., & Martin, R. B. (1990). The physiological and psychological effects of the expression and inhibition of emotion. *Behavioral Medicine, 16*(4), 182–189.

La Fave, L. (1972). Humor judgments as a function of reference groups and identification classes. In J. H. Goldstein & P. E. McGhee (Eds.), *The psychology of humor: Theoretical perspectives and empirical issues* (pp. 195–210). New York: Academic Press.

Lefcourt, H. M., & Martin, R. A. (1986). *Humor and life stress: Antidote to adversity.* New York: Springer-Verlag.

Losco, J., & Epstein, S. (1975). Humor preferences as a subtle measure of attitudes toward the same and the opposite sex. *Journal of Personality, 43,* 321–334.

Love, A. M., & Deckers, L. H. (1989). Humor appreciation as a function of sexual, aggressive, and sexist content. *Sex Roles, 20,* 649–654.

Mandese, J. (1993, September 6). *Home improvement* wins $ race. *Advertising Age,* 3, 26.

Martin, R. A., & Dobbin, J. P. (1988). Sense of humor, hassles, and immunoglobulin A: Evidence for a stress-moderating effect of humor. *International Journal of Psychiatry in Medicine, 18*(2), 93–105.

McDougall, W. (1908). *An introduction to social psychology.* London: Methuen.

McDougall, W. (1922). A new theory of laughter. *Psyche, 2,* 292–303.

McGhee, P. E. (1972). On the cognitive origins of incongruity humor: Fantasy assimilation versus reality assimilation. In F. H. Goldstein & P. E. McGhee (Eds.), *The psychology of humor: Theoretical perspectives and empirical issues* (pp. 61–80). New York: Academic Press.

McGhee, P. E., & Duffey, N. S. (1983a). Children's appreciation of humor victimizing different racial-ethnic groups: Racial-ethnic differences. *Journal of Cross-Cultural Psychology, 14*(1), 29–40.

McGhee, P. E., & Duffey, N. S. (1983b). The role of identity of the victim in the development of disparagement humor. *Journal of General Psychology, 108,* 257–270.

McGhee, P. E., & Lloyd, S. A. (1981). A developmental test of the disposition theory of humor. *Child Development, 52,* 925–931.

Meadowcroft, J. M., & Zillmann, D. (1987). Women's comedy preferences during the menstrual cycle. *Communication Research, 14,* 204–218.

Medoff, N. J. (1979). *The avoidance of comedy by persons in a negative affective state: A further study in selective exposure.* Unpublished doctoral dissertation, Indiana University.

Middleton, R. (1959). Negro and White reactions to racial humor. *Sociometry, 22,* 175–183.

Mundorf, N., Bhatia, A., Zillmann, D., Lester, P., & Robertson, S. (1988). Gender differences in humor appreciation. *Humor: International Journal of Humor Research, 1–3,* 231–243.

Nerhardt, G. (1976). Incongruity and funniness: Towards a new descriptive model. In A. J. Chapman & H. C. Foot (Eds.), *Humour and laughter: Theory, research and applications* (pp. 55–91). London: Wiley.

Nevo, O., Keinan, G., & Teshimovsky-Arditi, M. (1993). Humor and pain tolerance. *Humor, 6*(1), 71–88.

Nezu, A. M., Nezu, C. M., & Blissett, S. W. (1988). Sense of humor as a moderator of the relation between stressful events and psychological distress: A prospective analysis. *Journal of Personality and Social Psychology, 54,* 520–525.

Olson, E. (1968). *The theory of comedy.* Bloomington: Indiana University Press.

O'Neal, E. C., & Taylor, S. L. (1989). Status of the provoker, opportunity to retaliate, and interest in video violence. *Aggressive Behavior, 15,* 171–180.

Plato. (1871). Philebus. In B. Jowett (Ed. and Trans.), *The dialogues of Plato* (Vol. 3, pp. 531–630). Oxford, England: Clarendon.

Prerost, F. J., & Ruma, C. (1987). Exposure to humorous stimuli as an adjunct to muscle relaxation training. *Psychology: A Quarterly Journal of Human Behavior, 24*(4) 70–74.

Raskin, V. (1985). *Semantic mechanisms of humor.* Dordrecht, Holland: Reidel.

Repetti, R. L. (1989). Effects of daily workload on subsequent behavior during marital interaction: The roles of social withdrawal and spouse support. *Journal of Personality and Social Psychology, 57,* 651–659.

Robinson, V. M. (1983). Humor and health. In P. E. McGhee & J. H. Goldstein (Eds.), *Handbook of humor research: Vol. II. Applied studies* (pp. 109–128). New York: Springer-Verlag.

Rothbart, M. K. (1976). Incongruity, problem-solving and laughter. In A. J. Chapman & H. C. Foot (Eds.), *Humour and laughter: Theory, research and applications* (pp. 37–54). London: Wiley.

Rothbart, M. K., & Pien, D. (1977). Elephants and marshmallows: A theoretical synthesis of incongruity-resolution and arousal theories of humour. In A. J. Chapman & H. C. Foot (Eds.), *It's a funny thing, humour* (pp. 37–40). Oxford, England: Pergamon Press.

Rotton, J., & Shats, M. (1996). Effects of state humor, expectancies, and choice on postsurgical mood and self-medication: A field experiment. *Journal of Applied Social Psychology, 26,* 1775–1794.

Shultz, T. R. (1976). A cognitive-developmental analysis of humour. In A. J. Chapman & H. C. Foot (Eds.), *Humour and laughter: Theory, research and applications* (pp. 11–36). London: Wiley.

Simon, J. M. (1990). Humor and its relationship to perceived health, life satisfaction, and morale in older adults. *Issues in Mental Health Nursing, 11,* 17–31.

Spencer, H. (1888). The physiology of laughter. In *Illustrations of universal progress: A series of discussions* (pp. 194–209). New York: Appleton. (Original work published 1864)

Suls, J. M. (1972). A two-stage model for the appreciation of jokes and cartoons: An information-processing analysis. In J. H. Goldstein & P. E. McGhee (Eds.), *The psychology of humor: Theoretical perspectives and empirical issues* (pp. 81–100). New York: Academic Press.

Suls, J. M., & Miller, R. L. (1977). *Social comparison processes: Theoretical and empirical perspectives.* Washington, DC: Hemisphere.

Taylor, S. E., Wayment, H. A., & Collins, M. A. (1993). Positive illusions and affect regulation. In D. M. Wegner & J. W. Pennebaker (Eds.), *Handbook of mental control* (pp. 325–343). Englewood Cliffs, NJ: Prentice Hall.

Trice, A. D., & Price-Greathouse, J. (1986). Joking under the drill: A validity study of the coping humor scale. *Journal of Social Behavior and Personality, 1*(2), 265–266.

Weaver, J. B. (1991). Exploring the links between personality and media preferences. *Personality and Individual Differences, 12,* 1293–1299.

Weaver, J. B., & Zillmann, D. (1994). Effect of humor and tragedy on discomfort tolerance. *Perceptual and Motor Skills, 78,* 632–634.

Wicker, F. W., Barron, W. L., III, & Willis, A. C. (1980). Disparagement humor: Dispositions and resolutions. *Journal of Personality and Social Psychology, 39,* 701–709.

Wiener, T. (1989). *The book of video lists.* Lanham, MD: Madison Books.

Wolff, H. A., Smith, C. E., & Murray, H. A. (1934). The psychology of humor: I. A study of responses to race-disparagement jokes. *Journal of Abnormal and Social Psychology, 28,* 341–365.

Zelman, D. C., Howland, E. W., Nichols, S. N., & Cleeland, C. S. (1991). The effects of induced mood on laboratory pain. *Pain, 46*, 105–111.

Zillmann, D. (1980). Anatomy of suspense. In P. H. Tannenbaum (Ed.), *The entertainment functions of television* (pp. 133–163). Hillsdale, NJ: Lawrence Erlbaum Associates.

Zillmann, D. (1983). Disparagement humor. In P. E. McGhee & J. H. Goldstein (Eds.), *Handbook of humor research: Vol. 1. Basic issues* (pp. 85–107). New York: Springer-Verlag.

Zillmann, D. (1988). Mood management: Using entertainment to full advantage. In L. Donohew, H. E. Sypher, & E. T. Higgins (Eds.), *Communication, social cognition, and affect* (pp. 147–171). Hillsdale, NJ: Lawrence Erlbaum Associates.

Zillmann, D. (1991). Empathy: Affect from bearing witness to the emotions of others. In J. Bryant & D. Zillmann (Eds.), *Responding to the screen: Reception and reaction processes* (pp. 135–167). Hillsdale, NJ: Lawrence Erlbaum Associates.

Zillmann, D. (1994). Mechanisms of emotional involvement with drama. *Poetics, 23*, 33–51.

Zillmann, D. (1996). The psychology of suspense in dramatic exposition. In P. Vorderer, H. J. Wulff, & M. Friedrichsen (Eds.), *Suspense: Conceptualizations, theoretical analyses, and empirical explorations* (pp. 199–231). Mahwah, NJ: Lawrence Erlbaum Associates.

Zillmann, D. (1999). Does tragic drama have redeeming value? *Siegener Periodikum für Internationale Literaturwissenschaft, 16*(1), 1–11.

Zillmann, D., & Bryant, J. (1980). Misattribution theory of tendentious humor. *Journal of Experimental Social Psychology, 16*, 146–160.

Zillmann, D., & Bryant, J. (1991). Responding to comedy: The sense and nonsense in humor. In J. Bryant & D. Zillmann (Eds.), *Responding to the screen: Reception and reaction processes* (pp. 261–279). Hillsdale, NJ: Lawrence Erlbaum Associates.

Zillmann, D., & Bryant, J. (1998). Fernsehen [Watching television]. In B. Strauss (Ed.), *Zuschauer* (pp. 175–212). Göttingen, Germany: Hogrefe.

Zillmann, D., & Cantor, J. R. (1972). Directionality of transitory dominance as a communication variable affecting humor appreciation. *Journal of Personality and Social Psychology, 24*, 191–198.

Zillmann, D., & Cantor, J. R. (1976). A disposition theory of humour and mirth. In A. J. Chapman & H. C. Foot (Eds.), *Humour and laughter: Theory, research and applications* (pp. 93–115). London: Wiley.

Zillmann, D., de Wied, M., King Jablonski, C., & Jenzowsky, S. (1996). Drama-induced affect and pain sensitivity. *Psychosomatic Medicine, 58*(4), 333–341.

Zillmann, D., Hezel, R. T., & Medoff, N. J. (1980). The effect of affective states on selective exposure to televised entertainment fare. *Journal of Applied Social Psychology, 10*, 323–339.

Zillmann, D., & Paulus, P. B. (1993). Spectators: Reactions to sports events and effects on athletic performance. In R. N. Singer, M. Murphey, & L. K. Tennant (Eds.), *Handbook of research on sport psychology* (pp. 600–619). New York: Macmillan.

Zillmann, D., Rockwell, S. C., Schweitzer, K., & Sundar, S. S. (1993). Does humor facilitate coping with physical discomfort? *Motivation and Emotion, 17*(1), 1–21.

Zillmann, D., & Stocking, S. H. (1976). Putdown humor. *Journal of Communication, 26*, 154–163.

Zillmann, D., Taylor, K., & Lewis, K. (1998). News as nonfiction theater: How dispositions toward the public cast of characters affect reactions. *Journal of Broadcasting & Electronic Media, 42*(2), 153–169.

4
▼▼▼▼▼▼▼▼▼

Conflict and Suspense in Drama

Peter Vorderer
Silvia Knobloch
University of Music and Theater, Hannover

There can be no question that exposure to drama plays an important role in media users' everyday entertainment. A large number of TV and radio programs, books, movies, and even parts of the Internet provide what drama has to offer: "a state, situation, or series of events involving . . . intense conflict of forces" (Merriam-Webster, 1995, p. 351). To put it in media-related terms, drama dwells on conflict and its resolution by depicting events that impact the welfare of persons, animals, and animated things. At the core of each drama are characters, the protagonists and antagonists, who are affected by these events and who are witnessed by readers, viewers, and other media users. The characters may be shown as improving their lot in life or as experiencing a deterioration of their fortunes. As long as their actions can be observed and their intentions can be inferred, the audience is ready to morally evaluate the characters and to develop dispositions toward them (cf. Zillmann, 1996). Depending on these dispositions as well as on the depicted fate of the characters, drama may be enjoyed or deplored. Protagonists sometimes succeed and sometimes fail. They are loved by some and hated by others. The viewers, as a consequence of what they can see and hear, may be jubilant or they may suffer.

It is surprising to learn how much of their time individuals deliberately devote to consuming these dramas. When viewers are asked about their reasons for entertaining themselves with dramatic media content, they often refer to the fact that these dramas are suspenseful (i.e., that they can feel suspense when they read or witness a drama). It seems that suspense bears the same relevance to the understanding of what happens with the audience as conflict does to the definition of drama. Suspense might even be the viewer's or reader's appropriate response to the conflicts that are witnessed in the drama. Based on these considerations, this chapter discusses the following three questions:

1. Why does drama evoke suspense?
2. Why is suspense experienced as entertaining?
3. Why is suspense so often sought through drama?

To begin with the impact of drama (as a category of the text) on suspense (as a category of the user), we first refer to descriptions of what comprises drama. Next, we examine the audience's response to drama (i.e., suspense and entertainment). Finally, we address the issue of the underlying motivation of the viewer.

DRAMA AS GENRE

Drama includes literary texts and nonliterary performances, such as film. It covers subtypes such as tragedy, comedy, and mystery. It differs primarily from other forms of entertainment by the great importance it attaches to the overarching plot. Genres such as situation comedy, erotica, and horror and mayhem derive their appeal from discrete scenes. Knowing the background of the story usually is not a precondition for the amusing or exciting effect of the episodes. In contrast, the appeal of drama evolves with the plot. Of course, the term *plot* is ambiguous and rich in meaning, as it refers to both the specific events (actions or happenings) presented in a drama, and to the artistic arrangement of these events in the presentation. From a literary point of view, the plot conveys a certain moral (e.g., treachery leads to disaster), and thereby evokes the audience's emotions by a balanced and well-timed presentation of information about characters and events. In the significance of the plot, drama resembles narration. Both genres are narrative, in that they provide a representation of a series of causally and chronologically related events experienced or caused by actors (Bal, 1985; Onega & Landa García, 1996). However, they differ in their emphases on certain aspects of narration that are crucial for the audience's emotional response. As the traditional form of narration, the novel acquires its emotional vividness by revealing the inner experiential landscape of its characters ("telling"; cf. Onega & Landa García, 1996). As Bakhtin (1963) suggested, the novel is the genre of the dialogue—not only among characters, but also (in a metaphorical sense) between characters and readers or author and reader. More recent forms of narration in this sense are telenovelas and soap operas. In contrast, drama focuses on events with clear relations between cause and effect ("showing" instead of "telling"; cf. Onega & Landa García, 1996). In short, novels tell "how it feels," whereas drama shows "how it happens" (See for a similar distinction between "experience-texts" and "action-texts," Cupchik & László, 1994).

Given the centrality of events in drama, the definition of an event becomes crucial. Not every action in a drama counts as an event that is functional to the plot. Bal (1985) defined an event as transition from one state to another state that is caused or experienced by actors. This rather rough definition still covers actions of minor relevance and is therefore specified by the following three criteria: an event has to include a change of the situation, a choice on an actor's behalf, and confrontation between actors or groups of actors. All of these criteria refer more or less directly to conflict. In short, drama portrays events in relation to conflicts. It is important to note here that the way conflicts are depicted and the kind of resolution that follows these conflicts are decisive with regard to the response of the audience. As Aristotle (trans. 1951) emphasized, changes in the plot must follow principles of fairness in order to make a drama enjoyable for the audience (see chap. 3, this volume for more detail).

As the events are not always presented in chronological order, two levels of structure must be considered. On one level, the event structure (i.e., the story) contains the sequence of events as they would occur in real life. On the other level, the discourse structure may differ from the event structure by presenting ongoing events in a deviating order, that is, the outcome of the story might be presented at the beginning of a text or film. This differentiation is of particular importance because Brewer and his collaborators (Brewer, 1985, 1996; Brewer & Lichtenstein, 1982; Brewer & Ohtsuka, 1988) have demonstrated that particular relationships between event and discourse structure lead to certain emotional responses on the audience's part. Mystery, for example, often provides readers or viewers with an outcome (e.g., the presentation of the murder) at the beginning of the presentation but withholds a great deal of information (for the time being). The question "What has happened?" promotes the audience's interest in such instances. To use another subgenre as an example, tragedies usually imply or present an unfavorable ending in the beginning to haunt the audience by asking: "How could it happen?" Finally, drama in the form of what Brewer called suspense (as a category of texts) only indicates an upcoming resolution of a conflict in the beginning and depicts event and discourse structure in coincidence. The suspenseful question therefore is "What will happen?" Since viewers and readers are kept in the dark about the outcome, the decisive denouement may change the genre from suspense to tragedy. But in any case, by playing on the relationship between event and discourse structure, drama activates the audience's anticipations and/or speculations. Exposure to drama leads to either curiosity, sympathy, or suspense merely by witnessing the actions of others (cf. Brewer & Lichtenstein, 1982).

Conceptualizations such as Brewer's persuasively reveal the importance of conflict in drama and how conflicts depicted in drama lead to the readers' specific emotional responses. But by the same token, these concepts reduce the readers' response to the fulfillment of a rather passive role, in that their involvement with the text is more or less dependent on its specific structure. Other approaches have been more concerned with the audience's cognitive and emotional activities when dealing with texts or films. In particular, they emphasize how important characters are for readers or viewers. Protagonists and antagonists represent the element of drama that breathes life into the plot, which otherwise is nothing more than a sequence of invented happenings. Without the involvement of actors, an event would lack its connection with other elements of the plot and its emotional significance for the viewer. The relevance of these events to the characters makes them relevant for the audience as well. Characters are agents who perform actions, but they are not necessarily human. In this context, "to act" means to cause or to experience an event (Bal, 1985). If the audience is to feel more than spontaneous sympathy for an actor, an appealing character must personify appropriate attributes and intentions. The personal information known by the audience allows it to approach the character's position, cognitively and emotionally, in order to understand his or her feelings and actions. It is evident that we rarely get to know real people as thoroughly, comprehensively, and privately as we get to know characters in drama. Nevertheless, this "one-way intimacy" does not require extensive descriptions of the characters. Providing certain cues to the audience appears to be sufficient. Information about characters may allude to stereotypes. The character personally and/or others may provide such information, as do the character's actions in relation to others. In a complex interaction between the picture drawn by the actor and the personal understanding of the viewer or reader, an emotional bond between the viewer and the character is established. This instigates interest in the protagonist's welfare. It is the protagonist in the drama who is challenged by extreme life situations such as battles, murder, violent jealousy, neverending love, and the like. As fundamental human conflicts mark these "dramatic" fictional situations, the confrontation with severe conflicts between forces, personalities, emotions, and goals shifts the audience into emotional states of "heavy uneasiness."

CONCEPTUALIZATIONS OF SUSPENSE
AND ENTERTAINMENT

So far, we have discussed the importance of conflict for drama and why conflict is not only a feature of the text (film) but also lies within or is set into the viewer. Although these inner conflicts may lead to different emotional states and experiences on the audience side (Brewer, 1996), most prominent is suspense as a response to witnessing dramatic events. It was Carroll (1984, 1996), among others, who demonstrated how conflicts lead to suspense and how suspense is experienced as entertaining. His contribution derives from a philosophical conceptualization of entertainment. It does not come with empirical support, but it provides strong structural clarification.

Carroll (1996) defined suspense as "an emotional response to narrative fiction" (p. 74). This response may arise out of a whole narrative, or, in reaction to specific scenes or parts of a narrative that do not have to be suspenseful overall. He emphasized that suspense occurs before the audience is certain about the final outcome.

With the presentation of that outcome, the audience's affective state changes to feelings such as joy or sorrow (Carroll, 1996). Therefore, suspense as an emotion evolves during the anticipation of that crucial outcome. In contrast to other subtypes of drama, the suspenseful drama avails itself of only two outcomes, which are logically contrary to each other. In the end, the protagonist either defeats the opponent or does not; the heroine either survives the alien's attack or does not. Mystery or tragedy provide a multitude of possible answers to "What has happened?" or "How could it happen?" But suspense stories imply only two conflicting answers to "What will happen?" Surely, to affect the viewers' or readers' feelings through a suspenseful drama, the author has to involve the audience in anticipations about these two possible outcomes. According to Carroll, the means of choice is to generate a distinct preference for one of the possibilities. How does an author make a heterogeneous, anonymous audience care about the fate of fictional characters? Carroll proposed that morality is the common denominator to which different groups of onlookers relate similarly. General ideas about good and bad lead to the same preferences about feasible outcomes. However, the fiction may evolve to a specific moral setting, in which otherwise intolerable actions appear intelligible. In dramas with criminal protagonists, characters with certain virtues can personify the good side although they violate acceptable moral standards. In general the good guys treat inferiors well, whereas the bad guys do harm to their inferiors (Carroll, 1996). Once the preference about one of the two ending options is realized, the viewers or readers cognitively speculate about the outcome. This leads to emotional arousal experienced as suspense. From Carroll's point of view, these anticipations take into account the likelihood of different possible endings. The probabilities of the conflicting outcomes are not the same. The preferred outcome is far more unlikely than the evil ending. Yet the preferred outcome has to be possible, though it is less likely than the evil one. Carroll referred to a probability that is not a technical one. It depicts the subjective expectation in the view of the audience. In addition, this probability has a strong impact in terms of the fictional world in which the events of the drama take place. This conflict between preference and probability creates suspense as an emotional reaction.

Thus, Carroll showed how much conflict in the text relates to conflicts in the mind of the viewers. He could also demonstrate the relevance of the protagonists by explaining the cognitive and emotional experiences of the viewers with respect to the way characters are perceived. His approach offers clear progress in our understanding of suspense and entertainment. However, it lacks any empirical support and calls for more psychological theory-building that fits with his basic assumptions and turns these assumptions into experimentally testable hypotheses.

This type of theory-building has been done by Zillmann and his collaborators (for instance, Zillmann, 1996). The so-called disposition theory of drama resembles Carroll's philosophical approach in many aspects, but Zillmann also elaborated it in a psychological way. For example, Zillmann's theory agrees with the understanding of the suspenseful time slot of drama. It is that phase of anticipation prior to the climax resolving the conflict between a desired and a feared event. The conceptualization also expects the microstructure of a drama to evoke more suspense than the macrostructure. However, Zillmann's idea of suspense includes a more detailed model, incorporating elements that cooperatively compose the overall experience during media exposure. According to the disposition theory, a necessary condition for suspense is that the viewer witnesses the conflicting forces (Zillmann, 1996) without being able to intervene in the goings-on. If viewers could influence the plot, for example, the fate of the characters, their experiential state would change into actual fear or hope. Televised, literary, and cinematic drama, however, clearly does not imply interventions on the audience's part and therefore meets this condition for suspense. Given these restrictions, the question arises: Why should one get involved with the welfare of fictional strangers?

Zillmann (1996) opposed two theoretical approaches for "mechanisms" by which media users relate to the emotions in a drama. The concept of identification is very popular in publications about media use; it claims that respondents believe they are the protagonists. Therefore, identification exceeds mere admiration and imitation. It includes an adoption of features, or at least an attempt to do so. Yet, simple considerations point out the shortcomings of an application to media use. Usually the viewer or reader keeps clearly in mind the distinction between his or her person and the character in a drama. Very often cues in the drama will prevent the audience from feeling as the protagonist does, through information that the protagonist does not have (such as who plans to kill the hero or where the ticking bomb is hidden). In contrast to this idea of identification, Zillmann (1991, 1994) suggested the concept of empathy, which has been elaborated in psychology primarily within different contexts, but that seems to be applicable to the cognitive and emotional processes of audiences:

> Empathy is defined as any experience that is a response (a) to information about circumstances presumed to cause acute emotions in another individual and/or (b) to the bodily, facial, paralinguistic, and linguistic expression of emotional experiences by another individual and/or (c) to another individual's actions that are presumed to be precipitated by acute emotional experience, this response being (d) associated with an appreciable increase in excitation and (e) construed by respondents as feeling with or feeling for another individual. (Zillmann, 1994, p. 40)

Empathy certainly deals with exchange of meaning in everyday interpersonal communication. But, it also includes communication between a person observed and the observer. As the observer, that is, the viewer, witnesses the events that a character undergoes, he or she either applauds or condemns the character's actions and intentions. Approval of the character leads to dispositions of liking and caring, and the character becomes a friendlike hero. In contrast, condemnation generates dispositions of disliking and resentment, so that the character is seen as an enemylike villain. The affective disposition toward the protagonist triggers the respondent's hope for positive outcomes, and conversely, the fear of negative denouements. A disapprobation in the first step instigates this process reciprocally and causes a dislike and fear of the outcomes that are positive for an antagonist (Zillmann, 1994). Hence, like Carroll, Zillmann considered subjective probabilities of the two conflicting outcomes as crucial. The respondent's certainty that a threatening danger will violate the protagonist's welfare influences the degree of suspense. The more likely a negative outcome is anticipated for the protagonist and a positive outcome for the antagonist, the greater the empathic distress and suspense that are felt. Still, that outcome must not be certain, for with a reliably predictable denouement, suspense vanishes.

As can be seen, Zillmann believed that conflict forms the essence of drama, and in suspenseful drama that conflict is between good and evil. Yet in contrast to the importance that Carroll attached to morality, Zillmann suggested a broader concept. It explains the audience's emotionality about the conflict between protagonistic and antagonistic forces. He claimed that the affective disposition of the recipients toward the characters yields different levels of suspense. Although this disposition derives partly from moral considerations, the idiosyncrasy in ethic ideas is considered immense. In addition, nonhuman forces such as an earthquake can serve as an antagonistic force. In these instances, morality cannot convey preferences about outcomes, as Zillmann outlined (1996). However, the categorization of the characters' actions and attributes employs moral terms to create affective dispositions in the audience.

MOTIVATION: WHY DOES THE AUDIENCE SEEK SUSPENSE?

The preceeding paragraphs should demonstrate how drama, with its focus on conflict, is capable of inducing suspense; and the degree to which viewers, readers, or onlookers experience this suspense as entertainment. The question remains as to why the audience deliberately seeks this form of emotional involvement. As long as the emotional effects on the viewers are positive, the question can be answered easily. In fact, most of the research in media psychology has been based on the assumption that media users are hedonistic. They seek circumstances that serve their general well-being and they generally avoid distress (cf. Vorderer, 1996). The explanation for the onlookers who follow a happy story is obvious. They just use the story to feel good. Many (if not most) of the stories categorized as drama, however, portray rather undesirable vicissitudes. As described earlier, these depictions often lead to empathic distress, at least during exposure. Therefore, drama often fosters a rather unpleasant form of emotional experience for the viewers. The more likely the protagonist is to fail or the antagonist to succeed, the more intensive distress will be felt. But by the same token, more suspense usually also leads to a more positive assessment of the drama (see above). This apparent paradox calls for an explanation. Research provides at least the following four possibilities.

The oldest explanation for the often observable fact that many viewers seek exposure to drama, despite its potentially noxious effect, is the so-called catharsis doctrine. This doctrine goes back to Aristotle's attempt to deal with the redeeming value of tragedy. Aristotle's basic idea concerning tragedy was that exposure to it may in fact evoke undesirable experiences. But these experiences, nevertheless, help to diminish such negative emotions in the real life of the observers. Therefore, Aristotle thought that the audience seeks aversive experiences through tragedy and finds relief afterwards (cf. Scheff, 1979). There is hardly any other notion in drama theory that is as popular as this catharsis doctrine. It nevertheless has failed to gain any empirical support. It is similar to another popular explanation, which has also ignored the genuine enjoyment through drama and focused on its side effects: that is, the idea of *escapism*. Assuming that life can and will only be unsatisfactory and that individuals have only limited capacities to arrange themselves within their circumstances, the idea that people have to escape from reality was born (cf. Zillmann, chap. 1, this volume). Although traced back to Montaigne (1958), this notion became most popular within media research in the 1960s and 1970s. Also, assuming that most people, particularly those who are underprivileged in modern society, live an alienated life, it was not very difficult to consider media entertainment as a sedative. This type of entertainment is said to seduce and distract the public from the real problems of life and keeps people busy with what the entertainment industry has to offer (Katz & Foulkes, 1962; Pearlin, 1959). Entertainment, therefore, is regarded as an appropriate means by which to forget the shortcomings of everyday life, fulfilling both a psychological and a social function (cf. Loewenthal, 1961). Revealing these functions is one of the most prominent goals of the critical approach within the social sciences, and it has also been applied to media and audience research (cf. Vorderer & Groeben, 1992). Following this perspective, the psychological function is important enough to dominate the short-term effects of distress, which is part of entertainment. In other words, watching a sad movie might imply emotional distress, but it also enhances involvement with a fictional story. By being involved, the viewers are distracted from what is much more undesirable in their own life. Unfortunately, this explanation is, just like the catharsis doctrine, as much speculative as it is plausible. Very little research has been conducted to show whether, how, and with what effect individuals use the media for that purpose.

An empirically supported explanation is provided by Zillmann's idea of *excitation transfer* (Zillmann, 1978, 1983). According to this idea, physiological arousal during exposure is crucial for the appreciation of drama at its conclusion. Throughout exposure, arousal derives primarily from watching favorable agents who are in trouble. As the story approaches its final outcome, the viewers' arousal increases and is felt as empathic distress. With the final presentation of the desired, although unlikely, outcome, the environmental conditions change from negative to positive. The viewers' cognitive adjustment to this changing situation is very fast, whereas their excitatory adjustments are rather slow. Therefore, the residual excitation from the preceding distressing emotions is transferred into the subsequent euphoric emotion, based on the resolution of the drama. The intensity of the positive emotion is increased and experienced as extraordinarily positive. In other words, the viewers' experience switches from distress to euphoria, as the outlined backlog of intense excitation passes on to a positive emotional state. Not surprisingly, the greater the emotional distress prior to the resolution of the drama and the greater the residual excitation that is felt, the more positive is the emotion following the resolution and the greater the enjoyment that the viewer attains.

In contrast to the notion of "escapism," "excitation transfer" has repeatedly been demonstrated through experimental studies (cf., e.g., Zillmann, 1983). It is the primary answer to the question of why onlookers appreciate suspense despite its temporary negative effects. But does "excitation transfer" also explain the reason why people undergo rather long periods of suffering in order to gain a comparatively short moment of positive feeling? Is the audience really ready to suffer throughout the reading of an entire novel or throughout the watching of a long and suspenseful movie only to briefly feel good afterwards (cf. Vorderer, 1994)?

A fourth explanation is provided by Mares and Cantor (1992), who used social comparison theory (Festinger, 1954) to explain the selection and appreciation of a short movie by elderly viewers. Social comparison theory states that people in general need and wish to compare themselves with others in order to gain information about themselves. Mares and Cantor concluded that onlookers prefer TV programs that describe a setting comparable to their own life circumstances but that display this setting in an unfavorable manner. This situation provides the onlookers with an opportunity to compare themselves with characters on the screen. In particular, a so-called downward comparison is made, that is, a comparison with less-fortunate others, and contrasts the viewers' own circumstances positively with those depicted in the movie. This results in satisfaction with one's own situation and leads to greater well-being, based on the observation of an otherwise negative and distressing life. As we have seen, drama is often characterized by conflicts. The sheer observation of characters suffering from conflicts gives the audience a positive manipulation of their moods and well-being.

Of course, the latter two explanations for the audience's deliberate exposure to sometimes distressing entertainment are not contradictory. They complement rather than compete with each other. For example, Zillmann's notion of "excitation transfer" is based on the general idea that viewers are basically motivated to enhance their moods through selective exposure. And so is the hypothesis of Mares and Cantor (1992). Although their original goal was to test the theory of mood-management versus that of social comparison, in the conclusion of their analysis they suggested that their results support both the theory of social comparison and that of mood-management. Even considering the possible integration of these different explanations, some problems still remain unsolved.

BEYOND MOOD-MANAGEMENT

Envisioning the existing explanations does not sufficiently answer the question of why many media users tolerate rather long periods of time that are characterized by noxious emotional circumstances. Take, for example, a very long and suspenseful novel. Is it intelligible or at least plausible to follow such a story for weeks or months, only to finally experience relief and merriment through excitation transfer within a few minutes or seconds? Do viewers follow lengthy suspenseful movies with fearful negative consequences for their beloved heroes, only to see them finally succeed within the last two minutes (Vorderer, 1994)? And what about movies and books that leave recipients sad, irritated, or depressed? Is it not true that individuals often seek these negative experiences through the media, and that they are disappointed when drama evokes only weak sentiments?

The given lack of insight into this paradox may be due to a fundamental error in reasoning. Theorizing about entertainment so far has implicitly taken for granted a dichotomy that differentiates between entertainment (that may lead to escapism and suspense) and aesthetically valuable, "serious," ambitious literature, film, and TV programs. According to this dichotomy, only "high culture" provides users with a possibility to reflect on their own lives. Entertainment, in contrast, has nothing to offer but "shallow" merriment and enjoyment. Surely, some types of texts and media content support instead a reflective (analytical) or an escapist (involved) mode of reading. In fact, these prototypical examples of texts fit this dichotomy very well. Oatley (1994) followed this distinction in a way by also differentiating between what he called "internal" and "external" emotions. Internal emotions are those that occur when the reader enters the world of the text, depending on how strongly he or she is involved (p. 57). In contrast, external emotions are those a reader feels when approaching a text from an aesthetic distance. Cupchik and László (1994), as well as Vorderer, Cupchik, and Oatley (1997), found empirical support that so-called action-texts instead lead to a suspenseful and rapid reading, whereas so-called experience-texts, although less suspenseful, are evaluated more positively by readers. But despite all of these differences, there is no immanent distinction between aesthetically valuable cultural products and those that entertain. There is nothing that would determine how much suspense and how much self-reflection is possible.

The implicit assumption of the dichotomy "entertainment versus reflection" may be a pitfall. We suggest another starting point here. From our perspective, viewers or readers do not use what has been categorized as entertainment only to be amused shallowly. Just like dreams, daydreaming, memories, and anticipations, mediated experiences and interactions in drama are imaginary (Caughey, 1978) in the sense that the individual internally exceeds his or her actual situation. Although fictional, drama nevertheless relates closely to reality. Social interactions and relations in dramas are similar to real interactions and relations; they function with the same social "grammar." Certain dramatic genres like fantasy or science fiction deserve their names by being distinctly unreal at first glance, but draw their attractiveness from the interesting relationship between their presentation and what exists and what is, or will be, possible in real life. Social conflict and structures (e.g., war and hierarchies) are also easily recognizable in these subtypes of drama. As drama exceeds or exaggerates rules and structures of real life in social or physical matters, it reveals often overlooked aspects of reality. In order to understand the characters and the plot of a drama, readers and viewers apply rules of their everyday life and culture. During the decoding of fiction, they empathically feel with and feel for the protagonists of the stories presented, and often this empathy goes along with or is followed by contemplating about oneself. Literary studies and reader's psychology have repeatedly described how exposure to drama provides readers with cognitive and emotional states that cannot easily be experienced otherwise. It is assumed that these states, though sometimes distressing, have their own redeeming value for the reader, as various authors have outlined.

Oliver (1993; see also chap. 12, this volume) has offered an explanation for sad movies that are apparently appreciated by a large, often female, audience. Since emotions are based on evaluations and appraisal processes, she suggests that meta-emotions provide the pleasure of these films. According to this perspective, viewers appreciate the fact that they are capable of experiencing certain emotional states, even negative ones, and they therefore evaluate a distressing movie positively. In addition to positive assessment of empathic suffering, sad movies deliver an opportunity to express negative feelings that are already there. To put it simply: There is always some reason to cry, and finally, there is a chance and good reason to do so!

Oatley (1998) saw readers attaining simulations of critical life situations that allow an anticipatory enactment of situations and a reevaluation of the actual or imagined past. According to this perspective, drama offers an opportunity to vicariously enact border situations not provided in real life (see also Groeben & Vorderer, 1986, 1988). This means that there are situations where readers do not seek only positive moods but also the possibility to ingenuously examine feelings that are without consequences anyway (Mikos, 1994; Vorderer, 1992). How does this fit with the impressive body of literature that confirms mood-management (Zillmann, 1988a, 1988b) as a basic principle for selective exposure?

Vorderer (1998) differentiated between socioemotional and ego-emotional aspects of electronic media use, implying that socio-emotional experiences dwell on the viewer's moral assessments and empathic relationships with characters, while ego-emotional aspects refer to the personal and individual relevance a drama has for the viewer. He assumes that the audience selects and sticks with TV programs for different reasons. One reason is a TV program's potential to enhance the viewers' moods by using their socio-emotional bond with the characters on the screen. Another reason is to provide the onlookers with information relevant to their own lives, using their ego–emotional attention for specific contents. And exposure to such content may include unfavorable experiences.

It almost does not need mentioning that entertainment on the one hand, and learning, enlightenment, and self-reflection on the other, do not match. In particular, within audience research it has been implied that people can either entertain themselves or reflect on their own lives. But because this dichotomy is no longer based on psychological research, we must disagree strongly. We have learned from social psychology that positive moods may also foster information processing (see, e.g., Bless, 1997; Isen, 1987; Schwarz, 1990). If we only give up this neo-romantic dichotomy of learning versus feeling well, entertainment and self-reflection do not have to be contradictory. Instead, entertainment may be considered as a process in which individuals fluctuate between involvement with other worlds, which is rather escapist in nature, and a possible reflection of what this means to them personally. In fact, both tendencies may have negative consequences for the individual if not controlled by the respective other: Escapism may lead to a permanent alienation from the social world if not mediated by reality. By the same token, continuous self-reflection without the possibility of a transient escape from one's own life will be too demanding and exhausting for most individuals.

In summary, drama focuses on deplorable events that are meaningfully arranged in a plot. The most frequent effect of drama to which viewers explicitly refer is suspense. Suspense may be conceptualized by characteristics of the film or the text, but from a psychological point of view, it is primarily an affective and cognitive experience of media users. Though several approaches offer insight into the motivations for seeking suspense, the apparent enjoyment viewers derive from witnessing even negative events remains to be explained. The popular assumption that implies a dichotomy of entertainment versus reflection is no longer convincing. Instead, we propose to go beyond this theoretical distinction in order to broaden the perspective on entertainment as a multifaceted tool for coping with the shortcomings of life and oneself.

REFERENCES

Aristotle. (1951). The Poetics. In S. H. Butcher (Trans.), *Aristotle's theory of poetry and fine art* (pp. 7–111). New York: Dover Publications.

Bakhtin, M. (1963). *Problems of Dostoevsky's Poetics*. Minneapolis: University of Minnesota Press.

Bal, M. (1985). *Narratology: Introduction to the theory of narrative*. Toronto: University of Toronto Press.

Bless, H. (1997). *Stimmung und Denken: Ein Modell zum Einfluß von Stimmungen auf Denkprozesse*. Bern, Switzerland: Huber.

Brewer, W. F. (1985). The story schema: Universal and culture-specific properties. In D. R. Olson, N. Torrance, & A. Hildyard (Eds.), *Literacy, language, and learning* (pp. 167–194). Cambridge, UK: Cambridge University Press.

Brewer, W. F. (1996). The nature of narrative suspense and the problem of rereading. In P. Vorderer, H. J. Wulff, & M. Friedrichsen (Eds.), *Suspense: Conceptualizations, theoretical analyses, and empirical explorations* (pp. 107–127). Mahwah, NJ: Lawrence Erlbaum Associates.

Brewer, W. F. & Lichtenstein, E. H. (1982). Stories are to entertain: A structural-affect theory of stories. *Journal of Pragmatics, 6*, 473–486.

Brewer, W. F., & Ohtsuka, K. (1988). Story structure, characterization, just world organization, and reader affect in American and Hungarian short stories. *Poetics, 17*, 395–415.

Carroll, N. (1984). Toward a theory of film suspense. *Persistence of Vision, 1*, 65–89.

Carroll, N. (1996). The paradox of suspense. In P. Vorderer, H. J. Wulff, & M. Friedrichsen (Eds.), *Suspense: Conceptualizations, theoretical analyses, and empirical explorations* (pp. 71–91). Mahwah, NJ: Lawrence Erlbaum Associates.

Caughey, J. L. (1978). Artificial social relations in modern America. *American Quarterly, 30*(1), 70–89.

Cupchik, G. C., & László, J. (1994). The landscape of time in literary reception: Character experience and narrative action. *Cognition and Emotion, 8*(4), 297–312.

Festinger, L. (1954). A theory of social comparison process. *Human Relations, 7,* 114–140.

Groeben, N., & Vorderer, P. (1986). Empirische Literaturpsychologie. In R. Langner (Ed.), *Psychologie der Literatur* (pp. 105–143). Weinheim, Germany: Psychologie Verlags Union.

Groeben, N. & Vorderer, P. (1988). *Leserpsychologie: Lesemotivation— Lektürewirkung.* Münster, Germany: Aschendorff.

Isen, A. (1987). Positive affect, cognitive processes, and social behavior. In L. Berkowitz (Ed.), *Advances in experimental social psychology* (Vol. 20, pp. 203–253). San Diego, CA: Academic Press.

Katz, E., & Foulkes, D. (1962). On the use of the mass media as "escape": Clarification of a concept. *Public Opinion Quarterly, 26,* 377–388.

Loewenthal, L. (1961). *Literature, popular culture, and society.* Englewood Cliffs, NJ: Prentice-Hall.

Mares, M.-L., & Cantor, J. (1992). Elderly viewers' responses to televised portrayals of old age: Empathy and mood management versus social comparison. *Communication Research, 19*(4), 459–478.

Merriam-Webster's collegiate dictionary (10th ed.). (1995). Springfield, MA: Merriam-Webster.

Mikos, L. (1994). *Fernsehen im Erleben der Zuschauer. Vom lustvollen Umgang mit einem populären Medium.* Berlin: Quintessenz.

Montaigne, M. de (1958). *The complete works of Montaigne: Essays, travel journal, letters* (D. M. Frame, Trans.). Stanford, CA: Stanford University Press.

Oatley, K. (1994). A taxonomy of the emotions of literary response and a theory of identification in fictional narrative. *Poetics,* (23), 53–74.

Oatley, K. (1998). Meeting of minds. In S. Janssen & N. van Dijk (Eds.), *The empirical study of literature and the media: Current approaches and perspectives* (pp. 58–72). Rotterdam: Barjesteh van Waalwijk van Doorn & Co's.

Oliver, M. B. (1993). Exploring the paradox of the enjoyment of sad films. *Human Communication Research, 19*(3), 315–342.

Onega, S., & Landa García, J. A. (1996). Introduction. In S. Onega & J. A. Landa García (Eds.), *Narratology: An introduction* (pp. 1–41). London: Longman.

Pearlin, L. (1959). Social and personal stress and escape television viewing. *Public Opinion Quarterly, 23,* 225–259.

Scheff, T. J. (1979). *Catharsis in healing, ritual, and drama.* Berkeley: University of California Press.

Schwarz, N. (1990). Feelings as information: Informational and motivational functions of affective states. In R. M. Sorrentino & E. T. Higgins (Eds.), *Handbook of Motivation and Cognition: Foundations of social behavior* (Vol. 2, pp. 527–561). New York: Guilford.

Vorderer, P. (1992). *Fernsehen als Handlung: Fernsehfilmrezeption aus motivationspsychologischer Perspektive.* Berlin: Sigma.

Vorderer, P. (1994). "Spannung ist, wenn's spannend ist": Zum Stand der (psychologischen) Spannungsforschung. *Rundfunk und Fernsehen, 42*(3), 323–339.

Vorderer, P. (1996). Toward a psychological theory of suspense. In P. Vorderer, H. J. Wulff, & M. Friedrichsen (Eds.), *Suspense: Conceptualizations, theoretical analyses, and empirical explorations* (pp. 233–254). Mahwah, NJ: Lawrence Erlbaum Associates.

Vorderer, P. (1998). Unterhaltung durch Fernsehen: Welche Rolle spielen parasoziale Beziehungen zwischen Zuschauern und Fernsehakteuren? In G. Roters, W. Klingler, & O. Zoellner (Eds.), *Fersehforschung in Deutschland. Themen, Akteure, Methoden* (pp. 689–708). Baden-Baden: Nomos.

Vorderer, P., Cupchik, G. C., & Oatley, K. (1997). Reading and literary landscapes: Experience and action from self-oriented and spectator perspectives. In S. Totsy de Zepetnek & I. Sywenky (Eds.), *The systemic and empirical approach to literature and culture as theory and application* (pp. 559–571). Alberta: Research Institute for Comparative Literature and Cross Cultural Studies, University of Alberta.

Vorderer, P., & Groeben, N. (1992). Audience research: What the humanistic and the social science approaches could learn from each other. *Poetics,* (21), 361–376.

Zillmann, D. (1978). Attribution and misattribution of excitatory reactions. In J. H. Harvey, W. J. Ickes & R. F. Kidd (Eds.), *New directions in attribution research* (Vol. 2, pp. 335–368). Hillsdale, NJ: Lawrence Erlbaum Associates.

Zillmann, D. (1983). Transfer of excitation in emotional behavior. In J. T. Cacioppo & R. E. Petty (Eds.), *Social psychophysiology: A sourcebook* (pp. 215–240). New York: Guilford.

Zillmann, D., (1988a). Mood management: Using entertainment to full advantage. In L. Donohew, H. E. Sypher, & E. T. Higgins (Eds.), *Communication, social cognition, and affect* (pp. 147–171). Hillsdale, NJ: Lawrence Erlbaum Associates.

Zillmann, D., (1988b). Mood management through communication choices. *American Behavioral Scientist, 31,* 327–340.

Zillmann, D. (1991). Empathy: Affect from bearing witness to the emotions of others. In J. Bryant & D. Zillmann (Eds.), *Responding to the screen: Reception and reaction processes* (pp. 135–167). Hillsdale, NJ: Lawrence Erlbaum Associates.

Zillmann, D. (1994). Mechanisms of emotional involvement with drama. *Poetics, 23,* 33–51.

Zillmann, D. (1996). The psychology of suspense in dramatic exposition. In P. Vorderer, H. J. Wulff, & M. Friedrichsen (Eds.), *Suspense: Conceptualizations, theoretical analyses, and empirical explorations* (pp. 199–231). Mahwah, NJ: Lawrence Erlbaum Associates.

Violence, Mayhem, and Horror

Glenn G. Sparks
Cheri W. Sparks
Purdue University

A woman has seen the movie *Pulp Fiction* three times. She considers the movie to be outrageously amusing and inventively clever. Years ago, wanting others to share in this movie, she encouraged a group of graduate-school friends to attend it with her. As it turned out, her friends were completely perplexed by her attraction to such a violence-packed movie. They were particularly troubled by the fact that, during the viewing, many members of the college audience screamed out their approval and clapped wildly during the most violent scenes. After the movie, the avid *Pulp Fiction* fan received a stern lecture from her friends (all budding young social psychologists) about the negative effects of exposure to this type of media stimulus. At least one of these friends had never before attended such a violent movie and he reported that he would never do so again.

When we inquire after the particular reasons why the avid fan enjoyed *Pulp Fiction*, it turns out that she reports liking it in spite of, rather than because of, several long and violent scenes (including ones featuring male rape and gory beatings). She squinted her eyes during the most violent scenes of the movie and reacts to any other movies containing graphic violence in similar eye-squinting fashion.

The *Pulp Fiction* fan is the second author of this chapter. The first author does not share her fascination with this movie, but we do share a general preference to avoid explicit depictions of bashing, beating, knifing, punching, shooting, raping, and torturing. Only in rare circumstances, in which we are quite confident in advance of the excellence of other aspects of a movie, do we risk being exposed to graphic violence.

The *Pulp Fiction* episode illustrates a number of different responses to violent entertainment.[1] Some people may generally choose to stay away from violent movies (as was the case with the colleague who announced his intent to avoid any violent movies like *Pulp Fiction* in the future). Some may occasionally choose to view violent films and yet not find them very appealing (like most of the social psychology colleagues described above). Others appear to enjoy the violence wholeheartedly, as evidenced by the cheering crowd of university students who applauded wildly at the most violent scenes. Yet others may choose to view violent films and report enjoying them in spite of the fact that the violent scenes themselves do not bring feelings of pleasure, delight, or happy excitement (as in Cheri's case).

In this chapter, we want to think about the appeal of violence by considering three distinct ways of enjoying this type of entertainment. First, one might report enjoyment for a violent movie precisely because the violent images themselves evoke pleasure. Second, one might report overall enjoyment of a violent movie but find the violent scenes themselves to be unpleasant. In this case, the enjoyment of the movie may actually be due to enjoyment of things that tend to co-occur with violence. Finally, one might report overall enjoyment for a violent movie not so much because of the inherent appeal of the images, but because of various gratifications that are indirectly related to the viewing of the images and are actually experienced after the images themselves are viewed.

We address these three possibilities with respect to mayhem and horror as well. It is important to note that there is considerable, but not perfect, overlap in the conceptions of violence, mayhem, and horror (VMH). Before we consider the reasons for the appeal of this kind of entertainment, some definitional issues must be resolved.

DEFINITIONAL ISSUES

In general, we use the term *violence* to refer specifically to images in which the actions of one or more characters brings about physical injury to another character. We use *mayhem* to refer in general to images that might potentially be associated with bodily harm, but are not clearly initiated by a particular character (explosions, natural disasters, etc.). *Horror* is reserved for the media content that seems designed to induce a state of fear or terror.

While violence, mayhem and horror are conceptually distinct, there is also overlap between these categories. Attempts by characters to injure or harm another (violence) certainly qualify as mayhem, and horror films often contain violent images as one vehicle designed to arouse fear in viewers (Sapolsky & Moli-

---

[1]While parts of our analysis in this chapter may be appropriately applied to other forms of entertainment, we are especially concerned in this chapter with movies and TV programs.

tor, 1996).[2] But mayhem also might include such things as exploding volcanoes and subsequent lava flows, or buildings that explode even when no one is hurt as a result. Likewise, horror might involve grotesque images or anticipated outcomes that are unfavorable for the protagonist, but little explicit violence.

We attempt to distinguish among these different types of content if it becomes necessary; otherwise we treat them all similarly in our discussion. We turn now to a consideration of the first of the three possible ways in which individuals might find appeal in violent, horrific, and mayhem-involving entertainment.

ARE VIOLENCE, MAYHEM, AND HORROR INHERENTLY APPEALING?

One possibility is that media depictions of VMH contain properties that are inherently attractive or enjoyable. For example, some people may actually enjoy the sight of a bullet entering a body (an enjoyment manifested, perhaps, by the vocalization "Aha!"), quite apart from who shot the bullet or who suffered because of it. Or they may find the image of the White House exploding (*Independence Day*) to be aesthetically appealing in some way (the bright colors, the symmetry of the blast, etc.). One of us (Cheri) was completely captivated by the spectacle of the lava flows in the movie *Volcano*, quite apart from the way they fit into the movie's plot. The sensory appeal of the mayhem was enjoyed for its own sake and the plot details were of little concern to her. In the case of horror, individuals may specifically seek the feelings of thrill and excitement that horrific images evoke or they may be drawn in by the aesthetic appeal of scenes involving bizarre monsters. The next portion of this chapter describes several perspectives from which to consider the idea that images of VMH may be inherently pleasurable to view.

Sensory Delight

As just noted, images involving VMH may have sensory appeal. The enjoyment of the color and movement of a lava flow qualifies as an example. Some viewers may find particular sensory delight in the sound of an alien popping out of a person's stomach in the horror film *Alien*. Perhaps some are enamored with slow-motion shots of bodies being riddled with bullets and blood splashing into the air, as shown for one of the first times in movie history in the film *Bonnie and Clyde* (see Hoberman, 1998). An important dimension of this explanation is that these sensory experiences are enjoyed completely apart from the surrounding context, characters, plot, and so on that might be happening simultaneously. While there is little data to directly support the sensory delight explanation with respect to media VMH, Kagan

---

[2]Zillmann and Weaver (1997) suggested that violence in the context of the horror film may be more "purposeless" and less likely to involve the extent of social conflict that is typical in the "superviolence" genre.

(1996) has recently noted wide agreement among psychologists that one of the primary goals of human behavior is to maximize "sensory pleasure." If some individuals do experience sensory delight from these media themes, it could be a powerful motivator for repetitive consumption of this type of media content.

Aesthetic Theory of Destruction

One account of the pleasure that may exist in viewing VMH is advanced by Allen and Greenberger (1978, 1979). These authors explicated "an aesthetic theory of destruction" that attempts to explain the motivations involved in destructive behavior. The theory emphasizes that the same factors that contribute to aesthetic enjoyment (factors such as complexity, expectation, novelty, intensity, patterning, etc.) are also involved in destructive acts. Consequently, these authors held that there may be a powerful aesthetic pleasure elicited by acts of destruction. For example, when a pane of glass is struck by a hard object, it may or may not break. If it does break, the shattering of the glass is complex and unpredictable. The accompanying sound of the glass breaking is not exactly the same each time. These elements, the authors contended, all contribute to the enjoyment of destruction. Although the theory was formulated primarily to account for the motivations behind destructive behavior, the authors extended the basic principles to witnessing destructive acts. They stated:

> The aesthetic theory of destruction proposes that persons seek stimulation in the destruction of an object just as they seek stimulation in more socially acceptable aesthetic experiences (Berlyne, 1971). . . . Demolition derbies, disaster movies, and burning buildings are just a few examples of mundane situations in which persons intentionally choose to observe acts of destruction. (1979, p. 94)

Any attempt to evaluate the relative merits of this explanation for the appeal of VMH is severely limited by the lack of critical research. The strategy that has been taken in the few existing studies is to manipulate the uncertainty or the complexity of a destructive act and measure the relative appeal of the destruction. One study (Allen & Greenberger, 1979) appears to offer some support for the notion that uncertainty or surprise contributes to the enjoyment of a pane of glass breaking. Another study (Greenberger & Allen, 1980) uncovered a linear relation between the commitment on the part of subjects to break an object and that object's subjective complexity. More directly related to media consumption, Tamborini and Stiff (1987) found that one of the three major reasons that subjects reported for attending horror films was to see the destruction that these films often presented.

At this point, we find the ideas of sensory or aesthetic appeals of media VMH to be distinct possibilities that should be explored in future studies. However, the evidence in favor of other explanations (reviewed in the following sections) for the appeal of this type of entertainment along with there being little direct evidence for the importance of these variables causes us to be cautious in estimating the relative merits of the aesthetic or sensory delight positions.

Novelty

Perhaps some of the appeal of images of VMH can be explained by the fact that they are unusual or novel. The orientation to novel stimuli may have some evolutionary significance. Dangers often arise from a disruption of the status quo and those who survive best are those who can efficiently and quickly identify new and unusual events in the environment. Carroll (1990) commented on the inherent properties of horror that seem to be consistent with the idea that their appeal is found in their novelty. He stated that "horror attracts because anomalies command attention and elicit curiosity" (p. 195).

Novelty seeking, of course, has been identified as a fundamental dimension of personality on which individuals vary. Cloninger developed a tridimensional theory of personality and psychopathology as well as the Tridimensional Personality Questionnaire (TPQ) to assess the extent to which individuals were high on novelty seeking, harm avoidance, and reward dependence (Cloninger, Przybeck, & Svrakic, 1991). A number of researchers have used the TPQ to investigate the relationship between novelty seeking and substance abuse. For example, Wills, Vaccaro and McNamara (1994) studied 457 adolescents and found that substance use (tobacco, alcohol, and marijuana) was particularly high for those subjects who scored highest on the novelty seeking portion of the TPQ. In a review of studies between 1986 and 1995, Howard, Kivlahan, and Walker (1997) concluded that adolescent and adult scores on novelty seeking as measured by the TPQ predicted the early onset of alcohol abuse as well as criminality. In attempting to explain the relationship between novelty seeking and substance abuse, Bardo, Donohew, and Harrington (1996) proposed a biological mechanism. According to these authors, individual differences in novelty seeking and drug abuse may be explained, in part, by individual differences in the mesolimbic dopamine system of the brain. The authors suggest that while there appears to be some genetic component to novelty seeking, early developmental experiences may also be critical in modifying the brain system activity that governs these responses.

While a general preference for novel stimulation must be considered a possible explanation for the appeal of VMH, it appears to us that considerably more work needs to be done in this area before our understanding of this motivation is complete.

Sensation Seeking

One explanation that incorporates components of both the sensory delight and novelty explanations is the sensation-seeking view (Zuckerman, 1979). According to this explanation, VMH are enjoyed by some viewers because of their intrinsic capabilities to satisfy the need for arousing stimulation. One of Zuckerman's most recent statements on sensation seeking (Zuckerman, 1996) defines the concept in the following way: "Sensation seeking is a trait defined by the seeking of varied, novel, complex, and intense sensations and experiences, and the willingness to take physical, social, legal, and financial risks for the sake of such experience" (p. 148).

The fact that sensation seeking is related to preferences for arousing media seems to be well established. Zaleski (1984) exposed subjects to a variety of pictures that included torture scenes, hanging, and corpses, as well as to scenes of celebration and "mild love making." High sensation seekers preferred pictures that had been rated by a different group of subjects as highly arousing—regardless of whether the content was positive or negative. They preferred a group of neutral pictures the least. In contrast, low sensation seekers preferred the negatively arousing pictures the least and positively arousing pictures the most. Johnston (1995) studied high school students and found sensation seeking to be related to the preference for viewing horror films. Other researchers have also reported that sensation seeking is positively correlated with the preference for media horror (Edwards, 1984; Sparks, 1986; Tamborini & Stiff, 1987; Zuckerman & Litle, 1986). As Zuckerman (1996) observed, "Sensation seekers prefer being frightened or shocked to being bored" (p. 155).

According to Zuckerman, the basis for the sensation-seeking motive lies at the biological level. In one version of the theory, high sensation seekers are those who function better at high levels of cortical arousal. Subsequent research has suggested that the need for stimulation resides not in cortical arousal but in the subcortical limbic systems (Zuckerman, 1984). In view of the well-established literature that documents the existence of the sensation-seeking trait and the numerous studies that relate sensation seeking to preferences for violence and horror in entertainment, this explanation for the appeal of VMH must be considered seriously. However, we agree with Zuckerman when he pointed out, "As with other kinds of phenomenal expression, we must be cautious about interpreting a preference in terms of a single trait or any disposition at all. There are many social facilitating factors that bring young people into these films" (1996, p. 158).

Dispositional Alignments

One particularly satisfying explanation for the appeal of VMH is the disposition theory. According to this theory, viewers of media entertainment react to the events on the screen in much the same way that they would react to the events if they witnessed them in real life. A crucial component in such witnessing is the formation of dispositional alignments with various characters. That is, viewers form likes and dislikes for the characters involved in the drama. Zillmann (1998) summarized the dynamic of dispositional alignments:

> Specifically, a favorable disposition toward friendlike characters is thought to instigate hopes for benefaction and fears of aversive outcomes. Liked characters, in other words, are deemed deserving of good fortunes and undeserving of bad ones. In contrast, an unfavorable disposition toward enemylike characters is thought to instigate hopes for aversive, punitive outcomes and fears of benefaction. Disliked characters, then, are deemed deserving of bad fortunes and undeserving of good ones. (p. 201)

The theory of dispositional alignments has been used quite successfully to predict emotional reactions of consumers to a variety of types of entertainment (Zillmann

& Cantor, 1976; Zillmann & Paulus, 1993). In terms of the appeal of violence, the theory suggests that the typical viewer is willing (even eager) to witness various acts of violence so long as the ones who suffer from these acts are disliked and perceived as deserving of their punishment. As Zillmann (1998) stated, "Negative affective dispositions, then, set us free to thoroughly enjoy punitive violence" (p. 202).

A key component that permits the viewer to enjoy various acts of violence is the extent to which the acts are perceived to be appropriate and fair for those punished. Again, as Zillmann (1998) noted, "However, as we still adhere to concepts of 'fair retaliation,' any gruesome retributive killing has to appear just, and this appearance has to be prepared by witnessing the party to be punished perform increasingly despicable heinous crimes" (p. 206). Accordingly, the same violence might be either enjoyed or despised, depending fully on the extent to which a viewer believed that the acts were justified in the context of the dramatic events depicted.

The disposition theory explanation may seem a bit removed from the notion of the "inherent appeal" of violence, especially when compared to the sensory, aesthetic delight, or novelty accounts. But even though the enjoyment of violence is dependent on the various dispositional alignments that viewers form, these alignments, once in place, do seem to permit the viewer to thoroughly relish violence and mayhem if they cause havoc, pain, and so on for deserving antagonists.

Violating Social Norms

In discussing the appeal of novelty in violent entertainment, McCauley (1998) considered a view that he labeled "curiosity/fascination theory." But on close scrutiny, the curiosity or fascination of which he wrote is not so much a general curiosity or fascination but, rather, a very specific one. According to his analysis of the horror film, many of the images presented in this form of entertainment violate social norms. He states that the violation of norms "holds a fascination for people to the extent that they rarely see these violations in everyday experience" (p. 149). McCauley (1998) cited data reported by Tamborini, Stiff, and Zillmann (1987) that shows that the preference for horror films is significantly correlated ($r = .39$) with the deceit subscale of the measure for the Machiavellianism personality trait. What do high scores on the deceit dimension of Machiavellianism and the preference for horror have in common? According to the authors, the underlying common feature is "a desire to violate the norms of socially acceptable behavior, or to see them violated by others" (p. 548).

This view is not inconsistent with disposition theory. One possibility is that when viewers are encouraged through various cinematic techniques to form favorable alignments with characters who engage in rule-breaking behavior—characters who, according to mainstream social norms, might be considered to be despicable—their violent behaviors may be particularly appealing. This may be precisely the dynamic that worked in the movie *Bonnie and Clyde*. As Hoberman (1998) wrote:

It should not be surprising then that, for some, *Bonnie and Clyde* was not so much overly violent as excessively glamorous: "Pretty people who kill, and the killing they do is pretty too," wrote Jimmy Breslin in *New York* (July 8, 1968). . . . Good looks, swell clothes, and impossible cool set Bonnie and Clyde apart from their dowdy environment. . . . These were no ordinary delinquents. . . . Bonnie and Clyde were too beautiful to grow up, become domestic, join the middle class. (p. 131)

So, when viewers are encouraged to form positive dispositions with characters who make a habit of violating social norms by committing aggression, then pleasure may be taken from viewing these acts.

Sex Differences Based on Evolution

In a recent review of empirical evidence, Buss and Shackelford (1997) proposed that the psychological appeal of human aggression evolved as a result of adaptation to basic problems (gaining others' resources, defending against attack, negotiating status, dealing with same-sex rivals, etc.). The authors argued that after considering these problems and the adaptive, aggressive solutions that have evolved, there is evolutionary logic for the common finding that males are more aggressive than females. If the aggressive response has evolved over thousands of years of human existence as an efficient solution to various social problems, then it follows that the stimulus features of aggression (such as those in violent entertainment) have inherent attraction as generally valued commodities.

A host of findings in the mass media literature report sex differences that are certainly consistent with the logic of the evolutionary position. Cantor (1998) noted that "it is a truism that violence is much more a male than a female activity" (p. 99). She reviewed a variety of evidence showing that males are more attracted to media violence even as young children. Fenigstein (1979) demonstrated that behaving aggressively and thinking aggressive thoughts led to an increased preference for watching violent films—but only among males. Tamborini and Stiff (1987) found that males were more likely to prefer viewing horror films than females. Likewise, Sparks (1991) found that males were much more likely to express enjoyment after watching frightening movies.

As our understanding of evolutionary psychology increases, we suspect that the role of evolutionary predispositions will take on increasing importance in our understanding of behavior related to the mass media. As Guttmann (1998) noted, Konrad Lorenz apparently held the view that the attraction of violence for the human being was an "ineradicable part of human nature" (p. 18).

VIOLENCE CONFOUNDED WITH OTHER VARIABLES

As the formulations specified above demonstrate, there are a number of reasons for suggesting that VMH are inherently appealing. Notwithstanding these reasons, it is also plausible to suggest that this sort of entertainment is appealing not because of the inherent properties of violent or horrific content, but because of other features that seem to be naturally confounded with their occurrence. It is very difficult to judge the overall appeal of violent or horrific movies when we do not have quality control measures—perhaps violent movies are generally of better (or worse) quality than movies that are not violent. Perhaps quality is the critical variable that drives viewing selection and enjoyment. Alternatively, perhaps violent or horrific movies have more sexual content than other films and it is the sexual content that motivates viewing and supplies enjoyment. Or, perhaps it is the suspense generally associated with violence that elicits positive feelings and motivates viewing (chap. 4, this volume).

One obvious lack in the current research on the appeal of media violence is a systematic program of experimental research that assesses levels of enjoyment after manipulating levels of violence in program content while holding other variables constant. In one sense, it is remarkable that such studies have not yet been done. In Cantor's (1998) review of the literature, she noted only a single study with adults (Diener & DeFour, 1978) that pursued this strategy. The results revealed that a violent episode of *Police Woman* was not liked significantly more than a nonviolent episode. A second study done with children by Potts, Huston, and Wright (1986) did attempt to systematically vary levels of violence and action in program content. Similar to the study by Diener and DeFour (1978), children's interest in violent programs as measured by visual attention to the screen was not significantly higher than their interest in nonviolent programs. While the authors of both of these studies discussed their results in terms of how Hollywood could reduce violence without losing audience appeal, their conclusions are certainly premature without additional data that replicates the findings.

Both of us have occasionally sat through a movie that we wanted to see because of the actors, storyline, or artistic acclaim, but we chose to avert our gaze from the screen during particularly horrific or violent moments. To the degree that graphic depictions of VMH are invariably associated with stimulating and engrossing drama, it is difficult to ascertain the appeal of the violent scenes themselves, apart from the appeal of the movie as a whole. Since good entertainment often involves conflict (see chap. 4, this volume), it seems inevitable that some of that conflict will be physical. One thing that we really do not know from existing studies is the extent to which movies like *Casino*, *Pulp Fiction*, *Sleepers*, *Die Hard*, and *Gone with the Wind* would maintain their appeal if the scenes containing explicit gore, brutality, bodily injury, and so on were shortened or eliminated altogether. We regard this as a significant unanswered question in the literature.

THE APPEAL OF POST-VIEWING GRATIFICATIONS

A third general explanation for the appeal of VMH is that viewers might experience various post-viewing gratifications that are associated with these types of content. According to this formulation, viewers may not actually enjoy the watching of violent or horrific images. Instead, the appeal of this kind of entertainment is to be found in post-viewing gratifications that result in reports of overall viewing enjoyment and that motivate future encounters with the same type of material.

Catharsis

One early theory in the violence literature proposed by Feshbach (Feshbach, 1955, 1976; Feshbach & Singer, 1971) advanced the notion of symbolic catharsis. According to this view, exposure to media violence had potentially therapeutic properties for individuals who were angry and who, because of this emotional state, were inclined to behave aggressively. By viewing violent entertainment, regardless of its specific association with their own emotional state, individuals would leave the entertainment experience with their pent-up aggressive tendencies purged or cleansed. In short, they would feel better and certainly less inclined to act in an aggressive fashion. Presumably, witnessing others engage in violence provided the opportunity for individuals to fantasize about their own aggressive actions. Having engaged in such fantasy, the need to actually act out their anger was significantly reduced. Of particular importance for our consideration of reasons for the appeal of violence, Liebert & Sprafkin (1988) have observed that Feshbach believed that the positive feelings resulting from fantasy aggression could become habit-forming. They stated, "If the individual is rewarded often enough for fantasy aggression (he pushes his boss off a bridge in thought and feels better afterward), he gets into the habit of using fantasy aggression to "cathart" (drain off) his aggressive feelings" (p. 76).

Despite its early popularity, the theory of symbolic catharsis suffered from various flaws in the studies that were presumably supportive (for an analysis of these flaws, see Chaffee & McLeod, 1971; Liebert, Sobol, & Davidson, 1972). Most importantly, a number of other studies revealed that when angry individuals were exposed to media violence, their aggressive tendencies increased, in direct opposition to the theory's major prediction (Berkowitz & Geen, 1966; Siegel, 1956). Recent studies show the same finding (e.g., Bushman & Geen, 1990). Current assessments of the theory conclude that the prediction of diminished aggression after exposure to media violence was simply mistaken (Berkowitz, 1993).

Of course, if individuals do not end up feeling less angry as a result of a draining off of their aggressive impulses after exposure to media violence, the premise that violent entertainment might be enjoyed for this reason appears to crumble. Certainly, some individuals enjoy the fantasy aggression that exposure to media violence invites, but if such enjoyment does not result in a subsequent reduction of aggressive tendencies, the symbolic catharsis hypothesis fails.

Desensitization and "Flooding" in the Context of Horror

Although there is some consensus about the lack of merit of the catharsis theory in the context of purging anger by exposure to media violence, we might inquire about the merits of a catharsis-type process occurring in the context of horrific or frightening media. Could it be that one might seek out frightening entertainment as a way of attempting to overcome one's fears? If so, does such exposure provide any relief?

One of us (Cheri), found the experience of viewing *The Exorcist* unbearably scary, still reporting over 25 years later that it was the scariest movie she ever saw. In fact, she found it so scary that after a few weeks she went back to see it again, because she had some intuition that seeing it again would help her get over her recurring images of the possibility of people's eyes turning demon-yellow as they walked through the lounge of her undergraduate dormitory.

There is certainly some evidence that media exposure to objects that are feared can serve to reduce fear and anxiety of the same objects. The use of filmed models is a standard technique for the treatment of phobias (Hill, Liebert, & Mott, 1968; Ollendick & King, 1998) with the supposed mechanism of the successful treatment being gradual desensitization through repeated exposure. The intuition that repeated exposure to *The Exorcist* might help to diminish the same fears induced by the first exposure to the film seems consistent with emotional desensitization, but there appears to be little empirical evidence documenting a specific desire to engage in repeat viewing for this purpose. However, several studies do show clear evidence that repeated exposure to the same (or highly similar) media images of violence causes a diminished emotional reaction consistent with a desensitization effect (Cline, Croft, & Courrier, 1973; Linz, Donnerstein, & Adams, 1989; Linz, Donnerstein, & Penrod, 1988).

Another technique for the treatment of fears is imaginal flooding, which calls for the subject to flood the imagination with fear-provoking images (Lyons & Scotti, 1995; Saigh, 1998). In one study (Cooper & Clum, 1989), subjects suffering from posttraumatic stress disorder induced by war experiences in Vietnam were assigned to 14 sessions of imaginal flooding. Relative to a control group, the group that underwent imaginal flooding suffered fewer sleep disturbances and fewer symptoms associated with reexperiencing traumatic events. Taken together, the evidence from studies on desensitization and imaginal flooding suggests that direct exposure to images associated with one's fears might actually help to reduce them.

What is much less clear from the literature is whether individuals are actually motivated to voluntarily expose themselves to horrific images as a method of reducing fears. Notwithstanding the anecdotal experience of repeat viewing of *The Exorcist*, the empirical data on selective exposure for purposes of fear reduction suggests a slightly different kind of process. In a study by Wakshlag, Vial, and Tamborini (1983), viewer apprehension about becoming a victim of a crime was manipulated and film choices were subsequently observed. Subjects who were feeling the highest levels of apprehension preferred to view drama that was lower in images of violence victimization. These subjects preferred to view images where justice triumphed over evil. Zillmann and Bryant (1994) summarized this data by noting that the apprehensive viewers clearly showed a tendency "to minimize exposure to disturbing events" (p. 447). To summarize, our analysis suggests that there is little evidence that people commonly seek out scary films for the purpose of fear reduction, even though in some situations, the evidence suggests that it might be effective.

Excitation Transfer

One explanation for the enjoyment of horror is found in Zillmann's (1978) theory of excitation transfer. According to this theory, the viewer's encounter with frightening media stimuli induces elevated levels of physiological arousal. When these encounters conclude, viewers often experience a profound sense of relief that the film is over or even a strong positive feeling in response to a plot resolution in which the horrifying threat is, at last, defeated. Since the viewer remains in an elevated state of arousal from prior fear and anxiety and since arousal intensifies whatever emotion is subjectively experienced, the feelings of relief or positive affect are subsequently intensified. The euphoric feelings that viewers sometimes report after watching frightening films are undoubtedly a function of this transfer of residual excitation from prior feelings of fright. The empirical evidence in favor of the excitation transfer effect in the context of media stimuli is solid (Cantor, Zillmann, & Bryant, 1975; Reisenzein, 1983; Zillmann, 1978; Zillmann, Mody, & Cantor, 1974). Sparks (1991) used data from three different studies and found that especially for male viewers, self-reported ratings of distress to a frightening film were significantly correlated with ratings of delight. Consistent with the excitation transfer explanation, subjects' ratings of delight after the films were over varied as a function of the level of physiological arousal recorded during the films. Sparks's data involved subjects at three different universities and included reactions to three different frightening films. It would appear then that the excitation transfer effect has considerable support in this context.

Mastering Threats

Zillmann and Weaver (1996) recently explicated another theoretical framework that helps to explain the appeal of VMH—particularly for males. According to these authors, horror films may serve as a replacement in modern culture for ancient tribal initiation rites that served to bestow the status of "protector" on males and "protectee" on females. They state, "Adolescents of modern society have to demonstrate their compliance with societal precepts in alternative social contexts, and we suggest that going to the movies provides such a context" (p. 81). The authors go on to predict that watching horrific entertainment provides an opportunity for males to demonstrate their mastery over the various images. In contrast, the same entertainment provides females with an opportunity to demonstrate their relative helplessness and high levels of fear. To the extent that males and females are able to perform their appropriate roles in the context of frightening entertainment, the overall experience is pleasant. This pleasure in achieving the appropriate social displays is misconstrued as enjoyment of frightening films. Notice that this account of pleasure in the wake of media threats applies mainly to adolescents rather than other population groups. Adolescents are the ones who are most conscious of assuming their appropriate societal roles.

One conceptual advantage of this explanation for the appeal of media horror is that it fully acknowledges the experience of genuine fear reactions that the data clearly document. Cantor (1994) reviews a diverse set of studies conducted with children and adults that show that lingering fright reactions are prevalent. In a survey by Palmer, Hockett, and Dean (1983), one third of the children who were studied said that they were sometimes or frequently sorry that they had viewed scary programs. In a study with college students (Sparks, Spirek, & Hodgson, 1993), significant percentages of the respondents reported being nervous after viewing scary movies (44%); experiencing sleep trouble (42%); avoiding exposure to other scary movies (40%); and being afraid to go into certain rooms of one's own house (50%). The extent to which adults experience these lingering fears after media exposure suggests that something other than the willing suspension of disbelief occurs when audiences view horror films.

The emphasis on mastery of threats also explains how exposure to frightening entertainment can be enjoyed despite the fact that the content itself produces negative emotional reactions. Indeed, in order for males to experience the satisfaction that comes from mastering a threat, they must first experience the threat and its accompanying negative emotional reactions.

While Zillmann and Weaver (1996) reviewed a variety of types of evidence in favor of this gender-role-socialization account for the appeal of horror, the definitive study appears to be one conducted by Zillmann, Weaver, Mundorf, and Aust (1986). In this experiment, male subjects were paired together with a female confederate who displayed either fear, mastery of fear, or emotional neutrality during the movie *Friday the 13th, Part III*. Likewise, in other conditions, female subjects were paired together with a male confederate who displayed one of the three emotional reactions to the events in the film. After the film, the subjects provided ratings of the extent to which they enjoyed the film, the extent to which they liked their viewing partner, the extent to which they were romantically attracted to their viewing partner, and the extent to which they felt intimidated by their viewing partner. The major finding of this study was that males enjoyed the movie much more when they were paired together with a female who displayed fear. Likewise, females enjoyed the movie much more when they were paired together with a male who displayed mastery. In addition, for confederates who were quite ordinary in physical attractiveness, females were rated as being much more attractive when they displayed fear. Male confederates were rated as being much more attractive when they displayed mastery. In discussing the results of this experiment a decade later, Zillmann and Weaver concluded that:

> Emotional displays to horror thus have social consequences for the displayer, consequences that extend far beyond reactions to events on the screen as such. Most importantly, these consequences are predictable. As the discussed experimental evi-

dence is supportive of the gender-socialization model of horror, this model may be considered to predict many of these consequences accurately. (Zillmann & Weaver, 1996, pp. 97–98)

Clearly, it does appear that mastery of threatening images, particularly for male adolescents, plays a role in the appeal of horror.

To this point, we have considered three main categories for thinking about how people might enjoy movies or TV programs that contain VMH. A common assumption that seems to underlie our discussion is that there is considerable appeal in this sort of entertainment. Therefore, we would be remiss in our consideration of this topic without at least subjecting this common assumption to more careful scrutiny.

HOW POPULAR ARE VIOLENCE, MAYHEM AND HORROR IN THE MEDIA?

Some data suggests that the popularity of violence may be over-rated, perhaps due in part to the high profile that violent entertainment has occupied on the public and political agenda (American Psychological Association, 1993; Centers for Disease Control, 1991; National Academy of Science, 1993). In a recent video ("The killing screens," 1994), George Gerbner took a position that deemphasizes the popularity of violent entertainment. He said:

> Violence, in itself, is not a popular commodity. To be sure, there are some good stories and very strong stories that have a lot of violence, but their popularity does not rest in the violence. Most of the highly rated programs on television are non-violent.

We would also note that Gerbner's observation also holds for mayhem and horror. Gerbner explained the prevalence of violence in media entertainment according to its properties as a transportable marketing commodity. According to him, violence can help to liven up a boring plot scenario and can be produced relatively easily and economically. Most important, violence is easily understood by an international audience and is easily exportable. Since Gerbner contends that most media productions are made with this international audience in mind, Hollywood productions tend to contain higher levels of violence than might be expected based on domestic profits. Gerbner's observations certainly do not explain fully the prevalence and popularity of VMH, but they have some merit in putting this sort of entertainment into proper perspective. The prevalence of VMH entertainment is not necessarily a reliable gauge for its general appeal.

There is some other evidence to suggest that violent content is not generally the most appealing. Cantor (1998) noted that the Nielsen ratings for 1995 showed that children in the age range of 2 to 11 years old were much more likely to view situation comedies that focused on family issues than action-oriented violent cartoons on Saturday morning. Cantor's own data were also consistent with this point. In a random sample survey of parents, the most popular program reported as a favorite among children was *Full House* (a nonviolent situation comedy). It was mentioned spontaneously by 33% of the sample. In contrast, the violent cartoon *Mighty Morphin Power Rangers* was mentioned by only 26% of the parents. Cantor concluded that, "In evaluating the popularity of violent programming, it is important to keep in mind that there are other types of offerings that are even more popular with children" (p. 96). Goldstein (1998a) echoed this same theme in his recent book on the attractions of violent entertainment. He concluded, "It is worth remembering that violent entertainment is the preferred form of entertainment only for a minority of the general audience. Most viewers appear to prefer comedies and sitcoms to violent entertainment" (Goldstein, 1998b, p. 225).

One must consider the possibility that, left to their own writing and directing preferences, the average member of the viewing public would generate much less VMH than Hollywood currently makes available. If such a situation were possible, the average viewer might actually watch far less VMH than is currently the case. On the other hand, perhaps even more, not less, of this type of entertainment would be generated. The point here is that it is difficult to judge the relative overall appeal of violent movies if most movies currently available are either violent or nonviolent. Only if equal numbers of high quality violent and nonviolent movies were available to the viewing public would we be able to begin to untangle the question of the relative appeal of the various types of presentations. If a disproportionate number of available movies are violent and people want to watch something, then high quantities of violence will be consumed.

CONCLUSIONS

In this chapter, we have attempted a general exploration of the appeal of VMH in media entertainment. It should be evident from our discussion that the topic is not a simple one to contemplate. Indeed, Goldstein (1998b) listed 17 different explanations for the appeal of violence alone. We tend to view the various explanations for the appeal of VMH as falling into three main categories: inherent appeal of the content, appeal of variables that are naturally confounded with the content, and appeal of various post-viewing gratifications.

In thinking about these three types of explanations, it is important to note that they are not generally incompatible with one another. For example, one could find evidence for the notion that violent content is appealing because of its novelty (an example of the inherent appeal of violence) while simultaneously discovering that the same content is appealing because of an engaging, dramatic, conflict-filled story (an example of the appeal arising from other variables confounded with violence). Just as one may be able to explain aggressive behavior or alcohol use by appealing simultaneously to developmental factors, biological factors, or situational factors, it may be possible to explain the appeal of VMH by including all three of the general categories that we have outlined. However, just as scholars may argue about the relative contributions of development, biology, or situation to behaviors like aggression or alcohol use, the extent to which any of our three categories may ultimately explain the appeal of violence is very much an open question and subject to the results of future research that may explore these issues.

It is also important to note that there may be specific explanations or theories within the three categories that are incompatible with each other. For example, the experience of mastery (one of the post-viewing gratifications) requires some type of negative reaction to VMH (i.e., the experience of a true threat) as a prerequisite. This type of negative reaction appears to be incompatible with the idea that one would derive inherent pleasure (sensory delight, novelty, etc.) from the same content. Thus, while the three different types of explanations for the appeal of VMH are not generally incompatible, there may be particular ideas from different categories that would appear to stand in opposition to each other.

Finally, we also discussed reasons for why the appeal of this type of entertainment is something that should not be generally assumed. Moreover, we note that in considering VMH in the same essay, some important distinctions between these types of entertainment were not fully explored in terms of the relevance of each of the explanations for their appeal. As our understanding of the particular dynamics of media entertainment increases, these distinctions should become much more pronounced than they were in our analysis.

In the end, one point seems clear: For all of the research that has been done on media effects over the years, our analysis of this topic reveals the need for carefully controlled laboratory experiments on a number of critical issues. We are particularly interested in learning more about the inherent appeal of VMH. We would suggest studies that involve varying the length and explicitness of VMH while holding all other variables constant. In addition, we believe more work needs to be done incorporating individual differences in the areas of sensation and novelty seeking as well as the experiences of sensory and aesthetic delight. One thing is certain: If we have any hope of learning to control the impact of media violence on human beings, we must continue rigorous, empirical investigations on the diverse issues that arise in connection with the appeal of this type of entertainment.

REFERENCES

Allen, V. L., & Greenberger, D. B. (1978). An aesthetic theory of vandalism. *Crime and Delinquency, 24,* 309–321.

Allen, V. L., & Greenberger, D. B. (1979). Enjoyment of destruction: The role of uncertainty. *Journal of Nonverbal Behavior, 4,* 87–96.

American Psychological Association. (1993). *Violence and youth: Psychology's response.* Washington, DC: American Psychological Association.

Bardo, M. T., Donohew, R. L., & Harrington, N. G. (1996). Psychobiology of novelty seeking and drug seeking behavior. *Behavioural Brain Research, 77,* 23–43.

Berkowitz, L. (1993). *Aggression: Its causes, consequences, and control.* New York: McGraw-Hill.

Berkowitz, L., & Geen, R. G. (1966). Film violence and the cue properties of available targets. *Journal of Personality and Social Psychology, 3,* 525–530.

Berlyne, D. E. (1971). *Aesthetics and psychobiology.* New York: Appleton-Century-Crofts.

Bushman, B. J., & Geen, R. G. (1990). Role of cognitive-emotional mediators and individual differences in the effects of media violence on aggression. *Journal of Personality and Social Psychology, 58,* 156–163.

Buss, D. M., & Shackelford, T. K. (1997). Human aggression in evolutionary psychological perspective. *Clinical Psychology Review, 17,* 605–619.

Cantor, J. R. (1994). Fright reactions to mass media. In J. Bryant & D. Zillmann (Eds.), *Media effects: Advances in theory and research* (pp. 213–245). Hillsdale, NJ: Lawrence Erlbaum Associates.

Cantor, J. R. (1998). Children's attraction to television programming. In J. H. Goldstein (Ed.), *Why we watch: The attractions of violent entertainment* (pp. 88–115). New York: Oxford University Press.

Cantor, J. R., Zillmann, D., & Bryant, J. (1975). Enhancement of experienced sexual arousal in response to erotic stimuli through misattribution of unrelated residual excitation. *Journal of Personality and Social Psychology, 32,* 69–75.

Carroll, N. (1990). *The philosophy of horror, or paradoxes of the heart.* New York: Routledge.

Centers for Disease Control. (1991). *Position papers from the third national injury conference: Setting the national agenda for injury control in the 1990s.* Washington, DC: Department of Health and Human Services.

Chaffee, S. H., & McLeod, J. M. (1971, September). *Adolescents, parents, and television violence.* Paper presented at the meeting of the American Psychological Association, Washington, DC.

Cline, V. B., Croft, R. G., & Courrier, S. (1973). Desensitization of children to television violence. *Journal of Personality & Social Psychology, 27,* 360–365.

Cloninger, C. C., Przybeck, T. R., & Svrakic, D. M. (1991). The Tridimensional Personality Questionnaire: U.S. normative data. *Psychological Reports, 69,* 1047–1057.

Cooper, N., & Clum, G. A. (1989). Imaginal flooding as a supplementary treatment for PTSD in combat veterans: A controlled study. *Behavior Therapy, 20,* 381–391.

Diener, E. & DeFour, D. (1978). Does television violence enhance program popularity? *Journal of Personality and Social Psychology, 36,* 333–341.

Edwards, E. (1984). *The relationship between sensation-seeking and horror movie interest and attendance.* Unpublished doctoral dissertation, University of Tennessee, Knoxville.

Fenigstein, A. (1979). Does aggression cause a preference for viewing media violence? *Journal of Personality and Social Psychology, 37,* 2307–2317.

Feshbach, S. (1955). The drive-reducing function of fantasy behavior. *Journal of Abnormal and Social Psychology, 50,* 3–11.

Feshbach, S. (1976). The role of fantasy in the response to television. *Journal of Social Issues, 32,* 71–85.

Feshbach, S., & Singer, R. D. (1971). *Television and aggression.* San Francisco: Jossey-Bass.

Goldstein, J. H. (1998a). *Why we watch: The attractions of violent entertainment.* New York: Oxford University Press.

Goldstein, J. H. (1998b). Why we watch. In J. H. Goldstein (Ed.), *Why we watch: The attractions of violent entertainment* (pp. 212–226). New York: Oxford University Press.

Greenberger, D. B., & Allen, V. L. (1980). Destruction and complexity: An application of aesthetic theory. *Personality & Social Psychology Bulletin, 6,* 479–483.

Guttmann, A. (1998). The appeal of violent sports. In J. H. Goldstein (Ed.), *Why we watch: The attractions of violent entertainment* (pp. 7–26). New York: Oxford University Press.

Hill, J. H., Liebert, R. M., & Mott, D. E. (1968). Vicarious extinction of avoidance behavior through films: An initial test. *Psychological Reports, 22,* 192.

Hoberman, J. (1998). "A test for the individual viewer": *Bonnie and Clyde's* violent reception. In J. H. Goldstein (Ed.), *Why we watch: The attractions of violent entertainment* (pp. 116–143). New York: Oxford University Press.

Howard, M. O., Kivlahan, D., & Walker, R. D. (1997). Cloninger's tridimensional theory of personal-ity and psychopathology: Applications to substance use disorders. *Journal of Studies on Alcohol, 58,* 48–66.

Jhally, S. *The killing screens: Media and the culture of violence* [video]. (1994). Northampton, MA: Media Education Foundation.

Johnston, D. D. (1995). Adolescents' motivations for viewing graphic horror. *Human Communication Research, 21,* 522–552.

Kagan, J. (1996). Three pleasing ideas. *American Psychologist, 51,* 901–908.

Liebert, R. M., Sobol, M. P., & Davidson, E. S. (1972). Catharsis of aggression among institutional-ized boys: Fact or artifact? In G. A. Comstock, E. A. Rubinstein, & J. P. Murray (Eds.), *Television and social behavior: Vol. V. Television effects: Further explorations* (pp. 351–358). Washington, DC: U.S. Government Printing Office.

Liebert, R. M., & Sprafkin, J. N. (1988). *The early window.* New York: Pergamon Press.

Linz, D., Donnerstein, E., & Adams, S. M. (1989). Physiological desensitization and judgments about female victims of violence. *Human Communication Research, 15,* 509–522.

Linz, D. G., Donnerstein, E., & Penrod, S. (1988). Effects of long-term exposure to violent and sexu-ally degrading depictions of women. *Journal of Personality & Social Psychology, 55,* 758–768.

Lyons, J. A., Scotti, J. R. (1995). Behavioral treatment of a motor vehicle accident survivor: An illus-trative case of direct therapeutic exposure. *Cognitive and Behavioral Practice, 2,* 343–364.

McCauley, C. (1998). When screen violence is not attractive. In J. H. Goldstein (Ed.), *Why we watch: The attractions of violent entertainment* (pp. 144–162). New York: Oxford University Press.

National Academy of Science. (1993). *Understanding and preventing violence.* Washington, DC: Na-tional Academy Press.

Ollendick, T. H., & King, N. J. (1998). Empirically supported treatments for children with phobic and anxiety disorders: Current status. *Journal of Clinical Child Psychology, 27,* 156–167.

Palmer, E. L., Hockett, A. B., & Dean, W. W. (1983). The television family and children's fright reac-tions. *Journal of Family Issues, 4,* 279–292.

Potts, R., Huston, A. C., & Wright, J. C. (1986). The effects of television form and violent content on boys' attention and social behavior. *Journal of Experimental Child Psychology, 41,* 1–17.

Reisenzein, R. (1983). The Schachter theory of emotion: Two decades later. *Psychological Bulletin, 94,* 239–264.

Saigh, P. A. (1998). Effects of flooding on memories of patients with posttraumatic stress disorder. In J. D. Bremmer & C. R. Marmar (Eds.), *Trauma, memory, and dissociation. Progress in psychia-try, No. 54* (pp. 285–320). Washington, DC: American Psychiatric Press.

Sapolsky, B. S., & Molitor, F. (1996). Content trends in contemporary horror films. In J. B. Weaver, III & R. Tamborini (Eds.), *Horror films: Current research on audience preferences and reactions* (pp. 33–48). Mahwah, NJ: Lawrence Erlbaum Associates.

Siegel, A. E. (1956). Film-mediated fantasy aggression and strength of aggressive drive. *Child De-velopment, 27,* 365–378.

Sparks, G. G. (1986). Developing a scale to assess cognitive responses to frightening films. *Journal of Broadcasting and Electronic Media, 30,* 65–73.

Sparks, G. G. (1991). The relationship between distress and delight in males' and females' reactions to frightening films. *Human Communication Research, 17,* 625–637.

Sparks, G. G., Spirek, M. M., & Hodgson, K. (1993). Individual differences in arousability: Implica-tions for understanding immediate and lingering emotional reactions to frightening mass media. *Communication Quarterly, 41,* 465–476.

Tamborini, R., & Stiff, J. (1987). Predictors of horror film attendance and appeal: An analysis of the audience for frightening films. *Communication Research, 14,* 415–436.

Tamborini, R., Stiff, J., & Zillmann, D. (1987). Preference for graphic horror featuring male versus female victimization: Personality and past film viewing experiences. *Human Communication Re-search, 13,* 529–552.

Wakshlag, J. J., Vial, V., & Tamborini, R. (1983). Selecting crime drama and apprehension about crime. *Human Communication Research, 10,* 227–242.

Wills, T. A., Vaccaro, D., & McNamara, G. (1994). Novelty seeking, risk taking, and related constructs as predictors of adolescent substance use: An application of Cloninger's theory. *Journal of Substance Abuse, 6,* 1–20.

Zaleski, Z. (1984). Sensation-seeking and preference for emotional visual stimuli. *Personality & Individual Differences, 5,* 609–611.

Zillmann, D. (1978). Attribution and misattribution of excitatory reactions. In J. H. Harvey, W. Ickes, & R. F. Kidd (Eds.), *New directions in attribution research: Vol. 2* (pp. 335–368). Hillsdale, NJ: Lawrence Erlbaum Associates.

Zillmann, D. (1998). The psychology of the appeal of portrayals of violence. In J. H. Goldstein (Ed.), *Why we watch: The attractions of violent entertainment* (pp. 179–211). New York: Oxford University Press.

Zillmann, D., & Bryant, J. (1994). Entertainment as media effect. In J. Bryant & D. Zillmann (Eds.), *Media effects: Advances in theory and research* (pp. 437–461). Hillsdale, NJ: Lawrence Erlbaum Associates.

Zillmann, D., & Cantor, J. R. (1976). A disposition theory of humour and mirth. In A. J. Chapman & H. C. Foot (Eds.), *Humour and laughter: Theory, research, and applications* (pp. 93–115). London: Wiley.

Zillmann, D., Mody, B., & Cantor, J. R. (1974). Empathetic perception of emotional displays in films as a function of hedonic and excitatory state prior to exposure. *Journal of Research in Personality, 8,* 335–349.

Zillmann, D., & Paulus, P. B. (1993). Spectators: Reactions to sports events and effects on athletic performance. In R. N. Singer, M. Murphey, & L. K. Tennant (Eds.), *Handbook of research on sport psychology* (pp. 600–619). New York: Macmillan.

Zillmann, D., & Weaver, J. B., III. (1996). Gender-socialization theory of reactions to horror. In J. B. Weaver, III & R. Tamborini (Eds.), *Horror films: Current research on audience preferences and reactions* (pp. 81–101). Mahwah, NJ: Lawrence Erlbaum Associates.

Zillmann, D., Weaver, J. B., Mundorf, N., & Aust, C. F. (1986). Effects of an opposite-gender companion's affect to horror on distress, delight, and attraction. *Journal of Personality and Social Psychology, 51,* 586–594.

Zuckerman, M. (1979). *Sensation seeking: Beyond the optimal level of arousal.* New York: Wiley.

Zuckerman, M. (1984). Sensation seeking: A comparative approach to a human trait. *Behavioral and Brain Sciences, 7,* 413–471.

Zuckerman, M. (1996). Sensation seeking and the taste for vicarious horror. In J. B. Weaver III & R. Tamborini (Eds.), *Horror films: Current research on audience preferences and reactions* (pp. 147–160). Mahwah, NJ: Lawrence Erlbaum Associates.

Zuckerman, M., & Litle, P. (1986). Personality and curiosity about morbid sexual events. *Personality and Individual Differences, 2,* 49–56.

6

▼▼▼▼▼▼▼▼

Sex on Entertainment Television

Bradley S. Greenberg
Linda Hofschire
Michigan State University

As we wrote this chapter in mid-1999, the conception of sex as entertainment on television was undergoing a transformation that academic research continues largely to ignore. The country watched the dramatic federal inquiry into the sexual activities of the president of the United States. We all heard him define and describe a variety of heterosexual activities. We read the deposition of the woman with whom these activities had occurred; it described in precise detail the specific content of these activities. Was this not "entertainment" television? No, by some quaint definition created decades ago, this was "news and public affairs," somewhat sacred entities often left unexamined for political reasons. So we draw attention at the outset of this chapter that much sex on television that may be entertaining has been omitted in prior research because certain content genres have been isolated or exempted. Here, we focus on the fictional presentation of sex—the soap operas, the prime time television series, the music videos on MTV. The absence of analysis of real-life sex issues on television, however, appears to be a huge void. Yet not all real-life sex is ignored. Another television genre—the afternoon talk show—provides its own spectacle and has undergone some relatively sophisticated content analyses. But are talk shows real or fiction or both? Or is that answer in the eye and ear of the viewer?

Within the political panorama of presidential sex, we witnessed considerable confusion at the national level as to just how one might define *sex* and *sexual relations*. Perhaps many thought they "knew it when they saw it," a principle not well adapted to quantitative analyses. Difficult as it is to train coders to become reliable with our own somewhat arbitrary content definitions, consider the difficulty of training lawyers, jurists, and politicians! Bear in mind as well that social scientists likely have ignored legal definitions in framing their projects.

Nonetheless, the task of this chapter is to summarize what we know of the content of sex on television (for soap operas, talk shows, prime time television and MTV), paying some special attention to the alternative approaches and definitions used. Then, where effects studies exist, they will be linked to the content components, before we wrestle with an agenda for subsequent research.

SOAP SEX

Let us illustrate what sex is like on one soap, *Sunset Beach*, as a basis for digesting the somewhat sterile statistical results:

- Cole had sexual intercourse with a married woman, Olivia, and may have fathered her son
- Cole subsequently had sex with Olivia's daughter and later married her
- Michael had sex with Vanessa and is now engaged to her; she just aborted a fetus implanted in vitro from the sperm of a different man
- Ben had sex with Meg and then married her, but his once-dead wife showed up at the wedding ceremony, and the second marriage is now in limbo
- Antonio, a priest, has just had sex with Gabi, his brother's girlfriend; and Gabi had been having sex with the brother
- Annie, the most promiscuous woman on the show, seduced Gregory and then married him
- Gregory offered Francesca $5 million to seduce AJ.

Simply stated, each story line on the show offers a romantic relationship that becomes completely confounded with a sexual relationship.

More systematic content analyses of sex in the soaps can be obtained from studies done in 1985 (Greenberg & D'Alessio, 1985), partly replicated in 1994 (Greenberg & Busselle, 1996), and expanded in 1996 (Heintz-Knowles, 1996). First, we compare the replicated studies and then update them with findings from the 1996 study.

Ten episodes of each of five soaps in 1994 yielded 333 incidents of sexual activity, an average of 6.6 acts depicted or talked about each soap hour. Three soaps analyzed in both 1985 and 1994 showed a 35% increase in sexual activity. These studies looked for physical or verbal occurrences of sexual intercourse, prostitution, rape, "long" kisses, "petting" or other forms of foreplay, and homosexuality. The most common sexual activity in both decades was intercourse between two people not married to each other; there were 120 instances of unmarried intercourse (2.4 times per hour) in the 1994 sample. The second most common topic, rape, was presented 1.4 times per hour; rape story lines on two soaps accounted for all 71 references. Long kissing was seen once each hour. Intercourse between married couples was shown or referred to .72 times per hour. Prostitution and petting were infrequent and there was no homosexual activity.

Two substantial differences in sexual content emerged between 1985 and 1994 among the three soaps analyzed in both studies. Intercourse between unmarried partners increased from 1.56 to 1.83 instances per hour, or one more act every four episodes. Rape increased from one rape reference per 10 episodes to more than one per episode. Rape was not found in the 1985 soaps sample but was a major activity in the 1994 sample; its inclusion is indicative of the soaps' response to current issues in their story lines (another recent story line featured an intern seduced by her congressman). In the 1990s, news media attention focused on date rape, primarily on its occurrence among adolescents and young adults. Two soaps in the 1994 sample had story lines about the date rape of teenagers, which accounted for the temporary surge in this content category. In the 1996 study, there were no date rape story lines; it was no longer in the headlines. All other changes in findings between the 1985 and 1994 findings were trivial.

Soap operas talk about sex much more often than they show it. Of the 333 separate physical acts or verbal references to sex in the 1994 sample, 225 were verbal references, with no visual counterpart; soap viewers hear about sex twice as often as they see it. This is true of all the sexual content categories except long kisses, which were shown 57 times in the 1994 sample, or once per episode, but never talked about. The second most frequent sex topic to be seen by the viewer, in the sense of strong visual implications (e.g., partners are naked and in bed) was unmarried intercourse. This activity was visually portrayed 32 times (.64 times per hour), but talked about nearly three times as often (88 acts, 1.8 times per hour). Therefore, in a typical week of watching one's favorite soap opera, there would be talk of having sex nine times, and the opportunity to see it occur three or four times!

Heintz-Knowles (1996) provided a third point of comparison with an analysis of 10 hours each of the 10 nationally televised soaps sampled over a five-week period. She examined sexual intercourse, but her subset of other activities was quite different: intimate dancing, modest kisses, passionate kisses, petting, flirting, and romantic touching. Nonetheless, the overall rate of these activities (6.1) was quite comparable to the 1994 rate (6.6), given differences in time and sampling frame. Her primary findings include: (a) considerably greater frequencies of visual behaviors, many of which are attributable to the addition of largely visual content categories, for example, dancing, modest kissing; (b) that most sexual interactions were between participants involved in established relationships with each other, rather than one-night stands; (c) no change in the rate of discussion of safe sex or contraception, which was about one incident every other week; (d) zero homosexual activity; (e) the dropout of date rape story lines; and (f) that most sexual activity had a positive effect on the participants' relationships within the episode in which the activity occurred.

Additional information about the participants, their relationships, and their attitudes toward sexual activity is available. From the 1994 study (Greenberg &

Busselle, 1996), 50% of the participants engaging in the coded sexual activities were not married at the time or had never been married, 21% were married to each other, and 9% were known to be divorced or widowed. Only 8% were married to someone else, so that appears to be the soaps' baseline for the entire set of behaviors that involved at least one unfaithful, married partner.

Half the participants expressed positive attitudes toward their sexual activity; 20% were negative; the rest were noncommittal. Much of the sex viewers hear about comes from characters who talk about what other characters are doing. They were three times as likely to express negative comments (59%) and only 12% were positive in talking about other characters' sexual activities. Married couples having intercourse were overwhelmingly positive about their activity; all husbands were positive and only two wives were negative. Married men and women initiated sexual activity in equal proportions.

For unmarried intercourse partners, attitudes were more ambiguous: 46% of men and 40% of women were positive; 14% of men and 18% of women were negative; the attitudes of 40% of each gender were not apparent. When the instigator could be identified (half the time), initiation was evenly split between males and females. About 12% of the women and 15% of the men had sex with someone married to someone else at the time.

Soap Effects

Studies of the effects of watching soaps serve more to stimulate a research agenda than as definitive or consistent answers. Systematic efforts have examined the effects of soap operas within a cultivation paradigm. This theory proposes that heavy soap viewers will make estimates about the frequency of selected behaviors or groups that are more similar to the frequency of soap portrayals of these phenomena than their real life frequencies. Carveth and Alexander (1985) showed a soap cultivation effect on viewer estimates of the number of illegitimate children, number of divorces, and number of divorced males. Surveying college students, Buerkel-Rothfuss and Strouse (1993) found that viewing daytime soaps was positively correlated with respondents' perceptions of how often people have intercourse. Larson (1996) compared soap opera viewers' and nonviewers' perceptions of the lifestyles of single mothers among junior and senior high students. Viewers believed that single mothers were relatively well-educated and had good jobs and that their babies would receive love and attention from the mothers' male friends. As a parallel, Buerkel-Rothfuss and Mayes (1981) found that college students with higher exposure to soaps believed that more businessmen, men, and women have had affairs, have been divorced, and have had illegitimate children, and that women have had more abortions. Alexander (1985) also found that adolescent soap opera viewers had inflated estimates of the difficulty of maintaining a relationship.

Content analyses indicate little if any portrayal of safe sex and contraception, but many pregnancy stories (Greenberg & Busselle, 1994), and those themes provided the basis for Olson's (1994) cultivation hypotheses. She reported that college student soap viewers perceived (a) less need for contraception use than nonviewers, (b) higher rates of pregnancy, and (c) higher rates of adultery. They also made higher estimates of the presence of sexually transmitted diseases (STDs), a contrary result. In addition, viewers did not differ from nonviewers in their estimates of the risks associated with sexual behavior nor in the acceptability of premarital intercourse. The findings offer mixed support from the cultivation perspective.

TALK SHOW SEX

In the fall of 1995, 24 different daytime television talk shows specializing in interpersonal conflicts, emotional crises, and disclosure of very private information were available on broadcast and cable television. That season was the apex of abundance for this genre and generated the most public level of criticism. In the first months of 1999, the number of such shows is about half as large and the criticism is directed at a smaller number of hosts, Jerry Springer in particular. As talk show competitors became more brazen in their attempt to survive on television, increasing criticism of the content of these shows emerged from politicians and television critics. The popular press focused on outrageous topics and situations (Chad, 1995; Steenland, 1990; Zoglin, 1995), suggesting that talk shows are modern, mass-mediated freak shows (Andersen, 1993; Oliver, 1995). These critics stressed the dominance of sexual themes on the programs, especially the blunt discussions of sexual orientations and deviances that have been unavailable on television outside of restricted, pay cable channels. General literary analyses mirror claims of the popular press. They have characterized talk shows as sordid (Mifflin, 1995), immoral and sleazy (Gregorian & Kuntzman, 1995), degrading (Oldenburg, 1995), revolting (Alter, 1995), and rot (Cass, 1995).

What content do these shows actually contain? In contrast to several volumes of quantitative analyses of violent content on television (National Television Violence Study 2, 1998) and a smaller but informative number of systematic studies of sex content in different media (Greenberg, 1994), quantitative examinations of the content of television talk shows have been sparse. One project, funded by the Kaiser Family Foundation, generated a 1995 video sample of 10 episodes from each of 12 talk shows and a nonoverlapping sample of 10 transcripts from each of 8 talk shows (Greenberg et al., 1995), in addition to an examination of nearly 1000 TV talk show titles (Smith, Mitchell, et al., in press).

Sexual themes as major topics on television talk shows emerged as the second most common element in the video sample. Half the shows in the sample focused on parent–child relations (control, child care, working mothers) and one third dealt with spousal relations (problems, multiple marriages, divorce), making some aspect of family relations the most common facet of the talk shows. Sexual themes, however, were frequent; 34% of the shows had sexual activity (number of partners, being lovers, safe and unsafe sex, prostitution) as a major topic, 18%

had sexual infidelity (cheating on someone) and 11% had sexual orientation (homosexuality, transsexuals) as a major topic. The prevalence of these sexual topics did not vary by the gender or age of the guests on the shows, only by their ethnicity and by their relationship; sexual orientation as a topic was more likely a theme among African American guests, whereas sexual infidelity was rarely a theme among Hispanic guests; sexual topics were most prominent among lovers and former lovers. Shows most likely to feature one or more of the sexual topics were *Geraldo*, *Jenny Jones*, *Rolonda*, and *Springer*.

The transcript analysis of televised disclosures ("personal information usually revealed only to one's close friends, family, rabbi, minister, or therapist") identified a core format/content feature of the talk show genre. An average of 16 personal disclosures per episode hour were identified; 42% were self-disclosed, 28% were disclosed by the host or hostess, and 30% were disclosed by a third party. The disclosures were assembled in six categories; most prevalent was sexual activity (4 disclosures per hour), followed by abuse (3), criminal activity (2), embarrassing situations (2), and sexual orientation (1). A hodgepodge of all other personal attributes (4/hour) filled the sixth disclosure category. Within the sexual activity category, general sexual activity (frequency, regularity, number of partners) accounted for 44% of the disclosures; pregnancy and sexual infidelity disclosures also occurred frequently. In the sexual orientation category, disclosures about bisexual, transsexual and transvestite behaviors occurred more often than disclosures about gay and lesbian activities. Yet another disclosure category—abuse—revealed that sexual abuse accounted for 11% of all the abuse disclosures, lagging behind physical and general abuse. Talk shows most prone to sexual disclosures in the sampled time frame were *Jenny Jones* and *Jerry Springer*.

Subsequently, Smith, Ah Yun, et al. (in press) identified whether these disclosures occurred in the context of a family relationship or personal relationship, and whether the overall valence of each relationship was positive, negative, or neutral. When talk shows deal with sexual activity as a family relationship concern, there is a distinctly negative or neutral valence; when talk shows deal with the same activity in a personal relationship, it is equally likely to be positive, negative, and neutral. Sexual orientation is very seldom a subject of disclosure in the family relationship, and distinctively positive the vast majority of the time when disclosed in personal relationship contexts.

The Smith, Mitchell, et al. (in press) analysis of six months of talk show titles included the coding of 14 individual attributes from those titles, 2 of which paralleled their analysis of disclosures, that is, sexual activity (e.g., "Incest" was one show title) and sexual orientation ("Homosexuals with Crushes on Members of the Opposite Sex"). The analysis identified 785 instances of individual attributes and the most frequent one was sexual activity, 20% of the total, with sexual orientation contributing another 4%. No other single attribute made up as much as 10% of the total; all personality traits collectively accounted for 18%. This study also codified the valence of those attributes and determined that they were distinctly negative (74%), rather than neutral (16%) or positive (10%).

Talk Show Effects

Despite the recurrent criticism of talk shows and their alleged antisocial effects, studies of the audience of these shows are minimal. There is evidence that the audience that likes the personal disclosure format has high self-disclosure scores itself (Keao-Botkin, 1996). Why do people watch these shows? Undergraduates responded to a series of 27 gratification items from prior research with high scores on entertainment ("because it amuses me") and pass time ("nothing better to do") dimensions and comparatively low scores on other dimensions, for example, arousal, social interaction (Cress & Rapert, 1996).

One study examined audience responses that dealt with sexual issues. A survey of 282 high school students by Davis and Mares (1998) asked them to estimate the percentage of people who engage in activities commonly discussed on talk shows, for example, teen pregnancy and premarital sex; assessed possible desensitization to victim suffering and perpetrator blame in several common talk show scenarios; and had the students evaluate the seriousness and complexity of two topics often discussed on talk shows—drug abuse and pregnancy. Results indicated a significant and positive relationship between amount of viewing and frequency estimates for four of five teen-related topics, for example, teen pregnancy. Heavier viewers also were less likely to agree that "people are pretty decent," and "you can rely on people to be there when you need them." Heavier and lighter viewers did not differ in their judgments of victim suffering, nor in their assessment of the moral correctness of different scenarios; they also did not differ in their judgments of the complexity and severity of drug abuse and pregnancy issues.

PRIME TIME SEX

Sex on television in the evening has changed considerably from television's infancy in the 1950s (twin beds for married couples) to what may well be its pubescent hormonal apex a half century later. This report provides an overview from the 1980s forward. Disagreement as to what constitutes sex on television is apparent across these reports.

In 1979 and again in 1989, Sapolsky (1982; Sapolsky & Tabarlet, 1991) used the same scheme for analyzing sexual acts and references in one week of prime time television across what were then the three major broadcast networks. Overall, there was an increase from 13 to 16 sexual incidents per hour in that decade. In 1989, these incidents consisted primarily of noncriminal sex acts (kissing, touching, implied intercourse), an increase of one per hour from the earlier study; use of sexual language (about intercourse, prostitution, sexual anatomy), an increase of .7/hour; sexual innuendo (verbal innuendo and suggestive displays), an increase of .4/hour. In 1979, there was no examination of sexual responsibility, for example, safe sex or contraception, while in 1989, one could find some semblance of sexual responsibility two times in every three hours of prime time. Neither of these studies found much incidence of sexual intercourse, either implied or explicit (.06/hour in 1979 and .23/hour in 1989), although the authors noted that "characters speak about having sex on average more than once an hour. . . . The intimate act of intercourse is openly discussed in prime time . . . explicit intercourse, unseen in the 1970s, was observed four times in 1989" (p. 513). They did not code talking about intercourse as others have done, as an act itself.

Compare that finding with Greenberg, Stanley, et al. (1993) and their analysis of several episodes of the 19 TV series viewed most often by high school students in 1985. Using fewer but more manifest categories (intercourse, homosexuality, prostitution, rape, long kisses, and petting), on average each show offered three of these incidents per hour. Two acts—intercourse and long kisses—predominated. The combination of married and unmarried intercourse occurred 1.14 times per hour, or 39% of the total coded acts. Unmarried exceeded married intercourse by a ratio of 5:1, and one fifth of the participants were cheating on a spouse. Homosexuality and prostitution occurred once every two hours, with rape and petting virtually nonexistent. Aside from possible differences in coding procedures, these two studies suggest that preferred shows have more sexual content than an across-the-spectrum analysis of television's offerings.

Internal comparisons also offer additional insight. For example, the overall rate of sex acts found in action adventure series and in situation comedies was equivalent, at about 2.5 acts or references per hour. However, the action adventure series featured unmarried intercourse in nearly half of its total acts and prostitution in the major portion of the remainder; the situation comedies consisted mainly of kisses (42%), intercourse (30%), and homosexuality (21%). Finally, participants in sexual activity were positive toward those activities 80% of the time; in contrast, nonparticipants (those talking about someone else's sexual activities) were negative 80% of the time.

Similar results as to the frequency of sexual activity come from broader samples of prime time television shows that looked for incidents of sex, STDs, and pregnancy prevention (Lowry & Shidler, 1993; Lowry & Towles, 1989). Reference to pregnancy prevention occurred about once every five or six hours, reference to STD prevention only slightly more often than that, whereas indications of contracting STDs were essentially nil. These two studies also demonstrated that the shows included "erotic touching" at a rate of 2.5 times per hour and a litany of sexually suggestive language, ranging from 2.6 to 5 times per hour.

In a different vein, an analysis of the 12 most frequently watched TV programs by children and adolescents indicated that discussions and messages about sex and sexuality were common (Ward, 1995). In over one fourth of the interpersonal interactions, statements expressed were sexually oriented. Prevailing male sex role themes included the ideas that men view women as objects of sexual pleasure and value them accordingly, and that sex is inherently linked to masculinity. Added notions were that men are strategic in their attempts to attract women, that men will use any tactic necessary to convince a woman to have sex, and that men are the aggressors in sexual relations, although not all men are interested in sex at all times. Parallel themes about the female sex role emphasized that women are attracted to specific types of men for their physical appearances, their financial portfolio, their romantic appeal or their sensitivity. Further, not all women are sexually passive. An overall theme was that sex is fun for people of all ages.

The most recent and comprehensive analyses of sex on prime time television have emerged from the research team at the University of California at Santa Barbara (Kunkel, Cope, & Colvin, 1998; Kunkel et al., 1999). In their first study, they looked for verbal and physical sexual messages on television between 8 and 9 p.m., the "family hour." Although they made some attempt to compare their 1996 sample findings with 1976 and 1986, there were too few shows from the earlier decades for reliable or valid comparisons and we summarize their 1996 findings across 128 programs.

They found sexual content in some form on 75% of the 8 to 9 p.m. (EST) shows, and an average hour contained 8.5 sexual interactions; these consisted of 5.4 sexual behaviors and 3.1 verbal references to sexual activities. Situation comedies averaged 10.2 incidents per hour and dramas averaged 8.9 per hour.

Most prevalent among the behavioral messages (61% of the sex messages included a behavioral component) were physical flirting (2.4/hour) and kissing (2.1/hour). Sexual intercourse accounted for 3.3% of the sexual activity. Sexual talk (in 59% of the sexual messages) included suggestive commentary and discussions about sexual topics. The most common verbal behaviors were discussing another individual's sexual activity (1/hour) and comments on one's own current sexual activity (1/hour) or prior sexual activity (.6/hour).

For most sexual behaviors exhibited, there were no consequences. When there were consequences, 40% were positive, as reflected in greater personal satisfaction and self-confidence, 53% had unclear outcomes, and 7% were negative consequences. Only 5% of all scenes with sexual content stressed the themes of risk and responsibility. However, when sexual interactions involved teens (12% of all the sexual interactions and an average of 1/hour), 29% were in shows which emphasized risk/responsibility, compared to 9% of parallel interactions involving adults.

The single largest study of sexual content on television was released in February 1999 (Kunkel et al.), spanning 16 hours daily (7 a.m. to 11 p.m.) for 10 channels, sampling over a five-month period in 1998, and netting 942 shows, in addition to an oversampling of prime time television on ABC, CBS, Fox, and NBC, for an additional 274 shows. Omitted from this analysis were the daily newscasts and sports. We summarize the section of their study that focuses on prime time television and make meaningful comparisons between prime time and the rest of the television day they analyzed (excluding children's shows).

Two of every three prime time shows include sexual content and these average 5.3 scenes per hour, involving both sexual talk and sexual behavior, as compared with 56% and 3.2 scenes per hour in the overall program sample. The difference is located almost entirely in talking about sex, inasmuch as both program samples (prime time vs. overall) contain the same proportions of sexual behavior (24% vs. 23%). The incidence shows that prime time has one more sexual behavior (1.8/hour vs. 1.4/hour) every 2.5 hours.

As for the particular behaviors examined, 16% of the prime time shows contained only what were termed "precursory" behaviors—physical flirting, passionate kissing, intimate touching—the same figure obtained in the composite week sample. Those shows averaged 1.7 scenes with precursory behaviors. Nine percent of the prime time shows were found to contain implied or depicted sexual intercourse (1.8 scenes/hour), as compared with 7% across all the shows. In the composite week, 26% of the sexual behaviors were physical flirting, 50% passionate kisses, 7% intimate touching, 12% implied intercourse, 3% explicit intercourse, and 3% "other" activities. Comparable data for prime time shows alone are not reported.

A majority of each program genre analyzed in prime time contained sexual content, with situation comedies the leader at 77%, compared to 56% of comedies in the broader sample. In those shows with talk about sex, sitcoms and news magazines averaged 6.7 scenes/hour; for shows with sexual behaviors, sitcoms averaged 2.7 scenes per hour and exceeded dramas (1.9).

In looking for messages dealing with the risk and responsibility of sexual behavior, sitcoms provided one extreme—only 3% had such messages—whereas drama series (23%) and reality shows (22%) provided the opposite anchor. Risk and responsibility messages were more likely to occur in prime time shows than in the other day parts. For Kunkel et al., the fact that one in four drama series conveys risk and responsibility messages was a striking finding. This finding, however, was at the scene level. In examining the program overall, the authors report that just 3% of all programs including sexual content placed an overall emphasis on the risk and responsibility theme. Finally, what consequences, if any, are there to sexual intercourse? Composite week findings demonstrate that this question is ignored for the most part. No consequences were identifiable in 59% of the shows where intercourse was depicted or implied, consequences were distinctly positive in 27%, mixed in 7%, and distinctly negative in 7%.

Prime Time Effects

Because the literature on the effects of television sexual content is fragmented across different age groups, the focus here will be on adolescent responses to these messages.

Effects of exposure to media sexual content on adolescents' attitudes, perceptions, and behaviors can be encompassed around four general issues. First is the appeal of and appreciation for sexual content when recipients are asked to evaluate what they view. Second is the influence of such content on teens' general perceptions and beliefs about sexuality in our society (e.g., heavier TV viewers believe that more men have sexual affairs). The third area is the role of sexual content in the media on teens' attitudes and beliefs about their own sexuality (e.g., heavier television viewers are less satisfied with the quality of their own sex lives). Finally, we trace any relationships obtained between media content and adolescent sexual behavior.

Appreciation Function of Sexual Content

Greenberg, Linsangan, and Soderman (1993) measured high school students' reactions to televised scenes of homosexuality, prostitution, rape, married and unmarried intercourse, and heavy kissing. Participants reported that the prostitution scenes were the most enjoyable, acceptable, and funny, while the unmarried intercourse scenes were the sexiest. Married intercourse scenes were the least enjoyed and considered not sexy, and homosexual scenes were the least acceptable and the least sexy.

Beliefs About Sexuality in Society

A second area of research focuses on the cultivation effects of media sexual content, that is, do teens with heavier media diets accept more of television's sexual portrayals as real-to-life? Bryant and Rockwell (1994) found that teens exposed to television segments with pre-, extra- or nonmarital sexual relations evaluated them as significantly less bad activities than did teens exposed to marital sexual relations or to adults involved in nonsexual relations. Surveying college students, Buerkel-Rothfuss and Strouse (1993) found that exposure to popular media, rather than to sexually explicit media, was a stronger predictor of the perceived frequency of sexual behaviors among males and females in the real world. Signorielli (1991) reported a positive relationship between viewing television and ambivalence toward happy marriage as a way of life. In a study of a single series' impact on adolescent attitudes, Greenberg (1993) traced regular viewing of *Beverly Hills 90210* to stronger nontraditional sexual attitudes, as well as more materialistic attitudes.

Media sex content also can yield an educational opportunity for teens. For example, young teens who viewed television scenes with sexual content understood the meaning of terms such as homosexuality and prostitution better than nonexposed controls (Greenberg, Linsangan, & Soderman, 1993). Preteens who viewed TV shows designed to inform them about the sexual functions of the human body knew more factual information than nonviewers (Greenberg, Perry, & Covert, 1983).

Beliefs About Teens' Own Sexuality

Exposure to media sexual content influences teens' attitudes and expectations about their own sexuality. Baran (1976) found a positive relationship between perceived reality of televised sex and dissatisfaction with one's own sex life, regardless of whether or not the teen was sexually active. A significant relationship also was identified between heavy television viewing and negative attitudes toward remaining a virgin (Courtright & Baran, 1980). In a survey of more than 1,000 teens, television and pop music were identified as the two biggest sources of pressure to engage in sexual activity (Howard, 1985).

Behavioral Responses to Media

In addition to influencing adolescents' attitudes about their sexuality, media exposure impacts on their sexual experiences and behaviors. Brown and Newcomer (1991) identified a positive relationship between teenage viewing of sexually oriented television content and sexual activity. Peterson, Moore, and Furstenberg (1991) supported these results with a positive correlation between television viewing and sexual experience for teenage girls.

However, Huston, Wartella, and Donnerstein (1998) identify three factors that mediate the effects of exposure to sexual content: (a) Age: Older teens understand better, are more comfortable with, and are more likely to seek out media sexual portrayals than younger teens (Brown, White, & Nikopoulou, 1993; Kaiser Family Foundation & Children Now, 1996; Silverman-Watkins & Sprafkin, 1983); (b) Gender: Girls are more likely to use the media to educate themselves about sex and relationships (Thompson, Walsh-Childers, & Brown, 1993); and (c) Perceived realism and use of media: Media messages have the most impact when teens perceive them as realistic.

MTV SEX

Since its 1981 debut, Music Television (MTV) has been the subject of much criticism. Concerned parties argue that MTV is filled with sexual imagery and stereotypes, and that the prevalence of these portrayals has a negative effect on viewers. Because MTV is targeted at the 12–34-year-old demographic, parents and politicians have been among its loudest protesters, arguing that teenagers are negatively influenced by the messages of popular singers (Goodwin, 1992).

Research indicates that adolescents like to watch videos because the visual images enhance their appreciation of the music and help them to understand better the songs' messages (Goldberg, Chattopadhyay, Gorn, & Rosenblatt, 1993; Sun & Lull, 1986). Because many music videos tell ambiguous stories, teenagers use them to make inferences about the meanings of the songs (Blanchard-Fields, Coon, & Matthews, 1986). Given these attempts by adolescents to comprehend and draw their own conclusions about music videos, it is important to consider the types of sexual messages MTV sends its viewers.

A handful of studies over the past two decades to measure sexual content on MTV indicate its presence in the majority of videos. Three studies analyzed content from the 1984–1985 television season. From a sample of 49 MTV videos, Sherman and Dominick (1986) found that more than three fourths contained sexual behavior. Of these sexual acts, 77% were categorized as nonintimate behaviors (e.g., flirting, kissing, and hugging), while 23% were categorized as intimate ones (e.g., caressing and stroking).

Baxter, De Riemer, Landini, Leslie, and Singletary (1985) used a more stringent definition of sexual acts, coding only visual images of sexuality, such as provocative clothing, embraces and other physical contact, and sexually suggestive dance movements, in a 1984 MTV sample of 62 videos. In the 60% of the videos that contained sexual behaviors, the majority of these acts were implicit, relying on innuendo through clothing, suggestiveness, and physical behaviors such as kissing and hugging. However, in a study of six hours of MTV videos from 1985 (Greeson & Williams, 1987), sexual references (both visual and lyrical) were present in just 47% of the videos.

Sommers-Flanagan, Sommers-Flanagan, and Davis (1993) used a different unit of analysis to code sexual behavior: In a five-hour sample of MTV videos from 1990, they coded the presence of sexual activity per 30-second interval. Of 313 intervals, 90% contained implicit sexual acts (suggestive behaviors short of explicit sexual activity), whereas 4% contained explicit sexual acts.

A more recent analysis of sexual content on MTV indicates that it has not varied significantly in the past decade. With the coding categories used in Baxter et al.'s (1985) study, Pardun and McKee (1995) found sexual imagery (based on Baxter et al.'s definition) in 63% of a 1992 MTV sample of 160 videos (as compared to 60% in Baxter et al.'s study done in 1984).

Sexual stereotypic portrayals of men and women in music videos also have been analyzed. Sommers-Flanagan et al. (1993) found that women, compared with men, engaged in more implicitly sexual and subservient behavior and were more frequently the object of explicit, implicit, and aggressive sexual advances.

MTV Effects

Based on this research, MTV viewers are able to make certain inferences about sexuality. For example, they may be more accepting of sex since it appears to be a socially normative behavior. Studies that examine the effects of MTV on the sexual attitudes held by viewers support this proposition.

Some researchers have chosen to focus on how the attitudes of adolescents toward sexuality are affected by MTV. Strouse, Buerkel-Rothfuss, and Long (1995) found a positive relationship between MTV exposure and the acceptance of premarital sex among female junior and senior high school students. However, this effect was lessened when the females were from stable home environments.

The impact of family also was significant in another study of the effects of sexual content on adolescents (Thompson, Pingree, Hawkins, & Draves, 1991). Subjects were surveyed after viewing "Papa Don't Preach," a video about a young unmarried woman who becomes pregnant. The results indicated that for girls, family communication patterns and sexual and pregnancy experiences were significant predictors of enjoyment of the video. Specifically, strong family communication patterns lessened their enjoyment, while sexual and pregnancy experiences were positively correlated with enjoyment.

Greeson and Williams (1987) surveyed junior and senior high students about their attitudes toward sexuality after watching a collection of randomly selected music videos. They found that more adolescents agreed that premarital sex was acceptable after viewing MTV. A study using college undergraduates yielded similar findings. Calfin, Carroll, and Schmidt (1993) found that the college subjects reported more liberal sexual attitudes after viewing either erotic or nonerotic music videos when compared with the control group (who did not watch any videos). These findings indicate that MTV viewing in general is associated with more liberal attitudes about sexuality.

Other researchers have focused on how representations of sexual activity affect the appeal of music videos for college undergraduates. Hansen and Hansen (1990) found that visual depictions of sex increase the appeal of music videos for both males and females. Subjects exposed to greater levels of visual sex reported feeling happier and more sexual when compared to those in the control group. Zillmann and Mundorf (1987) also found that sexual imagery in music videos increased appreciation. In their study, subjects viewed music videos without sexual content or the same videos with added scenes depicting couples engaging in sexually suggestive behavior. While subjects rated the videos with added visual sex higher overall, females indicated that these videos were less romantic and more objectionable than videos without such images.

DISCUSSION

The following themes emerge from this review of the content and effects of TV sex.

. . . Sex, however defined, is more likely to be verbal than visual, with an average of more than six acts depicted or discussed per hour on the afternoon soaps. Sex is engaged in most frequently by unmarried participants, typically by at least a 6:1 ratio; this is the case for broadcast and cable television fare in all day parts.

. . . Sexual themes were the second most common topic of discussion on talk shows, and they encompassed a wide range of issues (e.g., sexual orientation, abuse, infidelity, safe and unsafe sex). In addition, sex content abounded in the disclosures made by the guests, their "friends," and the hosts of these shows.

. . . In a 1998 analysis of prime time TV shows, two of every three shows contained sexual content, with minimal emphasis on issues of risk and responsibility

. . . Similarly, music videos typically contained sexual content, ranging from innuendo to explicit sexual activity.

How does this content affect viewers? Researchers have identified several effects: cultivation effects to the extent that viewers overestimate the prevalence of sexually related activities in this society; disinhibition, as viewers express more liberal attitudes toward sexual issues and sexual diversity; appreciation, as derived from viewer interest in programming with a sexual component; and learning effects, as more of us are likely to know what "oral sex" is at an earlier age.

This review continues to reveal gaps in the content examined as well as the apparent scarcity of direct effects. In terms of content, most researchers have stayed largely within the confines of entertainment programming on the major broadcast networks, although Kunkel's 1999 report adds major cable networks to the mix. However, the television audience is increasingly turning to video as an entertainment alternative (Owen & Wildman, 1992). Given that videos are not subject to the indecency regulations of broadcast television, what is the sexual fare of the typical video rental outlet? More importantly, what is being rented and can such proprietary data reflecting the interests of the video audience become available for academic analysis? Owen and Wildman also talk of the drift to cable as an alternative, yet the cable networks likely to contain the most sexual content have been void of content analysis; these would include HBO and other movie channels, as well as the "adult" channels available in many cable systems, particularly in urban centers.

A relative of these adult channels may be the Internet and its surfeit of pornography. Not today, but in not so many tomorrows, the merging of television and computer technologies is likely to blur distinctions between the two. Kornblum (1999) reported that "sites selling porn—content perfectly suited for the anonymity and technology of the Net—earn about $1 billion a year" (p. 6B). She was bemoaning the fact that Microsoft had just canceled its political commentary magazine for lack of subscribers, while the porn sites were a boom. At the same time, Scott Sassa, the new entertainment president at NBC, was promising less emphasis on sex on NBC shows and less gratuitous sex when there is sex (Ostrow, 1999). Perhaps sex on broadcast television is so tepid compared with sexual content available elsewhere that some broadcasters perceive less need for it to attract viewers, or less ability to attract and sustain viewers.

The final content area to be singled out here is that of news and public affairs; this returns us to an opening theme in this chapter. No study to date reports on the presence, type, frequency, or form of sexual content in television news programming. The Kunkel et al. (1999) study taped daily newscasts, but excluded them from their analyses. The panorama of sexual content on television remains incomplete without such a report, and the study of television's effects on viewers' sexual inclinations and beliefs is incomplete for the same reason.

Part of the problem resides with different conceptions of what sexual content is: operational definitions differ across studies, even within entertainment programming analyses. These inconsistencies lead to mixed and sometimes contradictory results and make it difficult to chart content trends over time. The promise that the Kunkel et al. (1999) research will be biennial may rectify some of that difficulty, depending on how many biennials are forthcoming, whether they change portions of their scheme, and whether their scheme is generally accepted. Nevertheless all the content analyses reported in this chapter (and all those ignored because of age or methods) use content categories created by academics. They (and we) presume to define sexual activity and language, operationalize it, and train others to use our language scheme the same way. There is a need to bridge the gap between such analysts and the audience of interest. For instance, if we wish to assess the impact of television sexual content on adolescents, one might assemble a panel of teenagers to compare predetermined content definitions with content elements for purposes of assessing validity and reliability, or to help create the content definitions together with the academic specialists. Sexual content for a 16-year-old is not necessarily the same as for a 40-year-old, but all these analyses assume it is!

This suggestion provides a bridge to talking about effects. Knowing what a given segment of viewers considers as "sex" in television content permits more direct assessments of the relevance, importance, and meaning of that content for those viewers. Researchers in this area typically explain or predict the impact of viewing sexual content from either a cultivation or a social learning perspective. However, future effects research might wish to test the applicability of other theoretical perspectives, three of which are noted here. First, short-term effects of viewing sexual content may be assessed from a priming effects perspective (Jo & Berkowitz, 1994). Does exposure to sexual content activate related thoughts and action tendencies? Does watching two people entangled in a sexual embrace remind the viewer of a parallel actual or imagined incident from their past? If so, what happens as to behavior, tendencies, feelings, interests? To the extent that viewing sexual content may prime deviant, aggressive or irresponsible sexual responses, this effects perspective may be particularly useful.

For long-term effects paradigms, both the drench hypothesis and schema theory may be relevant. The drench hypothesis posits that some media portrayals, even if infrequent, "may be significantly strong, intense, or memorable that they create lasting impressions" (Greenberg & Brand, 1994, p. 304). Increasingly common, explicit (e.g., *NYPD Blue*) and even bizarre (e.g., the *Jerry Springer Show*) televised sexual portrayals may present novel or strong sexual experiences to some viewers, causing them to form their first and perhaps primary impressions about certain sexual issues, for example, the need for contraception, homosexuality, sexual abuse. In addition, schema theory (Fiske & Kinder, 1981) posits that viewers' sexual schemata can be shaped by the television messages they view, which in turn influences how they deal with sexual issues and how they process sexual messages in their own life. Both these conceptual perspectives suggest that television can be a primary reference point from which viewers make decisions about sexual matters. This would be so especially if the myriad of images they have received from television constitute a "norm" for them about sexual beliefs and behaviors. Understanding the processing of sexual content would add considerably to academic knowledge about the actual and potential influences of such messages.

What then do we have in sex as a form of entertainment on television? We have a noticeable trend for more sex (however defined), in more genres, in more channels. That sex content is increasingly visual and revealing. It focuses on intercourse as much as foreplay. That we have so few studies of its effects on viewers is a function of the difficulty of obtaining relevant data from that group in which considerable interest resides—the minor adolescent and preadolescent. Studies of young people's responses to sexual content appear to be more difficult to conduct than studies of their responses to violent and other antisocial content. All the content studies amount to little of importance without the required link to outcome. We have sparse evidence about the impact on postadolescent groups as well. If entertainment television content continues to prod us with sexual story lines, and it is likely to do so to remain competitive—the NBC entertainment president's disclaimer notwithstanding—there is an urgent need to delineate potential changes in beliefs, attitudes, values, and behaviors that may be linked to that content. If not, then we remain at the mercy of activists who claim personal knowledge of those outcomes.

REFERENCES

Alexander, A. (1985). Adolescents' soap opera viewing and relational perceptions. *Journal of Broadcasting & Electronic Media, 29*(3), 295–308.

Alter, J. (1995, November 6). Next: "The revolt of the revolted." *Newsweek*, 46–47.

Andersen, K. (1993, October 11). Oprah and Jo-Jo the dog-faced boy. *Time*, 94.

Baran, S. J. (1976). How TV and film portrayals affect sexual satisfaction in college students. *Journalism Quarterly, 53*(3), 468–473.

Baxter, R. L., De Riemer, C., Landini, A., Leslie, L., & Singletary, M. W. (1985). A content analysis of music videos. *Journal of Broadcasting & Electronic Media, 29*(3), 333–340.

Blanchard-Fields, F., Coon, R. C., & Matthews, R. C. (1986). Inferencing and television: A developmental study. *Journal of Youth and Adolescence, 15*(6), 453–459.

Brown, J. D., & Newcomer, S. F. (1991). Television viewing and adolescents' sexual behavior. *Journal of Homosexuality, 21*, 77–91.

Brown, J. D., White, A. B., & Nikopoulou, L. (1993). Disinterest, intrigue, resistance: Early adolescent girls' use of sexual media content. In B. S. Greenberg, J. D. Brown, & N. L. Buerkel-Rothfuss (Eds.), *Media, sex and the adolescent* (pp. 177–195). Creskill, NJ: Hampton Press.

Bryant, J., & Rockwell, S. C. (1994). Effects of massive exposure to sexually oriented prime-time television programming on adolescents' moral judgment. In D. Zillmann, J. Bryant, & A. C. Huston (Eds.), *Media, children, and the family: Social scientific, psychodynamic, and clinical perspectives* (pp. 183–195). Hillsdale, NJ: Lawrence Erlbaum Associates.

Buerkel-Rothfuss, N. L., & Mayes, S. (1981). Soap opera viewing: The cultivation effect. *Journal of Communication, 31*(3), 108–115.

Buerkel-Rothfuss, N. L., & Strouse, J. S. (1993). Media exposure and perceptions of sexual behaviors: The cultivation hypothesis moves to the bedroom. In B. S. Greenberg, J. D. Brown, & N. L. Buerkel-Rothfuss (Eds.), *Media, sex and the adolescent* (pp. 225–247). Creskill, NJ: Hampton Press.

Calfin, M. S., Carroll, J. L., & Schmidt, J. (1993). Viewing music-videotapes before taking a test of premarital sexual attitudes. *Psychological Reports, 72*, 475–481.

Carveth, R. A., & Alexander, A. (1985). Soap opera viewing motivations and the cultivation process. *Journal of Broadcasting & Electronic Media, 29*(3), 259–273.

Cass, C. (1995, October 27). Gangsta rap foes attack trash on TV. *Lansing State Journal*.

Chad, N. (1995, May). Talk stupid to me. *Gentlemen's Quarterly*, 156–159, 194.

Courtright, J. A., & Baran, S. J. (1980). The acquisition of sexual information by young people. *Journalism Quarterly, 57*(1), 107–114.

Cress, S. L., & Rapert, K. D. (1996, November). *Talk show viewing motives: Does gender make a difference?* Paper presented at the annual meeting of the Speech Communication Association, San Diego, CA.

Davis, S., & Mares, M.-L. (1998). Effects of talk show viewing on adolescents. *Journal of Communication, 48*, 69–86.

Fiske, S. T., & Kinder, D. R. (1981). Involvement, expertise, and schema use: Evidence from political cognition. In N. Cantor & J. F. Kihlstrom (Eds.), *Personality, cognition and social interaction* (pp. 171–190). Hillsdale, NJ: Lawrence Erlbaum Associates.

Goldberg, M. E., Chattopadhyay, A., Gorn, G. J., & Rosenblatt, J. (1993). Music, music videos, and wear out. *Psychology & Marketing, 10*(1), 1–13.

Goodwin, A. (1992). *Dancing in the distraction factory: Music television and popular culture*. Minneapolis: University of Minnesota Press.

Greenberg, B. S. (1994). Content trends in media sex. In D. Zillmann, J. Bryant, & A. C. Huston (Eds.), *Media, children, and the family: Social scientific, psychodynamic, and clinical perspectives* (pp. 165–182). Hillsdale, NJ: Lawrence Erlbaum Associates.

Greenberg, B. S., & Brand, J. E. (1994). Minorities and the mass media: 1970s to 1990s. In J. Bryant & D. Zillmann (Eds.), *Media effects: Advances in theory and research* (pp. 273–314). Hillsdale, NJ: Lawrence Erlbaum Associates.

Greenberg, B. S., & Busselle, R. (1994, October). *Soap operas and sexual activity*. Menlo Park, CA: Kaiser Family Foundation.

Greenberg, B. S., & Busselle, R. (1996). Soap operas and sexual activity: A decade later. *Journal of Communication, 46*(4), 153–160.

Greenberg, B. S., & D'Alessio, D. (1985). The quantity and quality of sex in the soaps. *Journal of Broadcasting & Electronic Media, 29*(3), 309–321.

Greenberg, B. S., Linsangan, R., & Soderman, A. (1993). Adolescents' reactions to television sex. In B. S. Greenberg, J. D. Brown, & N. L. Buerkel-Rothfuss (Eds.), *Media, sex and the adolescent* (pp. 196–224). Creskill, NJ: Hampton Press.

Greenberg, B. S., Perry, K. L., & Covert, A. M. (1983). The body human: Sex education, politics and television. *Family Relations, 32,* 419–425.

Greenberg, B. S., Smith, S. W., Ah Yun, J., Busselle, R., Rampoldi Hnilo, L., Mitchell, M., & Sherry, J. (1995, November). *The content of television talk shows: Topics, guests and interactions*. Menlo Park, CA: Kaiser Family Foundation.

Greenberg, B. S., Stanley, C., Siemicki, M., Heeter, C., Soderman, A., & Linsangan, R. (1993). Sex content on soaps and prime-time television series most viewed by adolescents. In B. S. Greenberg, J. D. Brown, & N. L. Buerkel-Rothfuss (Eds.), *Media, sex, and the adolescent* (pp. 29–44). Creskill, NJ: Hampton Press.

Greenberg, D. (1993). *The relationship between viewing "Beverly Hills 90210" and attitudes toward sexuality, materialism, and academic achievement*. Unpublished master's thesis, University of Wisconsin, Madison.

Greeson, L. E., & Williams, R. A. (1987). Social implications of music videos for youth: An analysis of the content and effects of MTV. *Youth & Society, 18*(2), 177–189.

Gregorian, D., & Kuntzman, G. (1995, October 28). Talk-TV titans meet in Apple to accentuate the positive. *New York Post.*

Hansen, C. H., & Hansen, R. D. (1990). The influence of sex and violence on the appeal of rock music videos. *Communication Research, 17*(2), 212–234.

Heintz-Knowles, K. E. (1996). *Sexual activity on daytime soap operas: A content analysis of five weeks of television programming*. Menlo Park, CA: Kaiser Family Foundation.

Howard, M. (1985). Postponing sexual involvement among adolescents: An alternative approach to prevention of sexually transmitted diseases. *Journal of Adolescent Health Care, 6,* 271–277.

Huston, A. C., Wartella, E., & Donnerstein, E. (1998). *Measuring the effects of sexual content in the media: A report to the Kaiser Family Foundation*. Menlo Park, CA: Kaiser Family Foundation.

Jo, E., & Berkowitz, L. (1994). A priming effect analysis of media influences: An update. In J. Bryant and D. Zillmann (Eds.), *Media effects: Advances in theory and research* (pp. 43–60). Hillsdale, NJ: Lawrence Erlbaum Associates.

Kaiser Family Foundation & Children Now. (1996). *The family hour focus groups: Children's responses to sexual content on TV and their parents' reactions*. Menlo Park, CA: Authors.

Keao-Botkin, M. L. (1996). *Television viewing habits, self-disclosure, and "liking" for talk show guests*. Unpublished master's thesis, California State University, Fullerton.

Kornblum, J. (1999, February 15). "Slate" lesson: Sex sells on net, news doesn't. *USA Today,* p. 6B.

Kunkel, D., Cope, K. M., & Colvin, C. (1998, July). *Sexual messages in "family hour" television*. Paper presented at the annual meeting of the International Communication Association, Jerusalem, Israel.

Kunkel, D., Cope, K. M., Maynard Farinola, W. J., Biely, E., Rollin, E., & Donnerstein, E. (1999). *Sex on TV: Content and context*. Menlo Park, CA: Kaiser Family Foundation.

Larson, M. S. (1996). Sex roles and soap operas: What adolescents learn about single motherhood. *Sex Roles, 35,* 97–110.

Lowry, D. T., & Shidler, J. A. (1993). Prime-time TV portrayals of sex, "safe sex," and AIDS: A longitudinal analysis. *Journalism Quarterly, 70*(3), 628–637.

Lowry, D. T., & Towles, D. E. (1989). Prime-time TV portrayals of sex, contraception, and venereal diseases. *Journalism Quarterly, 66*(2), 347–352.

Mifflin, L. (1995, October 28). Aim higher, forum urges talk shows. *New York Times*, p. A6.

National television violence study 2. (1998). Thousand Oaks, CA: Sage Publications.

Oldenburg, A. (1995, November 1). A click trip around the talk-show dial. *USA Today*, p. 3D.

Oliver, C. (1995, April). The sleazing of America. *Reason*, 142–144.

Olson, B. (1994). Soaps, sex and cultivation. *Mass Comm Review, 21*, 106–113.

Ostrow, J. (1999, January 18). NBC wants "balance" in its shows. *The Denver Post*, p. G05.

Owen, B. M., & Wildman, S. (1992). Introduction. In *Video economics* (pp. 1–25). Cambridge, MA: Harvard University Press.

Pardun, C. J., & McKee, K. B. (1995). Strange bedfellows: Images of religion and sexuality on MTV. *Youth and Society, 26*(4), 438–449.

Peterson, J. L., Moore, K. A., & Furstenberg, F. F. (1991). Television viewing and early initiation of sexual intercourse: Is there a link? *Journal of Homosexuality, 21*, 93–119.

Sapolsky, B. S. (1982). Sexual acts and references on prime-time TV: A two-year look. *Southern Speech Communication Journal, 47*, 212–226.

Sapolsky, B. S., & Tabarlet, J. O. (1991). Sex in prime time television: 1979 versus 1989. *Journal of Broadcasting & Electronic Media, 35*(4), 505–516.

Sherman, B. L., & Dominick, J. R. (1986). Violence and sex in music videos: TV and rock 'n' roll. *Journal of Communication, 36*(1), 79–93.

Signorielli, N. (1991). Adolescents and ambivalence toward marriage: A cultivation analysis. *Youth and Society, 23*(1), 121–149.

Silverman-Watkins, L. T., & Sprafkin, J. N. (1983). Adolescents' comprehension of televised sexual innuendoes. *Journal of Applied Developmental Psychology, 4*, 359–369.

Smith, S. W., Ah Yun, J., Orrego, V., Johnson, A. J., Mitchell, M., & Greenberg, B. S. (in press). The sources types, and frequencies of personal disclosures on talk television. In L. Klein (Ed.), *Talking up a storm: The social impact of daytime talk programs*. Westport, CT: Greenwood Press.

Smith, S. W., Mitchell, M. M., Ah Yun, J., Johnson, A. J., Orrego, V. O., & Greenberg, B. S. (in press). The valence of close relationships and the focus on individual attributes in six months of television talk show topics. In L. Klein (Ed.), *Talking up a storm: The social impact of daytime talk programs*. Westport, CT: Greenwood Press.

Sommers-Flanagan, R., Sommers-Flanagan, J., & Davis, B. (1993). What's happening on music television? A gender role content analysis. *Sex Roles, 28*(11/12), 745–753.

Steenland, S. (1990). Those daytime talk shows. *Television Quarterly, 24*(4), 5–12.

Strouse, J. S., Buerkel-Rothfuss, N., & Long, C. J. (1995). Gender and family as moderators of the relationship between music video exposure and adolescent sexual permissiveness. *Adolescence, 30*(119), 505–521.

Sun, S., & Lull, J. (1986). The adolescent audience for music videos and why they watch. *Journal of Communication, 36*(1), 115–125.

Thompson, M., Pingree, S., Hawkins, R. P., & Draves, C. (1991). Long-term norms and cognitive structures as shapers of television viewer activity. *Journal of Broadcasting & Electronic Media, 35*(3), 319–334.

Thompson, M., Walsh-Childers, K., & Brown, J. D. (1993). The influence of family communication patterns and sexual experience on processing of a movie video. In B. S. Greenberg, J. D. Brown, & N. L. Buerkel-Rothfuss (Eds.), *Media, sex and the adolescent* (pp. 248–263). Creskill, NJ: Hampton Press.

Ward, L. (1995). Talking about sex: Common themes about sexuality in the prime-time television programs children and adolescents view most. *Journal of Youth and Adolescence, 24*, 595–615.

Zillmann, D., & Mundorf, N. (1987). Image effects in the appreciation of video rock. *Communication Research, 14*(3), 316–334.

Zoglin, R. (1995, January 30). Talking trash. *Time*, 77–78.

7

▼▼▼▼▼▼▼▼▼

Affect-Talk and Its Kin

Gary Bente
Ansgar Feist
University of Cologne, Germany

The study of psychological processes implies limiting interpretation to the cultural settings in which the data are gathered. This is nowhere more true than in the area of cultural phenomena themselves, be it high culture or popular culture as manifested in the offerings and uses of mass media. This especially holds for TV. This chapter is based on research on German TV. Certainly there is a tendency toward the globalization of TV programming and an especially profound influence of American television on what can be seen on German TV screens. When we began our investigation of content, viewing motivation, and effects of so-called affect TV in the mid-1990s, we were actually wondering whether the study of overseas offerings could be regarded as peeking into our own TV future.

Although in the United States the term *trash TV* was coined at that time to describe the most extreme forms of self-disclosure and public mud battles, the German equivalents seemed more or less cultivated and harmless by comparison. Open confrontations between studio guests, mutual accusations, or revelations of personal secrets and intimate experiences did not occur as often on German TV. The participation of the studio audience as a TV jury, which was common on many U.S. talk shows, was unusual in Germany at that time. Although German talk shows have adopted some American elements during the last three years, the most extreme versions here are still way "behind" current American standards. Perhaps this is due to the fact that intense public discussion accompanied these talk shows from their first appearance on German TV screens. Even those talk shows that claimed to be informative, following basic rules of investigative journalism, like the classic *Hans Meiser*, came under fire from critics at a very early stage. "Embarrassing" was the word most often used by these critics, and the guests as well as the viewers were assigned to pathological categories such as the *exhibitionist*, with a sick need to expose himself in front of a mass audience, and the *voyeur*, striving for personal satisfaction while listening furtively to details from others' private lives and peeping at the most intimate encounters through the TV keyhole.

The scathing criticism issued mainly by the print media, however, contrasted sharply with the success of these shows as reflected in the daily ratings. Evidently, affect TV meets a very common need that, at least with respect to statistical norms, cannot be labeled as deviant, without assuming it to be a symptom of a global disease of Western society. Whereas this point of view has been widely explored in sociological approaches such as those by Sennett (1983) and Habermas (1990), there has been little psychological research on the individual motivational basis for viewing and on the specific effects of exposure to affect-TV offerings. Approaching the field from a psychological perspective, we isolated four characteristics common in public discussion and media criticism of the different offerings grouped under the heading of affect TV (see Bente & Fromm, 1997). These are:

- *Personalization:* The story relates a particular experience of an individual person. The focus is on the specifics of the case, not the generalizability of problems and solutions.
- *Authenticity:* True stories of real, nonprominent people—like you and me— are told or put on stage. Live characters foster the audience's impression of being an eyewitness.
- *Intimacy:* Traditional frontiers between the private and public sphere are crossed. Intimate aspects of interpersonal relationships and private affairs are made a public issue.
- *Emotionality:* Production methods and interpersonal communication styles within the shows are set up to produce emotional reactions and to reveal personal attitudes of the studio guests and of the audience.

In this sense we defined *affect TV* as "offerings that present the most private stories of nonprominent people to a mass audience, crossing traditional borders of privacy and intimacy." This definition, more or less, fits a series of different TV formats that have been broadcast in the last few years in Germany; for example, some game shows or so-called relationship shows in which lovers are (re-) united or relatives ask to be forgiven after family quarrels. Prototypical for this genre are the offerings that we categorized as *affect-talk shows*, that is, talk shows with a personalized presentation style, emotional climate, and intimate topics that are broadcast in the afternoon, most often on a daily basis. The show typically bears the name of the host, who guarantees a special socioemotional experience by means of his or her individual communication style, be it in the role of a public prosecutor, an attorney, a therapist, or a personal friend. Examples from German TV are Hans Meiser (the pioneer of German affect-talk shows), Ilona Christen, Arabella Kiesbauer, Magarete Schreinemakers, Bärbel Schäfer, and Sonya. American viewers have Oprah Winfrey, Jenny Jones, Geraldo Rivera, Sally Jessie Raphael, and Jerry Springer. These kinds of talk shows are at the core of this chapter, although we sometimes include other related shows in our discussion.

DEVELOPMENT OF AFFECT-TV OFFERINGS AND VIEWING PATTERNS

As mentioned previously, the relevant literature contains only a few empirical studies on affect-TV offerings. Actually, before 1995 there was no integrative study of affect TV, either with respect to viewing motivation and effect or a description of offerings and audiences. Most studies that do exist are limited to particular formats, like talk shows (Hutchby, 1996; Katriel & Philipsen, 1990), confrontation talk shows (Holly & Schwitalla, 1995), reality TV (Wegener, 1994; Winterhoff-Spurk, Heidinger, & Schwab, 1994) or even focus on singular offerings like *Wedding of your Dreams [Traumhochzeit]* (Berghaus & Staab, 1995) and *Only Love Counts [Nur die Liebe zählt]* (Pape, 1996). Also, the research field is characterized by a lack of theoretical and methodological integration. Hermeneutic approaches (Keppler, 1994; Reichertz, 1996) and qualitative methodology, such as interviews and descriptions predominate (Katriel & Philipsen, 1990; Livingstone & Lunt, 1994; Mehl, 1996; Pape, 1996). Content analysis (Winterhoff-Spurk, Heidinger, & Schwab, 1994) and controlled experiments (Grimm, 1995) are rare. Also the research questions and hypotheses cover a large range of singular interests, such as motives for appearing on the show (Pape, 1996; Reichertz, 1996), presentation techniques (Winterhoff-Spurk, Heidinger, & Schwab, 1994), communication styles (Hutchby, 1996) daily ratings (Wegener, 1994), viewing motives (Berghaus & Staab, 1995) and emotional effects (Grimm, 1995). For a closer look at the current research, see Bente and Fromm (1997).

   In a first approach we investigated quantitative and qualitative aspects of the development of affect-TV offerings using archive analysis, content analysis of titles, and daily ratings as a database (Bente, Jochlik, Adameck, & Grisard, 1997). There has been a dramatic increase in frequency and absolute transmission time of affect TV between 1987 and 1995. The biggest growth rate has been recorded for the talk shows. Before 1995 four of the five major channels in Germany (ARD, RTL, SAT1 and Pro7) introduced at least one affect-talk show into the early afternoon program. This trend has continued, with a tendency to expand the broadcast times into the afternoon and morning. In 1998 the second German public channel ZDF finally introduced a daily talk show.

   The age distribution of the audience proved to be nearly identical for three of the four daily talk shows analyzed (*Hans Meiser, Ilona Christen,* and *Fliege*) showing increasing consumption with increasing age. An exception is the show *Arabella*, which is specially tailored to a younger audience and mainly reaches viewers between 14 and 29. The youngest viewers (3–13 years old) play a marginal role as a potential talk show audience. Less than 5% of young children watch these offerings and we might assume that these are more accidental viewers, who are "victims" of their mothers' choices. Indeed, watching people talk does not seem to be of any interest to small children. Besides these differences in age we found a predominance of female viewers for most of the talk shows. Differences in educational level of the audiences are not systematic for the affect-talk shows.

With respect to content, there is also a striking similarity between the three talk shows *Hans Meiser*, *Ilona Christen*, and *Fliege*, showing a clear preference for the topics of family and relationships, which cover 30–35% of the offerings. Relationships are also an important topic on *Arabella*; however, the ranking of subjects here shows an accentuation of less psychological and more physical aspects, such as appearance, attractiveness, and sex. While these results are not surprising, the data concerning the audience's interest in different topics contradicted our expectations. There was no systematic relationship between content and daily ratings. Neither the so-called taboo topics, such as sex, death, and abuse, nor the frequent categories "relationships" and "family" showed significantly higher viewer levels. Table 7.1 gives an overview of topics, broadcast frequencies and average ratings for the four most important daily talk shows.

Overall, the data suggest that viewing behavior is determined more by opportunity (being at home in the afternoon) and viewing habits (TV as a background medium) than by specific interests. However, this thematically nonselective viewing behavior does not automatically mean that there is no content-related motivational basis for watching. Viewers at home could switch to another channel or turn the TV off when there is no subjectively relevant subject being discussed. The audience fluctuation, however, proved to be relatively low. Against this background, we might look for a common denominator in the content of these offerings that is not related to the specific subject presented in the title of an individual daily show. Perhaps there is a similarity of content between the situation of the audience and that of the protagonists. Jane and John Doe present themselves and their personal problems to a mass audience in interpersonal situations while talking about emotionally charged private affairs. The question remains, what is the benefit to the protagonists and viewers?

WHAT IS IT GOOD FOR? PSYCHOLOGICAL FUNCTIONS AND VIEWING MOTIVATIONS

The literature is very weak on this aspect. Microsociological approaches predominate, describing in more general terms the functional basis of communicating intimate matters to a mass audience. For example, the French sociologist Mehl (1996) differentiated between four functional aspects of what she called *intimacy TV* (La télévision de l'intimité) from the perspective of the protagonists and the corresponding roles for the audience:

TABLE 7.1
Ranking of Topics in German Affect-Talk Shows

Hans Meiser			Ilona Christen		
Topics	F%	V%	Topics	F%	V%
Family	13.2	30.3	Family	15.3	30.7
Relationships	12.7	30.9	Relationships	14.6	30.5
Society/economy	11.1	29.6	Health	10.0	28.2
Profession/work	10.1	29.4	Society/economy	8.9	28.8
Character/lifestyle	7.4	30.3	Criminal/victim	8.2	29.8
Health	7.2	29.5	Character/lifestyle	7.3	27.3
Sex	5.6	30.3	Sex	6.0	30.4
Body/beauty/fashion	5.2	30.9	Psychological problems	5.8	28.2
Not categorized	5.0	28.4	Not categorized	5.5	28.4
Psychological problems	4.9	28.7	Profession/work	5.1	28.8
Criminal/victim	4.3	30.9	Astrology/esoteric	3.5	28.6
Prominent people	3.6	30.9	Body/beauty/fashion	3.1	32.3
Astrology/esoteric	2.7	30.6	Religion/sects	2.2	29.2
Religion/sects	2.1	30.6	Prominent people	1.6	27.8
Death/loss	2.1	29.2	Death/loss	1.6	29.4
Animals	1.6	29.3	Animals	0.9	29.4
Alternative healing methods	1.3	29.1	Alternative healing methods	0.4	32.9

Fliege			Arabella		
Topics	F%	V%	Topics	F%	V%
Family	22.6	12.3	Body/beauty/fashion	28.0	11.1
Relationships	13.9	13.2	Relationships	21.3	9.3
Character/lifestyle	9.6	12.6	Sex	14.6	10.0
Health	9.6	11.8	Character/lifestyle	9.3	10.4
Society/economy	9.1	13.0	Family	7.5	10.3
Not categorized	5.3	12.9	Not categorized	6.0	10.1
Psychological problems	4.3	10.2	Profession/work	5.2	9.5
Alternative healing methods	4.3	14.3	Astrology/esoteric	3.0	10.6
Criminal/victim	3.8	12.3	Society/economy	1.9	10.9
Astrology/esoteric	3.4	10.7	Prominent people	1.5	10.1
Prominent people	2.9	15.8	Animals	1.1	10.0
Body/beauty/fashion	2.4	13.8	Alternative healing methods	0.7	13.7
Death/loss	2.4	14.9	Criminal/victim	0	0
Sex	1.9	11.8	Psychological problems	0	0
Animals	1.9	13.1	Health	0	0
Profession/work	1.4	12.2	Death/loss	0	0
Religion/sects	1.0	10.9	Religion/sects	0	0

Note.   Relative frequencies of emission (F%) and percentage of viewers in daily ratings (V%).

1. *The personal message (le message personnel):* The nonprominent guests address a concrete person or a group of persons with a personal message, one that has not been revealed before because of adverse circumstances or a disturbed relationship.

2. *The therapeutic interview (le verbe thérapeutique):* The communication process resembles that of a patient and a therapist. The guests do not only want to make their problems public, but also hope for a psychological or medical diagnosis and treatment.

3. *The TV confession (la confession cathodique):* The guests use the appearance for public self-accusation and to report a burdensome problem. Guilt and atonement are relevant aspects.

4. *The public speech (la parole publique):* The guests attempt to convert or educate the audience. They want to generalize a personal experience and to convey a message to the public (see also Reichertz, 1996).

Religious well-being and (psycho-)therapeutic help are the most frequently used comparisons when it comes to a microsociological analysis of the public and personal functions of affect-TV offerings. White (1992) described the practice of affect-talk shows: "Most immediately, the private exchange between two individuals—in a church or a doctor's office, for example—is reconfigured as a public event, staged by the technological and signifying conventions of the television apparatus" (p. 9), and Pape (1996) stated: "It has been shown that the mass media, as secondary institutions, contribute fundamentally to the creation of meaning and to the orientation of people and that they can be seen as a functional equivalent of counseling and therapy at the societal level" (p. 87). Based on a content analysis of 35 broadcasts of the American talk shows *The Phil Donahue Show* and *The Oprah Winfrey Show*, and the British equivalents *Kilroy* and *The Time, the Place*, Livingstone and Lunt (1994) came to a similar conclusion, differentiating three types of affect-talk shows: "We consider below three influences on the programs—the debate, the romantic narrative and the therapy session" (p. 56). With respect to the last type the similarity is regarded as structural rather than functional: "We would not argue that these programs offer 'good' therapy, but rather that any occasion on which painful emotional issues are discussed in a personal manner must at times resemble a therapeutic situation, recasting host (or sometimes, expert) and lay speaker as therapist and patient" (p. 63).

Although these reflections offer some evidence they most often lack a consistent theoretical framework and a convincing empirical basis. Also, the viewer's perspective is underrepresented in most approaches. It is hard to believe that all talk show guests expect to receive therapy and it is even more difficult to understand why an audience would watch a therapy session, assuming that they do not have the same problem and that the therapeutic method is not capable of vicarious treatment and remote healing. It remains unclear in most studies, what the different individual needs are that are satisfied by affect TV and what kind of information or emotional experience protagonists and audiences are looking for. The differentiations within the "uses and gratifications" literature (Katz, Blumler & Gurevitch, 1974) seem worth considerating in this context, not only with regard to the elaborate lists of possible motives, like "entertainment," "pastime," and "information" (Perse & Rubin, 1990), and "escape," "relaxation," and "status enhancement" (see also Conway & Rubin, 1991; Brown, Campbell, & Fischer, 1986; Ferguson & Perse, 1993; Frank & Greenberg, 1980; Perse, 1990; Rubin, 1983; Schorr & Schorr-Neustadt, 1994), but also with regard to the identification of distinct viewing patterns; for example, "instrumental" or "habitual" (Ferguson & Perse, 1993), "ritualized" or "ritualizing" viewing behavior (see also Cutler & Danowski, 1980; Perse, 1990; Rubin, 1984; Wenner, 1985).

One of the most important viewing motives in the context of talk shows seems to be what has been called *parasocial interaction* (Horton & Wohl, 1956). While this concept was originally developed to match symbolic interaction patterns between the news anchor and the audience as a consequence of the direct form of address and related communicative acts (Barloewen & Brandenberg, 1975; Berghaus & Staab, 1995; Foltin, 1994; Schumacher, 1992; Steinbrecher & Weiske, 1992; Sturm, 1991), it has received new meaning in the context of TV research in the last decade, and especially in the field of the personalized and emotional offerings that are the focus of this paper (Bente & Vorderer, 1997). Here it is less the relationship between the viewers and the anchorperson that counts but rather the relationship between the viewers and the studio guests, which is based on identification, empathy, social learning, or social comparison (Mares & Cantor, 1992; Strange, 1996; Vorderer, 1996). Herzog (1944) commented on the results of a questionnaire study of radio daytime serials: "They teach the listener appropriate patterns of behaviour" (p. 25). She also mentions the "psychohygienic" value of not being alone with one's problems: "Burdened with their own problems, listeners claim that it made them feel better to know that other people have troubles, too" (p. 24).

The results of our own questionnaire study, based on a sample of 624 subjects matched for sex, age, and education, confirm these earlier findings (Bente, Bahß, Dorando, & Hündgen, 1997). Using a combined 78-item TV motive questionnaire (Brown, Campbell, & Fischer, 1986; Conway & Rubin, 1991; Ferguson & Perse, 1993; Frank & Greenberg, 1980; Perse, 1990; Rubin, 1983; Schorr & Schorr-Neustadt, 1994) we found a four-factor solution accounting for 44.7% of the variance (see Table 7.2).

Regression analysis using these four factors to predict viewing behavior (frequency and time) and evaluation of the various affect-TV shows points to the importance of the first factor, (para-)social comparison and problem solving, for both attitude and behavior. As expected from the analysis of the daily ratings, pastime/habitual viewing played a significant role for actual viewing behavior, but was of only marginal importance for the evaluation of the shows. We found no systematic correlation between personality variables, socioemotional problems, and affect-TV viewing. Seemingly there is a general motivational basis for viewing these offerings that has to be conceived in accordance with processes of social comparison as they occur in real-life interactions. A deeper understanding of the underlying functional princi-

TABLE 7.2
Factor-Structure of Viewing Motivation

Factors	Items with Highest Loading (>.6)
(1) (para-)social comparison/ problem solving (25.1%)	1.) . . . because I get to know that other people have similar problems (.72)
	2.) . . . because it helps to solve my own problems (.71)
	3.) . . . because it reminds me of things that happened in my own life (.70)
(2) relaxation/escapism (9.9%)	1.) . . . because I can relax watching TV (.77)
	2.) . . . because I can really "turn off" (.71)
	3.) . . . to have a calm evening (.65)
(3) information/news (5.7%)	1.) . . . because it reports real events (.73)
	2.) . . . to learn something new (.72)
	3.) . . . to evaluate important events better (.69)
(4) pass time/habitual viewing (4.0%)	1.) . . . to pass time, when I feel bored (.81)
	2.) . . . because I have nothing else to do (.78)
	3.) . . . because nothing better comes to mind (.76)

ples, however, would require research on the process level of media viewing, focusing on the cognitive and emotional effects that are induced by typical offerings.

INVOLVEMENT AT A DISTANCE: EFFECTS OF DIRECT EXPOSURE TO AFFECT-TV OFFERINGS

As elaborate psychological approaches to affect TV do not currently exist, we have had to reformulate the research question on a more general level, looking at comparable viewing situations and relevant determinants for the psychological processes they induce. There is some evidence that the characteristics of affect TV described earlier are also recognizable in other TV formats; not only in entertainment offerings, but also in traditional information formats like TV news (see Bente & Frey, 1991; Masters, Frey, & Bente, 1991). Against this background, we might ask whether the purpose of personalization and emotionality is to make the transmitted content more digestible and enhance the depth of information processing, or whether we are dealing with a different quality of information, which is introduced by the concreteness of the visual display, in this case showing a concrete individual in a concrete situation with concrete behavior and concrete emotional responses (see Meyrowitz, 1987, p. 81). Wegener (1994) stated, "The published intimacy of personal emotions is providing an opportunity for the audience to participate in the fate of the exposed individual" (p. 54), and Burger (1991) came to the conclusion that TV transforms communication over any distance into a variety of face-to-face encounters" (p. 416). As previously mentioned, we might assume various processes on the viewers' side of the TV screen, which are triggered by the transmitted socioemotional information. Empathy, identification, or parasocial interaction (Bente & Vorderer, 1997; Vorderer, Cupchik, & Oatley, 1997) might account for the variance in the emotional experience of the audience. Mood management (Zillmann, 1978, 1979, 1983, 1988) and striving for suspense (Tan, 1996; Vorderer, 1996; Zillmann, 1996) could be the motivational basis for exposure as well as social comparison and learning (Herzog, 1944; Strange, 1996). Are people looking for an emotional, cognitive, or behavioral effect from these shows? In light of our data the traditional distinction between cognitive and emotional uses and effects, however, does not seem to make much sense for an understanding of the way affect TV works. Also it is not indicated to differentiate between social and parasocial reality in this context: When watching protagonists in emotional situations and especially in social interactions, the psychological processes during TV viewing are very similar to those that occur when observing other people in real life. We may choose to stay outside the action, but nevertheless we are able to take part emotionally by means of empathetic reactions or identification processes, or as Bischof (1989) would have put it from an evolutionary biological perspective, we may run a kind of "internal simulation" on this visual input, which can lead us through the most difficult situations without taking the risk of actually being harmed. Bischof described this capacity for internal simulation as humankind's most important evolutionary advantage. While this type of simulation is based primarily on creative thinking and fantasy, we may consider observations via the TV screen as a very convenient way to extend, substitute, or complement the possibilities of our own imagination. The shows described here are in many respects prototypical for this televised facilitation of emotional simulation.

However, when we started our research in 1995, there were no empirical data on the actual psychological effects that occur while viewing affect-TV. We focused on the following questions: What are the basic dimensions of cognitive, emotional, and behavioral responses to these TV programs? Are they mainly perceived as entertainment or information or as a mixture of both? What qualities are important for the positive evaluation of these offerings and actual viewing behavior? How does the choice of topic and behavior of talk show hosts and guests contribute to the attitudes of the viewers and their actual viewing behavior? Can subjective reports of stimulus qualities and personal feelings about them be validated through objective measures of emotional arousal? How do viewers process the incoming information; for example, are they emotionally involved with a high degree of immersion or are they viewing from a more distant analytical position? In the following we focus on the most important results of this study; for a further discussion of methodological and theoretical issues see Feist, Bente, and Hündgen (1997) and Feist (1999).

THE EXPERIMENTAL SETUP

An experimental design was chosen, in which a thematically broad spectrum of different affect-talk shows and some of the relationship shows was presented to a large group of TV viewers. Subjects (240) between the ages of 15 and 70 years ($M = 30.4$,

SD = 13.8) were recruited from the local area. Controlling for gender and age, the subjects were assigned randomly to five experimental groups. Stimulus material was randomly preselected from our video database. On the basis of content analysis, five sequences were then selected for each of five talk shows representing the topics health, death/loss, sexual abuse, sex, relationships/love. Additionally we chose five sequences from different relationship shows. Each group watched one clip of each show, varying over all five topics. Blood pressure was taken continuously during stimulus presentation as an indicator for sympathetic activity of the autonomous nervous system using a noninvasive measurement device (Portapres, Model 2, TNO-BioMedical Instrumentation, Amsterdam, Netherlands). For a detailed description of the method see Feist, 1999, and Schmidt and Jain, 1996.

Immediately after the presentation of each stimulus sequence the subjects filled out checklists and questionnaires assessing emotional experience as well as stimulus evaluation. The Self-Assessment Mannequin (SAM) (Hamm & Vaitl, 1993; Hodges, Cook, & Lang, 1985; Lang, 1980) was used as a global measure of emotional impact. Using three pictogram scales the system represents the basic dimensions of emotional experience: evaluation, activity, and potency or control, which were postulated by Osgood (1969). General attitude toward the stimuli (liking) was also measured by a one-dimensional pictogram. For a more differentiated judgment of stimulus quality and emotional response, as well as for the personal attributes of the protagonists, we used adjective checklists that had been developed previously in pilot studies (see Feist, Bente, & Hündgen, 1997). As zapping was not possible during stimulus presentation, we had no direct behavioral measure of viewing behavior. So, we substituted "attitude toward behavior" with the question: "Provided you had been watching this sequence at home: would you have continued watching it?"

As mentioned earlier, we were also interested in measuring the involvement of the audience. There is, however, no universal definition of involvement available at the moment (Tasche, 1996), so we decided to explore the phenomenon from several different perspectives. The *involved* and *analytical* reception modes as described by Vorderer (1992) were differentiated by the item, "How did you view this sequence?" (a) "emotionally involved" or (b) "critically." *Cognitive involvement* in the sense of "active information processing" (Perse, 1990, p. 560) was measured by the item, "Did you think about what you saw during the sequence?" *Experiential involvement* in the sense of relating the TV content to one's own life situation and personal problems (see Krugman, 1965) was represented by the item, "Did you think about yourself during this sequence?" Finally, as a measure of a *global lack of involvement*, we asked the subjects: "Did you think about other things during this sequence?"

BASIC DIMENSIONS OF EMOTIONAL RESPONSE
TO AFFECT-TV OFFERINGS

Twenty-three items as variables (the SAM and the 20-item adjective list) and the 30 stimuli as cases were analyzed using factor analysis. Since our analysis focuses here on the emotional quality of the stimuli rather than the individual variance in emotional experience, the measures taken from 48 subjects were averaged for each of the 30 stimuli before factor analysis (principal-components analysis). Using the scree plot criterion we found a four-factor solution accounting for 87.1% of the variance. The results of the varimax rotated solution are shown in Table 7.3.

Factors 1 and 3 are consistent with the basic dimensions *hedonistic tone* (pleasant vs. unpleasant) and *level of excitement* (boring vs. exciting) described in most dimensional approaches (see Russell, 1979). We did not find the dimension *potency* or *control* to constitute a factor of its own. In contrast, as in Hamm and Vaitl's (1993) results, the control dimension of the SAM showed a significant correlation with the pleasantness-unpleasantness dimension in the SAM and also with our hedonistic tone factor. *Information processing*, factor 2 (informative vs. embarrassing), might be interpreted as an emotionally based judgment about the

TABLE 7.3
Factors of Emotional Experience of Affect-TV Offerings

	Hedonistic Tone (pleasant-unpleasant)	Information Processing (informative-embarrassing)	Level of Excitement (boring-exciting)	Sentimentality (emotionally touching-intellectually appealing)	h^2
Entertaining *(unterhaltsam)*	**−.95**	.09	.10	.15	.95
delighted me *(erfreut)*	**−.94**	.11	−.06	−.12	.92
amused me *(amüsiert)*	**−.90**	.34	−.10	.11	.95
unpleasant (SAM)	**.89**	.01	.29	.00	.89
made me sad *(traurig)*	**.76**	−.02	.46	−.37	.93
worried me *(beunruhigt)*	**.76**	−.29	.51	.11	.93
strong (SAM)	**−.71**	.37	−.22	.39	.84
touched me *(nahegegangen)*	**.68**	−.14	.56	−.37	.93
embarrassing *(peinlich)*	−.07	**.97**	.06	−.08	.96
excessive *(übertrieben)*	−.14	**.93**	.06	.06	.89
artificial *(gestellt)*	−.23	**.84**	−.06	−.05	.77
superficial *(oberflächlich)*	−.41	**.82**	−.21	.15	.90
went to far *(zu weit gegangen)*	.32	**.76**	.26	−.32	.85
informative *(informativ)*	.43	**−.74**	.31	.31	.93
interesting *(interessant)*	.30	**−.65**	**.61**	.25	.94
made me curious *(neugierig)*	.12	−.59	.36	.56	.81
demanding *(anspruchsvoll)*	.58	−.59	.47	−.01	.91
made me angry *(geärgert)*	.47	.54	.45	.25	.78
bored me *(gelangweilt)*	−.05	.22	**−.88**	.19	.87
exciting *(spannend)*	.08	−.09	**.87**	.08	.78
calm (SAM)	−.31	−.18	**−.85**	.04	.86
unusual *(außergewöhnlich)*	.12	.06	**.72**	−.09	.55
emotionally touching *(rührend)*	.34	.20	.28	**−.80**	.88
Explained variance	**30.3%**	**27.1%**	**21.6%**	**8.1%**	

Note.   Factor loading > 0.6 appear in bold.

informational value of the stimuli, which could influence any of the following: continuing to watch, passing the input to deeper information processing, or rejecting the input and stopping further viewing. The factor shows an impressive similarity with the factor *attention-rejection* as described by Schlosberg (1952): "Attention is exemplified by surprise, in which all receptors are maximally open to stimulation. Rejection is the best term we have found for the other end of the axis; it is shown most clearly in contempt and disgust, in which eyes and nostrils appear to be actively shutting out stimulation" (p. 230).

Certainly, this neglected factor deserves special attention in future research. As discussed later, it proved to be of major relevance for our analysis. The fourth factor, which we named *sentimentality*, is specific to the stimulus material we used, for example, the emotion-laden dramaturgy of the relationship shows. It is represented by one item, *touching* (in German, rührend) in contrast to the item *made me curious*, which, however, did not reach the cut-off criterion of .6 factor loading. So the fourth factor should be interpreted with caution (see Guadagnoli & Velicer, 1988).

Over 90% of the attitude variance (liking) can be predicted by two factors. Information processing accounts for about 65% of the variance and level of excitement for another 26.4%. The results are very similar for prediction of the readiness to continue watching. Two factors can explain 87.5% of the variance. However, the importance of the two predictors is reversed. While informational gain and low embarrassment are of major importance for predicting attitude toward affect-talk shows, high excitement is the best predictor of viewing behavior (i.e., reported readiness to continue watching at home).

A TYPOLOGY OF AFFECT-TV OFFERINGS

In view of the very heterogeneous stimulus material, which was intended to represent the actual variation within the daily talk shows, it was of central interest to determine how these offerings are actually perceived by the audience, how they are classified with respect to these four dimensions of emotional experience, and how these factors contribute to evaluation and reception of these offerings. Searching for a reliable and meaningful classification of our stimulus material, we ran a hierarchical cluster analysis (Ward method, squared euclidean distance) based on the emotional factors. The analysis generated a clear-cut two-cluster solution (elbow criterion). Stepwise discriminant analysis demonstrates a 100% correct classification of the TV offerings based on the factor values of three of the four factors: hedonistic tone (45.7%), information processing (23.3%) and level of excitement (20.1%). The fourth factor did not reach the required level of significance.

We were able to classify the offerings into distinct categories, which we named, according to their specific emotional impact, *serious-talk* (unpleasant, informative, high excitement) and *small-talk* (pleasant, noninformative, low excitement). Relationship shows were grouped together with the small-talk shows. The clusters show a significant difference in liking and consumption readiness, indicating a general preference for the serious-talk shows, although they produce unpleasant feelings.

As can be seen in Table 7.3 the item *entertaining* has the highest loading on the hedonistic tone factor. This means that these offerings, which producers often classify as *infotainment*, are not really a mixture of both genres in the eyes of the audience. Rather, the viewers strictly classify each offering with respect to these two criteria, whether it is entertaining (produces good feelings) or whether it is seriously informative, which could include excitement, but also the experience of negative feelings (such as sadness and fear).

Indeed, it seems that with respect to these nonfictional offerings viewers prefer the serious information talk shows. It is questionable whether the meaning of the item *entertaining* would change in the context of fictional offerings, where we might expect a stronger correlation to feelings of suspense. In this context negative emotional qualities like anger, fear, and sadness could be temporary states derived from empathy or identification with the protagonists and thus part of the dramaturgy. If the plot leads to relief from distress, for example, in the classic happy ending, then the overall impression could be that this was good entertainment. But even if a serious-talk show, for example dealing with the loss of a beloved person, leads to a happy ending (finding her/him again), nobody—except perhaps TV producers and media researchers—would classify this offering as entertainment, although the audience might be emotionally touched and might feel relief and happiness at the end. This may be due to the lack of a meta-perspective, which is present in the fictional offerings, indicating that there has been a specific effort to create this emotional experience. While this hypothesis is rather speculative at the moment, our data support it to some degree.

EMOTIONAL STIMULUS QUALITY AND RECEPTION MODE

Based on Vorderer's (1992) distinction between a more emotionally involved and a more analytical reception mode, we looked at whether the different emotional qualities of the stimuli also lead to different reception modes. We found a significant positive correlation ($r = .41$) between the emotionally involved and the analytical (critical) reception modes (Table 7.4). We were not satisfied with our item *critically* for labeling the analytical reception mode, because it was perceived as negative by the subjects. So we decided to rely on the item "Did you think about what you saw?" as an indicator for the analytical mode as described by Vorderer (1992) see also Perse (1990). Here the correlation between emotional involvement and analytical reception mode proved to be even higher ($r = .76$).

Further analysis indicated that there is a direct influence of the emotional quality of the stimuli on the specific pattern of involvement. More than 80% of the variance for each of the reception modes could be predicted by the extracted emo-

TABLE 7.4
Intercorrelations of the Involvement-Items

	(1)	(2)	(3)	(4)	(5)
How did you view this sequence ...					
emotionally involved? (1)		.41*	.76***	.09	−.33
critically? (2)			.41*	−.02	−.24
During this sequence did you ...					
think about what you saw? (3)				.15	−.49**
think about yourself? (4)					.01
think about other things? (5)					

*$p < .05$. **$p < .01$. ***$p < .001$.

tional factors (see Table 7.5). The major factor in both cases is the level of excitement factor, followed by the hedonistic tone factor. Both kinds of immersion are facilitated by more serious (*unpleasant feelings*) but also *exciting* offerings. So if people are emotionally involved they also tend to think about what they see. This means that there is no contradiction between analytically and emotionally involved reception modes for the offerings under investigation. On the contrary, both modes coincide when there is an exciting presentation of a true story in which negative feelings are involved. Again, this result points to the importance of processes of social comparison and learning for the viewers of affect-TV offerings. Especially dangerous or threatening situations involving life or death and social success, which are part of a dramatic development, fulfill the requirements for emotional and cognitive involvement and are important contexts for social learning, simulation, and anticipation.

PSYCHOPHYSIOLOGICAL CORRELATES OF EMOTIONAL EXPERIENCE

With respect to the psychophysiological validation of emotional arousal, we focused on systolic blood pressure as a well-established parameter and relevant indicator for sympathetic activity. Indeed, systolic blood pressure shows significant correlations with a series of items (see Feist, Bente, & Hündgen, 1997). As expected there was a positive correlation with the subject-reported factor level of excitement, but there was even a stronger correlation with the factor information processing, indicating that noninformative, that is, embarrassing stimuli dramatically increase systolic blood pressure: information processing accounts for about 34.4% of the variance and level of excitement for 10.8%.

This result is consistent with data presented by Darrow (1929), who showed that blood pressure could be increased by simply presenting the word *embarrassment* or other embarrassing stimuli like the question "An inferiority complex?" Referring to our interpretation of the information-processing factor, this result

TABLE 7.5
Correlations Between Involvement-Items
and the Four Factors of Emotional Experience

Factors	I	II	III	IV
How did you view this sequence . . .				
emotionally involved?	.52**	−.06	.71***	−.34
critically?	.58**	.45*	.31	.43*
During this sequence did you . . .				
think about what you saw?	.52**	−.34	.67***	.08
think about yourself?	−.03	−.42*	−.07	.20
think about other things?	.11	.23	−.65***	−.21

I: pleasant-unpleasant; II: informative-embarrassing; III: boring-exciting; IV: touching-curious
*p < .05. **p < .01. ***p < .001.

can be explained by Lacey's revision of general activation theory (1967): "The input from pressoceptors, indeed, is the first known sensory input to the brain which inhibits (not activates) cortical activity" (p. 26). Following these findings an increase in systolic blood pressure cannot be seen as an index of general activation. Systolic blood pressure leads to the stimulation of baroreceptors, which then reduce neural brain activity and thus reduce the sensitivity to stimulation. These findings have been well replicated in the last 30 years (for an overview see Elbert & Schandry, 1998). Lacey (1967) named two information-processing states with respect to cardiovascular responses: *environmental intake* (low stimulation of baroreceptors) and *environmental rejection* (high stimulation of baroreceptors), which also show an impressive similarity to Schlosberg's *attention-rejection* and our information-processing factor. We assume that the information-processing factor represents a primary evaluation of the information content of the stimulus material—in the sense of good versus bad information—before it is processed in detail. So it might be associated with a fundamental decision to let sensory information in or to block it out. Especially when presented with embarrassing stimuli (in the experimental situation there was no real alternative to viewing, except to leave the room), the subjects may be able to continue watching but prevent their brains from thinking about what they are actually seeing or doing. Under more normal viewing conditions, they might instead turn away from the stimulus, switch to another channel, or switch off the TV.

INDIVIDUAL DIFFERENCES
IN AFFECT-TV RECEPTION

Up to this point we have focused on the emotional quality of the shows; however, the effects of individual differences and their influences on viewing experience are also of particular interest. As has been pointed out, viewer characteristics like gender, extroversion, neuroticism, and so on could offer some important hints about variance in attitude, viewing behavior, and emotional experience (see Bommert, Weich, & Dirksmeier, 1995; Sturm, 1989). No sequence was evaluated as better (attitude) by the male subjects and seven sequences were evaluated as better by the female subjects. In these sequences female guests were focusing on what can be seen as typically female issues (rape, diets, widows, etc.). Independent of their sex the subjects' extroversion seems to be especially important for the emotional experience of and the attitude toward sequences with the highest levels of pleasure (extroverts reported a higher degree of pleasure, and evaluated these sequences as better), whereas extroversion had no effect when viewing hedonistically unpleasant or neutral sequences.

It seems that specific stimulus intensities are necessary to trigger the specific response modes of neurotics and extroverts. The data suggest that for extroverts it is the hedonistic tone factor that plays the major role in stimulus evaluation, while for neurotics the specific combination of excitement and information rejection is most important. This could mean that neurotics are seeking autonomic arousal, while blocking off central information processing (cortical arousal). Certainly further analysis is required; for details, see Feist (1999).

DISCUSSION

The objective of the present paper was twofold. First, we sought to psychologically analyze a rapidly developing infotainment genre, which we named affect TV, focusing on the topics and emotional qualities of these offerings, as well as the possible motives for viewing and the concrete effects of direct exposure. Second, we tried to identify the basic psychological dimensions of the reception process, integrating aspects of information processing and emotional experience as well. As a common denominator of all shows subsumed under the heading of affect TV, we identified specific staging variables such as personalization, emotionalization, authenticity, and intimacy. With respect to these characteristics, the affect-talk shows proved to be prototypical for the genre under investigation. Although affect-talk shows cover a wide range of topics, from sexual adventure and esoteric experience to sexual abuse and death, we found clear thematic preferences (broadcast frequency) for issues related to relationships and interpersonal communication. Interestingly this preference, reflected in the broadcast frequencies, does not covary with the interest of the audience. There is no correlation between daily ratings and topics. Also, there is no preference for taboo topics like sex, sexual abuse, and death. Everything that is presented in the emotionally laden affect-TV manner, and that is related to a personal story about a concrete individual, receives the same level of attention from the audience.

The data indicate habitual, thematically nonselective viewing behavior, as well as a common motivational basis that is not dependent on the specific topic. Indeed, both aspects seem to play an important role in affect-TV viewing. As our questionnaire data clearly show, actual viewing behavior (frequency and time) is determined by *passing time habits* (opportunity to watch TV in the afternoon) and also by the motivation for *social comparison and problem solving*. This second factor, however, proved to be the only one of importance for attitudes toward affect TV, that is, the positive evaluation of these offerings.

These results could be confirmed in a controlled experimental study of the reception process and the effects of selected affect-TV sequences. Viewers discriminate between specific offerings based on the possibility they offer for social comparison and internal simulation of emotional, critical, or socially difficult situations. We found four factors accounting for 87.1% of the judgment variance, two of which were consistent with the literature: the dimensions hedonistic tone (pleasant/unpleasant) and level of excitement (exited/bored), but we also extended our view to a widely neglected dimension: information processing (informative/embarrassing) that has already been described by Schlosberg (1952) as attention/rejection. The factors information processing and level of excitement accounted for the majority of the variance of stimulus evaluation and the readiness to continue watching a specific offering at home (an indirect behavioral measure). While the major contribution to the prediction of attitude relates to the information-processing factor (not embarrassing, but informative and interesting) the behavioral variance was better predicted by a high level of excitement.

The factors extracted also allow for a 100% accurate classification of the heterogeneous stimulus material into two distinct clusters that we named serious-talk and small-talk according to the emotional quality that is characteristic for each category. Indeed, hedonistic tone contributed as much to the cluster solution (45.7%) as information processing (23.3%) and level of excitement (20.1%) together. Thus serious-talk shows produce negative feelings, are not at all amusing, are informative and not embarrassing, and are also presented in an exciting way. Small-talk shows are mainly defined by amusement and joy, they are not very exciting, and they are not informative. So we found that the audience identifies two very distinct genres within the single affect-TV genre as defined by the producers.

In our principal-component analysis, the item *entertaining* showed the highest loading on the hedonistic tone factor. Thus, our subjects' statements that they felt entertained by a sequence are clearly defined as an emotional experience of pleasure. However, the experience of pleasure has only a small effect on the attitude toward an affect-TV offering and no effect on the likely viewing behavior. We found two other components of emotional experience to be responsible for TV-offering evaluation and viewing behavior. These components are based on two independent activation systems (see Lacey, 1967): cortical arousal (information processing) and autonomous arousal (level of excitement), which were both high when the sequence was interesting. Interest is independent of *pleasure-displeasure*.

People can be interested in experiencing sad and fearful or delightful and amusing events in fictional or realistic media offerings by feeling with a protagonist, feeling themselves to be a protagonist, or imagining how an uncertain situation will be resolved. People can become interested in interacting (para-)socially with protagonists on the screen independent of the hedonistic tone of the content. But what is the motivation for this interest, if it is not to experience pleasure? According to concepts of social perception and cognition we can assume that people have specific drives to explore the world and to built concepts about the physical and especially the social environment. As Festinger (1954) put it: "There exists, in the human organism, a drive to evaluate his opinions and his abilities . . . (because the) holding of incorrect opinions and/or inaccurate appraisals of one's abilities can be punishing or even fatal in many situations" (p. 117).

The construction and evaluation of concepts is based on direct experience, but also on imagination (see Bischof, 1989). The use of media could be conceptualized as an imaginative technique or maybe better as something in between experience and imagination. Affect-talk shows provide an ideal stimulus material to investigate these hypotheses. If the avoidance of risk and punishment is the most important aspect of this striving, our subjects should be particularly interested in sequences where situations are portrayed in which the physical or social integrity of a person is challenged or damaged. That is exactly what happens. Out of the 10 most interesting sequences in our experiment, 9 involve a high level of danger up to and including the risk of death (death/loss, sexual abuse, health) and only one involves a relatively moderate level of violation (i.e., unfaithfulness). From the 10 sequences with the lowest level of interest, none involves a significant level of danger. (These 10 include all the relationship shows and talk show sequences on relationships/love and sex). The viewing-motivation factor *social comparison* is an important predictor for the evaluation of these TV offerings. The viewing motivation *relaxation/escape* has no relevant effect on evaluation. Since social comparison is the main course in these shows, we have to take a look at its ingredients.

Of course, comparing one's own opinion and appraisal with those of others is an act of imagination. We use the term *simulation* for this process, not merely due to theoretical considerations (see Bischof, 1989), but also because it is used in everyday language to characterize techniques like flight simulation, in which people are trained for potentially dangerous situations without taking the risk of actual harm during the rehearsal. Obviously, TV viewing is mainly an internal simulation and not interactive as with flight simulators. However, the simulation allows the viewers to interact (para-)socially with the protagonists, experience their feelings (empathy), identify with the protagonists' social roles, or participate in the dramatic process, that is, how the story would develop if the protagonist were to use the viewer's concepts and knowledge. A very important criterion for a successful simulation, that is, the *telepresence* and *immersion* it leads to, is its realism (Sheridan, 1992; Steuer, 1992; Zeltzer, 1992). Affect TV meets this criterion perfectly, with the elements of personalization, authenticity, intimacy, and emotionality. The satisfaction of viewing affect TV results in the experience of realistically simulating important social situations, which supports the development of concepts of the social world.

ACKNOWLEDGMENT

The authors gratefully acknowledge the financial support of the Landesanstalt für Rundfunk, Nordrhein-Westfalen, for the investigation of "Affect-TV." Most of the reported data have been collected in this project.

REFERENCES

Barloewen, C. v., & Brandenberg, H. (1975). Das Gespräch mit Gästen. Abgrenzungen. Die Entwicklung der Talk Show in Deutschland. In C. v. Barloewen & H. Brandenberg (Eds.), *Talk Show. Unterhaltung im Fernsehen = Fernsehunterhaltung?* (pp. 17–27). Munich, Germany: Hanser.

Bente, G., Bahß, C., Dorando, G., & Hündgen, B. (1997). Zuschauermerkmale und Affekt-TV-Konsum. In G. Bente & B. Fromm (Eds.), *Affektfernsehen: Motive, Angebotsweisen und Wirkungen* (pp. 142–186). Opladen, Germany: Leske & Budrich.

Bente, G., & Frey, S. (1991). Visuelle Zitate als Mittel der Fernsehberichterstattung in Deutschland, Frankreich und den USA. In W. Schulz (Ed.), *Medienwirkungen. Einflüsse von Presse, Radio und Fernsehen auf Individuum und Gesellschaft* (DFG Forschungsbericht, pp. 191–222). Weinheim, Germany: VCH Verlagsgesellschaft.

Bente, G., & Fromm, B. (Eds.). (1997). *Affektfernsehen: Motive, Angebotsweisen und Wirkungen.* Opladen, Germany: Leske & Budrich.

Bente, G., Jochlik, D., Adameck, C., & Grisard, T. (1997). Angebot und Nachfrage auf dem Affektfernsehmarkt. In G. Bente & B. Fromm (Eds.), *Affektfernsehen: Motive, Angebotsweisen und Wirkungen* (pp. 79–113). Opladen, Germany: Leske & Budrich.

Bente, G., & Vorderer, P. (1997). The socio-emotional dimension of using screen media. Current perspectives in German media psychology. In P. Winterhoff-Spurk & T. H. A. van der Voort (Eds.), *New horizons in media psychology: Research cooperation and projects in Europe* (pp. 125–144). Opladen, Germany: Westdeutscher Verlag.

Berghaus, M., & Staab, J. F. (1995). *Fernseh-Shows auf deutschen Bildschirmen: Eine Inhaltsanalyse aus Zuschauersicht.* Munich, Germany: Fischer.

Bischof, N. (1989). Emotionale Verwirrungen oder: Von den Schwierigkeiten im Umgang mit der Biologie. *Psychologische Rundschau, 40,* 188–205.

Bommert, H., Weich, K. W., & Dirksmeier, C. (1995). *Rezipientenpersönlichkeit und Medienwirkung. Der persönlichkeits-orientierte Ansatz der Medienwirkungsforschung.* Münster, Germany: Lit-Verlag.

Brown, J. D., Campbell, K., & Fischer, L. (1986). American adolescents and music videos: Why do they watch? *Gazette, 37,* 19–32.

Burger, H. (1991). *Das Gespräch in den Massenmedien.* New York: de Gruyter.

Conway, J. C., & Rubin, A. M. (1991). Psychological predictors of television viewing motivation. *Communication Research, 18,* 443–463.

Cutler, N., & Danowski, J. (1980). Progress gratification in aging cohorts. *JournalismQuarterly, 57,* 269–277.

Darrow, C. W. (1929). Electrical and circulatory responses to brief sensory and ideational stimuli. *Journal of Experimental Psychology, 12,* 267–300.

Elbert, T., & Schandry, R. (1998). Herz und Hirn. Psychophysiologische Wechselwirkungen. In F. Rösler (Ed.), *Ergebnisse und Anwendungen der Psychophysiologie* (Enzyklopädie der Psychologie, Band 5, pp. 427–477). Göttingen, Germany: Hogrefe.

Feist, A. (1999). *Emotionale Wirkungen von Fernsehtalkshows.* Unpublished doctoral dissertation, University of Cologne, Germany.

Feist, A., Bente, G., & Hündgen, B. (1997). Sozio-emotionale Wirkungsdimensionen des Affektfernsehens. In G. Bente & B. Fromm (Eds.), *Affektfernsehen: Motive, Angebotsweisen und Wirkungen* (pp. 242–285). Opladen, Germany: Leske & Budrich.

Ferguson, D. A., & Perse, E. M. (1993). Media and audience influence on channel repertoire. *Journal of Broadcasting and Electronic Media, 37*, 31–47.

Festinger, L. (1954). A theory of social comparison processes. *Human Relations, 7*, 117–140.

Foltin, H.-F. (1994). Zur Entwicklung der Talkshow in den USA. *Media Perspektiven, 8*, 477–487.

Frank, R. E., & Greenberg, M. G. (1980*). The public's use of television: Who watches and why.* Beverly Hills, CA: Sage Publications.

Grimm, J. (1995). Wirklichkeit als Programm? Zuwendungsattraktivität und Wirkung von Reality-TV. In G. Hallenberger (Ed.), *Neue Sendeformen im Fernsehen. Ästhetische, juristische und ökonomische Aspekte* (Arbeitshefte Bildschrimmedien, Heft 54, pp. 79–111). Universität Siegen, Germany.

Guadagnoli, E., & Velicer, W. F. (1988). Relation of sample size to the stability of component patterns. *Psychological Bulletin, 103*, 265–275.

Habermas, J. (1990). *Strukturwandel in der Öffentlichkeit. Untersuchungen zu einer Kategorie der bürgerlichen Gesellschaft.* Frankfurt a. M., Germany: Suhrkamp.

Hamm, H. O., & Vaitl, D. (1993). Emotionsinduktion durch visuelle Reize: Validierung einer Stimulationsmethode auf drei Reaktionsebenen. *Psychologische Rundschau, 44*, 143–161.

Herzog, H. (1944). What do we really know about daytime serial listeners'? In P. F. Lazarsfeld & F. N. Stanton (Eds.), *Radio research 1942–1943* (pp. 3–33). New York: Duell, Sloan, Pearce.

Hodges, R. L., Cook, E. W., & Lang, P. J. (1985). Individual differences in autonomic response: Conditioned association or conditioned fear? *Psychophysiology, 22*, 545–560.

Holly, W., & Schwitalla, J. (1995). Explosiv - Der heiße Stuhl - Streitkultur im kommerziellen Fernsehen. In S. Müller-Doohm & K. Neumann-Braun (Eds.), *Kulturinszenierungen* (pp. 59–89). Frankfurt a. M., Germany: Suhrkamp.

Horton, D., & Wohl, R. R. (1956). Mass communication and para-social interaction: Observations on intimacy at a distance. *Psychiatry, 19*, 215–229.

Hutchby, I. (1996). *Confrontation talk: Arguments, asymmetries, and power on talk radio.* Mahwah, NJ: Lawrence Erlbaum Associates.

Katriel, T., & Philipsen, G. (1990). "What we need is communication": "Communication" as a cultural category in some American speech. In D. Carbaugh (Ed.), *Cultural communication and intercultural contact* (pp. 77–93). Hillsdale, NJ: Lawrence Erlbaum Associates.

Katz, E., Blumler, J. G., & Gurevitch, M. (1974). Utilization of mass communication by the individual. In J. G. Blumler & E. Katz (Eds.), *The uses of mass communication: Current perspectives on gratifications research* (pp. 19–32). Beverly Hills, CA: Sage Publications.

Keppler, A. (1994). *Wirklicher als die Wirklichkeit? Das neue Realitätsprinzip der Fernsehunterhaltung.* Frankfurt a. M., Germany: Fischer.

Krugman, H. E. (1965). The impact of television advertising: Learning without involvement. *Public Opinion Quarterly, 29*, 349–356.

Lacey, J. I. (1967). Somatic response patterning and stress: Some revisions of activation theory. In M. H. Appley & R. Trumbull (Eds.), *Psychological Stress* (pp. 14–36). New York: Appleton.

Lang, P. J. (1980). Behavioral treatment and bio-behavioral assessment: Computer applications. In J. B. Sidowsky, J. H. Johnson, & T. A. Williams (Eds.), *Technology in mental health care delivery systems* (pp. 119–137). Norwood, NJ: Ablex.

Livingstone, S., & Lunt, P. (1994*). Talk on television: Audience participation and public debate.* London: Routledge.

Mares, M.-J., & Cantor, J. (1992). Elderly viewers' responses to televised portrayals of old age: Empathy and mood management versus social comparison. *Communication Research, 19*(4), 459–478.

Masters, R., Frey, S., & Bente, G. (1991). Dominance and attention: Images of leaders in German, French and American TV news. *Polity, 23*, 373–394.

Mehl, D. (1996). *La Télévision de L'intimité.* Paris: Seuil.

Meyrowitz, J. (1987). *Die Fernsehgesellschaft: Wirklichkeit und Identität im Medienzeitalter.* Weinheim, Germany: Beltz.

Osgood, C. E. (1969). On the why and wherefore of E, P, and A. *Journal of Personality and Social Psychology, 12*, 194–199.

Pape, I. (1996). *Verzweifelt gesucht! Typische Motive für die Teilnahme an der Sendung "Nur die Liebe zählt."* Unpublished master's thesis, Universität Gesamthochschule Essen, Germany.

Perse, E. M. (1990). Involvement with local television news: Cognitive and emotional dimensions. *Human Communication Research, 16,* 556–581.

Perse, E. M., & Rubin, A. M. (1990). Chronic loneliness and television use. *Journal of Broadcasting and Electronic Media, 14,* 37–53.

Reichertz, J. (1996). *Trauung, Trost und Wunder: Formen und Praktiken des Religiösen im Fernsehen.* Unpublished manuscript.

Rubin, A. M. (1983). Television uses and gratifications: The interactions of viewing patterns and motivations. *Journal of Broadcasting, 27,* 37–51.

Rubin, A. M. (1984). Ritualized and instrumental television viewing. *Journal of Communication, 34,* 67–77.

Russell, J. A. (1979). Affective space is bipolar. *Journal of Personality and Social Psychology, 37,* 345–356.

Schlosberg, H. (1952). The description of facial expressions in terms of two dimensions. *Journal of Experimental Psychology, 44,* 229–237.

Schmidt, T., & Jain, A. (1996). Continuous assessment of finger blood pressure and other hemodynamic and behavioral variables in everyday life. In J. Fahrenberg & M. Myrtek (Eds.), *Ambulatory Assessment: Computer-assisted psychological and psychophysiological methods in monitoring and field studies* (pp. 189–213). Seattle, WA: Hogrefe & Huber Publishers.

Schorr, A., & Schorr-Neustadt, M. (1994). *Fragebogen zur Erfassung allgemeiner Fernsehmotive* (Version 6/94). Unpublished manuscript, Katholische Universität Eichstätt, Germany.

Schumacher, H. (1992). Moderation im Magazin. In K. Hickethier (Ed.), *Fernsehen, Wahrnehmungswelt, Programminstitution und Marktkonkurrenz* (pp. 193–209). Frankfurt a. M., Germany: Lang.

Sennett, R. (1983). *Verfall und Ende des öffentlichen Lebens. Die Tyrannei der Intimität.* Frankfurt a. M., Germany: Fischer.

Sheridan, T. B. (1992). *Telerobotics, automation, and human supervisory control.* Cambridge, MA: MIT Press.

Steinbrecher, M., & Weiske, M. (1992). *Die Talkshow. 20 Jahre zwischen Klatsch und News.* Munich, Germany: Ölschläger.

Steuer, J. (1992). Defining virtual reality: Dimensions determining telepresence. *Journal of Communication, 42,* 73–93.

Strange, J. (1996). Leben in Bildschirmwelten - Formen der narrativen Involviertheit. Stellungnahme zu dem Beitrag von Peter Vorderer. In P. Vorderer (Ed.), *Fernsehen als "Beziehungskiste." Parasoziale Beziehungen und Interaktionen mit TV-Personen* (pp.173–180). Opladen, Germany: Westdeutscher Verlag.

Sturm, H. (1989). Medienwirkungen - ein Produkt der Beziehungen zwischen Rezipient und Medium. In J. Groebel & P. Winterhoff-Spurk (Eds.), *Empirische Medienpsychologie* (pp. 33–44). Munich, Germany: Psychologie Verlags Union.

Sturm, H. (1991). *Fernsehdiktate: Die Veränderung von Gedanken und Gefühlen.* Gütersloh, Germany: Bertelsmann.

Tan, E. S. (1996). *Emotion and the structure of narrative film: Film as an emotion machine.* Mahwah, NJ: Lawrence Erlbaum Associates.

Tasche, K. G. (1996). *Die selektive Zuwendung zu Fernsehprogrammen: Entwicklung und Erprobung von Indikatoren der selektiven Nutzung von politischen Informationssendungen des Fernsehens.* Munich, Germany: R. Fischer.

Vorderer, P. (1992). *Fernsehen als Handlung: Fernsehfilmrezeption aus motivationspsychologischer Perspektive.* Berlin: Edition Sigma.

Vorderer, P. (1996). Toward a psychological theory of suspense. In P. Vorderer, H. J. Wulff, & M. Friedrichsen (Eds.), *Suspense: Conceptualizations, theoretical analyses, and empirical explorations* (pp. 233–254). Mahwah, NJ: Lawrence Erlbaum Associates.

Vorderer, P., Cupchik, G. C., & Oatley, K. (1997). Reading and literary landscapes: Experience and action from self-oriented and spectator perspectives. In S. Totösy de Zepetnek & I. Sywenky

(Eds.), *The systematic and empirical approach to literature and culture as theory and application* (pp. 559–571). Research Institute for Comparative Literature and Cross-Cultural Studies: University of Alberta, Canada.

Wegener, C. (1994). *Reality-TV: Fernsehen zwischen Emotion und Information*. Opladen, Germany: Leske & Budrich.

Wenner, L. A. (1985). The nature of news gratifications. In K. E. Rosengren, L. A. Wenner, & P. Palmgreen (Eds.), *Media gratification research: Current perspectives* (pp. 171–194). Beverly Hills, CA: Sage Publications.

White, M. (1992). *Tele-Advising: Therapeutic discourse in American television*. Chapel Hill, NC: University of North Carolina Press.

Winterhoff-Spurk, P., Heidinger, V., & Schwab, F. (1994). *Reality TV. Formate und Inhalte eines neuen Programmgenres* (Schriften der LAR, Bd. 3). Saarbrücken, Germany: Logos.

Zeltzer, D. (1992). Autonomy, interaction and presence. *Teleoperators and virtual environments, 1,* 127–132.

Zillmann, D. (1978). Attribution and misattribution of excitatory reactions. In J. H. Harvey, W. J. Ickes, & R. F. Kidd (Eds.), *New directions in attribution research* (pp. 335–368). Hillsdale, NJ: Lawrence Erlbaum Associates.

Zillmann, D. (1979). *Hostility and Aggression*. Hillsdale, NJ: Lawrence Erlbaum Associates.

Zillmann, D. (1983). Excitation transfer in emotional behavior. In J. T. Cacioppo & R. E. Petty (Eds.), *Social psychophysiology: A source book* (pp. 215–240). New York: Guilford.

Zillmann, D. (1988). Mood management through communication choices. *American Behavioral Scientist, 31,* 327–340.

Zillmann, D. (1996). The psychology of suspense in dramatic exposition. In P. Vorderer, H. J. Wulff, & M. Friedrichsen (Eds.), *Suspense: Conceptualizations, theoretical analyses, and empirical explorations* (pp. 199–231). Mahwah, NJ: Lawrence Erlbaum Associates.

8

▼▼▼▼▼▼▼▼▼

Children's Likes and Dislikes
of Entertainment Programs

Patti M. Valkenburg
University of Amsterdam, The Netherlands

Joanne Cantor
University of Wisconsin

Most people seem to agree that children have distinct tastes when it comes to consuming entertainment. Although little is known about how these tastes are formed during childhood, it has been shown that even toddlers firmly express their tastes and preferences regarding what they want to eat, wear, watch, or play with (Bartsch & Wellman, 1995). It has also been shown that as children mature they become increasingly able to voice sophisticated and critical views about television entertainment programs (Clifford, Gunter, & McAleer, 1995). Program producers and marketers of child products have undoubtedly gathered valuable information about what children in different age groups like in commercials and entertainment programs. However, their research findings are, in most cases, not accessible to the academic world. In academic circles, there has been very little systematic research on children's opinions about and preferences for television entertainment programs, and no reviews organizing the existing literature.

One thing that makes the study of children's preferences for entertainment so interesting and so valuable is that children usually watch entertainment programming not because they are told to, but because they want to. Although children might tune into educational programs because of encouragement from their parents or teachers, children often choose entertainment programs without being encouraged by an authority figure—and sometimes despite being discouraged by an adult. Because children often choose entertainment programming for their own enjoyment, studying what children prefer to watch may give researchers insight into the various types of gratifications that viewing may provide.

Children might enjoy entertainment programs for a variety of reasons, including differences in experiences, differences in predispositions or temperament, and differences in cognitive and emotional development. According to research that has been conducted thus far, two factors that have been shown to be important antecedents of children's preference for entertainment are their age or developmental level (Mielke, 1983; Sheldon & Loncar, 1996; Valkenburg & Janssen, 1999) and their gender (Cantor, 1998a; Valkenburg & Janssen, 1999). Because of the important role of both age and gender in children's viewing preferences, we have organized this chapter according to these major themes.

COGNITIVE DEVELOPMENT AND CHILDREN'S LIKES AND DISLIKES

Cognitive developmental theories have been used to explain a variety of differences in the way children respond to mass media, including their comprehension of the motivations and consequences underlying stories, their reactions to television advertising, and their fright reactions. In this chapter, we investigate the extent to which cognitive developmental differences play a role in determining children's likes and dislikes for entertaining programming. On the basis of a review of the existing literature on preschoolers' (Acuff, 1997; Cupitt, Jenkinson, Ungerer, & Waters, 1998; Jaglom & Gardner, 1981; Rosengren & Windahl, 1989) and elementary school children's (Acuff, 1997; Gunter, McAleer, & Clifford, 1991; Valkenburg & Janssen, 1999) preferences for entertainment, we will discuss and hypothesize how children's developmental level might influence their preferences for different types of entertainment programs.

Early Childhood: Ages 2 to 7

Many theories of cognitive development distinguish the preschool and early elementary school years from the later elementary school years. Piaget refers to the younger age group as "preoperational," although many non-Piagetians attribute specific characteristics to this age group without using the preoperational label. Although a 2-year-old differs from a 7-year-old in many respects, preschoolers and young elementary school children do share certain cognitive-developmental characteristics that justify segmenting them in this way. We explain some of these characteristics and discuss how they might affect children's evaluative judgments of entertainment programs.

Limited Information-Processing Capacity.   Children of all ages strive to understand their environment, whether it surrounds them in real life or is presented to them on television. According to Piaget (1954), there seems to be an innate need in children to find order, structure, and predictability in their environment. When children can explain and process the events they experience, their world makes sense to them and they have equilibrium. When children cannot understand their external world, they are in a state of cognitive disequilibrium (conflict), and, to resolve this disharmonious state, they begin a search for a better level of understanding. Children have often been shown to display a preference for stimuli that they can understand or incorporate at least partially within their existing conceptual framework, and to show little preference for extremely simple or extremely complex stimuli (Flavell, Miller, & Miller, 1993; Siegler, 1991). According to the *moderate-discrepancy hypothesis*, which is formulated to explain these observations, infants and preschoolers prefer to look at objects that are moderately discrepant from what they know or are capable of (Siegler, 1991). Of course, the meaning of complexity changes dramatically as a child matures. Information that is too complex for a 2-year-old may seem overly simple to a 4-year-old.

Although we know of no research on the effect of children's cognitive abilities on their likes and dislikes in entertainment, some circumstantial evidence does exist. Observational studies of children's attention to television have shown, for example, that children prefer to watch television content that is easily understood (Anderson & Burns, 1991), and that children avoid television that they cannot understand (Wright & Huston, 1981). It must be noted, however, that although attention is a necessary condition for the appreciation of television content, it is not a sufficient one. It has been observed that children can involuntarily pay attention to certain aversive television content (e.g., starving children, survivors of a bombing) that they do not appreciate at all (Cantor, 1998b)—an issue we return to at the end of this chapter. Research on children's self-reports of what they like does suggest, however, that comprehension of entertainment shows is one of the most important determinants of selecting and enjoying them (Valkenburg & Janssen, 1999).

Because for young children, so much information goes beyond their existing knowledge and experiences, and because their information-processing capacity is limited, young children need more time than adults to interpret and make sense of television images. This is the reason why young preschoolers often are not attracted to fast-paced programming with rapidly changing images (Acuff, 1997). Programs with a slow pace and with lots of repetition, such as *Barney and Friends*, *Blue's Clues*, and *Mister Rogers' Neighborhood*, are more attuned to the needs of this age group (Acuff, 1997). Young preschoolers also, therefore, often prefer familiar contexts and visuals (Lemish, 1987). For instance, they like to watch programs that show babies and young children (Lemish, 1987), and they adore nonthreatening real or animated animals, such as kind birds, friendly dinosaurs, and babyish creatures like the Teletubbies (Acuff, 1997; Cupitt et al., 1998). By the time they are 5 or 6, children begin to develop a preference for more fast-paced programs. By that age, they often find slower-paced programs with friendly characters boring or childish (Acuff, 1997; Sheldon & Loncar, 1996). Because they are able to make sense of far more information, these children show greater persistence with content that is more difficult to understand (Anderson & Burns, 1991). At that time, they begin to prefer more adventurous themes located in foreign countries or in outer space, and more complicated characters (Acuff, 1997).

Unclear Fantasy–Reality Distinction.   For the preoperational child, there is an unclear demarcation between fantasy and reality. Virtually anything is possible in this child's imagination: A sponge can become a rock, bears can talk, and the wind can pick the child up and take him or her away. Research has shown that between the ages of 3 and 10 years, children gradually become more accurate in distinguishing fantasy from reality on television (e.g., Morrison & Gardner, 1978). At first, children believe that everything on television is real. Young preschoolers sometimes even think the characters live inside the TV set (Noble, 1975). Jaglom and Gardner (1981), for instance, observed that 2- to 3-year-olds ran to get a paper towel to clean up an egg they saw break on television. In addition, most 4-year-olds who participated in a study by Howard (1998) were convinced that Big Bird and Bugs Bunny were real.

As children grow older, they at first judge content as real versus unreal by focusing on perceptual cues. Children begin to judge marked violations of physical reality, such as animation and special effects, as unreal (Dorr, 1983), but they continue to consider something that looks real as real even if it is not. For example, although all of the 5- to 6-year-olds in Howard's (1998) study knew that Big Bird was a man dressed in a costume, many 9- to 10-year-olds thought that the Huxtables (on *The Cosby Show*) were a real family.

Children's failure to distinguish fantasy and reality can affect their likes and dislikes regarding television in important ways. First, because fantasy and cartoon characters are perceived as real, they can be just as attractive and engaging as real-life characters for preoperational children. By the time they are 3 years old, children start to make statements indicating attachment to television personalities (Jaglom & Gardner, 1981). But as they do not distinguish between fantasy and reality, they can just as easily focus their attraction on an animal or a fantasy character as on a real-life character. Another implication of children's limited understanding of fantasy and reality is that some special effects or stunts, such as a character vanishing in a puff of smoke, can have a great impact on preoperational children. Because they cannot put these events in perspective by understanding that they are cinematic tricks, young children may be more strongly affected by them.

Perceptual Boundedness and Centration.   Another quality of preschoolers' thinking is the tendency to center attention on the immediately perceptible attributes of a display, often ignoring other types of information that are less obvious or less visually prominent. This characteristic is sometimes referred to as perceptual boundedness (Bruner, 1966) or concreteness (Flavell, 1963). Research shows, for example, that in evaluating characters, preschoolers weigh a character's appearance more heavily than his or her behavior or motivations, information that is much less perceptually salient. In a controlled experiment in which a television character's appearance (attractive vs. ugly) and behavior (kind vs. cruel) were manipulated, preschool children were more inclined than older children to say that the ugly character was mean and the attractive character was nice, independently of how she had behaved. In contrast, older children's evaluations were more influenced by the character's behavior than by her looks (Hoffner & Cantor, 1985).

Closely related to perceptual boundedness is centration, the tendency to center attention on an individual, striking feature of an object or image, to the exclusion of other, less striking features. In other words, preoperational children are often unable to explore all aspects of a visual stimulus. When a child is presented with a stuffed bear with a big shiny bow, for example, the child may focus entirely on this bow, and ignore many other characteristics of the bear. In a qualitative study reported in Acuff (1997), 5- to 8-year-old girls were presented with three dolls. Two of the dolls were very expensive, had beautiful and realistic faces, and came with sophisticated mechanical effects. The third doll was much more cheaply made, but this doll had a big red sequined heart on her dress. To the surprise of the researchers, the majority of the girls preferred the cheap doll with the sequined heart. The researchers explained their results with Piaget's concept of centration. According to Acuff (1997, p. 75), the striking feature "became an object of centration . . . to the exclusion of all other attributes."

Young children's tendency to focus on immediately perceptible, striking features of images has important implications for children's entertainment programs. Children up to approximately 5 years old are very visual in their orientation to the world and certainly to characters. Their descriptions of television characters tend to fix on single, physical attributes, without integrating them into an overall picture (Jaglom & Gardner, 1981). They pay less attention to what characters are doing or saying, and pay most attention to simple, brightly colored visuals and colorful, uncomplicated, nonthreatening characters (Acuff, 1997; Jaglom & Gardner, 1981).

These tendencies have implications for emotional reactions as well. For example, children in this age group are more likely to be frightened by something in the media that is ugly or grotesque but is actually harmless, than by something that is dangerous but has a benign exterior (Cantor & Sparks, 1984).

Failure to Understand Transformations.   Another characteristic of preoperational children is the failure to understand transformations. In responding primarily on the basis of the immediately perceptual aspects of a situation, the young child is much less affected by depicted causal relationships or changes from past to future states. A study by De Vries (1969) provides a convincing example of this quality of children's thinking. In this study, 3- to 6-year-olds were allowed to pet a tame and friendly cat named Maynard. When the experimenter asked the children what Maynard was, all of them knew he was a cat. Then, while the children watched, the experimenter put a mask of a dog over Maynard's head. She found that many of the 3-year-olds thought that the animal had become a dog, whereas most 6-year-olds knew it was still a cat no matter what it looked like (De Vries, 1969). This study demonstrates that preschoolers tend to focus on static states rather than transformations. The preschoolers ignored (or possibly forgot) the transformational process, during which the researcher had put the mask on the cat's face.

Children's entertainment programs often use transformations as a means to attract children. One thing that popular children's programs such as *The Incredible Hulk*, *Power Rangers*, and the recent *Animorphs* have in common is that ordinary humans transform into very different-looking superheroes, complete with extraordinary talents, right before the viewers' eyes. These kinds of transformations have a very powerful impact on preoperational children, who often see a character's multiple forms as separate characters (Sparks & Cantor, 1986).

Visual transformational events, therefore, often surprise and impress preschoolers (Acuff, 1997). As children grow older, they still enjoy transformations, but because they have a better grasp of cinematic conventions, the transformations become less impressive. Unfortunately, transformations can also induce fright because young children are not able yet to dismiss the transformation as unreal, and the notion that a seemingly normal person could suddenly become a grotesque monster is especially unsettling (Cantor, 1998b). In a survey conducted at the time that *The Incredible Hulk* appeared on prime-time television, 40% of the parents of preschool children who responded to the questionnaire spontaneously listed *The Incredible Hulk* as a program that had frightened their child (Cantor & Sparks, 1984). Similarly, in a survey among Dutch parents conducted in 1997, *Power Rangers* was among the top three programs inducing fright in young children (Valkenburg, 1999).

Responsiveness to Language.   Children seem to have an innate tendency to respond to language. Long before infants talk, they are very responsive to human speech (Siegler, 1991), and they are especially attentive to a form of speech that is referred to as *motherese*. Motherese is characterized by a slower cadence, a higher pitch, and exaggerated intonations (Siegler, 1991). It has been shown that infants as young as 4 months clearly prefer to hear speech in motherese to speech in standard intonations (Fernald, 1985). Programs for toddlers sometimes make use of this style of speech (Cupitt et al., 1998).

Young preschoolers also like to listen to music, and they prefer rhythmic to non-rhythmic sounds (Siegler, 1991). In a study by Cupitt et al. (1998), almost half of the mothers of 2½-year-olds reported that their child had imitated music, rhymes, or songs from television. This study also showed that nearly all of the 2½-year-olds had interacted with television programs while watching, for instance, by singing, dancing, or clapping hands. Because young children are so responsive to songs, rhymes, and music, these devices are often used in educational and entertainment programs for young children (Wakshlag, Reitz, & Zillmann, 1982).

Younger preoperational children's limited language skills prevent them from appreciating some sophisticated forms of humor, such as world play, puns, and satire. Appropriate forms of humor for this age group are highly physical, visual forms of humor (e.g., clownish gestures), slapstick, and sudden surprises (Zillmann & Bryant, 1983). Preschoolers and young elementary school children dislike programs with humor that is too "grown-up" for them to understand (Sheldon & Loncar, 1996). Toward the latter part of the preoperational stage, however, children become more responsive to verbally oriented shows, with more sophisticated forms of humor (Jaglom & Gardner, 1981), like *The Simpsons*.

Middle Childhood: Ages 8 Through 12

Piaget believed that the cognitive systems of early childhood (preoperational) and middle childhood (concrete operational) thinkers are qualitatively different from one another. However, it is now generally believed that these differences are not that dramatic (Siegler, 1991). Still, many of the general trends that Piaget described hold up to empirical tests even today (Flavell et al., 1993). We discuss a number of qualities that characterize middle childhood and argue how these qualities may affect children's perceptions of and preferences for entertainment programs.

Appreciation of the Fantasy–Reality Distinction.   Throughout elementary school, children are increasingly able to distinguish the real from the unreal on television (e.g., Howard, 1998). Whereas the preoperational child's fantasies are not bound by logical rules, the fantasies in middle childhood more often entail realistic and plausible themes. In this period, children become interested in real-world phenomena (Mielke, 1983), and they seek to discover reality in their toys, books, and entertainment programs. According to Gunter et al. (1991), the realism of the setting and characters in entertainment programs is an important determinant of children's enjoyment of such programs. The children in their study were highly critical of entertainment that lacks realism, for instance, when actors behaved in an unlikely manner (Gunter et al., 1991). By the time children are 9 years old, they are mainly interested in entertainment designed for adults (Rosengren & Windahl, 1989). In a study by Rosengren and Windahl (1989), 87% of the boys and 80% of the girls in third grade had an adult program as their main preference. Children say that one of the reasons they watch such programs is to be taught social lessons, such as how to behave in relationships (Gunter et al., 1991). This may explain why situation comedies featuring families are so popular with children. In 1995 Nielsen ratings for children aged 2 to 11, for example, 9 of the top 10 programs were in that category (Cantor, 1998a). However, while seeking information about the real world, these children still appreciate dramatic conflict, fast-paced action, and comic escapism. Programs combining both appeals seem to be most successful (Mielke, 1983). Children in middle childhood continue to like to watch animals, but they are mainly interested in real-life animals rather than fantasy creatures (Mielke, 1983). Because most fantasy characters have been demystified (Fernie, 1981), concrete-operational children tend to become attached to real-life heroes, such as sports heroes, movie stars, and action heroes (Acuff, 1997).

Decentration.   With the developing ability to decenter, children come to appreciate details. As explained earlier, a preoperational child may focus on only one striking detail of a toy—a doll's clothing, for example. For the concrete-operational child, many characteristics of a toy may be carefully observed, from the face and body to details of the doll's clothing to how it moves (Acuff, 1997). At this age, children become progressively critical of programs of low quality, such as those that are poorly produced or repetitious (Gunter et al., 1991). They are no longer content with simple, salient characteristics, such as a colorful cartoon character. Unlike preoperational children, who are greatly impressed by special effects and characters with special powers, older children seem to agree that special effects by themselves are not enough (Gunter et al., 1991).

SOCIOCOGNITIVE DEVELOPMENT AND CHILDREN'S LIKES AND DISLIKES

Up to this point we have mainly discussed the impact of children's *cognitive* development on their preferences for entertainment. Of course, children strive to understand not only their physical surroundings but also their social environment. Social cognition includes recognizing and dealing with others' emotions and understanding social relations and social customs (Flavell et al., 1993). In the next sections, we focus on how children's social-cognitive level affects their preferences for entertainment.

Understanding Others' Emotions

Children's ability to recognize and interpret others' emotions gradually improves throughout early childhood. By age 4 or 5, children can provide explanations for why their playmates are happy, angry, or sad, although they tend to rely primarily on visible cues, such as facial expressions (Flavell et al., 1993). As children rely more and more on both internal and external cues to interpret emotions, they improve greatly in their understanding of emotions. For example, they eventually recognize that more than one emotion can be experienced at the same time and that an emotion can be feigned (Flavell et al., 1993). It is no accident, therefore, that at this level of sociocognitive development, children start to recognize and dislike poor acting by protagonists in entertainment programs, for example, when actors in soaps display emotions in an unlikely and unconvincing way (Sheldon & Loncar, 1996).

Social Role-Taking Perspectives

Children's ability to see the world from another's perspective steadily increases between the preschool and older elementary school years (Durkin, 1997). During early and middle childhood, children develop from mainly egocentric beings (roughly 3 years old), who are unaware of any social perspective (thoughts, feelings) other than their own, to advanced "role takers" (roughly 12 to 15+), who are capable of putting themselves in another person's shoes, can simultaneously consider different points of view, and anticipate and understand how others will react in different situations.

As children acquire role-taking skills, their understanding of human relationships changes. Whereas preschoolers think that any pleasant interaction with available playmates qualifies those playmates as friends, 8- to 10-year-olds appreciate how their interests and those of their peers can be similar or different, and they look for friends who are psychologically similar to themselves (Selman, 1980).

Children's growing abilities to role-take affect not only the way in which they deal with real-life persons, but also their likes and dislikes for characters in entertainment programs. Research has shown that children in middle childhood begin to enjoy watching television characters who seem psychologically similar to themselves (Hoffner & Cantor, 1991). Whereas preschoolers tend to rely on physical similarities between themselves and characters (e.g., I have eyes like Superman), or create them in their imagination, older children rely more heavily on psychological and social aspects of a character's personality (Fernie, 1981). Witnessing similar characters allows the child to observe a variety of events and outcomes that may be potentially relevant to his or her own life. It stands to reason, therefore, that children pay more attention to the actions of same-gender characters (Hoffner & Cantor, 1991), and that they dislike watching characters who are younger than themselves (Mielke, 1983). Research has shown that children prefer to watch actors at least their own age, or teenagers and young adults (Sheldon & Loncar, 1996). In a study that had children explain why they prefer to see adults, children indicated that adults were involved in more interesting and exciting activities, that they were better actors, and had better roles than children (Sheldon & Loncar, 1996).

Enjoyment of media entertainment is not always predicted by perceived similarity to a character (Hoffner & Cantor, 1991). Heroes like Superman and larger-than-life characters are undoubtedly dissimilar to most child viewers. Still, children are very much attracted to films and programs featuring characters like this. Rather than feeling similar, children see these characters as individuals to emulate. Children enjoy vicariously participating in the behaviors of someone they admire and would like to resemble but whom they do not have the capacity to imitate. *Wishful identification* (von Feilitzen & Linne, 1975) with admirable characters can help children feel more powerful at a time when they are struggling with real-life problems that are not instantaneously resolved. Because boys and girls differ in the media characters they admire (Hoffner, 1996), we discuss their preferences for characters in the next section of this chapter, on the relationship between gender and preferences for entertainment.

Influence of Peer Groups

Peer interactions become increasingly sophisticated among school-aged children (Durkin, 1997). A peer group in middle childhood is a stable confederation of children who share common interests and explicit norms that dictate how members should behave (Durkin, 1997). Members of peer groups in middle childhood share norms that they have created themselves. Because children in this age group develop such a strong sense of commitment and loyalty to the norms of their peer group, they are increasingly sensitive to the thoughts, opinions, judgments, and evaluations of other children, and become very sensitive to what's "cool" and what's "in." They therefore become alert to how to behave in public and how to avoid being ridiculed with respect to what they wear or prefer to watch on television. For example, older children feel the need to firmly demonstrate their aversion to programs designed for younger children or for shows that feature characters younger than they are (Mielke, 1983). Although some of them might still like to watch programs made for younger children when they are alone, they "wouldn't be caught dead" wearing a *Sesame Street* sweatshirt to school (Acuff, 1997).

Conversely, in some older peer groups it appears to be fashionable to watch entertainment programs made for preschoolers. For example, in Europe it is has become a rage among peer groups in middle childhood and adolescence to watch *Teletubbies*, and even in some adult subcultures the program is acclaimed. This striking phenomenon shows how easily and dramatically a child's individual taste for entertainment can be overruled by the norms of the peer group to which he or she belongs.

Peer pressure seems to be an especially strong force in children's exposure to frightening programs and movies. Although many children are attracted to something that produces a "good scare" that is not overwhelming, others, especially boys, often go along with their friends' preferences, even though they suffer nightmares afterward. These children often admit that they watched something scary because they did not want to be considered immature or unmanly, or, in their words, a "wimp" or a "wussy" (Cantor, 1998b).

GENDER DIFFERENCES AND CHILDREN'S LIKES AND DISLIKES

Despite the fact that being a girl in the year 2000 is very different from being a girl a generation ago, important and meaningful differences have been noted between the way boys and girls typically think, how they express themselves, and what they value (Guber & Berry, 1993). Many researchers have observed that in the first two years, there does not appear to be any significant gender difference in play style and toy preference (Fagot, 1994). Boys can enjoy make-believe cooking and girls can enjoy pounding on a toy workbench (Guber & Berry, 1993). Boys and girls in this age group also do not seem to differ in their liking for TV characters, such as Barney, Big Bird, and the Teletubbies (Acuff, 1997), and in their liking of computer games designed for preschoolers (Sanger, Willson, Davies, & Whittaker, 1997). Significant gender differences in toy preference have been observed as early as 2 years, however (Goldstein, 1998). And by the time they are 3, boys and girls frequently participate in different activities, avoid toys that are perceived to belong to the opposite sex, and play primarily in same-gender groups (Huston, 1983). This so-called process of gender segregation is found in a variety of cultures and settings (Leaper, 1994; Maccoby, 1994). As each gender group maintains different norms for social interaction, segregated peer groups become powerful socialization agents (Maccoby, 1990).

A factor that is believed to contribute to the emergence of gender segregation is *behavioral compatibility*, that is, the idea that at the ages of 2 and 3, boys and girls start to develop distinct interests and preferences, and that these interests and preferences are often not shared by opposite-gender peers (Martin, 1994). For example, it has repeatedly been found that boys engage in more physically aggressive forms of play, such as pretend fights and conquests and sports such as football (Goldstein, 1998). Girls' play, on the other hand, often involves fine motor skills (James & McCain, 1982), such as dressing dolls, making jewelry, and other crafts. The emerging differences between boys and girls are clearly reflected in their preferences for entertainment. In comparison to preschool girls, preschool boys have a strong preference for action and violence in books and entertainment programs (Cantor & Nathanson, 1997; Jaglom & Gardner, 1981; Rosengren & Windahl, 1989). They tend to prefer themes and content in entertainment such as sports, violent fantasy themes, and more dangerous scenarios, involving, for example, dinosaurs and aliens. They also are attracted to heroic male characters, including superhumans (e.g., the Power Rangers, Hercules), sports stars, knights, soldiers, doctors, and police officers (Acuff, 1997). Preschool girls are more interested in relationship-centered and nurturing themes. They prefer themes and contexts such as castles, dance studios, school, the circus, and farmyards (Acuff, 1997). Whereas boys focus mainly on male characters, girls become attached to characters of both sexes (Hoffner, 1996; Hoffner & Cantor, 1991). One explanation that has been advanced is that there are more male characters and that they generally have more exciting, interesting roles. Preschool girls generally focus on characters such as fashion models, ballerinas, dancers, good fairies, queens, and princesses (Acuff, 1997).

Children's awareness of societal stereotypes for gender roles continues to increase with age into adolescence, and in spite of the fact that cognitive flexibility increases in middle childhood and adolescence, boys' and girls' preferences diverge over time (Huston, 1983). Because children become increasingly involved with peers (Durkin, 1997), there is greater pressure to conform to "gender-appropriate" behavior (Matteson, 1975). It is not surprising, therefore, that differences in taste between boys and girls become stronger with age (Himmelweit, Oppenheim, & Vince, 1958).

Elementary school boys (Cantor & Nathanson, 1997; Valkenburg & Janssen, 1999) and adolescent males (Himmelweit et al., 1958) still have a comparatively strong preference for action-oriented and violent programs. They become strongly attached to male action heroes and power figures, although the heroes are now more realistic (e.g., Arnold Schwarzenegger, Bruce Willis). Watching adult television programs can also be considered daring and grown-up among boys (Rosengren & Windahl, 1989). Elementary school girls are in general more likely to react negatively to program scenarios involving action, violence, horror, and swearing (Valkenburg & Janssen, 1999), possibly because girls report more often being frightened by violent media depictions than boys do (e.g., LaFrance & Banaji, 1992). In a study that had children list characteristics of an entertainment program that they would produce if they were an assistant producer, only girls, but no boys, spontaneously referred to the absence of sex, violence, or coarse language in such a program (Valkenburg & Janssen, 1999).

What do girls like? Unfortunately, research on the program preferences of children has focused on gender differences mainly in the appeal of violent content (Cantor & Nathanson, 1997) and has largely ignored many other characteristics in entertainment programs that might be differentially preferred by male and female children. However, research on girls' preferences for computer games suggests that girls are less object-oriented than boys (Acuff, 1997). They are less interested than boys in devices, such as lasers, buttons, and futuristic weapons. For girls, it's not so much about winning or killing the enemy (Berselli, 1998); girls like a story line (Sanger et al., 1997); they like real-life situations; and they are interested in the development of relationships between characters (Maccoby, 1994). Elementary school girls also have a preference for family situations, and they enjoy serial dramas with realistic themes (Palmer, 1986). They are most interested in realistic, attractive characters, like actresses, movie stars, male and female sports and music celebrities, and models (Acuff, 1997).

Finally, research has found that girls attach more value than boys to the comprehensibility of an entertainment program (Valkenburg & Janssen, 1999). This could be because girls are more interested than boys in dramatic story lines. In comparison to teenage boys, teenage girls are more eager to look for actors or actresses they recognize, invest more time in searching for information about shows and characters, and prefer to watch an entertainment show from start to finish (Heeter, 1988).

The scarce research on gender-based preferences for romance in entertainment programs has yielded mixed results. Some studies suggest that girls like romantic themes in storybooks (Collins-Standley, Gan, Yu, & Zillmann, 1996) and television shows (Himmelweit et al., 1958), more than boys do, whereas other studies have not found any significant gender differences in preferences for romance in television entertainment (Valkenburg & Janssen, 1999). Still others have suggested that boys are more interested in such themes (Sheldon, Ramsay, & Loncar, 1994). One explanation for the divergent results may be the way romance has been operationalized in the various studies. Girls might be likely to favor romantic themes if the focus is on love and relationships; boys may prefer romance if the taboo nature of sexual activity is the focus. Further research should investigate in a more refined way how boys and girls in different age groups differ in their preference for various aspects of love and romance in entertainment shows.

THE SPECIAL CASE OF ATTRACTION TO SCARY IMAGES AND THEMES

One important area of children's attraction to entertainment that does not fit neatly into the age or gender analysis is the paradox of attraction to scary programs. What is perplexing about this area is that children are often drawn to scary television programs and movies even though they may suffer nightmares and severe anxieties afterward (Cantor, 1998b). One set of reasons for children's exposure has been alluded to already. These deal with social-group membership and the desire to be accepted by one's peers. Many children watch scary entertainment so as not to be ridiculed by their friends, who may consider the ability to withstand frightening fare a test of maturity, or perhaps, "manhood." Relatedly, children may watch scary shows and movies together for the "bonding experience" that often occurs when friends undergo an intense negative experience together.

Still, there are psychological reasons for children's enjoyment of scary programs that are not dependent on peer pressure or group interactions. There is something arresting or compelling about witnessing dangerous events. Morbid curiosity is one explanation that is frequently advanced for children's exposure to depictions of danger, mayhem, and death. From an evolutionary perspective, natural selection might make us innately predisposed to pay attention when violence, injury, disease, and death are occurring. Whether we enjoy that exposure is another issue, but it stands to reason that our curiosity is raised when we witness an accident or hear about a violent crime or life-threatening natural disaster. This curiosity is not just about real events that actually happened; it also extends to dramatic depictions of such events.

But another important aspect of the attraction of scary programs and movies for children seems to come from the fact that they are usually action-packed. It has been argued, for example, that action is a more important component of what attracts children to violent programming than the threatening or injurious behavior itself (Potts, Huston, & Wright, 1986). Certainly, we do not see children flocking to programs about elderly people passing away quietly or disease victims in the final stages of their illness. Such stories cannot hold a candle to those involving shoot-'em-ups, dinosaur attacks, and hand-to-hand combat in terms of appeal.

The arousing nature of scary programs seems to be an important component of children's attraction to it. As Zillmann and Bryant (1994) have argued, viewers often use entertainment for mood management, to calm them when they are overstressed and stimulate them when they are bored. Children should be a particularly good audience for arousing materials because they have been observed to be relatively high in the sensation-seeking motive (Zuckerman, 1979). Moreover, sensation-seeking is positively associated with attraction to horror films among adolescents (e.g., Tamborini & Stiff, 1987).

Another reason that is often advanced for children's attraction to frightening programming is that it helps children confront their fears and learn to control them. Many children report that they enjoy the feeling of power they get when the good guy, or the character they empathize with, overcomes dangers and triumphs over the forces of evil. There is some research that suggests that the right kind of scary program can help reduce viewers' feelings of anxiety. In a study by Bryant, Carveth, and Brown (1981), for example, college students who took a six-weeks' heavy dose of action adventure programs featuring good triumphing over evil showed reductions in their feelings of anxiety and an increase in their interest in seeing more of such programs. Other students, who were exposed to violence without justice restoration, did not show these effects. In a more recent survey of parents (Cantor & Nathanson, 1997), children who had been frightened by something on television were said to be more interested than others in violent television programs in which good triumphs over evil, but not particularly interested in other types of violent programs.

Many programs designed for children incorporate the theme of anxiety reduction into their content on a regular basis. The most obvious and long-running example is a program that began in the late 1960s with the title of *Scooby Doo, Where Are You?* This animated program features teenagers who solve mysteries involving monsters, ghosts, mummies, and the like. The central characters always show extreme fear, but then help solve the mystery and show that things are never quite as scary as they seem. *Mister Rogers' Neighborhood* frequently deals with children's fears, with episodes ranging from anxiety about going down the bathtub drain, to fear of the Incredible Hulk. Finally, the current sensation, *Teletubbies*, features a vacuum cleaner as a pet. Research has shown that fear of vacuum cleaners is one of the most common fears of young preschoolers (Fraiberg, 1966). The casting of this common household appliance in a friendly, nonthreatening role may have been designed to help children overcome their fear of vacuum cleaners.

There is some evidence, then, that children may expose themselves to scary programs in which a threatening agent is overcome because they find such stories reassuring. It is important to note, however, that not all stories end happily, and many that do show the triumph of good over evil will not necessarily be reassuring. Often, a drama ends happily by luck and the threatened protagonists are saved just in the nick of time. Also, much more story time is typically spent on the dramatization of danger than on the protective or retaliatory measures that produce the reassuring outcome.

Although some children are attracted to scary themes, others are not. Boys, for example, say they like horror more than girls do, and they are less likely to report long-term emotional reactions as a result of exposure (e.g., Harrison & Cantor, 1999). There is also evidence that children who are more violent are more attracted to violent, scary themes (e.g., Atkin, Greenberg, Korzenny, & McDermott, 1979). In addition, exposure to real-life violence has been shown to be positively correlated with interest in violent programs. A study in inner-city Milwaukee (Bruce, 1995), for example, showed that children who had been exposed to high levels of community violence were more interested than their peers in violent programming. Interestingly, the more these adolescents liked to view violence, the less interested they were in seeing justice restored. These children were apparently interested in violence for violence's sake and were not viewing these programs in search of anxiety reduction. In contrast, other adolescents in the same sample were not attracted to these programs. Those respondents who were experiencing acute anxiety symptoms from the violence in their environment were the least interested in viewing violent shows and the most upset when they did view them. Acute anxiety symptoms were also positively associated with saying that viewing violent television programming made them think about things in their own lives.

These data show that there are important individual differences in children's preferences for certain types of entertainment and that exposure to scary themes may serve various functions for different children.

CONCLUDING COMMENT

A basic assumption in modern theories of media effects is that children are active and motivated explorers of what they see on television. The research reviewed in this chapter suggests that even very young children are able to actively screen television content for attractiveness and understandability and make an effort to interpret the content in their own terms (Collins, 1981; Valkenburg & van der Voort, 1994). It also suggests that boys and girls in various age groups have very specific preferences for different types of entertainment, which confirms the assumption that gender and cognitive developmental level are important determinants of children's likes and dislikes of entertainment programs.

Another fundamental assumption of current media theories is that any effect of television entertainment on children is enhanced, channeled, or mitigated by what the child viewer makes of it (Clifford et al., 1995; Valkenburg & Janssen, 1999). So in order to understand television's effects on children, it is important to gain insights into the different motivations for children's selective exposure to entertainment. There is a need for further research, especially more controlled studies in which various aspects of programs are systematically manipulated, in order to understand more fully the elements of programs that attract children, and the functions that different types of content serve in children's lives.

REFERENCES

Acuff, D. S. (1997). *What kids buy and why: The psychology of marketing to kids*. New York: The Free Press.

Anderson, D. R., & Burns, J. (1991). Paying attention to television. In J. Bryant & D. Zillmann (Eds.), *Responding to the screen: Reception and reaction processes* (pp. 3–25). Hillsdale, NJ: Lawrence Erlbaum Associates.

Atkin, C., Greenberg, B. S., Korzenny, F., & McDermott, S. (1979). Selective exposure to televised violence. *Journal of Broadcasting, 23*(1), 5–13.

Bartsch, K., & Wellman, H. M. (1995). *Children talk about the mind*. New York: Oxford University Press.

Berselli, B. (1998, March 2). Are girlish computer games growing up? *Herald Tribune*, p. 11.

Bruce, L. (1995). *At the intersection of real-life and television violence: Emotional effects, cognitive effects, and the interpretive activities of children*. Unpublished doctoral dissertation, University of Wisconsin, Madison.

Bruner, J. S. (1966). On cognitive growth I & II. In J. S. Bruner, R. R. Oliver, & P. M. Greenfield (Eds.), *Studies in cognitive growth* (pp. 1–67). New York: Wiley.

Bryant, J., Carveth, R. A., & Brown, D. (1981). Television viewing and anxiety: An experimental investigation. *Journal of Communication, 32*, 109–119.

Cantor, J. (1998a). Children's attraction to violent television programming. In J. H. Goldstein (Ed.), *Why we watch: The attractions of violent entertainment* (pp. 88–115). New York: Oxford University Press.

Cantor, J. (1998b). *"Mommy, I'm scared": How TV and movies frighten children and what we can do to protect them*. San Diego, CA: Harcourt Brace.

Cantor, J., & Nathanson, A. I. (1997). Predictors of children's interest in violent television programs. *Journal of Broadcasting & Electronic Media, 41*, 155–167.

Cantor, J., & Sparks, G. G. (1984). Children's fear responses to mass media: Testing some Piagetian predictions. *Journal of Communication, 34* (2), 90–103.

Clifford, B. R., Gunter, B., & McAleer, J. (1995). *Television and children*. Hillsdale, NJ: Lawrence Erlbaum Associates.

Collins, W. A. (1981). Schemata for understanding television. In H. Kelly & H. Gardner (Eds.), Viewing children through television. *New Directions in Child Development, 13*, 31–45.

Collins-Standley, T., Gan, S., Yu, H. J., & Zillmann, D. (1996). Choice of romantic, violent, and scary fairy-tale books by preschool girls and boys. *Child Study Journal, 26*(4), 279–301.

Cupitt, M., Jenkinson, D., Ungerer, J., & Waters, B. (1998). *Infants and television*. Sydney, Australia: Australian Broadcasting Authority.

De Vries, R. (1969). Constancy of generic identity in the years three to six. *Monographs of the Society for Research in Child Development, 34*(3, Serial No. 127).

Dorr, A. (1983). No shortcuts to judging reality. In J. Bryant & D. R. Anderson (Eds.), *Children's understanding of television: Research on attention and comprehension* (pp. 199–220). New York: Academic Press.

Durkin, K. (1997). *Developmental social psychology: From infancy to old age*. Malden, MA: Blackwell.

Fagot, B. I. (1994). Peer relations and the development of competence in boys and girls. *New Directions in Child Development, 65*, 53–65.

von Feilitzen, C., & Linne, O. (1975). Identifying with television characters. *Journal of Communication, 25*(4), 51–55.

Fernald, A. (1985). Four-month-old infants prefer to listen to motherese. *Infant Behavior and Development, 8*, 181–196.

Fernie, D. E. (1981). Ordinary and extraordinary people: Children's understanding of television and real life models. *New Directions in Child Development, 13*, 47–58.

Flavell, J. H. (1963). *The developmental psychology of Jean Piaget*. New York: Van Nostrand.

Flavell, J. H., Miller, P., & Miller, S. A. (1993). *Cognitive development*. Englewood Cliffs, NJ: Prentice Hall.

Fraiberg, S. (1966). *The magic years*. New York: Charles Scribner's Sons.

Goldstein, J. H. (Ed.). (1998). *Why we watch: The attractions of violent entertainment*. New York: Oxford University Press.

Guber, S. S., & Berry, J. (1993). *Marketing to and through kids*. New York: McGraw-Hill.

Gunter, B., McAleer, J., & Clifford, B. R. (1991). *Children's view about television*. Aldershot, England: Avebury Academic Publishing Group.

Harrison, K., & Cantor, J. (1999). Tales from the screen: Enduring fright reactions to scary media. *Media Psychology, 1*(2), 97–116.

Heeter, C. (1988). Gender differences in viewing styles. In C. Heeter & B. Greenberg (Eds.), *Cable-viewing*. Norwood, NJ: Ablex.

Himmelweit, H. T., Oppenheim, A. N., & Vince, P. (1958). *Television and the child: An empirical study of the effect of television on the young*. London: Oxford University Press.

Hoffner, C. (1996). Children's wishful identification and parasocial interaction with favorite television characters. *Journal of Broadcasting & Electronic Media, 40*, 389–402.

Hoffner, C., & Cantor, J. (1985). Developmental differences in children's responses to a television character's appearance and behavior. *Developmental Psychology, 21*, 1065–1074.

Hoffner, C., & Cantor, J. (1991). Perceiving and responding to mass media characters. In J. Bryant & D. Zillmann (Eds.), *Responding to the screen: Reception and reaction processes*. Hillsdale, NJ: Lawrence Erlbaum Associates.

Howard, S. (1998). Unbalanced minds? Children thinking about television. In S. Howard (Ed.), *Wired-up: Young people and the electronic media*. London: UCL Press.

Huston, A. C. (1983). Sex-typing. In P. H. Mussen (Ed.), *Handbook of child psychology: Vol 4. Socialization, personality, and social development.* New York: Wiley.

Jaglom, L. M., & Gardner, H. (1981). The preschool viewer as anthropologist. *New Directions in Child Development, 13,* 9–29.

James, N. C., & McCain, T. A. (1982). Television games preschool children play: Patterns, themes and uses. *Journal of Broadcasting, 26,* 783–800.

LaFrance, M. & Banaji, M. (1992). Toward a reconsideration of the gender-emotion relationship. In M. S. Clark (Ed.), *Review of personality and social psychology: Emotion and social behavior* (pp. 178–201). Newbury Park, CA: Sage.

Leaper, C. (1994). Exploring the consequences of gender segregation on social relationships. *New Directions in Child Development, 65,* 67–85.

Lemish, D. (1987). Viewers in diapers: The early development of television viewing. In T. R. Lindlof (Ed.), *Natural audiences: Qualitative research of media uses and effects* (pp. 33–57). Norwood, NJ: Ablex.

Maccoby, E. E. (1990). Gender and relationships: A developmental account. *American Psychologist, 45,* 513–520.

Maccoby, E. E. (1994). Commentary: Gender segregation in childhood. *New Directions in Child Development, 65,* 88–97.

Martin, C. L. (1994). Cognitive influences on the development and maintenance of gender segregation. *New Directions in Child Development, 65,* 35–51.

Matteson, D. R. (1975). *Adolescence today: Sex roles and the search for identity.* Homewood, IL: Dorsey.

Mielke, K. W. (1983). Formative research on appeal and comprehension in 3-2-1 contact. In J. Bryant & D. Anderson (Eds.), *Children's understanding of television: Research on attention and comprehension* (pp. 241–263).

Morrison, P., & Gardner, H. (1978). Dragons and dinosaurs: The child's capacity to differentiate fantasy from reality. *Child Development, 49,* 642–648.

Noble, G. (1975). *Children in front of the small screen.* Beverly Hills, CA: Sage.

Palmer, P. (1986). *The lively audience.* Sydney, Australia: Allen & Unwin.

Piaget, J. (1954). *The construction of reality in the child.* New York: Basic Books.

Potts, R., Huston, A. C., & Wright, J. C. (1986). The effects of television form and violent content on boys' attention and social behavior. *Journal of Experimental Child Psychology, 41,* 1–17.

Rosengren, K. E., & Windahl, S. (1989). *Media matter: TV use in childhood and adolescence.* Norwood, NJ: Ablex.

Sanger, J., Willson, J. Davies, B., & Whittaker, R. (1997). *Young children, videos and computer games: Issues for teachers and parents.* London: The Falmer Press.

Selman, R. L. (1980). *The growth of interpersonal understanding.* New York: Academic Press.

Sheldon, L., & Loncar, M. (1996). *Kids talk TV: "Super wicked" or "dum."* Sydney, Australia: Australian Broadcasting Authority.

Sheldon, L., Ramsay, G., & Loncar, M. (1994). *"Cool" or "gross": Children's attitudes to violence, kissing and swearing on television.* Sydney, Australia: Australian Broadcasting Authority.

Siegler, R. S. (1991). *Children's thinking* (2nd ed.). Englewood Cliffs, NJ: Prentice Hall.

Sparks, G. G., & Cantor, J. (1986). Developmental differences in fright responses to a television program depicting a character transformation. *Journal of Broadcasting & Electronic Media, 30,* 309–323.

Tamborini, R., & Stiff, J. (1987). Predictors of horror film attendance and appeal: An analysis of the audience for frightening films. *Communication Research, 14* (4), 415–436.

Valkenburg, P. M. (1999). *Vierkante Ogen: Opgroeien met TV & PC* [Square eyes: Growing up with TV & PC]. Amsterdam: Rainbow Pocketboeken.

Valkenburg, P. M., & Janssen, S. (1999). What do children value in entertainment programs? A cross-cultural investigation. *Journal of Communication, 49,* 3–21.

Valkenburg, P. M., & van der Voort, T. H. A. (1994). The influence of television on daydreaming and creative imagination: A review of research. *Psychological Bulletin, 116,* 316–339.

Wakshlag, J. J., Reitz, R. J., & Zillmann, D. (1982). Selective exposure to and acquisition of information from educational television programs as a function of appeal and tempo of background music. *Journal of Educational Psychology, 74,* 666–677.

Wright, J. C., & Huston, A. C. (1981). Children's understanding of the forms of television. *New Directions in Child Development, 13,* 73–88.

Zillmann, D., & Bryant, J. (1983). Uses and effects of humor in educational ventures. In P. E. McGhee & J. H. Goldstein (Eds.), *Handbook of humor research: Vol. 2. Applied studies* (pp. 173–193). New York: Springer-Verlag.

Zillmann, D., & Bryant, J. (1994). Entertainment as media effect. In J. Bryant & D. Zillmann (Eds.), *Media effects* (pp. 437–462). Hillsdale, NJ: Lawrence Erlbaum Associates.

Zuckerman, M. (1979). *Sensation seeking: Beyond the optimal level of arousal.* New York: Wiley.

Sports on the Screen

Jennings Bryant
University of Alabama

Arthur A. Raney
Florida State University

This chapter addresses the enjoyment of sports presented on television. Televised sports permeate modern life from the family room to the newsroom and boardroom. Nevertheless, relatively few scientific researchers have applied either the binoculars of their theories or the crucibles of their methods in attempting to explain entertainment dimensions of this intriguing social phenomenon (Wenner, 1998b).

We begin with a brief note on participating in sports versus watching sports, with viewing initially considered both as physical presence at sporting events (nonmediated spectatorship) and as watching sports on the screen (mediated spectatorship). Evidence for the prevalence of mediated sports spectatorship in modern society is presented next. Then for the bulk of the chapter we address the enjoyment audiences apparently derive from watching a plethora of sports contests on the screen. We propose numerous factors that potentially contribute to the enjoyment of watching sports contests, and we present research findings pertinent to these proposals.

PARTICIPATION VERSUS SPECTATORSHIP

Although relatively little systematic research has been conducted on the enjoyment of watching sports, considerable research has examined active participation in sports (e.g., Goldstein, 1989). Moreover, whereas the value of sports spectatorship is frequently questioned, the widely presumed positive value of actively participating in athletic events is seldom challenged. Zillmann, Bryant, and Sapolsky (1989) identified six common claims for the benefits of sports participation:

1. To promote physical fitness and health
2. To produce mental benefits of fitness
3. To help control aggressive behavior
4. For recreational value (e.g., relaxing tensions, relief from boredom)
5. To teach a sense of fairness
6. To serve the control of unacceptable impulsive emotional behaviors

The authors indicated that some of these claims lacked convincing supportive evidence; nevertheless, taken together they are perceived to make a compelling case that vigorous activity through sports promotes physical fitness and good bodily health. Indeed, this has become a prominent social mantra of our age.

The situation is markedly different for sports spectatorship. Many popular discussions of sports spectatorship amount to moral condemnations of watching. In an early paper that seemingly set the stage for generations of negativity, Howard (1912) described participation in sports as good, spectatorship as bad, and partisan spectatorship as pure evil. Howard noted that involvement in play excites joyous emotions, and these pleasurable emotions build up energy and restore the "capacity for straight thinking" (p. 42) and productive human behavior. On the other hand, the "mob-mind of the athletic spectator" succumbs to "the elemental gaming and struggle-instinct of the human animal" (p. 43). This produces harmful emotions, which are said to tear down and diminish energy and undermine productive human behavior. Howard unabashedly condemned the watching of sports in religious terms: "Let the apostle of social righteousness break into Satan's monopoly!" (p. 41).

Several later commentators only slightly softened Howard's rhetoric of righteous indignation, similarly drawing distinctions between viewing sports and doing sports in ways that clearly relegate spectatorship to lower rungs on the ladder of social behaviors. For example, Stone (1958) identified spectatorship as a distinguishing characteristic of inferior cultures. He made a contrast common to those who report on the origins of organized sports in antiquity: Ancient Greece was seen as a superior culture of play (participation) and glory; in contrast, ancient Rome was a decadent culture of display (spectatorship) and vainglory. For Stone, play or participation in sports, as in the early Olympic Games, ennobled the players. The spectacle, in contrast, was said to be "inherently immoral and debasing" (p. 262). For this author, the spectator was said to forge inordinate demands for sensational play, thereby creating or enhancing demand for the spectacle. Stone noted that spectators should be viewed "as an agent of destruction as far as the dignity of sport is concerned" (p. 262).

Beisser (1967) took a similar stand. After identifying ancient Rome as a culture that suffered a precipitant decline due to its devotion to sports spectacles, Beisser added that "the United States is the second great nation in history to spend great amounts of time and resources in elaborately producing spectator sports" (pp. 13–14). Obviously some scholars think that a culture's devotion to viewing sports is a major step on the road to perdition.

For the sake of historical accuracy, it should be noted that some recent sports scholars have attempted to set the record straight regarding the alleged purity of the Olympians of ancient Greece as contrasted with the alleged barbarism of sports in the Roman Empire during its period of decline. For example, Guttmann (1998) has noted that " 'Olympian' detachment and disinterested curiosity were no more evident at Olympia than on the plains of Ilium" (p. 8). Guttmann also addressed the presumed absence of partisan spectatorship (i.e., "rooting") in ancient Greece—that "pure evil" that Howard (1912) claimed to be missing from early Olympian events. Guttmann (1998) noted that each Greek *polis* honored its winners with statues, odes, and material awards; that the spectators were closely linked with the athletes from their community; and that the spectators were "intensely partisan" (p. 12). This is in line with Finley and Pleket's (1976) contention that the Greek crowds for the early Olympics were "as partisan, as volatile, and as excitable as at any other period of time" (p. 57).

Guttmann (1998) also noted that whatever minimal decorum had been preserved at Olympia clearly had disappeared by the time of the chariot races in Hellenistic Alexandria. At least one commentator of that time, Dio Chrysostom, condemned the behavior of the ancient Greek race fans in terms that are highly similar to those used to decry soccer hooligans and eremitic wrestling fans today:

> When they enter the stadium, it is as though they had found a cache of drugs; they forget themselves completely, and shamelessly say and do the first thing that occurs to them. . . . At the games you are under the influence of some maniacal drug; it is as if you could not watch the proceedings in a civilized fashion. . . . When you enter the stadium, who could describe the yells and uproar, the frenzy, the switches of color and expression in your faces, and all the curses you give vent to? (Harris, 1976, p. 89)

Ironically, many of the apologias offered in defense of sports spectatorship have relied heavily if not exclusively on the alleged cathartic benefit of watching aggressive sporting events. In this view, watching combatants engage in violent sports serves to purge the spectators of any hostile predispositions through vicarious participation in the vigorous and aggressive sports competition. Roots of the catharsis argument run from Aristotle through Freud to modern psychology, but the most vocal proponent of the cathartic argument as applied to sports spectatorship has been Lorenz (1963). He has argued that spectators' vicarious participation in sports competition, especially in aggressive play that shares the general features of ritualized combat, is a sufficient condition for catharsis to occur. Obviously, if Lorenz's arguments hold true, watching violent sporting events should provide valuable psychological and social functions. It should make "the violent sports spectacle a valuable control mechanism for violence in society. The rougher, the better" (Zillmann et al., 1989, p. 248). "According to this line of reasoning, the more violent the action in a sports contest, the greater the pleasure that should result from the experience of relief" (Bryant, Zillmann, & Raney, 1998, p. 259). Unfortunately for Lorenz and his followers, the catharsis argument is beset with numerous conceptual difficulties and is refuted by a wealth of nonsupportive empirical evidence (e.g., Baron & Richardson, 1994).

FROM THE ARENA TO THE SCREEN

Audience Size

Prior to the modern electronic era of *Super Spectator and the Electric Lilliputians* (Johnson, 1971), the emphasis in sports was on the players and those spectators who attended their games. When compared with the size of the audiences for televised sporting events, relatively few spectators saw these athletes play their games. In fact, the size of the audiences for nonmediated sports at the time of the development of electronic media, and even today, typically was not much larger than the audiences for the sports spectacles of the Roman Empire. As Bryant et al. (1998) noted, the Roman blood sports were "super spectacles in terms of attendance, even by today's standards for non-televised sporting events" (pp. 256–257). Rome's Coliseum accommodated at least 40,000 spectators, and the largest Roman racetrack could host crowds of approximately 250,000 (Harris, 1976).

Today, of course, because of the vast number of competitive sporting events played at the high school, collegiate, and professional levels, the cumulative live attendance at team athletic contests is enormous. Without question, attending sporting events is a major pastime in the United States and much of the remainder of the world. For example, each year in the United States alone, more than 200 million spectators attend college and professional football games (Bryant et al., 1998). Nevertheless, the numbers for live attendance pale in comparison with the size of audiences for televised sporting events.

A recent example illustrates this phenomenon rather clearly. The 1999 Bowl Championship Series (BCS) title game of the 1998 NCAA football season (United States) was the Fiesta Bowl. This BCS game yielded an undisputed collegiate football champion—the University of Tennessee. It also yields a powerful statement for the place of television in modern sports. By our count, approximately 70 Tennessee and Florida State athletes got to play in the game.[1] In contrast, a Fiesta Bowl record 80,470 fans attended the game. In even more marked contrast, close to 17 million television households tuned into the prime time broadcast, yielding a 17.2 national Nielsen rating (Corbett, 1999). If these viewership figures are converted from household data to numbers of viewers,[2] and if estimates of viewership in bars, hotel rooms, airports, lounges, dorms, fraternity and sorority

---

[1]We watched the game on television and replayed a videotaped version of the telecast several times; however, because of selective camera coverage and commentary, we undoubtedly missed some players.

[2]In 1998, the number of persons per television household was 2.6 (Nielsen Media Research, 1998). Of course, not all of these household members watch football games. On the other hand, during championship games, household-based football parties are common, yielding a far larger number of household viewers than usual.

houses, and the like are added,[3] a conservative estimate of 30 million "Super Spectators" watched the 1999 Fiesta Bowl. We had hoped to illustrate these differences graphically, but the magnitude of the contrast defies the graphic capabilities of our statistical software. One way to look at the comparison between stadium versus television viewership, however, is to note that Sun Devil Stadium would have to be filled more than 372 times if the television audience was to be accommodated. In other words, a sold-out Fiesta Bowl game would have to be played every day for more than a year if the television audience were to fit into the stadium.

Of course, the audience for the telecast of the BCS championship game is relatively small when compared to viewership of the worldwide audiences for the Super Bowl, the Olympic Games, or the World Cup, which often attract more than 100 million, and sometimes more than a billion (Real, 1998), television spectators. The following catechism of statistics on viewership for sports on television provides a better-rounded profile of the magnitude of viewership for televised sports and its impact.

- Five of the Top 10 rated U.S. television programs of all time are sporting events (Super Bowl XVI, Super Bowl XVII, XVII Winter Olympics, Super Bowl XX, and Super Bowl XII; Nielsen Media Research, 1998).
- Only the final episode of M*A*S*H had more households tuned in than did the telecast of the ice-skating duel between Nancy Kerrigan and Tonya Harding at the 1994 Winter Olympics (Nielsen Media Research, 1998).
- More than one third of all programming on broadcast network television is devoted to sports events (Nielsen Media Research, 1998).
- During 1996, more than $4.75 billion was spent on sports advertising on television (Nielsen Media Research, 1998).
- The advertising rate for the 1999 Super Bowl was $1.6 million per 30-second ad. All advertising availability was sold weeks prior to the contest (Record ad revenue for Super Bowl, 1999).
- Of the six top-rated basic cable networks in prime time during the second quarter of 1997, only one did not regularly feature sports programming (Nielsen Media Research, 1998).
- For the week of November 30–December 6, 1998, all 10 of the top-rated basic cable shows were sportscasts. Five of those programs were telecasts of professional wrestling (Cable ratings, 1998).
- International viewership of U.S. sports has increased dramatically of late. Through ESPN International, telecasts of U.S. sports league play routinely reach nearly 160 million viewers in more than 10 countries (Pursell, 1998).

---

[3]A 1994 study conducted by Nielsen Media Research found that viewing of sports television outside of households was substantial. For example, for *ABC Monday Night Football*, an additional 930,000 adult men and 200,000 adult women 18+ were tuned in outside of households during an average minute of that sports telecast. Much "outside household" viewing took place in colleges, hotels, motels, restaurants, and bars (Nielsen Media Research, 1998).

Representative national surveys have consistently confirmed the popularity of sports spectatorship. Recent surveys have revealed that 73% of respondents either were "very interested" or "fairly interested" in watching sports (Lieberman, 1991; Madrigal, 1995). Nearly 50% of adults said they were watching "much more" or "somewhat more" sports on television now than in the past. Respondents also reported that if key sporting events were only available on pay-per-view, they would watch: 56.3% said they would pay to watch the Super Bowl; 49.3% said they would pay to watch the World Series. Moreover, of all adults surveyed, 70.8% said they watched 3 or more hours of sports on television each week throughout the year, and 83.1% said they followed sports daily through television, newspapers, or radio (*USA Today* Polls, 1999).

Pervasiveness of Sports Programming

Two other aspects of sports television should be mentioned briefly in order to more accurately profile the topic. Up to this point we have focused on viewership, but "audience size is but one index of the ascendancy of sports on television. The pervasiveness of sports programming on television is another index" (Bryant et al., 1998, p. 258). In 1960, the three major networks broadcast approximately 300 hours of sports programming (Lardner, 1982). By 1988, sports programming by the major broadcast networks had increased 500% to more than 1,800 hours (Madrigal, 1995). Nowadays, with 24-hour-a-day sports channels in abundance, approximately 7,000 hours of sports programming is on cable and broadcasting (Bryant et al., 1998; Eastman & Meyer, 1989). And that figure does not even count sports segments on local newscasts, cable and broadcast station coverage of local sports contests, and many other manifestations of the modern world of *MediaSport* (Wenner, 1998a). Unfortunately, as can be seen from Fig. 9.1, which profiles the Nielsen ratings of telecast coverage of professional championship play in three sports from 1980 through 1997, increased coverage does not translate into more viewership of specific events (i.e., to higher ratings and shares). Instead, the plethora of sports programming has contributed to the fragmentation of audiences.

The Selling Out of Sports by Television

The second additional dimension of sports television that is too blatant to ignore takes place both on the screen and behind the scenes. This is the increasing commercialization of televised sports. As Real (1998) noted, "The world of sports in the age of mass media has been transformed from nineteenth century amateur recreational participation to late twentieth century spectator-centered technology and business" (p. 18). The proliferation of sports coverage in the business sections of newspapers or on financial television networks is one marker of this commercialization. The fact that it is almost impossible to avoid corporate logos or product advertising in the background of any wide-angle camera shot of every sportscast is another. Sponsored replays or sponsored scoreboards seem omnipresent during televised sporting events. Add in the constantly increasing attention that is paid to salaries, strikes, and lockouts in professional sports by sports and news reporters. Factor in the focus on the salary packages and athletic shoe contracts of college— and in some instances, high school—coaches, and you have the mega-business off-spring of the marriage of sports and television. Commerce has long been part of the infrastructure of sports television. Of late, however, the commercial skeleton has become the all-too-obtrusive epidermis of sports on the screen. Its obtrusiveness calls into question the treatment of televised sports as *Sports, Games, and Play* (Goldstein, 1989). Many years ago, the notorious sportscaster Howard Cosell bragged, "We make sports entertaining." How prophetic he was. This New World of sports on the screen increasingly seems to be just another part of the entertainment business. Although the following claim goes beyond the empirical evidence presented in this chapter, a key question for future research seems to be: How does this affect spectators' enjoyment of televised sports contests?

THEORIES OF SPECTATORS' ENJOYMENT OF SPORTS ON THE SCREEN

The normative findings and trends we have reviewed have confirmed that watching sports on television is a prominent contemporary social phenomenon. What accounts for this social trend? Why are denizens of modern society willing to spend so much time sitting in front of screens large and small, watching grown (often overgrown) men and women throw, pass, kick, shoot, or dribble an object on grass, hardwood, or ice? Why do we gather around our electronic fires to watch others of our species run around in circles, jump over objects of various sizes and shapes, speed down hills, or engage in other related displays of physical prowess or reckless abandon? What factors help explain the widespread appeal of televised sports?

The relatively few social scientists who have devoted attention to these social phenomena have identified several factors that appear to be critical to spectators' enjoyment of televised sports contests. The most elementary of these factors seem to be:

1. Viewers' affective relationships to the players or teams involved in the contest;
2. The favorableness of the outcome of the contest to the spectator;
3. The amount of conflict and drama inherent in the contest or added to the sporting event by the sportscasting or production team;
4. The amount of suspense the contest has and how that suspense is resolved; and
5. The degree of novelty, riskiness, and effectiveness of play.

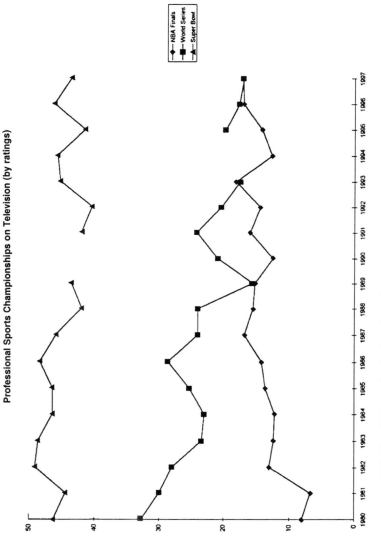

FIG. 9.1a   Nielsen national ratings for professional sports championships on television from 1980 to 1997. *Note:* Missing data are from seasons in which no championship games were played because of strikes.

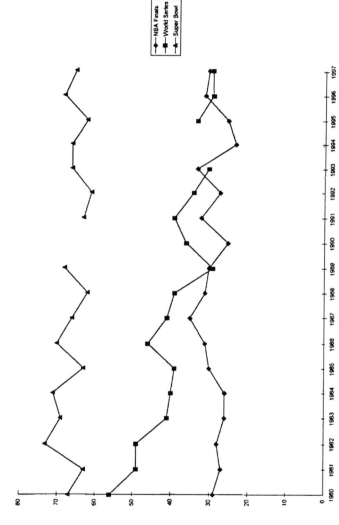

FIG. 9.1b   Nielsen national shares for professional sports championships on television from 1980 to 1997. *Note:* Missing data are from seasons in which no championship games were played because of strikes.

161

In addition, recent research has revealed gender differences that relate to several of the previous factors.

Disposition Theory of Sportsfanship and the Importance of Outcomes

The disposition theory of entertainment has been detailed elsewhere and has been summarized in two propositions:

1. Enjoyment derived from witnessing the success and victory of a competing party increases with positive sentiments and decreases with negative sentiments toward that party.
2. Enjoyment derived from witnessing the failure and defeat of a competing party increases with negative sentiments and decreases with positive sentiments toward that party. (Zillmann et al., 1989)

Several investigations conducted across a range of entertainment genres have provided strong support for these propositions. However, "the dispositional mechanics of enjoyment are most obvious in sports spectatorship" (Zillmann & Bryant, 1994, p. 450). Sportsfans are habitual "rooters." They have players and teams that they love, and they have players and teams that they hate (and love to hate). The affiliation with one's favorite team historically has been displayed by proudly wearing team colors (e.g., Cialdini et al., 1976). Today, team colors alone are not enough. Today's ardent sportsfan adds team and player jerseys, team hats of all shapes and colors, face and body paint, and weird but clearly identifiable costumes or apparel (e.g., cheeseheads, elephant trunks). These symbols clearly mark one not only as a fan, but as a diehard, true-blue, unadulterated, as-I-live-and-breathe, in-your-face fan.

Nirvana for these diehard fans is having one's favorite player or team not only defeat but humiliate and annihilate one's most hated player or team. Such is rooting; such are the manifestations of the disposition theory of sportsfanship circa the 21st century.

A wide variety of studies have supported disposition theory in team as well as in individual sports contests. Zillmann et al. (1989) presented the bulk of these investigations in considerable detail. We are less detailed and exhaustive in this chapter but include investigations that update their earlier report.

In the earliest study in this domain, research participants' preexisting affective dispositions toward professional football teams were assessed, and assignment to conditions were made so as to affect factorial variations in dispositions toward the two teams (negative, neutral, positive). The participants viewed a professional football game as it was telecast and rated their enjoyment of each play and the game overall. The findings supported the tenets of disposition theory of sports-fanship in that positive disposition toward a team enhanced spectators' enjoyment of successful offensive plays. The inverse prediction—disliking a team would produce disappointment when that team made successful offensive plays—was achieved only when the viewers disliked the offensive team intensely. Enjoyment of successful defensive plays was not as clearly differentiated by disposition toward the team, although the direction of the differentiation was in line with predictions from disposition theory (Zillmann et al., 1989).

An early study of men's high school basketball (Sapolsky, 1980) provided additional support for disposition theory. A basketball game between an all-White and an all-Black team was videotaped and edited to make (a) the White team defeat the Black team or (b) the Black team defeat the White team. White and Black male students who did not know these teams rated their enjoyment of the final series of baskets and their delight with, or disappointment about, the game's outcome. The results revealed that Black respondents, 89.6% of whom acknowledged rooting for the Black team, enjoyed baskets scored by Black players more than baskets scored by White players. Moreover, those Black respondents who saw the Black team win reported much more enjoyment for the game than did Black respondents who saw the White team win. The White respondents were not as dispositionally committed as Black respondents (only 45.7% of White respondents reported rooting for the White team), and the differentiations in enjoyment by race and outcome were not so strong for White respondents. Nonetheless, the results were in the direction predicted by disposition theory of sportsfanship.

A third early investigation of dispositional mediation of enjoyment in sports utilized nationalist loyalty to affect a dispositional variation to competing teams, and enjoyment of play in an Olympic basketball game was assessed (Zillmann et al., 1989). Male and female U.S. college students watched videotape of a portion of the championship game of the 1976 Olympics between the United States and Yugoslavia and rated their enjoyment of each play. Plays in which Yugoslav players scored were not enjoyed; in fact, female viewers reported mild disappointment when Yugoslavia scored. In contrast, substantial enjoyment was reported when the United States scored, supporting disposition theory of sportsfanship. A serendipitous element of this study yielded even stronger support for disposition theory. The investigation was conducted at Indiana University, and two very popular All-American members of the IU basketball team were members of the U.S. Olympic team. Baskets scored by these two players sparked more intense enjoyment from the IU students than baskets scored by other U.S. players. This finding further enhances our understanding of the sensitive nature of disposition in helping determine spectators' enjoyment of various dimensions of sports contests (Zillmann et al., 1989).

More recent investigations have not only supported but extended disposition theory of sportsfanship. Madrigal (1995) conducted a nonmediated spectatorship study of women's basketball, examining three possible predictors of enjoyment of play and overall fan satisfaction: expectancy disconfirmation, team identification (i.e., disposition), and quality of opponent. Disposition, assessed as team identification, "was found to have the dominant influence on affect, and enjoyment had the dominant influence on fan satisfaction" (p. 205).

Owens and Bryant (1998) studied the impact of hometown ("homer") announcers and color commentary on audience perceptions and enjoyment of a televised high school football game. As predicted by disposition theory, students from the home school found the game called by the homer announcer significantly more enjoyable and exciting than did all other respondents. The use of the hometown announcer, who used several different communication strategies to enhance the home fans' disposition to the team, also enhanced the fans' level of rooting for their team and their involvement with the game. As Pursell (1998) noted, "Sports is tribal. People want to root for the hometown guy" (p. 27).

Finally, an investigation by Hirt, Zillmann, Erickson, and Kennedy (1992) revealed that dispositional considerations transcend enjoyment per se. Enjoyment from seeing a beloved team win actually elevated the fans' self-esteem and enhanced their confidence in their physical, mental, and social skills. Moreover, despair from seeing their favorite team lose deflated their self-esteem and diminished confidence in their own abilities and talents. Findings from these three recent investigations indicate that disposition theory of sportsfanship is a particularly potent factor not only in enjoyment, but also in overall satisfaction and well-being. Clearly contemporary games are more than games.

DRAMA IN TELEVISED SPORTS

Social commentators have frequently likened athletic events to primitive conflict, often using war metaphors and referring to games as "battles" or "life-or-death struggles." The emphasis in such instances obviously is not on an artistic display of athletic skills, but on competitive conflict. As Guttmann (1996) noted, "Sports are, theoretically, a form of competition for which cooperation is a prerequisite. Opponents must agree to have a contest and to have it under certain mutually acceptable rules. Sports, however, can degenerate into bitter conflicts in which camaraderie justifies violence committed against a hated rival" (p. 147). Television seems to constantly push the "bitter conflict" button. Systematic research has shown that commentators use many dramatic statements and features to highlight actual or potential conflicts (Bryant, Comisky, & Zillmann, 1977). Consider how often play-by-play announcers and color commentators on radio and television use analogies such as "battles" to suggest the level of intensity of play, and how often they rely on hyperbole such as "the thrill of victory and the agony of defeat" to indicate how we should respond to the athletes who are giving their all.

The purpose of such "hype" appears to be to cause viewers to perceive the contests as high drama (see chap. 4, this volume). As Cheska (1902/1981) noted, "The elements of drama—participants, ritual, plot, production, symbolism, social message—are all brilliantly choreographed in the sports spectacular" (p. 376). This dramatizing of sports apparently works to infuse entertainment value into sports contests, because it elevates "deep play"—play in which the stakes are exceptionally high (Bentham, 1802/1931)—to high drama.

A few empirical investigations have tested the notion that special televisual features of sportscasts add elements of conflict to sports contests, which, in turn, enhances viewers' perceptions of high drama. Moreover, the research has further examined how this high drama leads to greater enjoyment for viewers. The initial study of the effects of sports commentary on audience perceptions and enjoyment was precipitated by a fortuitous observation (Comisky, Bryant, & Zillmann, 1977). While reviewing videotapes of ice hockey games for examples of varying degrees of violent interactions, the investigators found that the segments they had chosen as examples of aggressive behavior actually were not very extreme. After closer examination, they found that the play-by-play and color commentary had fooled them into thinking the game was more aggressive than the play warranted. Apparently the announcers had augmented normal action with dramatic commentary to keep the viewers' attention while adding little dramatic commentary to the genuinely violent hockey action. Taking their serendipitous discovery to the research laboratory, the investigators showed participants either the normal or rough play segments in one of two presentation styles: with commentary or without. Viewers' perceptions of play were affected by the commentary, much as the investigators' had been: Normal play coupled with commentary interpreting the play as aggressive was perceived as more intense and violent than rougher play with or without commentary. In terms of enjoyment, the condition yielding the highest entertainment scores was normal play with the commentary stressing rough action. Because the participants' perceptions of roughness of play were controlled primarily by the commentary, which, in turn, apparently affected enjoyment of the televised sporting event, Comisky et al. (1977) concluded, "these findings are suggestive of the great potential of sports commentary to alter the viewer's perception of the sports event" (p. 153).

Bryant, Brown, Comisky, and Zillmann (1982) more rigorously tested the proposition that dramatic conflict in sports enhances entertainment value in a study on the enjoyment of watching tennis. Three versions of a sportscast were prepared, using identical visual presentations of the tennis match in all of the versions. The sportscasters' commentary was different in each of the three versions, however, and created a differentiation in reported affective relationships between the two players. In one version, the players were described as the best of friends (amity), and anecdotes were offered to support the descriptive material. In a second version, the players were described as bitter enemies (enmity); again, anecdotes supported the description. The third version was a control version in which no affective relationship between the players was either stated or implied. Research participants viewed and evaluated one of the three versions of the televised tennis match. The results showed that the version presenting the opponents as bitter rivals was significantly more enjoyable, more exciting, more involving, and more interesting than the positive and neutral versions. Also, viewers' perceptions of the players as hostile, tense, and competitive was significantly greater for the enmity version.

A very different approach to examining dramatic aspects of sportscasts was taken by Bryant, Comisky, and Zillmann (1981). A number of plays from televised professional football games were presented to male and female research participants, who rated their enjoyment of each play. The plays differed widely in their degree of roughness/violence (low, intermediate, high). Enjoyment of plays was found to increase with the degree of their apparent roughness/violence. Some gender differences were found in that males enjoyed highly violent plays significantly more than females did.

An investigation by Sullivan (1991) provided further confirmation of the impact of dramatic commentary. In this study, commentary from a televised basketball game was manipulated to create three conditions (commentary stressing aggression, neutral commentary, no commentary). Respondent gender and degree of sportsfanship were also assessed. Once again, commentary was found to influence viewers' perceptions of sports violence, even among avid followers of sports. The author concluded, "Commentary can facilitate enjoyment of player violence" (p. 502).

In a state-of-the-art review of theory and research on "The Psychology of the Appeal of Portrayals of Violence," Zillmann (1998) noted that violence in sports is different from violence in other entertainment genres. In sports, "vigorous, potentially injurious behavior is a direct, if primitive, means to convince spectators of the combative disposition of competing athletes" (p. 209). In this sense, risky aggressive behavior provides a concrete indicator to viewers that the athletes are giving their all to defeat the enemy. Moreover, "to the extent . . . that athletic competition involves animosity that can erupt in hostile and injurious action, it creates tensions and distress capable of intensifying the enjoyment of play, especially when the play yields hoped-for outcomes" (Zillmann, 1998, p. 209).

THE ROLE OF SUSPENSE
IN SPORTS ENTERTAINMENT

Another element of drama that is useful in explaining the enjoyment of sports is suspense. In conceptualizing suspense, Zillmann (1991a) indicated that dramatic suspense is different from the popular notion that equates suspense with uncertainty. Instead, suspense is viewed as a high degree of perceived certainty of a negative outcome. The more the viewer anticipates this negative outcome, the higher the level of suspense that ensues. Disposition theory of sportsfanship is crucial to this explanation, because viewers have to care about this potential negative outcome if suspense is to reach optimal levels. A high degree of affinity for a team or player is perceived to work in concert with fear of a negative outcome for that player or team to create a high level of empathetic distress (Zillmann, 1980). This empathetic distress is said to create high levels of sympathetic excitation, which combine with the viewer's cognitive assessments of the outcome of the suspense to create either a dysphoric or euphoric emotional state. The hedonic valence of the resultant emotional state depends on the favorableness of the outcome for the player or team with whom the viewer is aligned. The mechanisms described are those of excitation-transfer theory (e.g., Zillmann, 1991b).

The earliest attempt to empirically examine the role of suspense in the enjoyment of sports contests (Sapolsky, 1980) failed to support predictions that degree of suspense in sports affects viewers' enjoyment. Two recent attempts to test these propositions have been more successful. Bryant, Rockwell, and Owens (1994) professionally videotaped a high school football game. The tapes were edited, and professional play-by-play and color commentary was added to create suspenseful and nonsuspenseful versions of the game. In addition to suspense, outcome of the game and gender of the viewer were examined. Viewing of the more suspenseful version of the sportscast made the game less boring and, more important, more enjoyable. Moreover, under conditions of high suspense, viewers reported being more anxious about the outcome, cared more whether their preferred team won, and liked the victorious team more than did viewers of the nonsuspenseful version of the sportscast.

A recent study of the enjoyment of men's basketball confirmed and clarified the role of suspense in facilitating enjoyment of sportscasts. Gan, Tuggle, Mitrook, Coussement, and Zillmann (1997) had respondents rate their enjoyment of one of the eight games of the 1995 NCAA basketball tournament as the games were played. The contests were subsequently categorized according to the point spread of the final score. It was assumed that the closer the final score, the more suspenseful the game. A four-way differentiation in suspense was affected: minimal (spread of 15 or more points), moderate (10–14 points), substantial (5–9 points), and extreme (1–4 points). For male viewers, the higher the suspense, the greater the enjoyment. For females, enjoyment increased as suspense increased up to the "substantial" level (point spread = 5–9); however, enjoyment by female viewers decreased substantially in the most suspenseful condition. The researchers suggest that the high level of suspense experienced during viewing might have resulted in distress, which could have been irritating to female viewers, thereby hampering their enjoyment. Another interpretation could be that women were unwilling to suffer high degrees of distress while viewing sports (Gantz & Wenner, 1995), and basically "tuned out" the game.

NOVEL, RISKY, AND EFFECTIVE PLAY

Aestheticians often emphasize the importance of novelty in sports, suggesting that uncommon play may facilitate enjoyment. Bense (1954, 1956, 1958), for example, developed a mathematical theory of aesthetics, which he applied to sports contests. He argued that the uncertainty of the outcome of sports contests contributes to spectators' excitement and, ultimately, to their enjoyment of the sporting event. Sportscasters seem to agree, because they often promote upcoming games based on the novelty and unpredictability of a coach's game plan (e.g., Bobby Bowden) or the unpredictable nature of a player's behavior (e.g., Deion Sanders). Moreover, the director frequently replays novel plays while the commentators rehash them, emphasizing their surprise value. Of course, novelty can also affect outcome of play, because defenses are set up to defend against the most likely offensive strategies and vice versa. Novel plays often catch opponents off guard and yield considerable success.

Zillmann et al. (1989) argued that uncertainty rationales can be applied to sports play in at least two different ways: "First, a play can be uncertainly-laden in that it is rarely used and thus comes unexpected when it comes. The more often a play is used, the more it is expected and the less it surprises" (pp. 271–172). In this rationale, plays featuring low frequency behaviors should be liked better than common plays. "Second, a play can be uncertainly-laden in that it entails a high risk of failure" (p. 272). When this risky play—the pass from the end zone in football, the behind-the-back pass in basketball—succeeds, enjoyment should be unbridled.

Zillmann et al. (1989) explored the relationship between novelty, riskiness, and enjoyment of play in a correlational study of the enjoyment of football. In addition to novelty and riskiness, effectiveness of play was an additional factor that was incorporated to determine the degree to which enjoyment of play is simply a function of a preferred team's progress toward the successful outcome of defeating an opponent. In addition to rating their enjoyment of a wide constellation of football plays, research participants estimated the average frequency of that type of play's successful or unsuccessful usage during a game (a measure of commonness and uncommonness, respectively), the failure percentage of such plays (a measure of riskiness), and the average gain of yardage per such plays (a measure of effectiveness). As can be seen from the left portion of Fig. 9.2, the enjoyment of play can be predicted with considerable accuracy on the basis of the risk of failure it entails, corroborating the proposition of proportionality between risk and enjoyment in the appreciation of plays successfully executed by a team the viewer likes. A more recent study (Sargent, Zillmann, & Weaver, 1998) supports the finding that riskiness of play is an important factor in the enjoyment of sportscasts.

The central portion of Fig. 9.2 shows that commonness of play (the frequency with which a play is used) essentially was unrelated to enjoyment. In other words, the frequency of the use of a play considered alone was a poor predictor of enjoyment.

Finally, the pattern of results displayed on the right side of Fig. 9.2 shows that a strong positive relationship exists between effectiveness of play and enjoyment. Obviously, fans love whatever plays work. The magic formula would appear to be: Always win; constantly find new ways to do so.

GENDER DIFFERENCES IN THE ENJOYMENT OF SPORTS ON TELEVISION

The aforementioned study by Sargent et al. (1998) was a macroanalytic investigation in which salient characteristics (e.g., violence, speed, risk, artistry) were evaluated in 25 different sports that are televised. Male and female respondents re-

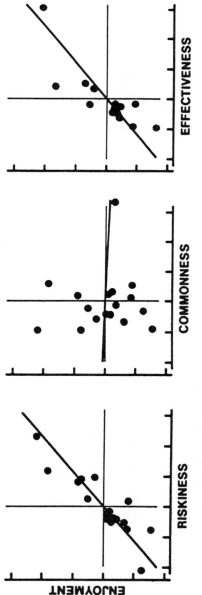

FIG 9.2 Enjoyment of offensive plays in football as a function of riskiness, commonness, and effectiveness of play. The data are presented in z-scores. For *riskiness*, $r = .90$, $\beta = .87$, variance accounted for = 76%; for *commonness*, $r = -.11$, $\beta = -.05$, variance accounted for = .2%; and for *effectiveness*, $r = .81$, $\beta = .81$, variance accounted for = 65%. The multiple-regression analysis involving all three predictor variables yielded $R = .91$. The data and graphs are from Zillmann et al. (1989); reprinted here with permission.

ported their enjoyment for all of these sporting events. As can be seen in Fig. 9.3, on some factors (e.g., team, animal), few or no gender differences in enjoyment were found. However, on other factors, gender differences were quite substantial. Factors that were enjoyed more by males than by females included violent play, risky play, speed, and mechanical elements (e.g., automobiles, bikes). In contrast, female viewers rated plays featuring artistic factors and more activity in general (e.g., gymnastics, figure skating) as more enjoyable than male viewers did.

Several other investigations into the enjoyment of watching sports contests have revealed intriguing gender differences (see also chap. 12, this volume). Two factors appear to consistently produce rather pronounced differences in enjoyment by males and females. The first is suspense. Both Bryant et al. (1994) and Gan et al. (1997) found that female viewers like the extremely suspenseful versions of televised sporting events less than the versions with moderate suspense. In contrast, for male viewers, the higher the level of suspense the better.

The second factor that consistently has produced gender differences in enjoyment is sports violence. Several investigations have produced results similar to those depicted in Fig. 9.4, which is derived from the findings of Bryant et al. (1981). In this investigation, male and female respondents rated their enjoyment of a wide variety of plays from televised professional football games, which varied in their degree of roughness and violence. Two findings from this investigation exemplify typical gender differences in viewers' enjoyment of sports con-

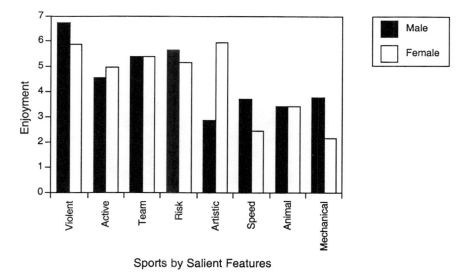

FIG 9.3   Enjoyment of sports differing in salient characteristics as a function of gender of respondent. The data were originally presented in Sargent et al. (1998). Presented here with permission.

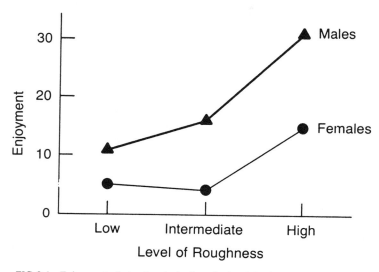

FIG 9.4 Enjoyment of play in televised professional football by roughness/violence of play. The data were originally presented in Bryant et al. (1981). Presented here with permission.

tests. First, as they did in this investigation, male viewers typically enjoy televised sports more than female viewers do. Obviously, tremendous individual differences lurk beneath the surface of these findings, but a "male bias" in watching and enjoying sports television has consistently been found. Secondly, whereas females may enjoy watching rough play in sports more than they enjoy seeing milder play, the magnitude of that difference is not as great for females as it is for males. In this investigation, the finding that violence and roughness facilitated enjoyment was statistically significant for male viewers only.

The surface has only been scratched as far as gender differences in the enjoyment of sportscasts is concerned. Wenner and Gantz (1998) pointed out a number of differences in the usage of sports by men and women, not just in viewing athletic contests per se, but in readership and viewership of news reports of sports contests, knowledge about sports, motives for watching sports, and the like. Historically, the decidedly masculine bias of sportscasting in America has been manifest in many realms. These areas include bias in terms of the gender of the announcers and color commentators, differential levels of coverage of the games of male versus female athletes, and bias in the use of stereotypically masculine themes and motifs in sportscasting. As the face of sports television undergoes subtle changes—with the WNBA, the newfound prominence of ice skating, the introduction of capable and respected female sportscasters, and the like—the nature of viewership and enjoyment is likely to evolve as well. As far as research in the arena of gender differences in the enjoyment of televised sports is concerned, undoubtedly the best is yet to be.

THE FUTURE OF SPORTS ON TELEVISION

The nature of television's presentation and coverage of sporting events has undergone dramatic shifts in recent years. The presence of 24-hour-a-day sports channels and the development of sports-news channels were early markers of sea changes in sports television. More recently, the introduction of specialized magazines and web sites derived from televised sports, the "discovery" of women's sports, the ascendancy of motor sports and wrestling, the "wars" over network contracts for sports coverage, and many other tremblings are visible manifestations of a ferment that is occurring in what has historically been one of the most tradition-bound genres of television. These dramatic changes all merit systematic study in their own right. They must also be studied as phenomena that may well alter the way the "Sovereign Consumer" of the information age uses and enjoys sports.

At one level or another, each of these shifts in sports television is a part of the larger picture of audience fragmentation—or the other side of the coin, audience segmentation. In other words, viewers for particular sporting events are becoming more authoritative "specialists" in the events in which they choose to participate as observers. For entertainment theory, this can be good. More entertaining sports productions can be delivered to relatively homogeneous segments of sportsfans by meeting their needs, interests, and aesthetic and content preferences more precisely. Ignoring at this point the foreboding issues of the economics of this equation, reaching smaller audiences more effectively should provide a wonderful opportunity for scholars to systematically study the evolution of "Super Spectator."

REFERENCES

Baron, R. A., & Richardson, D. R. (1994). *Human aggression* (2nd ed.). New York: Plenum.

Beisser, A. R. (1967). *The madness in sports: Psychosocial observations on sports.* New York: Appleton-Century-Crofts.

Bense, M. (1954). *Aesthetica: Metaphysische Beobachtungen am Schönen* [Aesthetics: Metaphysical observations on beauty]. Stuttgart, Germany: Deutsche Verlags-Anstalt.

Bense, M. (1956). *Ästhetische Information* [Aesthetic information]. Krefeld, Germany: Agis.

Bense, M. (1958). *Ästhetik und Zivilisation: Theorie der ästhetischen Kommunikation* [Aesthetics and civilization: Theory of aesthetic communication]. Krefeld, Germany: Agis.

Bentham, J. (1931). *The theory of legislation.* London: Kegan Paul. (Original work published 1802)

Bryant, J., Brown, D., Comisky, P. W., & Zillmann, D. (1982). Sports and spectators: Commentary and appreciation. *Journal of Communication, 32*(1), 109–119.

Bryant, J., Comisky, P., & Zillmann, D. (1977). Drama in sports commentary. *Journal of Communication, 27*(3), 140–149.

Bryant, J., Comisky, P. W., & Zillmann, D. (1981). The appeal of rough-and-tumble play in televised professional football. *Communication Quarterly, 29,* 256–262.

Bryant, J., Rockwell, S. C., & Owens, J. W. (1994). "Buzzer beaters" and "barn burners": The effects on enjoyment of watching the game go "down to the wire." *Journal of Sport & Social Issues, 18,* 326–339.

Bryant, J., Zillmann, D., & Raney, A. A. (1998). Violence and the enjoyment of media sports. In L. A. Wenner (Ed.), *MediaSport* (pp. 252–265). London: Routledge.

Cable ratings. (1998, December 14). *Electronic Media*, p. 36.

Cheska, A. T. (1981). Sports spectacular: The social ritual of power. In M. Hart & S. Birrell (Eds.), *Sports in the sociocultural process* (pp. 369–386). Dubuque, IA: Wm. C. Brown. (Original work published 1902)

Cialdini, R. B., Borden, R. J., Thorne, A., Walker, M. R., Freeman, S., & Sloan, L. R. (1976). Basking in reflected glory: Three (football) field studies. *Journal of Personality and Social Psychology, 34,* 366–375.

Comisky, P., Bryant, J., & Zillmann, D. (1977). Commentary as a substitute for action. *Journal of Communication, 27*(3), 150–153.

Corbett, P. (1999, January 10). An excess of Tostitos? *The Arizona Republic*, p. D1.

Eastman, S. T., & Meyer, T. P. (1989). Sports programming: Scheduling, costs, and competition. In L. W. Wenner (Ed.), *Media, sports, & society* (pp. 97–119). Newbury Park, CA: Sage.

Finley, M. L., & Pleket, H. W. (1976). *The Olympic Games.* New York: Viking.

Gan, S., Tuggle, C. A., Mitrook, M. A., Coussement, S. H., & Zillmann, D. (1997). The thrill of the close game: Who enjoys it and who doesn't? *Journal of Sport & Social Issues, 21,* 53–64.

Gantz, W., & Wenner, L. A. (1995). Fanship and the television sports viewing experience. *Sociology of Sport Journal, 12,* 56–74.

Goldstein, J. H. (1989). *Sports, games, and play: Social and psychological viewpoints*, 2nd ed. Hillsdale, NJ: Lawrence Erlbaum Associates.

Guttmann, A. (1996). *The erotic in sports.* New York: Columbia University Press.

Guttmann, A. (1998). The appeal of violent sports. In J. H. Goldstein (Ed.), *Why we watch: The attractions of violent entertainment* (pp. 7–26). New York: Oxford University Press.

Harris, H. A. (1976). *Green athletics and the Jews.* Cardiff: University of Wales Press.

Hirt, E. R., Zillmann, D., Erickson, G. A., & Kennedy, C. (1992). Costs and benefits of allegiance: Changes in fans' self-ascribed competencies after team victory versus defeat. *Journal of Personality and Social Psychology, 63,* 724–738.

Howard, G. E. (1912). Social psychology of the spectator. *American Journal of Sociology, 18,* 33–50.

Johnson, W. O., Jr. (1971). *Super spectator and the electric Lilliputians.* Boston: Little, Brown.

Lardner, R., Jr. (1982). An overview of network television sports. In M. Etzel & J. Gaski (Eds.), *Applying marketing technology to spectator sports* (pp. 201–220). South Bend, IN: University of Notre Dame Press.

Lieberman, S. (1991). The popular culture: Sports in America—a look at the avid sports fan. *The Public Perspective: A Roper Center Review of Public Opinion and Polling, 2*(6), 28–29.

Lorenz, K. (1963). Das sogenannte Böse: Zur Naturgeschichte der Aggression [The so-called evil: On the natural history of aggression]. Wien: Borotha-Schoeler.

Madrigal, R. (1995). Cognitive and affective determinants of fan satisfaction with sporting event attendance. *Journal of Leisure Research, 27,* 205–227.

Nielsen Media Research. (1998). *1998 report on television.* New York: Author.

Owens, J. W., & Bryant, J. (1998, July). *The effects of a hometown ("Homer") announcer and color commentator on audience perspectives and enjoyment of a sports contest.* Paper presented at the annual meeting of the International Communication Association, Jerusalem, Israel.

Pursell, C. (1998, June 29). Fields of competition: American pastimes going for o'seas gold. *Variety,* pp. 27, 30.

Real, M. R. (1998). MediaSport: Technology and the commodification of postmodern sport. In L. A. Wenner (Ed.), *MediaSport* (pp. 14–26). London: Routledge.

Record ad revenue for Super Bowl. (1999, January 20). *AP Sportswire*, p. 1.

Sapolsky, B. S. (1980). The effect of spectator disposition and suspense on the enjoyment of sport contests. *International Journal of Sport Psychology, 11*(1), 1–10.

Sargent, S. L., Zillmann, D., & Weaver, J. B. (1998). The gender gap in the enjoyment of televised sports. *Journal of Sport & Social Issues, 22,* 46–64.

Stone, G. P. (1958). American sports: Play and dis-play. In E. Larrabee & R. Meyersohn (Eds.), *Mass leisure* (pp. 253–264). Glencoe, IL: Free Press.

Sullivan, D. B. (1991). Commentary and viewer perception of player hostility: Adding punch to televised sport. *Journal of Broadcasting and Electronic Media, 35,* 487–504.

USA Today polls (1999). Public opinion polls of sports on television. (www.irss.unc.edu/CAT/search.fullrec.cgi.).

Wenner, L. A. (1998a). *MediaSport.* London: Routledge.

Wenner, L. A. (1998b). Playing the MediaSport game. In L. A. Wenner (Ed.), *MediaSport* (pp. 3–13). London: Routledge.

Wenner, L. A., & Gantz, W. (1998). Watching sports on television: Audience, experience, gender, fanship, and marriage. In L. A. Wenner (Ed.), *MediaSport* (pp. 233–251). London: Routledge.

Zillmann, D. (1980). Anatomy of suspense. In P. H. Tannenbaum (Ed.), *The entertainment functions of television* (pp. 133–163). Hillsdale, NJ: Lawrence Erlbaum Associates.

Zillmann, D. (1991a). The logic of suspense and mystery. In J. Bryant & D. Zillmann (Eds.), *Responding to the screen: Reception and reaction processes* (pp. 281–303). Hillsdale, NJ: Lawrence Erlbaum Associates.

Zillmann, D. (1991b). Television viewing and physiological arousal. In J. Bryant & D. Zillmann (Eds.), *Responding to the screen: Reception and reaction processes* (pp. 103–133). Hillsdale, NJ: Lawrence Erlbaum Associates.

Zillmann, D. (1998). The psychology of the appeal of portrayals of violence. In J. H. Goldstein (Ed.), *Why we watch: The attraction of violent entertainment* (pp. 179–211). New York: Oxford University Press.

Zillmann, D., & Bryant, J. (1994). Entertainment as media effect. In J. Bryant & D. Zillmann (Eds.), *Media effects: Advances in theory and research* (pp. 437–461). Hillsdale, NJ: Lawrence Erlbaum Associates.

Zillmann, D., Bryant, J., & Sapolsky, B. S. (1989). Enjoyment from sports spectatorship. In J. H. Goldstein (Ed.), *Sports, games, and play: Social and psychological viewpoints* (2nd ed., pp. 241–278). Hillsdale, NJ: Lawrence Erlbaum Associates.

Music and Music Videos

Christine H. Hansen
Ranald D. Hansen
Oakland University

This chapter explores the state of empirical knowledge of contemporary popular music. We begin with a discussion of the factors contributing to the appreciation of popular music and proceed to an exploration of music videos. From here, we progress to differences among currently popular music genres and their devotees, tracing social and personality correlates. Finally, we highlight the increasing body of research designed to demonstrate the effects of popular music on young people.

THE APPEAL OF POPULAR MUSIC
FOR ADOLESCENTS AND YOUNG ADULTS

Listening to popular music is one of the most preferred leisure activities reported by young people around the globe, particularly those living in westernized societies (Fitzgerald, Joseph, Hayes, & O'Regan, 1995; Wicke, 1985; Zillmann & Gan, 1997). During the 1960s and 1970s, most young people in the United States were listening to rock music emanating from the United States and Great Britain. It was only a matter of a few years, however, before large numbers of European adolescents were listening to the same (English language–based) popular music. There was a simultaneous rush toward "Americanization" by many European young people (Englis, Solomon, & Olofsson, 1993; Roe, 1985; Wicke, 1985).

An important trend in popular music began in the United States with the advent of Music Television (MTV) in 1981, playing music videos 24 hours a day. A smattering of American music videos began to appear around the world in the early 1980s, and some countries began to create music videos featuring their own popular performers. In 1987, MTV Europe was launched. In addition to spreading American musical taste around the globe through music videos, MTV Europe is a powerful vehicle for exporting American culture (Englis et al., 1993). Orman (1992) has argued, rather persuasively, that American popular music has even impacted recent global changes toward democracy and capitalism, such as the collapse of the Soviet Bloc:

> Some analysts have observed that the collapse of the Eastern European bloc countries, and indeed the collapse of the Soviet political economy itself, was not so much the failure of Marxist systems but rather the inability of these systems to deliver Big Macs, Levis, and rock music. Karl Marx in his political theory never anticipated the problem that "I WANT MY MTV" could create for decision-makers in socialist countries. (pp. 281–282)

What lies behind the tremendous appeal of contemporary popular music? First (and perhaps foremost), the music is pleasurable to the body, as well as the mind, of young people (Rowe, 1995). Despite vast differences in musical styles among contemporary musical genres, forms of contemporary popular music are physiologically arousing, and all induce varied, but generally pleasurable, mood states in listeners (Wells, 1990). Moreover, listening to one's preferred music can reduce unpleasant feelings of anxiety (Peretti & Zweifel, 1983), lift the spirits (Wells, 1990) or get someone pleasantly "pumped up" (Wells, 1990).

Listening to popular music also has psychosocial benefits. For adolescents, music may play a role in the development of both self- and group-identity (Christenson, DeBenedittis, & Lindlof, 1985). Popular music is also an important component of teen culture, influencing the choice of peer groups (Frith, 1978) and friends (Ball, 1981). Even though young people may be from different social strata, a shared music preference can bring them into the same cultural subgroup (Denisoff & Levine, 1972), and being part of a musical subculture can ease the transition away from parents toward peers (Zillmann & Gan, 1987). Furthermore, once a music preference is established in young adulthood, it appears to predominate throughout a person's life (Holbrook & Schindler, 1989).

The content of popular music also provides young people with information about society, social and gender roles, and behavior (Christenson et al., 1985), in essence acting as an "agent of socialization" (Lull, 1985, p. 368). Popular music provides commonly shared meanings that may ease peer-group identification (Russell, 1997) and facilitate social communication among subgroups of peers. Further, adolescents learn to define themselves by their music, imitating the speech, dress, and even actions of their favorite musicians (Baizerman, 1996). Music videos, which provide additional social information in the visual imagery, can be an especially potent source of information about social roles, consumerism, and culture (Sun & Lull, 1986).

THE CONTENT OF POPULAR MUSIC
AND MUSIC VIDEOS

Song Lyrics

Styles of popular rock music have changed rapidly and dramatically over the past 50 years, but the lyrical themes have remained remarkably constant. Most songs, then and now, speak of being in love. As sex has become more open in American society, song lyrics have become more sexually explicit (Hirsch, 1971; Prinsky & Rosenbaum, 1987; Rice, 1980). In the 1940s and 1950s, romantic love was the dominant theme. Folk and folk rock music of the 1960s brought other themes reflective of the times, such as drugs, protest against war, and a greater focus on physical love. In the 1970s, romance and having fun made a brief comeback in the dance music of disco. Then, rock music of the 1980s brought greater emphasis on physical aspects of love and infatuation (Fedler, Hall, & Tanzi, 1982). Punk rock and heavy metal rock in the '80's generated themes of violence, and the occult began to appear more frequently in song lyrics. It was during this decade that the lyrics of popular music became a matter of strong public controversy. Groups such as the Parents' Music Resource Center (PMRC) came out strongly against popular music lyrics describing sex, violence, satanism, and drugs or alcohol (Gore, 1987), resulting in voluntary labeling of record albums to warn parents about songs containing explicit lyrics. The 1990s saw the birth of rap music, and "gangsta rap" brought violent, sexual, and misogynistic themes to their highest levels ever (Hansen, 1995). In contemporary music, love is free to be expressed as lust, and thinly veiled lyrical descriptions of sexual acts are not uncommon.

Cooper (1985) conducted an interesting analysis of song lyrics from four different points in time: 1946, 1956, 1966, and 1976. Her results are generally consistent with the trends reported above. She reported, for example, that references to women's physical characteristics rose significantly from each decade to the next; they were mentioned in 6.4% of songs sampled from 1946 and 11.7%, 13.6%, and 20.4% of songs from 1956, 1966, and 1976, respectively. Characterizations of "woman as childlike" by use of terms such as *baby* or *girl* increased from about 25% to close to 50% during the last two decades, but "woman as sex object" (references to a woman's sexual desirability) remained steady at around 20%.

In counterargument to critics of the lyrics, some researchers have made the point that adolescent listeners do not seem to perceive song lyrics in the same ways that adults (particularly adult researchers) do. In one study by Rosenbaum and Prinsky (1987), descriptions by junior and senior high school students of their three favorite songs were coded by researchers into one of seven categories (sex, violence, satanism, drugs, love/feelings, other, and don't know). Only 7% of the descriptions included themes that fell into the four categories of greatest concern to the PMRC: sex, violence, satanism, and drugs or alcohol. When these same students were asked to rate 35 popular groups or performers on the extent to which the performers sang about sex, the students overwhelmingly reported that the performers were singing about love—and not sex. These results have been interpreted as evidence that adolescents do not perceive the same high levels of sexual content in popular song lyrics that adults do.

Other music researchers have reached similar conclusions. One study, for example, demonstrated that young listeners do not comprehend the meaning of all of the words in popular songs (Greenfield et al., 1987). Others have found that adolescents cannot accurately describe the meaning of their favorite songs (Denisoff & Levine, 1971; Gantz, Gartenberg, Pearson, & Schiller, 1978; Yee, Britton, & Thompson, 1988). According to Greenfield et al. (1987), the dangerous influence of music lyrics asserted by the PMRC and other watchdog organizations may be unfounded. They pointed out that "if rock lyrics are to have the effects charged by the PMRC, they must first be comprehended by their audience" (p. 316). In a review, Desmond (1987) reported that only about one third of young listeners can accurately describe the meanings of frequently played, popular songs.

Accurate comprehension of lyrics and song meanings, however, may not tell the entire story. In our own laboratory, for example, we found that despite low levels of lyric comprehension and recall of song lyrics, listeners were able to extract themes of sex, suicide, violence, and satanism from songs by popular heavy metal groups using schematic processing (Hansen & Hansen, 1991a). Even though accurate comprehension was poor, they were able to use common schemas for sexual behavior, suicide, violence, and the occult to construct meaning for the songs. Interestingly, when the songs were processed schematically, the meaning subjects constructed was frequently more negative than the actual song lyrics expressed.

What do young listeners think about the potential effects of their own music? The results are mixed. Gantz et al. (1978) found that adolescents view popular music as "a socially acceptable and prosocial force" (p. 85). For example, over 60% of their respondents reported that popular music "helps a person become more sympathetic and sensitive to the needs of others"; although about 65% showed agreement with the statement that popular music "stimulates sexual activity." Other researchers have reported that listeners believe that popular music lyrics influence values, attitudes, and behaviors (Toohey, 1982; Wass, Miller, & Stevenson, 1989). At the same time, however, listeners have reported that song lyrics are not particularly important to them and that they are more attracted to qualities of the music than they are to the lyrics (Rosenbaum & Prinsky, 1987; Wass et al., 1988).

Music Videos

There has been very little research designed to investigate differences between recorded music and music videos, and fans of contemporary popular music tend to experience both at different times (Hansen & Hansen, 1991b). Research suggests, however, that music videos are generally liked more than the music alone

(Rubin et al., 1986). Because music videos add a dramatic visual dimension to the music, it would seem likely that both the potential for learning social information and the potential for physiological excitation and mood effects would be increased in the newer medium (Desmond, 1987). In addition, music videos allow viewers a glimpse of the musicians, augmenting the potential for adoration and idolization of the performers. Sun and Lull (1986) found that MTV viewers reported that they wanted to hear the music, and they wanted to be able to see the groups, singers, and concert performances. These viewers also felt that the visual content gave meaning (or added a different meaning) to the songs, and they evaluated the visual dimension extremely positively.

The content of music videos, particularly sexual and violent content, has been the target of strong public criticism (Gore, 1987; National Coalition on Television Violence, 1984; Steinem, 1988; Strasburger, 1988). In 1984, the National Coalition on Television Violence repudiated music videos for their high levels of violence. In 1988, the National Academy of Pediatrics came out strongly against music videos (Strasburger, 1988), arguing that the high levels of both sexual and violent content makes music videos unwholesome viewing for children. Indeed, published content analyses conducted over the last 15 years have generally documented high levels of sex and violence (Baxter, De Riemer, Landini, Leslie, & Singletary, 1985; Brown & Campbell, 1986; Sherman & Dominick, 1986; Sommers-Flanagan, Sommers-Flanagan, & Davis, 1993, among others). In addition, researchers have found that music videos contain significant amounts of antisocial (rebellious and socially unacceptable) behavior (Brown & Campbell, 1986) and are replete with sexist and sex-role stereotypic treatment of women (Sommers-Flanagan et al., 1993).

Researchers have reported that between 40% and 75% of music videos sampled contained sexual imagery (Baxter et al., 1985; Gow, 1990; Greeson & Williams, 1986; Sherman & Dominick, 1986). Although prevalent, the sexual imagery in music videos was found to be generally mild and nongraphic, consisting mostly of touches, kisses, embraces, and suggestive movements. Sexual imagery typically contained scantily or provocatively clad women. More recently, a small number have shown nudity, but sexual areas of the body were mostly blocked from the view of the camera. Sherman and Dominick (1986) reported that half of all women in the videos they rated were dressed provocatively (compared with about 10% of the men). By far the majority of music videos are performed by male groups (Baxter et al., 1985), and beautiful women are used to showcase these male stars in much the same way as they showcase products in television commercials.

Women were much more likely than men to be treated as sex objects in music videos, and when women were dressed provocatively, they were more likely to be given sexist treatment (Vincent, Davis, & Boruszkowski, 1987). Vincent et al. (1987) reported that women were "put down" or dominated by men in approximately three fourths of music videos sampled. Both women and men in music videos are portrayed at the extreme ends of sex-role stereotypic dimensions:

Women are portrayed as more affectionate, nurturing, dependent, and fearful; men are portrayed as more adventuresome, aggressive, and domineering, "the more valued traits in American society" (Seidman, 1992). Occupational roles were similarly polarized in terms of sex-role stereotypes (Seidman, 1992). Women, for example, were more likely to be portrayed as waitresses, hairstylists, dancers, or fashion models; men had roles as police officers, scientists, athletes, and business executives. Many of the men held white-collar jobs, but women's jobs were more often blue collar. White characters were older and of higher status than nonwhites, and White characters were less often depicted in lower class roles (64% vs. 75%) than were nonwhites (Sherman & Dominick, 1986).

Violence has also been prevalent in music videos. The lowest figure comes from Greeson and Williams (1986), who reported that 15% of videos sampled contained violent acts. Others have reported much higher figures. Gow (1990) found that almost one third of the music videos sampled contained violence. Over half the videos sampled in other content analyses contained violent imagery (Baxter et al., 1985; Brown & Campbell, 1986; Sherman & Dominick, 1986). For videos containing violence, Gow (1990) reported an average of 2.7 violent acts per video; Sherman and Dominick (1986) reported an average of 2.86 violent acts.

Even though varied coding schemes and different sampling procedures make comparisons between studies tenuous, the consensus seems to be that a significant number of music videos contain sex and violence, and it is not uncommon for sexual and violent imagery to appear in the same video. Sherman and Dominick (1986) found that 45% of the 166 videos in their sample contained both violent and sexual images. In contrast, Gow (1990) reported only 11% in a sample of 36 "most requested" videos. Does this mean that the combination of sexual and violent imagery in music videos is generally unappealing? Perhaps.

Zillmann and Mundorf (1987) edited R-rated sexual images, violent images, or both into a rock music video to test viewers' appreciation of music containing different types of visual content. Sexy visuals increased liking; violence was equivocal; and the combination of sexual and violent visuals actually decreased liking for the music. We found similar results in our laboratory (Hansen & Hansen, 1990a). In a study using videos selected for high, moderate, and low levels of both sex and violence, we found that liking for both the visuals and the music increased as the level of sex increased. Violence, however, had the opposite effect; liking decreased as the level of violence increased. The least-liked videos were those containing both sexual and violent imagery, particularly at high levels.

The proportion of videos containing antisocial (rebellious, socially unacceptable) content has been found to be about the same as that of sexual content. Brown and Campbell (1986) found that slightly over half the videos they sampled contained antisocial content. In addition, a significant proportion of videos (24% as reported by Baxter et al. 1985) contained characters using artificial substances (narcotics, stimulants, and other artificial substances); although their article does not describe what these substances were. Greeson & Williams (1986) reported that none of their videos contained any mention of drug use in either lyrics or visuals; therefore it may be that Baxter et al.'s (1985) substances category represents the presence of tobacco and/or alcoholic beverages. And, in fact, Sherman & Dominick (1986) reported that 21% of videos they rated had scenes of people in bars—a likely location for drinking and smoking. Similarly, smoking was found to occur in 25.7% of videos from a more recent MTV sample; alcohol use was depicted in 26.9% (DuRant et al., 1997). Clearly, measuring prosocial content has not been the focus of past studies, but depictions of friendship were also common in music videos and occurred in 41.9% of Baxter et al.'s sample.

Characteristics of MTV Fans

A number of studies have found that among young women, liking for MTV is correlated with attitudes toward sexuality. A study by Greeson (1991), for example, found that young women who watch MTV regularly find the sex in music videos more enjoyable. Strouse and his colleagues have found that among college-age women, sexual permissiveness (Strouse and Buerkel-Rothfuss, 1987; Strouse, Buerkel-Rothfuss, & Long, 1995) and more accepting attitudes toward sexual harassment (Strouse, Goodwin, & Roscoe, 1994) could be predicted by their exposure to MTV. Also, heavy viewers of both genders reported greater prevalence of a number of sexual behaviors in the real world (Strouse, Goodwin, & Roscoe, 1994). Tiggemann and Pickering (1996) found that watching music videos also predicted a "drive for thinness" among young women (an important indicator for anorexia nervosa). One rationale for an influence of MTV's sexy portrayals of women comes from a study by Kalof (1993). She found that women interpret a sexy woman (but not a sexy man) in a music video very differently from men: For women, a sexy woman is equated with power; for men, a sexy woman is merely a tease.

BEYOND MTV: COMPARING THE NEW
MUSIC VIDEO CHANNELS

The 1990s have brought a number of new music video channels to American television. MTV has added VH-1 and M2. MTV itself has changed dramatically, adding more non-music, youth-oriented programming and videos from new music genres. CMT (Country Music Television) and TNN (The Nashville Network) now present country music videos, and BET (Black Entertainment Network) offers music videos for a (mostly) Black audience.

There have been only a couple of published content analyses sampling the newer video channels. Tapper, Thorson, & Black (1994) conducted a content analysis of 144 videos taken from four music video channels (MTV, VH-1, TNN, and BET). They grouped the videos into eight types of music (rap, soul, country, heavy metal, pop, classic rock, alternative rock, and other) and reported percentages for each type of music sampled from each of the channels. While not a perfect measure, the figures give a sense of the kinds of music played on different music channels. From

MTV, videos included alternative rock (29%), rap (23%), heavy metal (21%), pop (16%), classic rock (9%), and other (2%). VH-1 videos included pop (65%), classic rock (9%), heavy metal (7%), country (7%), soul (2%), alternative rock (2%), and other (7%). TNN videos were 98% country music with a single pop video (2%). BET videos included rap (40%), soul (36%), pop (17%), and other (7%).

Tapper et al. (1994) were most interested in stylistic features of the videos (slow motion, digital video effects, visual montages, etc.); however, they did code the videos for the presence of sexual appeal (sexual innuendo, symbolism, and explicit sexual references), violence (physical or verbal aggression or the presence of weapons), and the race and gender of the lead performer. They found that country, heavy metal, classic rock, and alternative rock videos were performed by White musicians, predominantly male; although country and alternative had some White female performers (21% and 15%, respectively). In contrast, the majority of rap and soul videos had Black male performers; 13% of the rap videos and 38% of the soul videos had Black female leads. Pop was the most diverse category: White male (50%), White female (10%), Black male (18%), and Black female (18%). For videos with sexual appeal, rap (46%), soul (50%), and pop (45%) ranked highest; alternative rock was intermediate (23%); country (14%), heavy metal (8%), and classic rock (14%) ranked lowest. They found that more rap videos contained violence (29%); classic rock contained none (0%); others varied between 6% and 17%; however, these differences were not statistically significant.

Another across-channels content analysis (DuRant et al., 1997) looked only at tobacco and alcohol use and sexuality. 518 music videos from four channels (MTV, VH-1, CMT, and BET) were sampled. The analysis used five categories of music (adult contemporary, country, rock, rap, and rhythm & blues). Adult contemporary is closest (although not identical) to Tapper et al.'s category of pop. Rock is probably a combination of Tapper et al.'s heavy metal, classic rock, and alternative rock. Rhythm & blues (R & B) is closest to Tapper et al.'s soul category. Because different categories were used, DuRant et al.'s figures for the percentages of each genre within each channel look quite different. About 75% of the videos on MTV were rock, and 15.8% were rap; 0% were country, and there were very few adult contemporary (5.3%) or R & B (3.9%). For VH-1, most were rock (56.6%), followed by adult contemporary (22.9%), country (10.8%), and R & B (9.6%). Videos sampled from CMT were almost exclusively country (99%), 1% was adult contemporary. Finally, 48.9% of the videos from BET were rap, 47.8% were R & B, and 1.7% were adult contemporary.

Sexuality was rated on a four-point ordinal scale: no reference, present but minor, moderate level, or significant-major part. In brief, the percentages of videos from each channel that contained any level of sexuality were as follows: MTV (26.3%), VH-1 (31.3%), CMT (19.8%), and BET (60.7%). By genre, these percentages translate to the following: adult contemporary (65.2%), country (18.9%), rock (23.5%), rap (28.3%), and R & B (54.5%). When present, sexuality in adult contemporary tended to be either present but minor or moderate. When present in country and rock, sexuality tended to be present but minor.

When present in rap, sexuality was likely to be either minor or significant, and when present in R & B, it could be minor, moderate, or a significant-major part.

In our laboratory, we have been engaged in a large-scale content analysis across several channels (MTV, VH-1, CMT, and BET), and we report here a few results in their preliminary form. We sampled 192 music videos, representing 53.08% of the videos shown across the four channels during a two-day period in September 1997. Six pairs of trained judges coded the videos, and differences were resolved through discussion. Analyses indicated the continued prevalence of sexual imagery and sex-role stereotypes. Results for the appearance of nudity and sexually provocative clothing can be seen in Fig. 10.1. The incidence of nudity was relatively low. It was about equal for men and women, but was more prevalent in VH-1 and MTV videos than in those from BET and VH-1. The most striking finding for sexually provocative clothing was the obvious appearance of sexual stereotypes—women were much more likely than men to be shown in sexually provocative dress. Beyond this, the most obvious effect was the much higher prominence of sexual dress in BET and VH-1 videos than in CMT videos; MTV videos were intermediate. Similar rankings were found across the four networks in the incidence of sexual behaviors, such as eye contact, sexual gestures, and touching. These results are quite similar to findings of sexuality reported by DuRant et al. (1997).

Dramatic effects were also found in the incidence of sexual stereotypes. As can be seen in Fig. 10.2, men were more likely than women to be portrayed as sexual animals; women were more likely than men to be shown as sex objects. This pattern was particularly prominent in BET videos. Indeed, the incidence of sexual stereotypes was highest in BET videos and lowest in CMT videos. Stereotyping of women as sexual objects and possessions was significantly more common in BET videos than in videos from any other channel. The same pattern emerged in the stereotyping of men as sexual animals. Finally, across all video outlets, sexual portrayals of women were more common than sexual portrayals of men. In addition, gambling, alcohol, and smoking (but not drug use) were quite prevalent in videos shown on three channels—BET, VH-1, and MTV—and these behaviors were almost always presented as part of the social milieu, rather than as problematic behaviors (findings similar to those reported by DuRant et al., 1997). To date, then, our findings suggest that sexual imagery and sex-role stereotypic portrayals of both women and men remain prevalent in music videos, but appear highest on BET, which shows rap, soul, and pop videos (results that are remarkably consistent with DuRant et al., 1997 and Tapper et al., 1994).

CHARACTERISTICS OF DIFFERENT MUSICAL GENRES AND THEIR FANS

Clearly, music video channels differ in their focus on specific musical genres; as a result, there are strong content differences across channels. In addition, the channels target different audiences. MTV targets young people, whereas VH-1's audi-

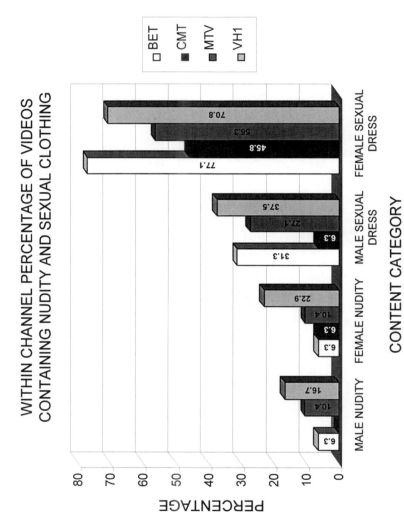

WITHIN CHANNEL PERCENTAGE OF VIDEOS
CONTAINING NUDITY AND SEXUAL CLOTHING

BET
CMT
MTV
VH1

PERCENTAGE

80
70
60
50
40
30
20
10
0

MALE NUDITY
6.3
10.4
16.7

FEMALE NUDITY
6.3
6.3
10.4
22.9

MALE SEXUAL
DRESS
31.3
6.3
27.1
37.5

FEMALE SEXUAL
DRESS
77.1
45.8
56.3
70.8

CONTENT CATEGORY

Fig. 10.1.   Percentage of music videos containing nudity and sexual attire on BET, CMT, MTV, and
VH-1.

184

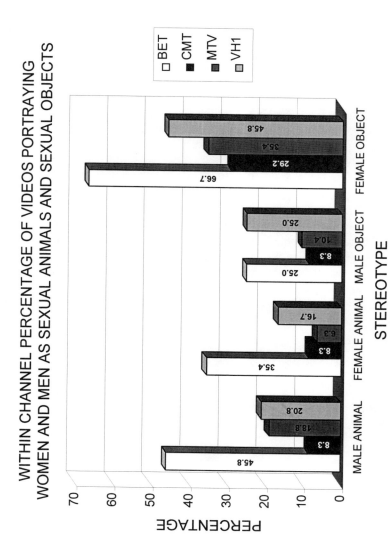

WITHIN CHANNEL PERCENTAGE OF VIDEOS PORTRAYING WOMEN AND MEN AS SEXUAL ANIMALS AND SEXUAL OBJECTS

Legend:
- □ BET
- ■ CMT
- ■ MTV
- □ VH1

PERCENTAGE

STEREOTYPE

MALE ANIMAL
- 45.8
- 8.3
- 18.8
- 20.8

FEMALE ANIMAL
- 35.4
- 8.3
- 6.3
- 16.7

MALE OBJECT
- 25.0
- 8.3
- 10.4
- 25.0

FEMALE OBJECT
- 66.7
- 29.2
- 35.4
- 45.8

Fig. 10.2.   Percentage of music videos portraying women and men as sexual animals and sex objects on BET, CMT, MTV, and VH-1.

185

ence is generally older. BET is targeting a Black audience, and CMT is exclusively courting country music fans. Liking for different kinds of music can cross genres, but strong fans of certain types of music tend to be disparaging of other kinds of music (Frith, 1981). In a study conducted in the early 1980s, Deihl, Schneider, and Petress (1983) found that music video fans clustered into three groups with different sets of music preferences. The clusters would differ today, but we suspect that they would tend to mimic music genres presented on the video channels. Research has focused on differences among fans of different kinds of music, and some evidence has accumulated that fans of different genres may have different personality characteristics, values, and attitudes and very different views of social reality. These differences are described below, but a summary of characteristics associated with fans of various types of music may be found in Table 10.1.

Punk Rock

For example, when we compared fans of late 1980s punk rock music with nonfans, a number of interesting differences emerged (Hansen & Hansen, 1991b). Fans of punk music were significantly less accepting of authority (Bales & Couch, 1969) than nonfans. In addition, punk fans estimated significantly higher prevalence of antiauthority behaviors among young people than did nonfans. Fans estimated that many more young people owned weapons, had vandalized something, had committed a crime, and had gone to jail. Moreover, fans' antiauthority attitudes and their frequency estimates were related to self-reported exposure to the music; the more

TABLE 10.1
Personality Characteristics of Music Fans by Genre

Hard Rock and Heavy Metal	*Punk Rock*
High in machiavellianism	Less accepting of authority
High in machismo	Say that family was not close while
Low in need for cognition	growing up
High in toughmindedness	Feel misunderstood by parents
High in excitement seeking	Report high estimates of young people who:
High in sensation seeking	own weapons
High in recklessness	have vandalized something
High in risk taking	have committed a crime
High in delinquency	have gone to jail
Greater use of tobacco, alcohol, and marijuana	
Report high estimates of young people who:	*Rap*
have premarital sex	May be understimulated
use cocaine and marijuana	Low in need for cognition
have satanic beliefs	
have stolen parent's car	*Pop*
Report low estimates of young people who:	High in empathy for characters
have been involved in date rape	in books and movies ("fantasy")

time subjects spent listening to punk music, the higher the levels of antiauthority attitudes and estimates for behaviors. In a study of young people detained as juvenile delinquents, Gold (1987) found evidence that fans of punk music also differed in family dynamics believed to be related to personality development. Significantly more fans than nonfans reported that their families were not close when they were growing up and that they felt misunderstood by their parents. While a causal direction cannot be established in studies of these types, the personality and attitudes of punk rock fans seem to relate directly to the genre, whose most prevalent themes are characterized by antiestablishment messages, alienation from society, and rebelliousness against authority (Bodinger-deUriarte, 1985; Gold, 1987).

Hard Rock and Heavy Metal

Correlates of liking for hard rock and heavy metal rock music have been explored by quite a few researchers. In another part of our study (Hansen & Hansen, 1991b), reported earlier, fans of heavy metal were shown to differ from nonfans on several personality characteristics and held different views of social reality. Fans of both genders, for example, scored higher in machiavellianism (Christie, 1968) and machismo (male hypersexuality combined with a lack of respect for women) (Mosher & Sirkin, 1984) than nonfans. Male and female heavy metal fans also scored lower in the need for cognition (Cacioppo, Petty, & Kao, 1984). When queried about their views of social reality, heavy metal fans generated much higher estimates among young people for premarital sex, using cocaine and marijuana, satanic beliefs, and stealing parents' cars. The latter two effects were particularly strong for female fans. Heavy metal fans also made much lower estimates of the number of other young people who had been involved in date rape. Again, exposure to the music predicted scores on the personality and attitude measures.

A number of other correlates of a preference for heavy metal music have been reported in the literature. Rawlings, Hodge, Sherr, and Dempsey (1995) investigated Eysenck's Psychoticism (P) dimension (more informatively known as Toughmindedness). High P individuals are characterized as being high in the following traits: aggressive, cold, egocentric, impersonal, impulsive, antisocial, unempathic, creative, and toughminded. They found that toughminded (high P) subjects showed a preference for hard rock and heavy metal music and disliked pop music. It should be noted that, in general, adolescent and young adult males tend to score higher on P than any other age or gender group. They also tend to like heavy metal in greater numbers than young women (Christenson & Peterson, 1988). However, in this study the association between toughmindedness and preference for hard rock/heavy metal music remained significant even when gender and age were statistically controlled. In other studies, preference for hard rock/heavy metal music has been shown to be related to excitement seeking (Dollinger, 1993), sensation seeking (Arnett, 1992; Zuckerman, 1979), recklessness (Arnett, 1991, 1992), risk taking (Martin, Clarke, & Pearce, 1993), and delinquency (Martin et al., 1993), as well as greater use of tobacco, alcohol, and marijuana (Martin et al., 1993). Interestingly, a study by Stack, Gundlach, and Reeves (1994) found that across the 50 United States, the number of statewide subscriptions to heavy metal magazines was significantly related to rates of suicide.

Heavy metal music has been severely criticized by music industry watchdogs and parents' groups for its violent, drug-related, sexual, antisocial, and occult lyrics (Gore, 1987). Common themes of the music might be characterized as violent, apocalyptic, sexual, occult, antisocial, and callous toward women (Bashe, 1985; Hansen & Hansen, 1991a). There is some evidence that ardent heavy metal fans are perceived as deviant and perhaps even mentally ill by mental health workers (Rosenbaum & Prinsky, 1991). In Rosenbaum and Prinsky's (1991) study, supervisors in 83% of inpatient facilities treating adolescents recommended hospitalization for a hypothetical young man who listened to a lot of music with lyrics about suicide and the devil, spiked and colored his hair, dressed in ragged jeans and T-shirts with skulls, and wore studded bracelets—even though the young man kept his grades up and was not depressed, violent, or taking drugs. As an interesting counterpoint to these findings, Zillmann and Bhatia (1989) discovered that, for young men, being perceived as a heavy metal fan can actually have social benefits. Specifically, they found that young women were more attracted to a potential date when he expressed a preference for heavy metal music than when he claimed to be a fan of country music or classical music or expressed no preference.

Naturally, the fans see little wrong with their music. For example, they were significantly less likely than nonfans to believe that the music was harmful to children or that listeners would be negatively impacted by the music (Wass et al., 1989). To counter criticism of heavy metal lyrics, Epstein and Pratto (1990) pointed out that, in reality, many heavy metal songs have socially constructive lyrics expressing "concern for the world that youth will inherit" (p. 74). These authors believe that listeners who are behaving negatively might be "misunderstanding the lyrics" (p. 74). We agree that listeners can easily misunderstand or misinterpret the lyrics in heavy metal songs. A number of subjects in one of our experiments, discussed earlier (Hansen & Hansen, 1991a), greatly misunderstood the lyrics of Ozzy Osbourne's song, *Suicide Solution*. The song is about the evils of alcohol, equating drinking with suicide, but many of our listeners thought that the lyrics actually advocated suicide. The lyrics in heavy metal music are commonly subordinate to the complex, loud, and frequently discordant music, placing a high cognitive load on listeners and making it difficult to comprehend the correct meanings of the songs. In this situation, listeners are forced to rely on their own cognitive schemas to give meaning to the song, and (as happened with *Suicide Solution*) they may use the wrong schema, interpreting the theme incorrectly (and, perhaps, more negatively).

Rap Music

This decade has seen the birth of a controversial new kind of music: rap. Rap, particularly gangsta rap, has been characterized as extremely ethnocentric, violent, misogynistic, sexually explicit, politically radical, and oriented toward the gang and drug cultures (Rule, 1994). Rap music, or hip-hop as it is sometimes called, is clearly distinct from other forms of music. The beat is strong and percussive (Thompson, 1996), and the lyrics are not so much sung as spoken. When present, the melody patterns the spoken lyrics. Thus, rap differs from other kinds of popular music because the lyrics are a strong focus of attention (Barongan & Hall, 1995); rhyme, playful use of language, and double meanings are important features. Even though they have the same delivery and musical style, male and female rappers have distinctly different agendas. Male rappers often protest police harassment and racism within the economic and political systems. Female rappers protest against racism too, but their platform is one of sexual power (Roberts, 1991). Female rappers use sexual provocation to challenge the misogyny of male rappers. At the same time, they appear to contradict the challenge by personifying sex objects (Rose, 1994).

Little is known about the characteristics and attitudes of rap fans. Most published material takes the form of essays, not empirical investigation. Pressley (1992), a Black psychologist and pastor, described his observations of young Black fans in clinical settings:

> It was found that the adolescents who reported listening to more hours of rap music daily also had a tendency to seek other forms of external stimulation through motor activity or extroverted behavior. . . . Further, the increased need for external stimulation correlates strongly with psychological traits of low self-acceptance, impulsive behavior and difficulty dealing with feelings of anxiety or guilt. These teenagers also held the belief that luck is more important than hard work. (pp. 94–95)

Pressley believed that these youths are internally understimulated and that rap music raises their arousal to more optimal levels (Zuckerman, 1979). The same theory (Litle & Zuckerman, 1986) has been used to explain the relationship between sensation seeking and liking for heavy metal music. Who listens to rap music? Bryson (1996) reports that only 26% of rap fans are Black, and we have almost no information yet about the characteristics of other fans. In our laboratory, we are currently undertaking a conceptual replication of Hansen & Hansen (1991b) comparing fans and nonfans of rap, pop, and heavy metal music. Preliminary data analyses have indicated that among our current sample of approximately 100 (predominantly female and 96% White) university undergraduates, liking for rap music appears to be significantly negatively correlated with the need for cognition.

Pop and Other Contemporary Music

Pop music, or contemporary adult rock music, differs from other musical genres in an important way. Punk, heavy metal, and rap music all reject the dominant culture; pop embraces it (Epstein, Pratto, & Skipper, 1990). Pop songs are about love, courtship, friendship, and having fun. Pop is sex-role stereotyped, but not violent. Perhaps because pop is considered mainstream music for adolescents and young adults, it has not received the attention of music researchers. The themes are generally prosocial, although they frequently include references to sexual feelings. From our own ongoing content analysis (discussed previously), we have some preliminary findings indicating that time spent listening to pop is related to the ability to empathize strongly with characters in books and movies (a type of empathy called "fantasy"). Assuming a significant relationship holds after the completion of the study, pop fans (who are largely female) also may feel a strong connection to the characters in pop music videos, making it probable that they would share the same mainstream beliefs and attitudes found in the music. The characteristics of fans of country, soul, classic rock, and alternative rock have not been studied.

EFFECTS OF MUSIC AND MUSIC VIDEOS

There is now a great deal of evidence that listeners can be affected by even a brief exposure to popular music and music videos. Most researchers have investigated music with high levels of sexual, violent, sexist, and antisocial content. Greeson and Williams (1986), for example, found that subjects were more likely to endorse violent and sexually permissive attitudes after watching rock music videos with these themes than after neutral rock videos. Others have reported similar findings (e.g., Calfin, Carroll, & Schmidt, 1993; Johnson, Jackson, & Gatto, 1995; Peterson & Prost, 1989).

In our own research, we have found that the effects of rock music videos can be predicted by the thematic content of the videos. For example, exposing college undergraduates to rock music videos with antisocial themes produced greater liking for antisocial behavior (Hansen & Hansen, 1990b). In other experiments (Hansen, 1989; Hansen & Hansen, 1988), subjects reported much greater liking for sex-role stereotypic (e.g., male-dominant, female-submissive) behavior after exposure to rock music videos selected for their sex-role stereotypic portrayals of women and men. Compared with subjects who watched music videos with neutral themes, sex-role stereotypic videos produced more positive impressions of people engaging in sex-role stereotypic behaviors. For example, a young man who was coming on strongly to a young woman he had just met was viewed in a much more favorable light after sex-role stereotypic videos than after neutral videos. When the woman reciprocated his advances, she was liked much more after sex-role stereotypic videos than she was after neutral videos. Interestingly, after neutral videos, subjects actually liked the young woman more when she fended off his advances.

We have amassed a fair amount of evidence now that thematic content of music videos "primes" viewers' cognitive schemas, influencing subsequent impressions and social judgments in highly predictable ways (Hansen, 1995, 1989; Hansen & Hansen, 1988; Hansen & Hansen, 1990b; Hansen & Krygowski, 1994). According to contemporary theories of social-cognitive information processing, impressions, evaluations, and other kinds of judgments can be influenced by priming (Bargh, 1984; Berkowitz & Rogers, 1986). The simple, common themes of much of contemporary music prime listeners' schemas for social behavior, making these schemas temporarily highly accessible. Once primed, the schema is more likely to be used to encode and interpret ongoing and subsequent social behaviors that share a phenotypic similarity with schematic content. Gan, Zillmann, & Mitrook (1997) found similar priming effects for music videos by Black female artists. Sexually enticing rap videos (but not other videos by Black female performers) primed an extremely negative schema for Black women in White subjects, one in which Black women were appraised as sluttish and sleazy. Once primed by the videos, the same schema was used to appraise other Black women, making subjects' evaluations much more negative.

THE AROUSAL COMPONENT

As Cantor and Zillmann (1973) hypothesized, physiological arousal is likely to be an important component of music appreciation. Cantor and Zillmann (1973) demonstrated that subjects who were already in a state of increased arousal prior to listening to music liked the music better than subjects who were not already aroused. Hansen & Hansen (1990a) also found that self-reported levels of arousal were important predictors of a music video's appeal as well as of the intensity of the affect produced. Higher arousal was related to stronger emotions (both positive and negative) and was predictive of greater liking for songs that elicited positive emotions and decreased liking for songs that produced negative emotions. Unfortunately, arousal has not been generally considered by most music researchers. In fact, a number of experiments showing effects for music video content have inadvertently confounded their manipulations by showing videos with different levels of arousal as well as different kinds of content; frequently this occurs because the selected content comes from different genres. For example, Peterson & Prost (1989) reported that subjects who watched a violent rock video reported significantly more aggressive attitudes toward women than did subjects who watched a nonviolent video. Given the videos selected, it is highly likely that the violent video was more physiologically arousing than the nonviolent video; therefore, effects on attitudes may have been produced by differences in arousal rather than differences in violent video content.

Zillmann's theory of *excitation transfer* (Zillmann, 1983) is particularly useful for understanding the contribution of physiological arousal to music appreciation and to the effects of music on listeners. Popular music and music videos are complex, affective stimuli, containing many potential sources of arousal. Individuals typically do not discriminate arousal produced by one source from arousal produced by another; therefore, arousal from multiple sources tends to be additive, increasing the effects of the music on the listener. Hansen and Krygowski (1994) demonstrated that under conditions of higher levels of physiological arousal, schemas primed by music also tend to be more extreme, producing even stronger priming effects. We found that sex object videos produced predictable schema-priming effects on attribute judgments of an ambiguous (but phenotypically similar) TV commercial shown after the video. And, more importantly, subjects who were physiologically aroused by exercise while watching the video and the commercial showed exaggerated priming effects. For example, after watching a male sex object video, aroused subjects judged a male actor in the ambiguous commercial to be a stronger sex object than did nonaroused subjects.

Many experiments have produced robust priming effects on attitudes and social judgments from music, but how long do these effects last? Do they have an influence on personality and stable attitudes? If these sorts of effects are merely short-term, transitory phenomena that dissipate rapidly, music researchers should have little cause for concern. Contemporary social psychological theories of information processing, however, suggest that this is probably not the case. These theories posit that schemas for violence, antisocial behavior, sexism, and so on, tend to become chronically accessible with frequent priming. The more often a schema is activated by themes of popular music (or other media stimuli), the more likely it is to become a stable aspect of the listener's disposition. In addition, popular music and music videos may be particularly likely candidates for producing lasting changes because schema activation is typically accompanied by strong, positive emotions. The positive affect produced by the music is likely to become associated with the schema through classical conditioning.

Let us look at an example of how this might work. Imagine that Johnny watches a lot of MTV and BET because he likes rap music. Many of the music videos played on these channels portray women as sex objects, so Johnny's schema for women as sex objects will be frequently primed. The positive emotions he feels when watching the videos become associated in memory with a cognitive schema for women as sex objects, resulting in the following: Johnny feels positively about women as sex objects, and these attitudes become a stable part of his personality. Incidentally, if we ask Johnny whether he thinks music has influenced his attitudes or behavior, he will say, "No." And, he will be giving an honest—though incorrect—answer. Perhaps the most problematic aspect of music influence is that effects occur at the unconscious level. In the same way that individuals are unaware of excitation transfer, they are also unaware of priming effects when these occur; thus, they are not aware that their judgments are being influenced by priming or that frequent priming by music is changing their attitudes. We have accumulated a large body of evidence suggesting that popular music influences young people, and we can predict its influence fairly well if we understand three of its components: arousal, affect, and content. Now that American contemporary popular music has found its way around the world, understanding and predicting its effects becomes exceedingly important, and, without a doubt, there will be a new cadre of international scholars to help us focus on the problem.

REFERENCES

Arnett, J. (1991). Heavy metal music and reckless behavior among adolescents. *Journal of Youth and Adolescence, 20*(6), 573–593.

Arnett, J. (1992). The soundtrack of recklessness: Musical preferences and reckless behavior among adolescents. *Journal of Adolescent Research, 7*(3), 313–331.

Baizerman, M. (1996). Comment on Seelow: What does it mean for kids? For us? *Child and Youth Care Forum, 25*(1), 55–57.

Bales, R., & Couch, A. (1969). Value profile. *Sociological Inquiry, 39*, 3–17.

Ball, S. G. (1981). *Beachside comprehensive.* Cambridge, MA: Cambridge University Press.

Bargh, J. A. (1984). Automatic and conscious processing of social information. In R. S. Wyer & T. K. Srull (Eds.), *Handbook of social cognition: Vol. 3* (pp. 1–44). Hillsdale, NJ: Lawrence Erlbaum Associates.

Barongan, C., & Hall, G. C. N. (1995). The influence of misogynous rap music on sexual aggression against women. *Psychology of Women Quarterly, 19*, 195–207.

Bashe, P. (1985). *Heavy metal thunder.* Garden City, NY: Doubleday.

Baxter, L., De Riemer, C., Landini, A., Leslie, L., & Singletary, M. (1985). A content analysis of music videos. *Journal of Broadcasting & Electronic Media, 29*, 333–340.

Berkowitz, L., & Rogers, K. (1986). A priming effect analysis of media influences. In J. Bryant & D. Zill-mann (Eds.), *Perspectives on media effects* (pp. 57–81). Hillsdale, NJ: Lawrence Erlbaum Associates.

Bodinger-deUriarte, C. (1985). Opposition to hegemony in the music of Devo: A simple matter of re-membering. *Journal of Popular Culture, 18*(2), 57–71.

Brown, D., & Campbell, K. (1986). Race and gender in music videos. *Journal of Communications, 36*, 94–106.

Bryson, B. (1996). "Anything but heavy metal": Symbolic exclusion and musical dislikes. *American Sociological Review, 61*, 884–899.

Cacioppo, J. T., Petty, R. E., & Kao, C. F. (1984). The efficient assessment of need for cognition. *Journal of Personality Assessment, 48*, 306–307.

Calfin, M., Carroll, J., & Schmidt, J. (1993). Viewing music-videotapes before taking a test of pre-marital sexual attitudes. *Psychological Reports, 72*, 475–481.

Cantor, J. R., & Zillmann, D. (1973). The effect of affective state and emotional arousal on music ap-preciation. *Journal of General Psychology, 89*, 97–108.

Christenson, P. , DeBenedittis, P., & Lindlof, T. (1985). Children's use of audio media. *Communica-tion Research, 12*(3), 327–343.

Christenson, P. G., & Peterson, J. B. (1988). Genre and gender in the structure of music preferences. *Communication Research, 15*(3), 282–301.

Christie, R. (1968). *Machiavellianism.* Unpublished manuscript. New York: Columbia University.

Cooper, V. W. (1985). Women in popular music: A quantitative analysis of feminine images over time. *Sex Roles, 13*(9/10), 499–506.

Deihl, E. R., Schneider, M. J., & Petress, K. (1983). Dimensions of music preference: A factor ana-lytic study. *Popular Music and Society, 9*(3), 41–49.

Denisoff, S., & Levine, M. (1971). The popular protest song: The case of "Eve of Destruction." *Pub-lic Opinion Quarterly, 35*, 117–122.

Denisoff, R. S., & Levine, M. (1972). Youth and popular music: A test of the taste culture hypothesis. *Youth and Society, 4*, 237–255.

Desmond, R. (1987). Adolescents and music lyrics: Implications of a cognitive perspective. *Commu-nication Quarterly, 35*(3), 276–284.

Dollinger, S. J. (1993). Research note: Personality and music preference: Extraversion and excite-ment-seeking or openness to experience. *Psychology of Music, 21*, 73–77.

DuRant, R. H., Rome, E. S., Rich, M., Allred, E., Emans, S. J., & Woods, E. R. (1997). Tobacco and alcohol use behaviors portrayed in music videos: A content analysis. *American Journal of Public Health, 87*(7), 1131–1135.

Englis, B. G., Solomon, M. R., & Olofsson, A. (1993). Consumption imagery in music television: A bi-cultural perspective. *Journal of Advertising, 22*(4), 21–33.

Epstein, J. S., & Pratto, D. J. (1990). Juvenile delinquency and satanic identification. *Popular Music and Society, 14*(4), 67–76.

Epstein, J. S., Pratto, D. J., & Skipper, J. K. (1990). Teenagers, behavioral problems, and preferences for heavy metal and rap music: A case study of a southern middle school. *Deviant Behavior, 11,* 381–394.

Fedler, F., Hall, J., & Tanzi, L. (1982). Analysis of popular music reveals emphasis on sex, de-emphasis of romance. Paper presented at the annual meeting of the Association for Education in Journalism. Athens, OH.

Fitzgerald, M., Joseph, A. P., Hayes, M., & O'Regan, M. (1995). Leisure activities of adolescent children. *Journal of Adolescence, 18,* 349–358.

Frith, S. (1978). *The sociology of rock.* London: Constable.

Frith, S. (1981). *Sound effects: Youth, leisure, and the politics of rock 'n' roll.* New York: Pantheon.

Gan, S.-L., Zillmann, D., & Mitrook, M. (1997). Stereotyping effect of black women's sexual rap on white audiences. *Basic and Applied Social Psychology, 19*(3), 381–399.

Gantz, W., Gartenberg, H. M., Pearson, M. L., & Schiller, S. O. (1978). Gratifications and expectations associated with pop music among adolescents. *Popular Music in Society, 6,* 81–89.

Gold, B. D. (1987). Self-image of punk rock and nonpunk rock juvenile delinquents. *Adolescence, 22*(87), 535–543.

Gore, T. (1987). *Raising PG kids in an X-rated society.* Nashville, TN: Abingdon.

Gow, J. (1990). The relationship between violent and sexual images and the popularity of music videos. *Popular Music and Society, 14*(4), 1–10.

Greenfield, P. M., Bruzzone, L., Koyamatsu, K., Satuloff, W., Nixon, K., Brodie, M., & Kingsdale, D. (1987). What is rock music doing to the minds of our youth? A first experimental look at the effects of rock music lyrics and music videos. *Journal of Early Adolescence, 7,* 315–330.

Greeson, L. E. (1991). Recognition and ratings of television music videos: Age, gender, and sociocultural effects. *Journal of Applied Social Psychology, 21*(23), 1908–1920.

Greeson, L. E., & Williams, R. A. (1986). Social implications of music videos for youth. *Youth and Society, 18,* 177–189.

Hansen, C. H. (1989). Priming sex-role stereotypic event schemas with rock music videos: Effects on impression favorability, trait inferences, and recall of a subsequent male-female interaction. *Basic and Applied Social Psychology, 10*(4), 371–391.

Hansen, C. H. (1995). Predicting cognitive and behavioral effects of gangsta rap. *Basic and Applied Social Psychology, 16*(1&2), 43–52.

Hansen, C. H., & Hansen, R. D. (1988). How rock music videos can change what is seen when boy meets girl: Priming stereotypic appraisal of social interactions. *Sex Roles, 19*(5/6), 287–316.

Hansen, C. H., & Hansen, R. D. (1990a). The influence of sex and violence on the appeal of rock music videos. *Communication Research, 17*(2), 212–234.

Hansen, C. H., & Hansen, R. D. (1990b). Rock music videos and antisocial behavior. *Basic and Applied Social Psychology, 11*(4), 357–369.

Hansen, C. H., & Hansen, R. D. (1991a). Schematic information processing of heavy metal lyrics. *Communication Research, 18*(3), 373–411.

Hansen, C. H., & Hansen, R. D. (1991b). Constructing personality and social reality through music: Individual differences among fans of punk and heavy metal music. *Journal of Broadcasting & Electronic Media, 35*(3), 335–350.

Hansen, C. H., & Krygowski, W. (1994). Arousal-augmented priming effects: Rock music videos and sex object schemas. *Communication Research, 21*(1), 24–47.

Hirsch, P. (1971). Sociological approaches to the popular music phenomenon. *American Behavioral Scientist, 14,* 371–388.

Holbrook, M., & Schindler, R. (1989). Some exploratory findings on the development of musical tastes. *Journal of Consumer Research, 16,* 119–124.

Johnson, J. J., Jackson, L. A., & Gatto, L. (1995). Violent attitudes and deferred academic aspirations: Deleterious effects of exposure to rap music. *Basic and Applied Social Psychology, 16,* 27–41.

Kalof, L. (1993). Dilemmas of feminity: Gender and the social construction of sexual imagery. *The Sociological Quarterly, 34*(4), 639–651.

Litle, P., & Zuckerman, M. (1986). Sensation seeking and music preferences. *Personality and Individual Differences, 7*(4), 575–577.

Lull, J. (1985). On the communicative properties of music. *Communication Research, 12*(3), 363–372.

Martin, G., Clarke, M., & Pearce, C. (1993). Adolescent suicide: Music preference as an indicator of vulnerability. *Journal of the American Academy of Child and Adolescent Psychiatry, 32*(3), 530–535.

National Coalition on Television Violence. (1984, January 14). *Rock music and MTV found increasingly violent.* Press Release.

Orman, J. (1992). Conclusion: The impact of popular music in society. In K. J. Bindas (Ed.), *America's musical pulse: Popular music in twentieth-century society* (pp. 281–287). Westport, CT: Praeger.

Peterson, J. L., & Prost, K. S. (1989). Influence of rock videos on attitudes of violence against women. *Psychological Reports, 64,* 319–322.

Pressley, A. (1992). Rap music by black male artists: A psychotheological interpretation. *The Western Journal of Black Studies, 16*(2), 92–97.

Prinsky, L. E., & Rosenbaum, J. L. (1987). "Leer-ics" or lyrics: Teenage impressions of rock 'n' roll. *Youth & Society, 18*(4), 384–397.

Rawlings, D., Hodge, M., Sherr, D., & Dempsey, A. (1995). Toughmindedness and preference for musical excerpts, categories, and triads. *Psychology of Music, 23,* 63–80.

Rice, R. (1980). The content of popular recordings. *Popular Music and Society, 7,* 140–158.

Roberts, R. (1991). Music videos, performance and resistance: Feminist rappers. *Journal of Popular Culture, 25,* 141–152.

Roe, K. (1985). Swedish youth and music: Listening patterns and motivations. *Communication Research, 12*(3), 353–362.

Rose, T. (1994). *Black noise: Rap music and black culture in contemporary America.* Hanover, NH: University Press of New England.

Rosenbaum, J., & Prinsky, L. (1987). Sex, violence, and rock 'n' roll: youth's perceptions of popular music. *Popular Music and Society, 11,* 79–90.

Rosenbaum, J., & Prinsky, L. (1991). The presumption of influence: Recent responses to popular music subcultures. *Crime and Delinquency, 37*(4), 528–535.

Rowe, D. (1995). *Popular cultures: Rock music, sport and the politics of pleasure.* London: Sage Publications.

Rubin, R., Rubin, A., Perse, E., Armstrong, C., McHugh, M., & Faix, N. (1986). Media use and meaning of music video. *Journalism Quarterly, 63,* 353–359.

Rule, S. (1994, April 3). Generation rap. *The New York Times,* Section 6, pp. 41–45.

Russell, P. A. (1997). Musical tastes and society. In D. J. Hargreaves & A. C. North (Eds.), *The social psychology of music* (pp. 141–159). Oxford, England: Oxford University Press.

Seidman, S. A. (1992). An investigation of sex-role stereotyping in music videos. *Journal of Broadcasting & Electronic Media, 36,* 209–216.

Sherman, B. L., & Dominick, J. R. (1986). Violence and sex in music: TV and rock 'n' roll. *Journal of Communication, 36,* 79–93.

Sommers-Flanagan, R., Sommers-Flanagan, J., & Davis, B. (1993). What's happening on Music Television: A gender role content analysis. *Sex Roles, 28,* 745–753.

Stack, S., Gundlach, J., & Reeves, J. L. (1994). The heavy metal subculture and suicide. *Suicide and life-threatening behavior, 24*(1), 15–23.

Steinem, G. (1988). Six great ideas that television is missing. In S. Oskamp (Ed.), *Television as a social issue: Applied social psychology annual issue (#8)* (pp.18–29). Newbury Park, CA: Sage.

Strasburger, V. C. (1988, November 17). Rock videos may harm kids' health. *USA Today,* Section D., p. 1 (Report on findings of the American Academy of Pediatrics' subcommittee on TV and children).

Strouse, J. S., & Buerkel-Rothfuss, N. (1987). Self reported media exposure and sexual attitudes and behaviors of college students. *Journal of Sex Education and Therapy, 13,* 43–51.

Strouse, J. S., Buerkel-Rothfuss, N., & Long, C. J. (1995). Gender and family as moderators of the relationship between music video exposure and adolescent sexual permissiveness. *Adolescence, 30*(119), 505–521.

Strouse, J. S., Goodwin, M. P., & Roscoe, B. (1994). Correlates of attitudes toward sexual harassment among early adolescents. *Sex Roles, 31*(9/10), 559–577.

Sun, S.-W., & Lull, J. (1986). The adolescent audience for music videos and why they watch. *Journal of Communication, 36,* 115–125.

Tapper, J., Thorson, E., & Black, D. (1994). Variations in music videos as a function of their musical genre. *Journal of Broadcasting & Electronic Media, 38,* 103–113.

Thompson, R. F. (1996). Hip hop 101. In W. E. Perkins (Ed.), *Droppin' science: Critical essays on rap music and hip hop culture* (pp. 211–219). Philadelphia: Temple University Press.

Tiggemann, M., & Pickering, A. S. (1996). Role of television in adolescent women's body dissatisfaction and drive for thinness. *International Journal of Eating Disorders, 20*(2), 199–203.

Toohey, J. V. (1982). Popular music and social values. *Journal of School Health, 42,* 582–585.

Vincent, R. C., Davis, D. K., & Boruszkowski, L. A. (1987). Sexism on MTV: The portrayal of women in rock videos. *Journalism Quarterly, 64,* 750–755, 941.

Wass, H., Miller, M. D., & Stevenson, R. G. (1989). Factors affecting adolescents' behavior and attitudes toward destructive rock lyrics. *Death Studies, 13,* 287–303.

Wass, H., Raup, J. L., Cerullo, K., Martel, L. G., Mingione, L. A., & Sperring, A. M. (1988). *Omege, 19,* 177–186.

Wells, A. (1990). Popular music: Emotional use and management. *Journal of Popular Culture, 24*(1), 105–117.

Wicke, P. (1985). Young people and popular music in East Germany: Focus on a scene. *Communication Research, 12*(3), 319–325.

Yee, S., Britton, L., & Thompson, W. C. (1988, April). *The effects of rock music on adolescents' attitudes and behavior.* Paper presented at the meeting of the Western Psychological Association.

Zillmann, D. (1983). Transfer of excitation in emotional behavior. In J. T. Cacioppo & R. E. Petty (Eds.), *Social psychophysiology: A sourcebook* (pp. 215–240.) New York: Guilford Press.

Zillmann, D., & Bhatia, A. (1989). Effects of associating with musical genres on heterosexual attraction. *Communication Research, 16*(2), 263–288.

Zillmann, D., & Gan, S.-L. (1997). Musical taste in adolescence. In D. J. Hargreaves and A. C. North (Eds.), *The social psychology of music* (pp. 161–187). Oxford, England: Oxford University Press.

Zillmann, D., & Mundorf, N. (1987). Image effects in the appreciation of video rock. *Communication Research, 14,* 316–334.

Zuckerman, M. (1979). *Sensation-seeking: Beyond the optimal level of arousal.* Hillsdale, NJ: Lawrence Erlbaum Associates.

Video Games and the Pleasures of Control

Torben Grodal
University of Copenhagen, Denmark

Video games are remarkable new forms of entertainment. Video games import and customize many different forms of entertainment, from games related to jigsaw puzzles and chess simulations to games related to novels or to action films. Video games provide simulations of a series of aspects of reality, like racing, flying, or playing soccer, or simulations of complex social developments, from urban development to the evolution of civilization. The hallmark of most video games is that they transform these traditional forms of entertainment into an interactive form that enables the player actively to participate in shaping the games. Films or videos enable their viewers to interact only passively, by following the narrative and predicting possible outcomes, whereas video games provide the player with interactive means to change the course of the narrative. The interaction with such possible audiovisual worlds provides the player with an experience of being immersed in a "virtual reality," because our experience of reality is linked not only to the possible salience of what we see and hear, but is also centrally linked to whether we are able to interact with such perceptions. A key to explaining why video games have become very popular forms of entertainment is to explore those gratifications that are linked to the interactive form.

Most scholarly studies of video games have focused on the possible negative effects of video games, especially of the violent "shoot-'em-up" games. The perceptual salience of such games is very much inferior to that of, for instance, a gory movie played in a wide-screen THX-sound movie theater. However, the argument has been that the interactivity of the video games would make the player personally responsible for the atrocious acts and implicate the player in the morally dubious actions. In this chapter I supplement some of the findings of studies aimed at measuring possible negative effects of video games with an analysis of a series of gratifications derived from the interactivity of the video games in comparison with film (as a term covering film, TV, and video fiction).

This chapter concentrates on games that provide *narrative simulations*, that is, fictitious actions. The narrative games can be subdivided into two groups. One subgroup within narrative video games could be called adventure–mystery games. These games tend increasingly to emulate the more complex world of films in respect to themes, character complexity, and so on. In order to do so, some experiences are provided by inserting non-interactive film sequences. However, the time is often player-generated; that is, time progresses only when the player makes a move, and the game narration is often partly shown from an exterior, third-person point of view. The other subgroup consists of action games, centered on interactive realism, often shown in a three-dimensional world and by point of view. Games like *Wolfenstein*, *Mortal Kombat*, and *Quake* belong to this subgroup. They elicit strong arousal because of their combination of violent images, strong aggressive player reactions, and point-of-view editing. I use those games as material for my analysis, because they are the best matches to an interactive simulation of an "online" reality, and because those games have caused most public concern, due to their portrayal of violence. My prototype for the analysis will be *Quake*.

THE IMPACT OF VIOLENCE ON FILM AND IN VIDEO GAMES

The public debate about the possible impact of violent video games has had a precursor in the heated debate of similar features in film. Those in favor of violent or sexual films have used different arguments. One line of defense is the catharsis argument: Fictions serve as safety valves for aggression or sexual urges. A variant of this theory is an equilibrium theory, which claims that people use films in order to control their level of arousal, a position that could be explained by uses-and-gratification theories (Rubin, 1994). Another theory is that the fictional nature dissociates the film experience from real-life experiences. Those concerned by violent or sexually explicit films have other arguments. One is the desensitizing argument: Exposure to violence or strong sex will accustom viewers to such phenomena. Another argument is that such exposure provides social learning: People will learn violent behavior from films and copy the violent behavior in real life (Bandura, 1994). A variant of this argument is a priming argument: Violence activates and strengthens violence-related associations and emotional charges. A third argument is the arousal argument: Violent films raise the level of arousal and will therefore provide a basis for violent acts if they are put into a violent context.

Contrary to studies of the impact of film violence, several studies of video games have found either catharsis effects, equilibrium effects, or lack of any significant increase in aggressive tendencies (e.g., Calvert & Tan, 1994; Graybill, Strawniak, Hunter, & O'Leary, 1987; Kerstenbaum & Weinstein, 1985). Graybill, Kirsch, and Esselman (1985) found that children who played the violent video game showed fewer defensive fantasies and tended to show more assertive or need-persistent fantasies than did children who played the nonviolent game. Other studies have found aggression, arousal effects, and social learning induced by playing violent video games more similar to those found in film and television studies (Ballard & Wiest, 1996; Hoffman, 1995; Shutte, Malouf, Post-Gorden, & Rodasta, 1988; Silvern & Williamson, 1987). No studies have proven any long-term effects.

A series of studies have addressed computer games from the point of view of cognitive and perceptual development. This is, for instance, the case with two studies by Loftus and Loftus (1983) and Greenfield (1984). They each analyzed how video games enhanced perception, attention, spatial skills, memory, and motor performance. In a more recent collection of studies (*Journal of Applied Developmental Psychology, 15,* 1994) Greenfield and associates have come up with additional experimental evidence for the role of video games as part of learning processes.

However, most studies do not consider any positive gratifications from playing violent video games. Although most children and adolescents use a lot of time playing such games, this only causes concern, not any interest in the fascination. A reason for this lack of interest is that the fascination is regarded as one focused on violence and aggression per se. It might, however, be argued that the fascination consists of many different elements. A central fascination with violent games is linked to the strong arousal caused by the dangerous situations portrayed. The playful simulation of dangerous situations is often gratifying because such simulations allow the player to cope with strong aversive sympathetic reactions. Coping with situations linked to strong aversive arousal is not only linked to criminal behavior; firefighters, drivers, rescue workers, or victims of violence will often experience dangerous situations. Daily life is based not only on empathy, cooperation, and compromise, but also on aversive situations that demand assertiveness. Respectable forms of entertainment like chess or fairy tales are often centered on confrontation and aversion.

The arousal motivates a series of cognitive and motor responses, some of which are violent. Many of these responses are defensive, other responses are linked to violent reactions to fantasy creatures, yet other responses are directed at humans, although even games like *Mortal Kombat* portray the possible victims of violence in a rather exotic, stylized manner, very different from the realist portrayal of victims in, for instance, splatter films. It is reasonable to be concerned that strong video game violence may be harmful for players disposed toward violence by other factors. However, there is no conclusive evidence for the impact on normal players.

There are some clearly immoral games, like the car game *Carmageddon*, in which the player gets points for killing innocent pedestrians. Such games raise problems similar to those raised by comic fictions in which the pain and abuse of clowns and other comic figures cue pleasurable viewer reactions. The ability to get comic pleasure out of such reversals of normal empathic relations between viewers (or players) and fictitious characters is based on innate dispositions. Comic reversals presuppose some kind of moral maturity that prevents viewers and players from experiencing such reversals as normal interpersonal relations. The limits to such comic reversals clearly depend on moral evaluations of the limits for what kinds of themes are acceptable, and on commonsense assessments of to what extent some reversals may lead to moral confusion.

In general we may assert that we possess aggressive potential, which we have inherited because aggression had a clear survival value for our ancestors. Many reactions supported by such inherited mechanisms are clearly harmful in our present environment (murder and other violent acts). However, it is not clear whether other types of "aggressive" behavior that does not lead to physical abuse of other people serve possible beneficial mental mechanisms; for instance, assertiveness, need-persistence, and emotional control in confrontation with aversive stimuli. It is not obvious that the media society only supports lack of empathy due to an overload of violence; on the contrary, more people than ever are deeply concerned with the well-being of other people, and empathic concerns are increasingly also directed at animals and lower life-forms. Intuitively this seems partly to be an effect of the way in which modern audiovisual media increasingly make it possible to empathize with other beings. In this larger context the aggression displayed in some types of media products and the comic reversal of empathy might partly be explained as negotiations and regulations of the level of empathy.

In the rest of this chapter I explore the hypothesis that danger and violence in video games serve as part of cognitive and emotional learning processes. I will analyze some reasons why the interactivity of video games supports emotional control by linking the experience of strong emotion-eliciting stimuli to cognitive and physical interaction with the game world. I further analyze some of the gratifications that are elicited by the playful simulations of "live" interactive processes.

EMOTIONS IN REAL LIFE, ON FILM
AND IN VIDEO GAMES

In order to provide a framework for understanding possible differences between the emotional impact of film and interactive video games I recapitulate some fundamentals in emotion theory (cf. Grodal, 1997) and relate these to film and video games. A precondition for eliciting strong emotions is to present some stimuli that are central concerns of living beings, for instance threats on life or health. Such stimuli will elicit physical arousal. Arousal is a very general physiological process, and, as argued by cognitive labeling theorists of human emotions, in order to create emotions out of arousal you need cognitively to specify, to contextualize the arousal, in order to elicit emotions. The situational context cues a dominant action tendency by means of a cognitive analysis of the situation, resulting in a cognitive labeling of the arousal. As described, for instance, by the Dutch psychologist Frijda, emotions are "modes of relational action readiness, either in the form of tendencies to establish, maintain, or disrupt a relationship with the environment or in the form of mode of relational readiness as such" (1986, p. 71).

A simple example: If you suddenly meet a lion on a savannah it would create arousal. The context will determine how the arousal is molded into an emotion. If you are armed, you may feel aggression and shoot the lion, but if unarmed you might feel fright and look for escape, or you might feel that you are unable to cope with the situation and feel despair. If you are safely placed in a photo safari jeep, the arousal is transformed into delight. These emotions are phasic, that is, there is an eliciting cause of arousal, followed by an appreciation of what to do, which then leads to actions that will eventually transform the emotion by removing or transforming the causes of the emotions. The emotional experience will therefore consist of phases: a cause, an arousal, a cognitive appreciation and a labeling, followed by some actions that remove the cause of arousal. In order to elicit phasic emotions in relation to fiction we need a focusing character, because without such a character we cannot specify any coping strategies.

The emotional experience of a given situation will consequently be different according to whether it is cued by a film or by a video game. When viewing a film the labeling of the emotions felt is determined by the viewer's passive appreciation of the film character's coping potentials. But when the situation is part of a video game, it is the player's assessment of his own coping potentials that determines the emotional experience. The unskilled player may feel despair when confronted with the lion, but the skilled player will fuel the arousal into a series of courageous actions. Video games therefore simulate emotions in a form that is closer to typical real-life experiences than film: Emotions are motivators for actions and are labeled according to the player's active coping potentials.

THE INPUT–OUTPUT PROBLEM AND THE GAME
PLAYER'S VIRTUAL REALITY SIMULATION

A film viewer has no control over the direction of his or her perceptions and no control over possible reactions to possible arousing events. However, the viewer can bridge the gap between perceptions and actions by several cognitive and affective strategies. The viewer can think up several coping strategies and hope for given outcomes. The terms *interest* and *suspense* often cover these passive viewer expectations. Films shown in the cinema are especially, so to speak, input-driven: the salience and magnitude of the screen in combination with engrossing events ensure a strong input, and often whole genres like melodrama are constructed in order to overwhelm the viewer, eventually by cuing strongly passive emotional responses like crying or great fear. The viewer may thus experience the film from a third-person position of being a witness to events (Carroll, 1990). The passive third-person aspects of film viewing are often partly masked by providing close links between the point-of-view presentation of emotion-eliciting elements and the protagonist's concerns and possible or effected actions. If there are a close knit and fast-paced relation between these three factors, the viewer is led into simulating such sequences of perceptions, concerns and actions as if they were performed actively by the viewer (Grodal, 1997; Smith, 1995). However, the coping potentials of the viewer are mostly very general and are linked to mental simulations.

Compared with cinema films and even with TV screen–transmitted fictions, video games have a less salient input, although sound and graphics have improved significantly. But the games make up for this by providing more sophisticated devices for processing the input in relation to output. A video game provides an interactive interface, which enables the player to control actions and often also perceptions by an ability to control the point of view, that is, to control the point from which, and the direction by which, the game world is represented. This leads to several dramatic changes compared to film viewing:

- The player needs to use attention in order to control perception, including the point of view.
- The player needs to make mental maps of the game-space as if it were a real three-dimensional world. He or she needs to notice landmarks, significant causal relations, and so on.
- The player needs to actively coordinate visual attention and motor actions (by mouse, joystick, or keyboard). The feedback from the activation of these procedural schemata will create additional arousal. The activation and coordination of the different mental functions and representations will compete with limited capacity in working memory and possibly cause mental overload.
- The emotional significance and labeling of a certain event-induced arousal are linked to the player's own ability to cope with a given problem. It will therefore vary over time (and vary from player to player).
- The player will get a continuous satisfaction from his performance. Therefore, the pleasure is derived not only from the global performance, but also from a series of local achievements, local sequences of arousal leading into coping actions.
- The game processes are driven by the player's motivation for performing, and success and failure is partly attributed to the player, not to the game-world. The length of the home video game relates to the player's own motivation.

All these characteristics emphasize that video games are much more focused on the relation between input and output, the relation between perception, attention, emotion, and motor control, than films (Kubey & Larson, 1990). Therefore the arousal is not only derived from input but also experienced in relation to processing the input in a more profound way than just guessing the probable outcome. The player participates in a virtual reality simulation of a possible real world. When a player accepts to play a given character in a game, it is done from the inside as a temporal fusion with a given world, with some game-defined perception capabilities and action capabilities. It is well documented that the interactions between persons and computers and with computers as platforms for video games are experienced as an involvement on a first-person level (Reeves & Nass, 1996; Shapiro & McDonald, 1992; Turkle, 1984). These studies emphasize that a naturalistic conception of the interaction with media, and especially with computer media, is the typical attitude.

The computer media experience underlines that actions and interactions are very strong components in our experience of reality. The fascination many players felt with the (by modern standards) often crude visual interfaces of the first video games of the early 1970s showed that the salience of the perceptual input was powerfully enhanced by feedback from the interactive output capabilities.

TYPES OF INTERACTION IN VIDEO GAMES

Our experience of our relations to reality may have three main forms. The first form consists of being a passive, perceptual witness to spaces, actions, and processes, as when we are viewing a film. Some video games have inserted such film-type sequences with which the player cannot interact. Because such sequences do not afford interaction, they are experienced as subjective (Grodal, 1997). The second form is based on an active exploration of spaces, actions, and processes that are fully self-controlled, as when we take a walk, whether this walk is taken in real life or in a virtual reality. Mystery games like *Myst* typically possess such a player-generated time, in which processes take off when the player performs some actions and stop when the player stops. Action-centered video games like *Quake* also have some sequences in which the player is in total control over the actions and processes. The third form is not only active, but also centrally interactive, because the player is confronted with other processes and agencies that are only partly under the control of the experiencing agency. The player has to perform actions at a certain pace, because otherwise he or she will "die," for instance, because he or she cannot prevent his or her vehicle from crashing. Furthermore, in centrally interactive sequences, it is not only the player who can seek out events, other agencies like monsters can seek out the player (or the player's character). The player has to cope with antagonistic forces and processes according to some game-world time. The sense of realism is enhanced because the player's control is not absolute, but relative to his skills.

Video sequences that are based on player-generated time support exploratory gratifications; for instance, curiosity and cognitive problem solving. The game proceeds at a speed that suits the player's sense of control. When a player has solved a problem, he can proceed to the next set of stimuli, the next problem. Game-world–generated time provides other gratifications because it evokes much stronger emotions. The problems need to be solved under severe time constraints similar to those in emotional peak situations in real life. The player has to integrate perceptions, cognitions, emotions, and actions fast in order to survive and is provided with a strong feeling of interaction. The closer a game experience gets to the player's optimal mental and motor capacity the less capacity is available for being conscious about the game being just a game: the game provides total immersion.

Such strong interaction will, however, also cause fatigue and eventually a sense of lack of control. Most action video games are therefore constructed in such a way that they provide the player with choices between playing in a player-generated and a game-world–generated time. Some spaces in the game-world are defined as player-controlled. In such spaces (zones) the player may "rest," perform strategic thinking, or carry out exploratory actions, by which he can control motion, and point of view, or explore objects. Other zones, other spaces, are defined as having game-world–defined times and processes; here the monsters can seek out the player-character and here the processes cannot be stopped, only mastered by some actions. If, for instance, the player falls into a pool of slime, he needs to get out "before he is out of air."

To control all the different activities of playing video games presupposes training by repetitive playing. Training will enable the player to transfer some of the activities from conscious control into a control by nonconscious procedures. The perfect mastering of such tasks will lead to the experience of mental flow, as described by Turkle (1984). The player who has perfectly learned all the different complex procedures can play in a highly active, but semiconscious, state. The performance demands total concentration in order to integrate a series of automated and nonconscious processes within a conscious framework. By having learned a series of procedural schemata the player will gain the necessary capacity for effortless voluntary control.

Thus video games are structured according to a principle of uses and gratifications similar to that of real life: We can seek out stimulating spaces when bored and take shelter in some other spaces when overstimulated and in need of rest. The video game enables the player to control his or her perceptual, emotional, and enactional activation. The feeling of being able to customize one's control over the relation between challenge and personal control is further enhanced by three additional features of most video games: the existence of a pause button, the possibility of saving intermediate results, and the existence of different levels of difficulty. Thus the player can choose the level of difficulty in relation to skill that the player considers to be optimal.

REPETITIVE GAME-PLAYING, CURIOSITY, SURPRISE, AND SUSPENSE

The typical film is viewed one time only, whereas the typical video game is played many times, and the cognitive and emotional differences between these two modes of reception accounts for central differences in the experience of the two media.

In a film there is a big difference between the first viewing and the following viewing(s) (Brewer, 1996). For most viewers the first viewing is the central film experience. The first-time viewing of a narrative takes place with an uncertain narrative future. This cues curiosity, surprise, and suspense. As the narrative proceeds, the film will make the narrative factual. When the film viewing is finished, the viewer has received the final and irreversible version of the narrative. Our cognitive, emotional, and enactional experience of a film will therefore be determined by the fact that any given film sequence presents a final version of events. Mutilations or deaths during the film are mostly final and unchangeable facts.

In contrast to this, a video game is played many times and many events can be altered by the player's interactions. Thus a given sequence in one game performance of a given video game-world by a given player is different from a similar sequence in the following game. A given game not only exists as a factual event, related to a given game, but also provides important feedback in the following games. Or phrased differently: Video games are learning processes. A given game will typically not lead the player through the whole game; only a series of games will provide the player with the necessary skills to complete the game. Even when completing the game the game-world will be a series of spaces, objects, and actions, a virtual reality, with many possibilities for making linear narratives from beginning to end. Because video games are repetitive learning processes, the emotional experience is different compared with the film experience. I explain this difference in relation to the experience of three central arousal-evoking elements: curiosity, surprise, and suspense. I mostly follow the definitions of curiosity, surprise, and suspense provided by Brewer (1996).

A film will often elicit curiosity, because a viewer is aware that vital information concerning narrative past or present events is withheld. The film will induce arousal until the information is disclosed and then the information will lose its interest. In a video game the satisfaction of curiosity is part of a process of learning and mastery. The player needs to remember the disclosed information in order to use it in a second game. A central factor in playing video games is to remember information from previous games, slotting the information into cognitive maps. Because curiosity in action video games (as opposed to mystery video games) is mostly prospective, curiosity is often linked to properties of the game-world as possible elements of future actions. I discuss curiosity in relation to suspense later in this chapter.

A film will create surprise by sudden events. It will create a momentary arousal jag, which will then disappear. But when playing video games, what was surprising in the first game is transformed into a suspenselike coping anticipation in the following games. When the player advances toward the space/time in which the surprising event has previously occurred, say the sudden appearance of a fierce antagonist, an increased arousal is induced. The arousal will diminish over time as the player learns some coping mechanisms, for instance, fast routines for shooting the monster despite the surprising speed or the surprising location of the monster. When hearing horrible dogs growling from behind, the player will learn to turn quickly. Because of capacity constraints imposed on the brain when playing games, it is not at all certain that a player is able to understand and remember the cause of a given surprise; only consecutive games will provide the necessary knowledge and motor skill (for instance, to control point of view in such a way that the circumstances of a surprising event can be discovered).

A film will create arousal related to the viewer's expectations of what will happen to the central protagonists. The expectations can be linked to knowledge of dangers or positive events disclosed to the viewer but not to the protagonists. Some theorists (Brewer, 1996) use the word *suspense* exclusively to describe such emotional concerns for protagonists if they are derived from knowledge not shared by protagonists. For good reasons such suspense does not exist in video games, because the game character and the player are fused. In everyday use of the term in respect to film, however, suspense also applies to strong concerns about the future destiny of the protagonists. I will therefore use suspense in this broad sense. (Zillmann [1996] provides a broad definition of suspense that is similar to mine, but he does not consider the role of the viewer's simulation of the characters' coping potentials.) Video games certainly evoke suspense related to the outcome of local sequences as well as the final outcome of the game. But just as we saw in relation to interest and surprise, suspense in video games is interwoven with the interactive and repetitive nature of the game.

Because of the interactive aspect of the game, the outcome in a given game is in principle just as uncertain the second time as the first time. The player might in the first game by chance shoot an important antagonist or by chance stand in a protected area, or the player may make a perceptual or motor mistake. The player will only by training achieve such an expertise that the game will lose its suspense, and thereby its ability to arouse and stimulate the player.

The suspense is often based on a series of different factors, such as the ability to perform spatial mapping, to detect the different capabilities and locations of antagonists, and to guess what weapons to use or what strategy to use. The player's exploration of the game-world by means of trial and error as well as by means of constant assessments of causes and effects is linked to a suspenseful curiosity. Contrary to a film narrative, which shows all aspects of the narrative world in the first viewing, because its narrative is based on a linear space-time, a video game often supports many different ways of proceeding through the game-world.

A characteristic aspect of video game suspense is the way in which it is molded by the player's coping motivation, including the wish for achievement. A film will go on irrespective of the viewer's degree of curiosity or suspense, but a video game is actively driven by the viewer's explorative activities. A term like *explorative coping* might therefore be a useful supplement to the terms curiosity, surprise, and suspense in order to describe video games.

In video games, curiosity, surprise, suspense and explorative coping are not fixed entities, causing fixed types of arousal and fixed emotions as a consequence of cognitive labeling linked to affordances. On the contrary: The experience of given situations will change over time, due to learning processes that will change arousal and will change the cognitive labeling of the arousal. The emotional experience is not primarily input-driven, but driven by the wish for an active control, and thereby also driven by a wish for emotional control. The aggressive game-induced arousal is therefore possibly more closely linked to the player's own activity and less directed at the hostile others than in film. When a player has been shot by an enemy, he can press a button to play a new game. Therefore, that arousal is fueled into further play is a more adequate coping reaction than aggression toward the "enemy." In video games, the antagonists are often a multitude of hostile others, and there are therefore no focusing antagonists (except maybe the computer itself as host for the hostile software).

VIDEO GAMES AND SELF-ESTEEM

In video games the blame for defeat is predominantly directed at the players themselves, because the players are well aware of the fact that the evil forces act according to encoded software scripts and that other, better-skilled players are able to succeed. The variable is the player's skill. To link defeat with personal humiliation is therefore a more adequate reaction than hate toward all the different evil forces. In many games a player can choose different skill levels and thus choose a level that provides an adequate balance between challenge and personal performance. These structural factors in violent video games accord with theories that hypothesize that entertainment serves as a means for controlling the level and the variation of arousal. The arousal is increased by exposure to adverse situations but reduced and relabeled as the learning processes enhance coping. Aggression is primarily linked to coping. And the player's exposure to arousing phenomena might—from a uses-and-gratification point of view—be seen as part of mood management (cf. Rubin, 1994; Zillmann & Bryant, 1994). But on the other hand, the effects are very much linked to the player's assessment of his or her own performance, and the effect on aggression could therefore be linked to individual differences. In films the viewer gets a vicarious satisfaction in seeing a protagonist succeed. The degree of satisfaction is—besides the narrative factors—probably linked to the degree to which the protagonist matches values of concern for the viewer's self-appreciation. The vicarious self-esteem derived from films may depend on the viewer's ability to empathize with characters and thematic values as well as on the display of mastery by violence. But the viewing process as such in a mainstream film does not demand any special skills and is therefore not a self-test. Exceptions are very violent films, which can test the stamina of the viewer.

In violent video games there are only rudimentary links to social themes. The player-character is mostly defined as a relatively unspecific warrior. The central factor for self-esteem is linked to the player's skill in mastering the game. It could therefore be hypothesized that playing video games would have very different effects on different players. Good players should get more self-esteem out of playing video games than bad players. Even if game playing is part of a learning process, in which more time spent on playing will lead to better results, there would still be significant individual differences (contrary to viewing films). But the possibilities for choosing an adequate level of difficulty in relation to the player's skills should lead to a diminishing of differences in self-esteem as a consequence of playing video games. It is furthermore not clear whether video games would attract people with self-esteem problems because of the possibility for creating an alternative way of mastery, as suggested by Dominick (1984) or attract people with strong self-esteem who are motivated by an additional way of coping. Fling et al. (1992) found no correlation between the amount of playing time and self-esteem. A study by Funk and Buchman (1996) found no effects on self-esteem on boys playing violent video games, but some correlations between girls playing violent video games and a lowered self-esteem.

VIDEO GAMES AND EMOTIONAL CONTROL

Following is a summary of some of the points discussed earlier.

1. The interactive interface between player and game-world makes the coping reactions to arousing events into concrete coping procedures. Therefore, video games elicit fluctuating emotional labeling procedures in relation to coping potentials in the given situation. This labeling will change over time as a function of the player's learning. They will activate a series of mental and bodily functions: attention, arousal, cognitive appraisals of arousal, cognitive mapping, procedural schemata, and motor performance. A given arousal-eliciting event will continuously be relabeled. A panic-evoking situation can, by learning processes, be transformed into a fear-evoking or aggression-evoking event, or eventually be totally controlled and be interpreted as a cause for playful mastery.

Contrary to film, video games are output-driven. Furthermore a game is meant to be played several times, and therefore a given outcome is not final, but part of cognitive and emotional learning processes similar to everyday learning. The input-mastering by coping reactions will influence the experience of curiosity, surprise, suspense, and explorative coping in the player's different performances in a given video game.

2. The games are constructed to make it possible for players to gain control over the elicited arousal by means of the learning processes. Besides the central interface that controls perception and action, the games typically possess a series of additional control devices, from being able to choose several levels of difficulty, to time out features and the possibility of saving a positive intermediate result. Video games are therefore often "mood managers;" that is, they allow the player to participate in a self-controlled arousing experience. The time spent on a given game is player-controlled, and therefore it may be suggested that the player will continue to play until he or she has achieved an optimal arousal equilibrium. The game is emotionally, cognitively, and physically demanding, and may cause fatigue.

3. The point-of-view video games activate the player on a first-person basis and are experienced as part of a self-testing, which links the player's performance to his personal self-esteem. As a consequence, the video game experience may be more individualized than film viewing because of a greater variation in a player's ability to master a game than to view a film, especially because video play mastery is objectively evaluated (by degree of scores, kills, number of secrets found, etc.), whereas a film viewer has no such objective evaluation of performance.

4. The violent action game is often experienced as a simulation of interacting with an online reality, because the player's mental flow of perceptions that cause emotions and cognition that causes action that again causes perceptions, is very similar to real-life interaction.

Seen from one perspective, violent video games look very much like a playful enactment of skills and dispositions central to our gatherer-warrior-hunter ancestors. The players cope with a hostile environment by quick perception and by spatial and motor skills, they notice landmarks and gather objects that may be useful. However, seen from another perspective, video games are ways in which players learn to master facets of computers. Video games thus mold the biological inheritance in a way that accords with present-day cultural needs. As pointed out in several studies (Greenfield, Brannon, & Lohr, 1994; Greenfield, Camaioni, et al., 1994, for example), computer games are important playful tools for learning to interact with the computer medium and its graphic interface, just as the games enhance spatial skills and eye–hand coordination. Those studies also show that boys on average perform significantly better in action-oriented computer games, partly because of better spatial skills, but also for motivational reasons, because boys have a stronger preference for violent games than girls, maybe for biological reasons (Kubey & Larson, 1990). This accords closely with evolutionary theories of sex differences in spatial abilities due to division of labor in gatherer-hunter societies (Silverman & Eals, 1992) and to motivational features that supported hunting. It is deplorable that the video game industry has not yet invented games that cater to those gatherer skills and motivations that are attractive to girls (verbal skills, object memory, location memory, and a series of social skills and pro-social motives).

When most children and adolescents in the industrialized world spend considerable time playing video games, and very often violent video games, pessimists argue that this was a dangerous trap by a greedy video game industry to evoke primitive and antisocial features of our biological inheritance. They further question that those games provide real creative interactive experiences. They argue that the interactivity is only a surface phenomenon that veils indoctrination because "most games require the player to take part in developing the game scenario, but players are routinely rewarded for identifying and selecting the strategies built in by the game designer" (Funk & Buchman, 1996). However, this is also the case in most culturally produced games and fictions and does not show whether video games are putting narrower constraints on personal creativity than other games and fictions. Pessimists further argue that the scenarios and themes provide an impoverished experience. Provenzo (1991) states, "Compared to the worlds of imagination provided by play with dolls and blocks, games such as those reviewed in this chapter [popular Nintendo games] ultimately represent impoverished cultural and sensory environments" (p. 97). Provenzo further points

TABLE 11.1
A Feature Comparison of Film Viewing and Video-Game Playing

Entertainment Medium	Film	Video Game
Perceptual quality	High visual salience	Medium visual salience
Interactive control of:		
Visual input (point of view)	None	Controlled by player via interface
Story events	None	Controlled by player via interface in interaction with game agency
Temporal progression	None	Controlled by player's explorative coping and time-out devices
Emotional significance of events	Controlled by film and characters	Emotional arousal is labeled according to the player's action skills and varies over time due to learning processes. Curiosity, surprise, and suspense are molded by repetitive interaction.
Supports mainly:	One viewing	Multiple games
	Mental and bodily simulations of cued events	Concrete interactive simulations based on extensive cognitive mappings of space and the learning of procedural schemas, leading to motor reactions via interface
	Vicarious simulation of characters	First-person simulation of roles, leading to immersion in game world
Evaluation of viewer/ player performance	None	Yes, by game success, and eventually by score mechanism

out the way in which video games rely on cultural stereotypes. These arguments, however, beg the question of why so many children choose such games, why they play with a Barbie Doll computer game instead of playing with the physical doll, or why they choose to fight galactic wars on computers instead of playing with physical blocks or all kinds of physical guns and tanks. Provenzo's portrayal of the impoverishment of the game leaves something out. Most video games or fairy tales are certainly more impoverished than a complex social melodrama or a novel by James Joyce, but the interaction with science fiction worlds or audiovisual re-makes of fairy tale worlds may be more gratifying than passively viewing a cops and robbers show on TV.

Optimists can argue that video games fulfill positive functions that mold our biological inheritance to fit present-day needs. I have argued for the pleasures de-rived from video games as tools for emotional control, which adds a new cultur-al artifact to those means of mood management that have been developed by the entertainment industry, for instance, film and TV (Grodal, 1997; Zillmann & Bryant, 1994). Video games are learning processes that develop a series of cog-nitive skills (Loftus & Loftus, 1983), just as video games enhance mastery of the computer (Greenfield, Camaioni, et al., 1994).

The themes and actions of most video games are updated versions of fairy tales and Homer's *Odyssey*, enhanced by modern audiovisual salience and inter-active capabilities. Central themes are the fights with dragons and evil monsters in combination with quests through dangerous and exotic scenarios. It is further-more important for many games that the hero rescues damsels in distress. That there are only a few basic narrative patterns in video games is not surprising be-cause there are not many basic narrative patterns in fiction. Of those basic narra-tive patterns only action-adventure and mystery plots are suitable for interactive narratives, whereas romances, comedies, and tragedies rely centrally on passive recipients for the emotional build-up (Grodal, 1997). Certainly there are degrees of freedom in the way in which action-adventure narratives are provided with themes; in principle it is easy to imagine games in which women save men in dis-tress, or games that provide scores for feeding hungry children in Africa. Criti-cism that points out stereotypes, prejudices, and antisocial behavior in video games puts a healthy pressure on the industry to come up with better themes.

Video games do not replace the traditional forms of entertainment but rather provide a supplement to, for instance, reading, watching film and television, and participating in sports. The pleasure derived from an interactive immersion in a virtual reality competes with pleasures derived from other types of entertainment that emphasize passive pleasures, like film and television. Interactive media like video games create a further sophistication of media consumption by enabling consumers to switch between a passive control of their emotional and cognitive states (by actively selecting one-way media) and an active control of these states (by choosing interactive media). These interactive media are still in their infancy for reasons related to the kinds of stories that, for technical reasons, can be en-acted. But interactive media have already provided quite new pleasures due to the way in which they enable players to simulate an interactive control of human faculties and emotions in possible worlds.

REFERENCES

Ballard, M. E., & Wiest, J. R. (1996). Mortal Kombat™: The effects of violent videogame play on males' hostility and cardiovascular responding. *Journal of Applied Social Psychology, 26*(8), 717–730.

Bandura, A. (1994). Social cognitive theory of mass communication. In J. Bryant and D. Zillmann (Eds.), *Media effects: Advances in theory and research* (pp. 61–90). Hillsdale, NJ: Lawrence Erlbaum Associates.

Brewer, W. F. (1996). Narrative suspense and rereading. In P. Vorderer, H. J. Wulff, and M. Friedrichsen (Eds.), *Suspense: Conceptualizations, theoretical analyses, and empirical explorations.* Mahwah, NJ: Lawrence Erlbaum Associates.

Carroll, N. (1990). *The philosophy of horror, or paradoxes of the heart.* London: Routledge.

Calvert, S. L., & Tan, S.-L. (1994). Impact of virtual reality on young adults' physiological arousal and aggressive thoughts: Interaction versus observation. *Journal of Applied Developmental Psychology 15,* 125–139.

Dominick, J. R. (1984). Videogames, television violence and aggression in teenagers. *Journal of Communication, 34*(2), 136–147.

Fling, S., Smith, L., Rodriguez, D., Thornton, D., Atkins, E., & Nixon, K. (1992). Videogames, aggression, and self-esteem: A survey. *Social Behavior and Personality, 20*(1), 39–46.

Frijda, N. H. (1986). *The emotions.* Cambridge, England: Cambridge University Press.

Funk, J. B., & Buchman, D. D. (1996). Playing violent video and computer games and adolescent self-concept. *Journal of Communication 46*(2), 19–32.

Graybill, D., Kirsch, J., & Esselman, E. (1985). Effects of playing violent versus nonviolent video games on the aggressive ideation of aggressive and nonaggressive children. *Child Study Journal 15,* 199–205.

Graybill, D., Strawniak, M., Hunter, T., & O'Leary, M. (1987). Effects of playing versus observing violent versus nonviolent video games on children's aggression. *Psychology: A Quarterly Journal of Human Behavior 24*(3), 1–8.

Greenfield, P. M. (1984). *Mind and media: The effects of television, computers and video games.* Cambridge, MA: Harvard University Press.

Greenfield, P. M., Brannon, C., & Lohr, D. (1994). Two-dimensional representation of movement through three-dimensional space: The role of video game expertise. *Journal of Applied Developmental Psychology 15,* 87–103.

Greenfield, P. M., Camaioni, L., Ercolani, P., Weiss, L., Lauber, B. A., & Perucchini, P. (1994). Cognitive socialization by computer games in two cultures: Inductive discovery or mastery of an iconic code? *Journal of Applied Developmental Psychology 15,* 59–85.

Grodal, T. (1997). *Moving pictures: A new theory of film genres, feelings and cognition.* Oxford, England: Oxford University Press/Clarendon.

Hoffman, K. (1995). Effects of playing versus witnessing video game violence on attitudes toward aggression and acceptance of violence as a means of conflict resolution (Doctoral dissertation, University of Alabama, 1994). *Dissertation Abstracts International, 56/03,* 747.

Journal of Applied Developmental Psychology, 15 (1994).

Kerstenbaum, G. I., & Weinstein, L. (1985). Personality, psychopathology, and developmental issues in male adolescent video game use. *Journal of the American Academy of Child Psychiatry 24*(3), 329–337.

Kubey, R., & Larson, R. (1990). The use and experience of the new video media among children and young adolescents. *Communication Research, 17*(1), 107–130.

Loftus, G. R., & Loftus, E. F. (1983). *Mind at play: The psychology of video games.* New York: Basic Books.

Provenzo, E. F. (1991). *Video kids: Making sense of Nintendo.* Cambridge, MA: Harvard University Press.

Reeves, B., & Nass, C. (1996). *The media equation: How people treat computers, television, and new media like real people and places.* Cambridge, England: Cambridge University Press.

Rubin, A. (1994). Media uses and effects: A uses-and-gratifications perspective. In J. Bryant and D. Zillmann (Eds.), *Media effects: Advances in theory and research.* Hillsdale, NJ: Lawrence Erlbaum Associates.

Schutte, N. S., Malouf, J. M., Post-Gorden, J. C., & Rodasta, A. L. (1988). Effects of playing videogames on children's aggressive and other behaviors. *Journal of Applied Social Psychology, 18*(5), 454–460.

Shapiro, M. A., & McDonald, D. G. (1992). I'm not a real doctor, but I play one in virtual reality: Implications of virtual reality for judgements about reality. *Journal of Communication 43*(4), 94–114.

Silverman, I., & Eals, M. (1992). Sex differences in spatial abilities: Evolutionary theory and data. In J. H. Barkow, L. Cosmides, and J. Tooby (Eds.), *The adapted mind: Evolutionary psychology and the generation of culture* (pp. 533–553). New York: Oxford University Press.

Silvern, S. B., & Williamson, P. A. (1987). The effects of videogame play on young children's aggression, fantasy, and prosocial behavior. *Journal of Applied Developmental Psychology, 126,* 273–284.

Smith, M. (1995). *Engaging characters: Fiction, emotion and the cinema.* Oxford, England: Oxford University Press/Clarendon.

Turkle, S. (1984). *The second self: Computers and the human spirit.* New York: Simon & Schuster.

Zillmann, D. (1996). The psychology of suspense in dramatic exposition. In P. Vorderer, H. J. Wulff, and M. Friedrichsen (1996). *Suspense: Conceptualizations, theoretical analyses, and empirical explorations.* Mahwah, NJ: Lawrence Erlbaum Associates.

Zillmann, D., & Bryant, J. (1994). Entertainment as media effect. In J. Bryant and D. Zillmann (Eds.), *Media effects: Advances in theory and research* (pp. 437–461). Hillsdale, NJ: Lawrence Erlbaum Associates.

12
▼▼▼▼▼▼▼▼

The Respondent Gender Gap

Mary Beth Oliver
Penn State University

Any trip to a local video rental store reveals the complexities of individuals' enjoyment of media entertainment. The videos are neatly arranged according to genre, and the customers wander around the aisles, much like in a grocery store, in search of that morsel of cinematic pleasure that will satisfy their entertainment needs. What type of media programming best serves these goals? The possible answers to this question are seemingly endless, as illustrated throughout the chapters in this book. However, a cursory observation of video seekers often reveals a common "he said–she said" debate concerning the evening's entertainment choices. Whereas "he" drifts toward the action movies and horror films, "she" pores over the romances and tearjerkers. Although this picture is admittedly simplistic in its stereotypes, the frequency with which this sort of scenario occurs serves as an illustration of the important role that gender plays in viewers' responses to entertainment. This chapter first reviews several types of media portrayals that appear to be differentially appealing to male and female audiences: melodramatic tearjerkers, sporting events, violent content, horror films, and pornography. Subsequently, this chapter explores possible explanations for why these gender differences may exist.

GENDER DIFFERENCES IN RESPONSE TO DIFFERENT
TYPES OF MEDIA ENTERTAINMENT

Melodramatic Tearjerkers

The sad film or tearjerker is an appropriate starting place for a discussion of gender and entertainment because this particular genre is commonly referred to in gender-related terms specifically. Namely, the phrase "chick flick" is popularly understood to mean those melodramatic films that many females adore but that males only tolerate at best, if not abhor (Gelernter, 1996; Goodman, 1998). Films that are readily identified as being in this category include *Steel Magnolias*, *Beaches*, *Fried Green Tomatoes*, and, of course, *Love Story*. Although the phrase "chick flick" can refer to many types of genres, including romances and female "buddy" films (e.g., *Thelma and Louise*; see Capwell, 1998), sad films or tear-jerkers are prototypical examples of these types of movies that appear to hold particular appeal to the female audience.

Viewers' responses to sad films have received considerably less research attention than have responses to other genres. However, the small number of studies that have explored this particular type of entertainment tend to report robust and consistent gender differences in viewer responses. First, research strongly supports the popular notion that these types of films are enjoyed more by female than by male viewers. For example, Oliver (1993b) reported that the females in her sample indicated a greater overall enjoyment of sad films than did the males, a more frequent exposure to this type of entertainment, and a larger consumption of specific films from a list of movie titles. Similar findings were obtained by Oliver, Sargent, and Weaver (1998) in their study that examined responses to segments from a sad film (*Beaches*), a violent film (*Friday the 13th, Part III*), and a neutral film (*Yentl*). Females reported greater enjoyment of the sad film than did males, whereas males reported greater enjoyment of the violent film than did females.

Curiously, in addition to reporting greater enjoyment of sad films, females also tend to report more intense negative affect than do males. For example, Choti, Marston, Holston, and Hart (1987) assessed males' and females' emotional responses to the film *The Champ*. Females reported higher levels of sadness and lower levels of happiness after viewing the film than did males, and they also reported more frequent crying (consistent with observers' ratings). These findings parallel the results obtained in the previously mentioned study examining responses to film segments (Oliver, Sargent, & Weaver, 1998). In that study, females not only reported greater enjoyment of *Beaches* than did males, but they also reported being more disturbed by the film. Although self-report measures should be interpreted with caution, these studies suggest that, particularly among females, enjoyment of this specific form of entertainment may be a function of the negative affect that these films elicit. This idea is consistent with Oliver's (1993b) research that found positive correlations between retrospective ratings of enjoyment and ratings of sadness in response to 18 different sad films.

Although research concerning gender differences in response to sad films suggests that the phrase "chick flick" may be an apt descriptor of this form of entertainment, it is important to note that the documentation of gender differences does not, in and of itself, solve the paradox that this genre represents. In other words, the idea that females appear to respond more favorably to these types of media portrayals does not explain why individuals experience gratification from viewing entertainment that prominently features beloved protagonists who suffer from a host of horrible ills including terminal illness, loss of family members, and heartbreak. While possible answers to this question have been considered from both philosophical and psychological traditions (e.g., Feagin, 1983; Zillmann, 1998a) unambiguous explanations of the appeal of tragedy are still wanting.

Sports

Turning from the cinematic pleasures that appeal to female viewers to media content that appears to be more gratifying to males, it is difficult to imagine any type of programming that is more stereotyped as masculine than the ever-popular sporting event. Indeed, the widespread cultural image of the football widow suggests that this particular form of entertainment is not only appealing to males, but is so appealing as to be able to draw men away from their familial relationships. Although this portrait is obviously extreme, research concerning viewers' responses to televised sports supports the idea that males do tend to enjoy this form of entertainment more than do females, but that gender differences in enjoyment may vary as a function of the type of sporting event and the degree of violence involved.

In a recent study, Sargent, Zillmann, and Weaver (1998) asked males and females to report their enjoyment of, frequency of viewing, and perceptions of 25 different types of sports (e.g., football, boxing, gymnastics, etc.). While males reported greater overall viewing of televised sports than did females, gender differences in viewing, enjoyment, and perceptions of sports performance varied as a function of the type of sport in question. Specifically, males reported greater viewing and enjoyment of sports categorized as combative (e.g., football, hockey) and mechanized (e.g., golf, mountain biking), whereas females reported greater viewing and enjoyment of sports categorized as stylistic (e.g., gymnastics, figure skating). These authors interpreted their findings as suggesting that the violence and action involved in many sporting events serves to enhances males' but not females' enjoyment.

The popularity of violent sporting events among male viewers does not necessarily imply that it is the violence itself that is enjoyable to fans. Rather, Zillmann and Bryant have argued convincingly that violence may increase enjoyment because it serves to heighten perceptions of the suspense and drama involved in the sporting event (Bryant & Zillmann, 1983; Comisky, Bryant, & Zillmann, 1977; Zillmann, Bryant, & Sapolsky, 1989). Nevertheless, the relationship between sports conflict and viewer enjoyment appears to be stronger among male than female fans. For example, Bryant, Comisky, and Zillmann (1981) reported that the degree of violence involved in professional football plays increased viewers' reported enjoyment, but significantly so among males only.

Together, these studies lend support to the stereotype of the male sports fanatic and the football widow. However, this research also suggests that many gender differences in sportsfanship may not necessarily indicate an indifference among female viewers, but rather a greater appreciation among males for the drama and tension that is often associated with aggression in the types of sports typically receiving the greatest media coverage (e.g., football, boxing, etc.).

Media Violence

Studies of media sporting events highlight the important role that violence plays in predicting males' and females' responses. Similarly, research on viewers' reactions to media violence in other types of entertainment suggest similar patterns, with males indicating greater appreciation and females reporting more aversive responses.

Gender differences in reaction to media violence have been observed across a variety of genres. Blanchard, Graczyk, and Blanchard (1986) showed college students a series of violent excerpts, including scenes from a cartoon, a spy movie, a western, a wilderness film, and a war movie. Men reported both greater enjoyment and amusement than did women, and particularly so for the non-cartoon violence. Other studies have reported similar gender differences, even for genres that are not necessarily thought of as being particularly aggressive. For example, Zillmann and Mundorf (1987) showed college students a music video that factorially varied both sexual and violent visual imagery (the music itself was held constant). Overall, the inclusion of violent imagery did not affect music appreciation among male subjects, but resulted in significantly lower scores among female subjects.

Gender differences in appreciation of violent content have also been observed among younger viewers. Cantor and Nathanson (1997) conducted a telephone survey of the parents of children in grades ranging from kindergarten though sixth grade. Parents were asked to indicate their child's interest in four types of violent programming, including classic cartoons, action cartoons, live action programs, and reality-based action programs. Parents of males reported higher interest scores for their children for both action cartoons (e.g., *GI-Joe*) and live action programs (e.g., *Mighty Morphin Power Rangers*) than did parents of females. Gender differences for the other two types of programs were not significant.

Not only does children's interest in media violence parallel adults' responses, at an early age children also appear to stereotype programming as more appropriate for males than for females largely on the basis of its inclusion of violent portrayals. Oliver and Green (1998) showed movie trailers to children in nursery school through third grade. These movie trailers included both a romance-centered cartoon (*Beauty and the Beast*) and an action cartoon (*Teenage Mutant Ninja Turtles Movie*). After each trailer, children reported whether they believed the movie would be enjoyed more by boys, by girls, or by both boys and girls equally. The majority of children (64.2%) indicated that the *Turtles* movie would be enjoyed more by boys than girls, and almost one third of the children (32.4%) spontaneously mentioned the violence in the cartoon as their reason.

Horror Films

As the previously mentioned studies imply, violence can permeate almost any popular entertainment offering. However, media violence is arguably nowhere more graphic or gratuitous than in the genre commonly referred to as the slasher movie. As one film critic noted, " 'Stalk-and-slash' and 'splatter' movies have gone as far as they can go . . . disembowelments, beheadings, amputations, entrail eating. Nothing is out of bounds" (Schoell, 1985, p. 149). Given the extreme portrayals of violence in this genre and the amount of research attention that it has generated, it is useful to consider this form of entertainment separately from other, related studies on media violence per se.

Consistent with other media violence research, studies of graphic horror consistently report strong gender differences in reaction to this film genre. First, males tend to report greater enjoyment of horror films than do females, both in general and in response to specific films (Cantor & Reilly, 1982; Oliver, 1994a; Sparks, 1986). In addition to greater enjoyment, males also tend to report lower levels of fear and disturbance than do females. Sparks (1991) showed subjects scenes from *When a Stranger Calls* (Study 1) and *Nightmare on Elm Street, Part I* (Study 2). Males not only scored lower on self-reported measures of distress than did females, their level of physiological arousal while viewing the frightening scenes was also significantly lower.

In addition to reporting gender differences in enjoyment and distress, several studies have also found that the relationship between these two variables differs for male versus female viewers. Although excitation transfer would suggest a positive correlation between disturbance and enjoyment, at least under some circumstances (Zillmann, 1980, 1991, 1998b), this relationship appears to be significant among male viewers only. Zillmann, Weaver, Mundorf, and Aust (1986) first reported this gender difference in a study in which males and females rated their responses to a scene from *Friday the 13th, Part III*. Among males, ratings of distress and ratings of delight were positively correlated ($r = .47$), whereas among females, the relationship between these two ratings was negligible ($r = .14$). Similar findings were reported by Sparks (1991), both in terms of self-report measures and in terms of physiological responses. Zillmann et al. (1986) interpreted this gender difference as suggesting that for females, strong distaste for images of violence prohibits the easy transition from negative to positive affect in the aftermath of horrific scenes.

Males' and females' differential response to the violent images contained in horror films is consistent with research concerning gender differences in motivations for viewing these types of films. For example, Johnston's (1995) survey of 220 high school students found that males scored significantly higher than females on a motivation scale labeled "gore-watching." Higher scores on this scale reflected agreement with items such as "I like to see blood and guts" and "I like to see the victims get what they deserve." Males were also more likely than females to report greater appreciation for the violence contained in horror films, to report more empathic responses to the killers, and to report less empathic responses to the victims. In contrast, no gender differences were obtained on some measures, including a motivation scale labeled "thrill-watching" (e.g., "To freak myself out"). These results parallel Tamborini and Stiff's (1987) survey of horror film moviegoers that found a greater enjoyment of horror films and a greater appreciation of the images of destruction contained in these movies among males, and a greater appreciation of horror film plots featuring restorations of justice among females.

Although violent images are perhaps the most salient aspect of horror films, researchers have also noted that these movies often contain sexual or erotic images, many of which are associated with displays of aggression. For example, Molitor and Sapolsky's (1993) content analysis of 30 slasher films found that sexual behaviors (e.g., nudity, kissing) occurred an average of 9.3 times per film, and sexual behaviors occurring prior to or during victimization occurred 3.1 times per film (see also Cowan & O'Brien, 1990). Although considerable research attention has been devoted to exploring the extent to which these films may desensitize viewers to aggression and to sexual aggression in particular (see Donnerstein & Linz, 1986; Linz, Donnerstein, & Penrod, 1987), considerably less attention has examined the role that sexual portrayals may play in viewers' enjoyment of these types of movies.

Research that has explored the effects of sexual images on viewers' responses to graphic horror suggests that such portrayals may increase enjoyment, but particularly among male viewers. In one study, Oliver (1994a) assessed enjoyment of a horror film segment that varied whether or not sexual scenes were present prior to portrayals of violence. Whereas sexual scenes had no effect on females' responses to the horror films, males' enjoyment ratings were significantly higher for the sexual than the nonsexual films. Although these results were interpreted, in part, as suggesting that males derive greater enjoyment from viewing sexually explicit portrayals per se, an alternative interpretation may be that males derive greater enjoyment from viewing portrayals of sexualized violence (see also Tamborini, Stiff, & Zillmann, 1987). Clearly, additional research is needed to further examine the appeal of sexualized violence. This is particularly important given that the horror film genre is targeted at and apparently most enjoyed by adolescent viewers who are in the midst of developing their attitudes, beliefs, and behaviors concerning sexuality.

Pornography

The prior discussion of sexual images in the context of horror leads to the final type of entertainment addressed in this chapter, pornography. Although many different terms have been used to refer to this genre (e.g., erotica, adult materials, X-rated content), the word pornography will be employed here very broadly to refer to sexually explicit materials including magazines, books, films, and photographs that are primarily designed to elicit sexual arousal on the part of the consumer.

In terms of one-time or limited exposure to pornographic materials, most research reports minimal gender differences. For example, Bryant and Brown's (1989) extensive review of research concerning the use of pornography reported that the majority of individuals indicated having seen at least some sexually explicit materials (e.g., *Playboy* or *Playgirl*) at some point in their lives. Nevertheless, while males and females may be similar in their one-time exposure to pornographic entertainment, their frequency of exposure tends to show considerable differences. Thompson, Chaffee, and Oshagan (1990) reported that among the college students in their sample, males indicated reading a larger number of sexually explicit magazines than did females and were three times more likely to report watching X-rated movies on video or pay television. Similar findings were obtained by Perse (1994), though her results showed that gender differences in use varied according to the type of pornography in question. Males reported more frequent use of X-rated movies and of most sexually explicit magazines (e.g., *Penthouse*, *Playboy*), whereas females reported more frequent use of *Playgirl* and of erotic books and novels. Despite these variations, males' overall frequency in pornography use exceeded that of females'.

Self-reported frequency of use parallels research concerning males' and females' affective responses to sexually explicit materials. For example, Fisher, Byrne, White, and Kelley (1988) reported significantly higher scores among males than females on the Sexual Opinion Survey, which assesses positive affective and self-reported physiological responses to erotic displays (e.g, "Seeing an erotic movie would be sexually arousing to me," "Almost all erotic material is nauseating"). Furthermore, these authors reported that similar gender differences on this measure have been observed across many different age ranges and in several different countries, including Canada, India, Hong Kong, and Israel. Females' greater disapproval of sexually explicit materials is consistent with numerous surveys that have reported greater perceptions of harm and more support for restrictions of pornographic materials among female than male respondents (Fisher, Cook, & Shirkey, 1994; Gunther, 1995; Lottes, Weinberg, & Weller, 1993).

Despite these general gender differences in reactions to pornography, some researchers have pointed out that erotic materials vary in terms of the types of portrayals that they feature most prominently, and they have suggested that these variations in portrayals may lead to different male and female reactions compared to those commonly observed in the literature (e.g., Quackenbush, Strassberg, & Turner, 1995). For example, Mosher and MacIan (1994) measured college students' affective reactions and subjective sexual arousal in response to sexually explicit films that were either intended for a female audience (i.e., written and directed by women) or for a male audience (i.e., written and directed by men). Although males reported more positive responses (e.g., interest, joy), less negative responses (e.g., shame, disgust), and more sexual arousal overall than did females, males' responses did not differ significantly between film types. In contrast, females' responses on all measures were significantly more favorable in the female-targeted than in the male-targeted film condition. These authors interpreted females' differential responses to the film types as reflecting the relative absence of offensive portrayals (e.g., closeups of genitals) and the inclusion of more intimate portrayals (e.g., discussions of emotions) in the female-targeted movies.

The importance of specific types of portrayals in pornography was also highlighted in Murnen and Stockton's (1997) recent meta-analysis of gender differences in subjective sexual arousal in response to sexually explicit materials. A total of 46 studies were included in their analysis, all of which assessed the self-reported sexual arousal of males and females to explicit portrayals featuring both male and female actors. The results showed that across all studies, males reported significantly higher levels of arousal than did females ($d = .31$). However, this gender difference was significantly larger among those studies that employed stimuli coded as "pornography" (i.e., depicting force, violence, or unequal power; $d = .41$) than among studies employing stimuli coded as "erotica" (i.e., not depicting force, violence, or unequal power; $d = .28$). While the validity of self-report measures as accurate indicators of physiological arousal has been questioned by some researchers (e.g., Heiman, 1977), the results of this study strongly imply that future research on responses to pornography would be well advised to consider the specific types of portrayals that women may find particularly appealing or distasteful.

Summary

Gender differences in response to media entertainment are evident across a variety of genres. This review, while clearly not exhaustive, illustrates the scope and the consistency of the types of content that hold greater and lesser appeal to male versus female audiences. In general, this review suggests that the romantic yet heart-wrenching world of the melodramatic tearjerker belongs to females, whereas the more action-packed and explicit world of sports, violence, and pornography belongs to males. However, this characterization of entertainment in terms of strict dichotomies should not be understood as ignoring the subtleties of portrayals within each genre, nor the variations that exist within same-gender groups. In addition, the demonstration of gender differences in response to media entertainment does not, in and of itself, address why these gender differences may exist. Consequently, the last portion of this chapter explores various possible explanations for why males and females seem to experience the world of entertainment in different ways.

EXPLANATIONS FOR GENDER DIFFERENCES

To suggest that there is any single reason for males' and females' differential response to media entertainment would be simplistic and naive. As with most phenomena, there are likely a host of explanatory mechanisms, all of which probably work together to varying degrees in different situations. However, for purposes of organizational clarity, it is useful to divide this discussion into two sections, the first of which examines possible content-related characteristics that may exacerbate gender differences in reactions and the second that examines viewer-related characteristics associated with differential responses.

Content-Related Characteristics

Because gender differences in reactions are evident across a variety of entertainment contexts, comments concerning content characteristics need to be somewhat general in order to encompass the diversity of entertainment types. However, two content-related characteristics that appear to apply to many, though not all, of the genres discussed in this chapter concern the gender of the characters portrayed in the entertainment programming and the primary nature of the thematic focus on affiliation versus aggressive conflict.

Gender of Media Characters

The importance of perceived similarity to media characters has been noted by many researchers. Hoffner and Cantor (1991) explained that viewers may perceive themselves as similar to media characters on the basis of numerous characteristics, including age, personality disposition, social class, and gender, among others. Furthermore, these authors pointed out that viewers seem to attend more closely to characters who are perceived as similar, and to enjoy watching and to have more intense empathic reactions to similar than to dissimilar characters (see also Feshbach & Roe, 1968).

An examination of several of the genres discussed in this chapter suggests that the gender of the primary media characters typically portrayed may help to explain some of the differences in males' and females' responses. For example, in terms of male-oriented entertainment, content analyses of sports clearly shows that males' athletic events receive greater coverage than do females' events (Tuggle, 1997). Similarly, content analyses of other action-oriented television programming, including prime time police shows and Saturday morning cartoons, also show an overrepresentation of male characters (Oliver, 1994b; Thompson & Zerbinos, 1995). Finally, while content analyses of graphic horror films tend to report an equal number of male and female victims, they also report that more screen time is devoted to the victimization of females than males, and that the killers in these films are most likely to be male (Cowan & O'Brien, 1990; Sapolsky & Molitor, 1996). In terms of female-oriented entertainment, there have been very few analyses of the tearjerker genre discussed in this chapter. However, prototypical examples of these types of films (e.g., *Steel Magnolias*, *Beaches*) suggest that these movies frequently, if not typically, focus on the plights of female protagonists specifically. Consistent with this idea, content analyses of daytime soap operas, the televised counterpart to cinematic melodramas, show significantly larger numbers of female characters in this genre compared to other television entertainment offerings (Gerbner, 1993).

Do these differences in portrayals of male and female characters play a role in viewers' responses to media entertainment? The results here are somewhat mixed. On the one hand, research does support the idea that viewers may notice these differences and more strongly attend and relate to same-sex characters, though this may be more pronounced among male than female viewers (Hoffner, 1996; Thompson & Zerbinos, 1997). On the other hand, research on affective responses to media entertainment featuring male versus female characters has revealed mixed results. For example, Oliver, Weaver, and Sargent (in press) assessed viewers' enjoyment of sad films in three separate studies. In the first two studies, subjects viewed actual films or film segments, and in the last study viewers indicated their anticipated enjoyment of written descriptions of films featuring male versus female protagonists. Responses to the actual films offered some support for the hypothesized importance of the characters' gender, at least among male viewers. Although females reported significantly greater enjoyment of the film featuring females most prominently (*Beaches*), there were no gender differences in enjoyment of the sad film featuring male characters (*Brian's Song*). However, the last study employing written descriptions of films revealed no gender differences in anticipated enjoyment of descriptions featuring male versus female characters.

Mixed results have also been reported in several studies that have examined viewers' enjoyment and distress in response to graphic horror featuring male versus female victims (Oliver, 1993a, 1994b; Tamborini et al., 1987). In general, these studies reported no main effects of victims' gender on viewers' responses, though interactions were obtained between the victim's gender and viewer characteristics such as consumption of pornography and attitudes toward sexuality, particularly among male subjects. Together, these results are somewhat ambiguous concerning the role that gender similarity may play in viewers' responses to entertainment. However, it is important to note that many of these studies have employed only film segments or written descriptions and may therefore not allow the opportunity for viewers to develop a strong emotional relationship with the characters portrayed. Nevertheless, research in this area does appear to imply that the gender of media characters may affect viewers' responses, but in ways that appear to be more complex than in terms of simple similarity to the viewer.

Entertainment Themes

Along with characters' gender, the dramatic themes featured in entertainment may be an additional content-related characteristic that serves to exacerbate differences in males' and females' responses. Although categorizations of dramatic themes could take hundreds of different forms, an examination of the common elements characteristic of "female" versus "male" entertainment suggests a differential focus on themes related to relationships versus themes related to aggressive conflict. Whereas females appear to enjoy dramatic content that most prominently features issues related to intimacy and interpersonal relationships, males appear to enjoy dramatic content that features characters overcoming obstacles, defeating (often violently) their opponents, or demonstrating their domination. Oliver, Weaver, and Sargent (in press) employed this interpretation in their research mentioned previously concerning gender differences in response to sad films. Although the last study employing written descriptions of movies showed little effect of characters' gender on males' and females' anticipated enjoyment, strong viewer gender differences were obtained as a function of the film's theme. When the tearjerker focused on the plight of a paralyzed basketball center, anticipated enjoyment was equal for male and female subjects. However, when the tearjerker focused on a group of friends who suffer heartbreak when one of them develops leukemia, females' enjoyment ratings were significantly higher than were males' ratings. These results, while exploratory, imply that gender differences in response to the female-oriented genre of tearjerkers may not necessarily reflect a strong distaste for relational themes among male viewers, but rather a particular affiliation for these themes among female viewers.

Similarly, gender differences in response to many forms of male-oriented entertainment may not necessarily reflect that females have a strong distaste for conflict per se. Rather, many of the gender differences observed in the literature suggest that males' and females' responses likely reflect differential reactions to the violent images that often accompany displays of conflict. This distinction between conflict and violence is an important one to make, particularly given that many forms of entertainment traditionally associated with female viewers, such as daytime soap operas, contain a great deal of conflict between characters, though not the level of explicit aggression typical of more masculine genres (Sutherland & Siniawsky, 1982).

The idea that it is the violence in male-oriented entertainment that females find objectionable is consistent with many of the studies discussed in this chapter. This idea is particularly evident in the studies pertaining to sports and pornography, where gender differences were substantially smaller when the media content was devoid of explicit portrayals of aggression, physical conflict between individuals, or domination. Females' assumed distaste for violent content may also help explain why males and females appear to have similar thrill-seeking motivations for viewing graphic horror films, but differ in their reactions to the aggressive portrayals that these films display so prominently. If these assumptions are correct, they may imply that females can actually enjoy the experience of fear or suspense elicited by frightening films, but not if the films do so through explicit displays of gruesome violence (see Zillmann & Weaver, 1996). Indeed, the recent popularity of adolescent horror films such as *Scream* among female viewers (Weeks, 1997) suggests that future research would benefit from explorations of both the cinematic elements of related genres that females seem to enjoy and the distinctions that viewers make between horror and other types of frightening or suspenseful entertainment.

Viewer-Related Characteristics

Although the content-related factors briefly discussed in the previous section may help predict when gender differences are most likely to occur, they still lack an explanatory element. That is, attempts to explain males' and females' differential response to horror in terms of violence, for example, still begs the question as to why males and females respond in different ways to violent portrayals. Consequently, the last section of this chapter shifts from a focus on aspects of media portrayals and instead explores what the viewer brings to the entertainment experience. Specifically, this last section considers both biological and gender role approaches.

Biological Approaches

Firmly entrenched in our culture is the idea that most gender differences in behavior and disposition reflect biological distinctions. From nursery rhymes that explain what "boys and girls are made of," to popular psychology claiming that men and women are from different planets, beliefs in seemingly innate differences are widely accepted and celebrated by many people. Similarly, within the social science community, many researchers have employed biological explanations for a variety of behaviors, but particularly for behaviors related to sexuality and aggression.

In terms of sexual behaviors, sociobiological explanations typically stress the differential investment that males and females play in ensuring the survival of their offspring (e.g., Buss, 1989; Buss & Barnes, 1986). From this perspective, given that females make larger physical and time-related investments in child-rearing, it is to their benefit to select a mate who is likely to reliably provide resources for them and their offspring. In contrast, males' lower level of investment implies that it is to their benefit to maximize their number of offspring and to select (multiple) mates who are most likely to be fertile (i.e., young, healthy). As Malamuth (1996) argued, this perspective has clear applications to males' and females' differential responses to pornography. That is, sociobiological approaches would imply a greater male interest in media content that provides a multitude of sexually available "partners," even if only at the level of fantasy. Sociobiological approaches are also consistent with females' seemingly greater appreciation of pornographic materials that more prominently feature displays of affection.

In terms of violent behaviors, most biological explanations of gender differences point out the importance of testosterone in intensifying aggression. Research on both animals and humans suggests that prenatal exposure to testosterone can increase fighting behavior and "rough play," though this effect seems to be more pronounced in animals than in humans (see Hines, 1982). Recently,

Goldstein (1998) employed this biological perspective in his discussion of gender differences in enjoyment of violent video games and aggressive play involving war toys such as guns and action figures. Although Goldstein's discussion did not focus specifically on other forms of violent entertainment featured in films or in television programming, the application of this perspective to other forms of media content is a natural extension of this line of reasoning.

Although biological approaches are consistent with research on responses to a variety of genres, these approaches have been criticized for ignoring the importance of socialization and for "justifying" or making "natural" interpersonal and political oppression (Bleier, 1984). Consequently, it is important to note that many of the theorists who employ such approaches acknowledge that while biological differences may create different behavioral tendencies for males and females, these differences are amplified by cultural factors concerning "appropriate" gender role behaviors.

Gender Role Approaches

Most models of gender role behaviors share the idea that many, if not most, differences in males' and females' behaviors and dispositions are a reflection of culturally prescribed norms. From a cognitive perspective, children's development of gender constancy (the understanding that their gender is stable over time and over superficial changes in appearance) serves as a motivator for them to attend to and imitate same-sex models (Kohlberg, 1966). From a social-learning perspective, gender differences in behavior result from children's observation of same-sex models and from rewards and punishments that often accompany displays of appropriate and inappropriate gender role behaviors, respectively (Mischel, 1966). From both perspectives, gender differences both reflect and perpetuate cultural norms concerning what is appropriate for males and females, and these differences develop over time as children age. This section considers how theories of gender role development may be useful in examinations of (a) viewers' attention to same-sex characters, (b) gender differences in emotional responses to media entertainment, and (c) gender differences in reactions to sexually explicit materials.

Attention to Same-Sex Models.   Using cognitive-developmental models, several studies have explored the idea that, at a very young age, children are more likely to attend to same-sex rather than opposite-sex models. For example, Slaby and Frey (1975) measured children's visual attention to portrayals of pairs of males and females performing various tasks. Among the boys, gender constancy was associated with significantly greater attention to the male models. Girls' attention to same-sex models also increased with gender constancy, but not significantly so. A similar pattern of results was obtained in a more recent study that analyzed the videotaped TV viewing behaviors of 5-year-old children in their homes over the course of 10 days (Luecke-Aleksa, Anderson, Collins, & Schmitt, 1995). Among boys, gender constancy was associated with greater visual attention to male but not female characters.

In addition, parents' diaries of their children's viewing habits showed significantly greater sports viewing among gender-constant boys than among pre-constant boys. These authors speculated that attention to televised portrayals of same-sex characters may be more pronounced for boys than for girls because girls may have greater real-life interaction with same-sex adults (e.g., mothers, teachers, etc.).

These studies concerning attention to same-sex media characters are consistent with gender differences in media preferences, but it would be difficult to maintain the position that gender constancy explains differences in adult male and female responses. Rather, it seems more plausible that the development of gender constancy may lead to early gender differences in media attention, and these early differences may subsequently develop into differential media habits and preferences.

Emotional Responses.   Gender role approaches to media-related behaviors are relevant not only to issues related to attention, but particularly to issues concerning viewers' emotional responses. Specifically, research exploring the sex-typing of emotional displays reports strong and consistent cultural norms concerning appropriate male versus female emotions, many of which parallel gender differences in responses to and enjoyment of media.

Studies concerning sex role stereotyping report that females are believed to be more emotional in general than are males, and that males are more likely to suppress their emotions than are females (Brody & Hall, 1993). However, stereotyping of emotions along gender-linked lines varies according to the specific emotion in question. That is, sadness and fear are more likely to be associated with females than males, and anger and hostility are more likely to be associated with males than females (Birnbaum, Nosanchuk, & Croll, 1980; Shields, 1987). Consistent with these gender stereotypes of emotional displays, surveys of childrearing practices report that parents tend to show greater warmth, to encourage greater empathy, and to expect greater control of anger among their daughters than their sons, and to encourage more competitive behaviors, to tolerate greater aggression, and to more strongly discourage displays of fear and sadness among their sons than their daughters (Block 1973; Garner, Robertson, & Smith, 1997).

Gender differences in emotional responding to entertainment parallel many of these stereotypes concerning emotional displays, and particularly so for females' greater sadness and distress in response to tearjerkers and to frightening films respectively, and males' greater enjoyment of violence and of destructive themes contained within horror. In addition, Zillmann et al. (1986) argued that gender-related expectations concerning emotional displays can also have implications in terms of co-viewing situations. Specifically, these authors argued that violent horror films may be enjoyed by many viewers because they provide the opportunity for males to display their calmness and bravado in the face of danger and for females to display high levels of distress that presumably require male protection. Consistent with this reasoning, these authors found that male subjects' enjoyment of a horror film was greatest when in the company of distressed female co-viewers, whereas female subjects' enjoyment was greatest when their male co-viewers expressed mastery.

Further support for the importance of emotion socialization can be obtained from research concerning children's media preferences. Consistent with models of gender role development, gender differences in responses to media entertainment appear to increase with age. For example, Oliver and Green (1998) found that among older children (ages 7 through 9), girls reported greater sadness and enjoyment in response to scenes from sad movies (i.e., *Lion King* and *Fox and the Hound*) than did boys, but among younger children (ages 3 through 6), gender differences were nonexistent. Similar age differences were obtained by Collins-Standley, Gan, Yu, and Zillmann (1996) who presented preschool children with a series of fairy tale books featuring romantic, violent, and scary stories. Gender differences in book preferences were not present among the youngest children. However, by age 4, girls were significantly more likely than boys to prefer romantic themes, whereas boys were significantly more likely than girls to prefer violent themes.

Responses to Pornography.   In addition to predicting gender differences in emotional displays, gender role models have clear implications for responses to sexually explicit materials. Numerous studies that have examined the sexual double standard report that individuals generally make more harsh judgments of females' than of males' sexuality, and particularly so when the sexual behaviors occur in casual or noncommitted relationships (Garcia, 1982; Sprecher, McKinney, & Orbuch, 1987). These cultural norms concerning the acceptability of male versus female sexuality imply that females should experience less enjoyment of pornography. Not only does this form of entertainment feature an abundance of portrayals of women that are otherwise deemed objectionable, these media portrayals also are presumably intended to arouse sexual feelings that women may associate with social disapproval, at least in some contexts.

Although this interpretation has not received a great deal of formal exploration, Leonard and Taylor's (1983) research offers support for this position. In their study, male subjects viewed a pornographic film with a female confederate who responded in a neutral manner to the film, in a disapproving manner, or in an enthusiastic manner. In a subsequent learning task involving shock trials, males responded most aggressively to the females who showed enthusiasm for the pornography and least aggressively to the females who showed disapproval.

Gender Role Self-Perception

Gender role approaches to understanding males' and females' reactions to media entertainment apply to a variety of genres and viewer responses. However, it is important to note that while cultural norms concerning gender role behaviors are widespread, considerable variation exists in terms of the internalization of such norms. Typically the internalization of gender role norms has been conceptualized along two dimensions, each of which define positive personal attributes (Bem, 1974, 1985; Eagly, 1987). Femininity (also called the communal dimension) consists of qualities such as nurturance, empathy, and emotionality, while masculinity (also called the agentic dimension) consists of qualities such as independence and self-assertion. Although actual gender differences in femininity and masculinity levels tend to mirror cultural expectations, variations exist within and between same-gender groups such that some females report higher levels of masculinity than do males, and some males report higher levels of femininity than do females. Consequently, under some circumstances, an individual's gender role self-perception, or the internalization of masculine and feminine qualities, may be a better predictor of responses to media entertainment than an individual's biological sex.

The importance of gender role self-perceptions has been illustrated in numerous studies, and particularly studies that have examined responses to entertainment that typically elicits strong emotional responses. For example, Oliver (1993b) reported that, controlling for gender, higher levels of femininity were positively associated with greater overall enjoyment and frequency of viewing sad films or tearjerkers. Similarly, Oliver, Sargent, and Weaver (1998) reported that subjects classified as communal (high on femininity, low on masculinity) differed from subjects classified as agentic (high on masculinity, low on femininity) in terms of their greater disturbance and greater enjoyment of a tragic film segment, and in terms of their greater disturbance but lesser enjoyment of a violent film segment. This type of research on gender role self-perceptions suggests that future studies of gender differences in response to media entertainment would benefit from considerations not only of biological sex alone, but also of the extent to which individuals internalize what is thought to be appropriate or acceptable for males versus females.

POSTSCRIPT

It is somewhat odd to end this chapter on gender differences and media entertainment with a suggestion that researchers consider variables other than gender in their studies of males' and females' responses. However, such a suggestion should be understood as illustrating that while gender differences are so widespread and robust that they are often considered obvious, the subtleties involved in these differences and the reasons why they arise are far from simple. Consequently, the he said–she said debate that often occurs in the video rental store should not be seen as a commonplace example of the war between the sexes, but rather a manifestation of the complexities of biological and culture forces that lead her to the melodramas and him to the action adventures.

REFERENCES

Bem, S. L. (1974). The measurement of psychological androgyny. *Journal of Consulting and Clinical Psychology, 42,* 155–162.
Bem, S. L. (1985). Androgyny and gender schema theory: A conceptual and empirical integration. In T. B. Sonderegger (Ed.), *Nebraska symposium on motivation: Vol. 32. Psychology of gender* (pp. 179–226). Lincoln: University of Nebraska Press.

Birnbaum, D. W., Nosanchuk, T. A., & Croll, W. L. (1980). Children's stereotypes about sex differences in emotionality. *Sex Roles, 6,* 435–443.

Blanchard, D. C., Graczyk, B., & Blanchard, R. J. (1986). Differential reactions of men and women to realism, physical damage, and emotionality in violent films. *Aggressive Behavior, 12,* 45–55.

Bleier, R. (1984). *Science and gender: A critique of biology and its theories on women.* New York: Pergamon.

Block, J. H. (1973). Conceptions of sex role: Some cross-cultural and longitudinal perspectives. *American Psychologist, 28,* 512–526.

Brody, L. R., & Hall, J. A. (1993). Gender and emotion. In M. Lewis & J. M. Haviland (Eds.), *Handbook of emotions* (pp. 447–460). New York: Guilford.

Bryant, J., & Brown, D. (1989). Uses of pornography. In D. Zillmann & J. Bryant (Eds.), *Pornography: Research advances & policy considerations* (pp. 25–55). Hillsdale, NJ: Lawrence Erlbaum Associates.

Bryant, J., Comisky, P., & Zillmann, D. (1981). The appeal of rough-and-tumble play in televised professional football. *Communication Quarterly, 29,* 256–262.

Bryant, J., & Zillmann, D. (1983). Sports violence and the media. In J. H. Goldstein (Ed.), *Sports violence* (pp. 195–211). New York: Springer-Verlag.

Buss, D. M. (1989). Sex differences in human mate preferences: Evolutionary hypotheses tested in 37 cultures. *Behavioral and Brain Sciences, 12,* 1–49.

Buss, D. M., & Barnes, M. (1986). Preferences in human mate selection. *Journal of Personality and Social Psychology, 50,* 559–570.

Cantor, J., & Nathanson, A. I. (1997). Predictors of children's interest in violent television programs. *Journal of Broadcasting & Electronic Media, 41,* 155–167.

Cantor, J., & Reilly, S. (1982). Adolescents' fright reactions to television and films. *Journal of Communication, 32*(1), 87–99.

Capwell, A. E. (1998, November). *Chick flicks: An analysis of self-disclosure in female friendships.* Paper presented at the meeting of the National Communication Association, New York.

Choti, S., Marston, A. R., Holston, S. G., & Hart, J. T. (1987). Gender and personality variables in film-induced sadness and crying. *Journal of Social and Clinical Psychology, 5,* 535–544.

Collins-Standley, T., Gan, S., Yu, H. J., & Zillmann, D. (1996). Choice of romantic, violent, and scary fairytale books by preschool girls and boys. *Child Study Journal, 26,* 279–302.

Comisky, P., Bryant, J., & Zillmann, D. (1977). Commentary as a substitute for action. *Journal of Communication, 27*(3), 150–152.

Cowan, G., & O'Brien, M. (1990). Gender and survival vs. death in slasher films: A content analysis. *Sex Roles, 23,* 187–196.

Donnerstein, E., & Linz, D. (1986). Mass media sexual violence and male viewers: Current theory and research. *American Behavioral Scientist, 29,* 601–618.

Eagly, A. H. (1987). *Sex differences in social behavior: A social-role interpretation.* Hillsdale, NJ: Lawrence Erlbaum Associates.

Feagin, S. L. (1983). The pleasures of tragedy. *American Philosophical Quarterly, 20,* 95–104.

Feshbach, N. D., & Roe, K. (1968). Empathy in six and seven year olds. *Child Development, 39,* 133–145.

Fisher, R. D., Cook, I. J., & Shirkey, E. C. (1994). Correlates of support for censorship of sexual, sexually violent, and violent media. *The Journal of Sex Research, 31,* 229–240.

Fisher, W. A., Byrne, D., White, L. A., & Kelley, K. (1988). Erotophobia–erotophilia as a dimension of personality. *The Journal of Sex Research, 25,* 123–151.

Garcia, L. T. (1982). Sex-role orientation and stereotypes about male–female sexuality. *Sex Roles, 8,* 863–876.

Garner, P. W., Robertson, S., & Smith, G. (1997). Preschool children's emotional expressions with peers: The roles of gender and emotion socialization. *Sex Roles, 36,* 675–691.

Gelernter, C. Q. (1996, January 28). Chick guy flicks. *The Seattle Times,* p. L1.

Gerbner, G. (1993). *Women and minorities on television: A study in casting a fate.* Report to the Screen Actors Guild and the American Federation of Radio and Television Artists.

Goldstein, J. H. (1998). Immortal kombat: War toys and violent video games. In J. H. Goldstein (Ed.), *Why we watch: The attractions of violent entertainment* (pp. 53–68). New York: Oxford University Press.

Goodman, E. (1998, May 7). In the new way of chick flicks, a new kind of man. *The Boston Globe*, p. A19.

Gunther, A. C. (1995). Overrating the X-rating: The third-person perception and support for censorship of pornography. *Journal of Communication, 45*(1), 27–38.

Heiman, J. R. (1977). A psychophysiological exploration of sexual arousal patterns in males and females. *Psychophysiology, 14*, 266–274.

Hines, M. (1982). Prenatal gonadal hormones and sex differences in human behavior. *Psychological Bulletin, 92*, 56–80.

Hoffner, C. (1996). Children's wishful identification and parasocial interaction with favorite television characters. *Journal of Broadcasting & Electronic Media, 40*, 389–402.

Hoffner, C., & Cantor, J. (1991). Perceiving and responding to mass media characters. In J. Bryant & D. Zillmann (Eds.), *Responding to the screen: Reception and reaction processes* (pp. 63–101). Hillsdale, NJ: Lawrence Erlbaum Associates.

Johnston, D. D. (1995). Adolescents' motivations for viewing graphic horror. *Human Communication Research, 21*, 522–552.

Kohlberg, L. (1966). A cognitive-developmental analysis of children's sex-role concepts and attitudes. In E. E. Maccoby (Ed.), *The development of sex differences* (pp. 82–173). Stanford, CA: Stanford University Press.

Leonard, K. E., & Taylor, S. P. (1983). Exposure to pornography, permissive and nonpermissive cues, and male aggression toward females. *Motivation and Emotion, 7*, 291–299.

Linz, D., Donnerstein, E., & Penrod, S. (1987). Sexual violence in the mass media: Social psychological implications. In P. Shaver & C. Hendrick (Eds.), *Review of personality and social psychology: Vol. 7. Sex and gender* (pp. 95–123). Newbury Park, CA: Sage.

Lottes, I., Weinberg, M., & Weller, I. (1993). Reactions to pornography on a college campus: For or against? *Sex Roles, 29*, 69–89.

Luecke-Aleksa, D., Anderson, D. R., Collins, P. A., & Schmitt, K. L. (1995). Gender constancy and television viewing. *Development Psychology, 31*, 773–780.

Malamuth, N. M. (1996). Sexually explicit media, gender differences, and evolutionary theory. *Journal of Communication, 46*(3), 8–31.

Mischel, W. (1966). A social-learning view of sex differences in behavior. In E. E. Maccoby (Ed.), *The development of sex differences* (pp. 56–81). Stanford, CA: Stanford University Press.

Molitor, F., & Sapolsky, B. S. (1993). Sex, violence, and victimization in slasher films. *Journal of Broadcasting & Electronic Media, 37*, 233–242.

Mosher, D. L., & MacIan, P. (1994). College men and women respond to X-rated videos intended for male or female audiences: Gender and sexual scripts. *The Journal of Sex Research, 31*, 99–113.

Murnen, S. K., & Stockton, M. (1997). Gender and self-reported sexual arousal in response to sexual stimuli: A meta-analytic review. *Sex Roles, 37*, 135–153.

Oliver, M. B. (1993a). Adolescents' enjoyment of graphic horror: Effects of viewers' attitudes and portrayals of victim. *Communication Research, 20*, 30–50.

Oliver, M. B. (1993b). Exploring the paradox of the enjoyment of sad films. *Human Communication Research, 19*, 315–342.

Oliver, M. B. (1994a). Contributions of sexual portrayals to viewers' responses to graphic horror. *Journal of Broadcasting & Electronic Media, 38*, 1–17.

Oliver, M. B. (1994b). Portrayals of crime, race, and aggression in "reality-based" police shows: A content analysis. *Journal of Broadcasting & Electronic Media, 38*, 179–192.

Oliver, M. B., & Green, S. (1998, April). *Development of gender differences in children's responses to animated entertainment.* Paper presented at the National Association of Broadcasters, Las Vegas, NV.

Oliver, M. B., Sargent, S. L., & Weaver, J. B., III. (1998). The impact of sex and gender role self-perception on affective reactions to different types of film. *Sex Roles, 38*, 45–62.

Oliver, M. B., Weaver, J. B., III, & Sargent, S. L. (in press). An examination of factors related to sex differences in enjoyment of sad films. *Journal of Broadcasting & Electronic Media.*

Perse, E. M. (1994). Uses of erotica and acceptance of rape myths. *Communication Research, 21,* 488–515.

Quackenbush, D. M., Strassberg, D. S., & Turner, C. W. (1995). Gender effects of romantic themes in erotica. *Archives of Sexual Behavior, 24,* 21–35.

Sapolsky, B. S., & Molitor, F. (1996). Content trends in contemporary horror films. In J. B. Weaver III & R. Tamborini (Eds.), *Horror films: Current research on audience preferences and reactions* (pp. 33–48). Mahwah, NJ: Lawrence Erlbaum Associates.

Sargent, S. L., Zillmann, D., & Weaver, J. B., III. (1998). The gender gap in the enjoyment of televised sports. *Journal of Sport and Social Issues, 22,* 46–64.

Schoell, W. (1985). *Stay out of the shower: 25 years of shocker films beginning with* Psycho. New York: Dembner Books.

Shields, S. A. (1987). Women, men, and the dilemma of emotion. In P. Shaver & C. Hendrick (Eds.), *Review of personality and social psychology: Vol. 7. Sex and gender* (pp. 229–250). Newbury Park, CA: Sage.

Slaby, R. G., & Frey, K. S. (1975). Development of gender constancy and selective attention to same-sex models. *Child Development, 46,* 849–856.

Sparks, G. G. (1986). Developing a scale to assess cognitive responses to frightening films. *Journal of Broadcasting & Electronic Media, 30,* 65–73.

Sparks, G. G. (1991). The relationship between distress and delight in males' and females' reactions to frightening films. *Human Communication Research, 17,* 625–637.

Sprecher, S., McKinney, K., & Orbuch, T. L. (1987). Has the double standard disappeared? An experimental test. *Social Psychology Quarterly, 50,* 24–31.

Sutherland, J. C., & Siniawsky, S. J. (1982). The treatment and resolution of moral violations on soap operas. *Journal of Communication, 32*(2), 67–74.

Tamborini, R., & Stiff, J. (1987). Predictors of horror film attendance and appeal: An analysis of the audience for frightening films. *Communication Research, 14,* 415–436.

Tamborini, R., Stiff, J., & Zillmann, D. (1987). Preference for graphic horror featuring male versus female victimization: Personality and past film viewing experiences. *Human Communication Research, 13,* 529–552.

Thompson, M. E., Chaffee, S. H., & Oshagan, H. H. (1990). Regulating pornography: A public dilemma. *Journal of Communication, 40*(3), 73–83.

Thompson, T. L., & Zerbinos, E. (1995). Gender roles in animated cartoons: Has the picture changed in 20 years? *Sex Roles, 32,* 651–673.

Thompson, T. L., & Zerbinos, E. (1997). Television cartoons: Do children notice it's a boy's world? *Sex Roles, 37,* 415–432.

Tuggle, C A. (1997). Differences in television sports reporting of men's and women's athletics: ESPN *SportsCenter* and CNN *Sports Tonight. Journal of Broadcasting & Electronic Media, 41,* 14–24.

Weeks, J. (1997, December 12). "Scream" movies cultivate special audience: Girls. *USA Today,* p. 1A.

Zillmann, D. (1980). Anatomy of suspense. In P. H. Tannenbaum (Ed.), *The entertainment functions of television.* Hillsdale, NJ: Lawrence Erlbaum Associates.

Zillmann, D. (1991). The logic of suspense and mystery. In J. Bryant & D. Zillmann (Eds.), *Responding to the screen: Reception and reaction processes* (pp. 281–303). Hillsdale, NJ: Lawrence Erlbaum Associates.

Zillmann, D. (1998a). Does tragic drama have redeeming value? *Siegener Periodikum für Internationale Literaturwissenschaft, 16,* 1–11.

Zillmann, D. (1998b). The psychology of the appeal of portrayals of violence. In J. H. Goldstein (Ed.), *Why we watch: The attractions of violent entertainment* (pp. 179–211). New York: Oxford University Press.

Zillmann, D., Bryant, J., & Sapolsky, B. S. (1989). Enjoyment from sports spectatorship. In J. H. Goldstein (Ed.), *Sports, games and play: Social and psychological viewpoints* (2nd ed., pp. 241–278).
Hillsdale, NJ: Lawrence Erlbaum Associates.

Zillmann, D., & Mundorf, N. (1987). Image effects in the appreciation of video rock. *Communication
Research, 14,* 316–334.

Zillmann, D., & Weaver, J. B., III. (1996). Gender-socialization theory of reactions to horror. In J. B.
Weaver III & R. Tamborini (Eds.), *Horror films: Current research on audience preferences and
reactions* (pp. 81–101). Mahwah, NJ: Lawrence Erlbaum Associates.

Zillmann, D., Weaver, J. B., Mundorf, N., & Aust, C. F. (1986). Effects of an opposite-gender companion's affect to horror on distress, delight, and attraction. *Journal of Personality and Social Psychology, 51,* 586–594.

13
▼▼▼▼▼▼▼▼

Personality and Entertainment Preferences

James B. Weaver III
Virginia Polytechnic Institute and State University

This chapter examines various media entertainment preferences within the conceptual framework of the psychobiological model of personality developed by H. Eysenck (1947, 1990). First, several commonalities between contemporary mass-media theories and personality theories are highlighted. Next, empirical evidence of linkages between three personality dimensions—psychoticism, extraversion, and neuroticism—and several measures of media entertainment preferences is detailed. Overall, the data provide informative initial sketches of distinctive media-preference profiles for each personality dimension.

PERSONALITY: AN OFTEN IGNORED CONCEPT IN MEDIA RESEARCH

Consideration of the personality characteristics of media audiences has long been recognized as a key component to understanding both the uses and effects of the mass media. Early research, for example, identified numerous unique individual characteristics—such as emotional insecurity (Cantril, 1940); social isolation (Herzog, 1944); intellectual ability (Hovland, Janis, & Kelly, 1953); and "predispositions, group membership, personality patterns, and the like" (Klapper, 1960, p. 251)—that influence preferences for media content and the consequences of exposure.

Building from these initial findings, contemporary theorists have focused considerable conceptual attention on the role of personality characteristics in modern mass communication theory (e.g., Katz, Blumler, & Gurevitch, 1974; McGuire,

1974; Wober, 1986). For example, working within the uses and gratifications paradigm, Rosengren (1974) argued that audience personality characteristics have a pervasive impact throughout the various stages of media selection, use, and consequence. He concluded that the need to incorporate such individual difference factors in media research seems "almost self-evident" (p. 273). More recently, these sentiments were echoed by Palmgreen, Wenner, and Rosengren (1985), who proposed that psychologically rooted individual differences, such as personality characteristics, must be conceptualized as being within "close causal proximity" of any media uses and gratifications model (p. 21). Similarly, Wober (1986), pointing to the necessity of including personality characteristics in media research, has observed that "adequate, let alone, full understanding of how individuals interact with mass media will not be reached without a good account of those individuals' fundamental attributes" (p. 206).

In most personality–media use models, media preferences are conceptualized as reflecting an individual's beliefs about and expectations of both the media and their various content themes (e.g., Conway & Rubin, 1991; Finn & Gorr, 1988; Nolan & Patterson, 1990; Rosengren & Windahl, 1977; Stanford, 1984). Media perceptions, in other words, are attitudes; evaluative judgments summarizing the gratifications that consumers anticipate receiving from their interaction with the media (Palmgreen, 1984). Within this framework, personality characteristics are seen as influencing perceptions of the media via cognitive, affective, and physiological mechanisms (H. Eysenck, 1990; McGuire, 1974; Zuckerman, 1991). Specifically, personality characteristics are conceptualized as the nexus of attitudes, beliefs, and values that guide our interactions with and interpretation of the social environment (cf. Allport, 1937; Blumer, 1969; Marlowe & Gergen, 1969; Mead, 1934). Within this framework—and given that the selection and use of the mass media has become, especially in Western cultures, an integral part of most individuals' social environment (Kubey & Csikszentmihalyi, 1990; Robinson, 1981)—the expectation that personality characteristics should be directly linked to our orientation toward and perceptions of the mass media seems prudent.

Interestingly, although recognition of the potential mediating influence of personality characteristics is a conceptual cornerstone of much mass communication theory, surprisingly little contemporary research has examined this issue (cf. Palmgreen et al., 1985; Webster & Wakshlag, 1983). Palmgreen et al. (1985) concluded, for example, that evidence of "empirical connections between [media] gratifications and their psychological roots" (p. 21) is very limited. Equally important, argues Wober (1986), of the available research many "projects relating patterns of viewing behavior (and other media preferences) to psychological variables have tended to be piecemeal" (p. 211) and often produce inconsistent results.

An illustrative example of this problem is derived from several studies examining graphically violent media presentations. Specifically, a great variety of personality characteristics—sensation seeking (Zuckerman & Litle, 1986), the

Machiavellian trait of deceit (Tamborini, Stiff, & Zillmann, 1987), and "coping style" (Sparks & Spirek, 1988)—have been shown to influence cognitive and affective responses to contemporary horror films. Unfortunately, while it can be intuitively argued that these personality dimensions are intertwined, theoretical and empirical evidence of such commonality is lacking. Indeed, consolidation of these divergent findings has been hampered by the seemingly haphazard manner in which personality variables have been selected and operationalized. Daly (1987) framed this dilemma perceptively:

> Communication research emphasizing personality has had no obvious structure or "master plan" associated with it. Each individual investigator selects his or her favorite trait and proceeds to explore the measurement, manifestations, or consequences of the disposition without much regard for how it fits within some larger domain. (p. 31)

Furthermore, Daly concluded that casting future research within an integrated model of personality was a theoretically critical challenge facing communication scholars (see also Klapper, 1960; Wober, 1986). It was this notion that grasped my intellectual curiosity and fostered the work summarized here.

CONTEMPORARY PERSONALITY THEORY

Most popular ideas about personality, many of which are rooted in antiquity, reflect the transcultural desire of societies and institutions to understand the " 'true' or 'innate' nature of human beings" (Stevenson & Haberman, 1998, p. 3). Distillation of these diverse notions of personality—ranging from the ancient traditions of India (Hinduism) and China (Confucianism) to twentieth-century thinkers such as Freud (psychoanalytical theory) and Skinner (behavioral psychology)—provides much of the conceptual foundation informing modern inquiry (cf. Eysenck & Eysenck, 1985).

Many contemporary theories of personality are built on the pioneering "dispositional model" advanced by Allport (1937). Recognizing the heuristic value of natural language terms, Allport and his colleagues identified more than 18,000 English words they believed described common personality characteristics. Approximately one fourth of these terms—including *friendliness*, *ambitiousness*, *cleanliness*, *enthusiasm*, *shyness*, *talkativeness*—were considered of particular importance because they had the potential "to distinguish the behavior of one human being from another" (Allport & Odbert, 1936, p. 24).

Grounded on a common foundation, most modern dispositional models of personality continue to share two common characteristics (cf. John, 1990). One is the assumption that central dispositions are relatively stable over time and relatively consistent across situations, although an individual's dispositions are not expected to manifest themselves all the time or in every situation (Liebert & Spiegler, 1994). A second shared characteristic concerns the strategy through which the most important or central dispositions on which people can be compared are isolated. Specifically, most contemporary theories of personality have been constructed within hierarchical structural models (John, 1990; Liebert & Spiegler, 1994).

The hierarchical structure in most contemporary dispositional models of personality involves three distinct levels. At the lowest level are "habitual cognitions or behaviors" (Eysenck, 1990, p. 244). These everyday "habits" are conceptualized as specific mental or behavioral responses to social stimuli that an individual experiences and exhibits across a variety of circumstances.

Personality traits are conceived as the next, intermediate level. Personality traits are seen as emerging from sets of habits that are "generalized and personalized determining tendencies—consistent and stable modes of an individual's adjustment to his environment" (Allport & Odbert, 1936, p. 26). For example, if a person is described as "talkative," then several consistent habits—such as always talking to people despite the situation and always having something to say—typically come to mind as underlying such a personality trait.

Predominant personality dimensions are conceptualized at the highest level of dispositional models of personality. Although a variety of labels have been assigned to these personality dimensions—for instance, *central dispositions* (Allport, 1937), *primary factors* (Cattell, 1946, 1990), *supertraits* (McCrae & Costa, 1985, 1987), and *personality types* (Eysenck, 1947, 1990)—theorists agree that they emerge from clusters of personality traits. Eysenck and Eysenck (1985), for example, referred to personality dimensions as second-order factors that reduce "the total complexity of sometimes thousands of intercorrelations to the relative simplicity of a few factors" (p. 19). The notion of personality dimensions, in other words, permits classification of individuals into a small number of distinct groups based on their similarities and differences across several personality trait characteristics.

Of the variety of personality models (cf. John, 1990), the one developed by H. Eysenck (1947, 1990) provides an excellent framework for examining potential interrelationships between personality characteristics and preferences for the mass media contents. Working since the late 1940s with extensive, culturally diverse samples, H. Eysenck demonstrated that numerous personality traits consistently cluster into three essentially orthogonal personality types: *extraversion*, *neuroticism*, and *psychoticism* (cf. Eysenck, 1990; Eysenck & Eysenck, 1985). Equally important, other research (e.g., Zuckerman, Kuhlman, & Camac, 1988; Weaver, 1998) provides considerable validation of H. Eysenck's integrated model and has further illuminated the definition of each of the three personality types.

Two dimensions of H. Eysenck's model are consistent with those isolated in essentially all contemporary disposition-based personality theories (cf. John, 1990). The *extraversion* (E) personality type is conceptualized as tapping trait characteristics such as an individual's level of sociability or social adaptability, affiliation, and positive self-esteem. The *neuroticism* (N) personality type, on the other hand, involves traits such as high levels of anxiety and emotionality, shyness, social isolation, and a negative self-image (cf. Weaver, 1998).

Differing from the other dimensions, and unique to H. Eysenck's conceptualization, the *psychoticism* (P) personality type is defined as accessing traits such as an individual's tendencies toward egocentricity, sensation-seeking, and autonomy (i.e., internal locus of control). More specifically, individuals evidencing the P personality type typically display a high level of social deviance, impulsivity, and "a lack of restraint, responsibility, need for cognitive structure, and willingness to live by society's rules and mores (socialization)" (Zuckerman, Kuhlman, & Camac, 1988, p. 104; see also Richendoller & Weaver, 1994).

Within this framework, we must ask: To what extent does consideration of the personality characteristics exhibited by mass media consumers influence their perceptions of the media and preferences for their contents? More specifically, are there unique profiles of media and content perceptions associated with the three predominant types—extraversion, neuroticism, and psychoticism—emerging from H. Eysenck's (1947, 1990) integrated model of personality? In order to address these questions, several recent studies of the link between personality characteristics and our orientation toward the mass media are examined in the following sections.

PERSONALITY AND MEDIA USE

Over the last decade, considerable empirical attention has been focused on the psychological predictors underlying self-reported television viewing motivations (e.g., Conway & Rubin, 1991; Finn & Gorr, 1988; Perse & Rubin, 1990). Common to all these investigations is the exploration of correlations between responses to the Television Viewing Motives questionnaire developed by Rubin (1981, 1983) and several, often interrelated, personality traits.

The work of Finn and Gorr (1988) provides an informative example of these studies. Specifically, relationships between two constructs isolating TV viewing motives—social-compensation (defined by companionship, pass time, habit, and escape motivations) and mood-management (defined by relaxation, entertainment, arousal, and information motivations), derived via factor analysis and six personality trait measures, including shyness, loneliness, self-esteem, and social-support—were examined. Finn and Gorr found that the traits of self-esteem and social-support were linked positively with the mood-management motive and negatively with the social-compensation motive. Further, they discovered that both shyness and loneliness personality traits correlated positively with the social-compensation viewing motive.

In light of this previous research, it seemed that further examination of various motives for television watching within H. Eysenck's integrated model of personality could prove insightful. To this end, responses to a self-administered questionnaire were obtained from a large sample of undergraduates recruited from a variety of disciplines at a large state university (Weaver, 1999b). Respondents voluntarily completed a broad-ranging questionnaire during the first weeks of two academic terms.

Embedded among other inventories within the "Communication Preferences" questionnaire were both the Television Viewing Motives inventory (TVM; Rubin, 1981, 1983) and a 36-item version of the Eysenck Personality Questionnaire (EPQ-R; S. Eysenck, Eysenck, & Barrett, 1985). A 20-item inventory adapted from Rubin (1981, 1983) was used to assess television viewing motivations. A principal components factor analysis of this TVM inventory yielded a five-factor solution that accounted for 61.6% of the variance. Consistent with Rubin's initial articulation, the factors, in the order of their extraction, were labeled Pass-time, Companionship, Relaxation, Information, and Stimulation. Direct factor scores were then computed for subsequent analyses. Also, as outlined elsewhere (Weaver, Walker, McCord, & Bellamy, 1996), responses to the EPQ-R were transformed to produce a categorical measure that classified each respondent into one of three discrete personality type groups: extraversion (E), neuroticism (N), and psychoticism (P).

As can be seen in Table 13.1, when subjected to a respondent gender by personality analysis of variance, significant differences across the three personality types emerged for four of the five television viewing motive indices. In many ways, the findings are congruous with earlier research examining personality traits such as loneliness and self-esteem. In particular, notice that respondents in the N group—a personality type defined by traits such as emotionality, shyness,

TABLE 13.1
Media Preferences as a Function of Personality Type

Media use preferences	Predominant personality type		
	Psychoticism	Extraversion	Neuroticism
Television Viewing Motives			
Pass time	−0.12a	−0.13a	0.29b
Companionship	−0.08b	−0.23a	0.39c
Relaxation	−0.15a	−0.04a	0.22b
Information	−0.09	0.04	0.03
Stimulation	−0.10a	−0.05a	0.15b
n	284	342	285
Remote Control Device Motives			
Content avoidance	−0.14[a]	−0.02[ab,A]	0.16[b,B]
Viewing satisfaction	−0.01	−0.08	0.01
Control of others	0.13[b]	−0.15[a]	−0.03[ab]
n	153	186	167

Note. Means, which were derived from standardized factor scores, with different superscripts differ at $p < 0.05$ by the Student-Newman-Keuls two-tailed t test. Means with different uppercase superscripts differ at $p < 0.10$.

and social isolation—reported television viewing motives that were consistently positive and substantially different from their counterparts in the E and P groups. Equally interesting is the significant disparity across the personality types on the Companionship television viewing motive. In this instance, respondents in the E group—a personality type defined by traits such as sociability and social affiliation—are those who strongly rejected the notion that television can serve as an adequate substitute for interpersonal interactions.

A similar pattern of findings was discovered by Weaver, Walker, McCord, and Bellamy (1996) in their exploration of links between personality and preferences for television remote control device (RCD) use. The means for three RCD perceptions displayed across the three personality types are included in Table 13.1. As can be seen, respondents in the N group, who strongly endorsed using the RCD to avoid apparently objectionable commercial and program content, differed substantially from those in the P group. Equally important is the considerable divergence between E and P respondents in their perceptions of the RCD as a means to controlling the viewing experience of others. In this case, the sociable Es rejected the notion that the RCD should be used to both annoy and dominate others, whereas the more egocentric, socially deviant Ps expressed strong endorsement.

PERSONALITY AND MEDIA-CONTENT PREFERENCES

The idea that stable and enduring patterns of media-content preferences might emerge from consideration of the demographic and psychological characteristics of the audience is a time-honored tradition within the media industry. Essentially all decisions concerning the success or failure of radio and television programs, for example, are aided by extensive surveys that break down the audience into subgroups defined by respondent sex and age (Beville, 1985). On the other hand, consideration of psychological aspects of audiences—often referred to as "psychographics"—appears to have been of only limited utility (Eastman & Ferguson, 1997). In many ways, the application of psychological characteristics to pragmatic endeavors such as audience analysis has suffered from the same dilemma of haphazard operationalizations articulated above by Daly (1987). Indeed, despite increasing content specialization and audience fragmentation, analysis of the content preferences of media audiences solely on the basis of demographic strata remains the modus operandi for most media organizations.

Some research suggests, however, that consideration of the personality characteristics of an audience can offer considerable illumination of many content preferences (Weaver, 1991; see also Nolan & Patterson, 1990; Stanford, 1984). Weaver (1991), for example, assessed the linkages between extraversion, neuroticism, and psychoticism and preferences for various genres of prime-time television programs, contemporary movies, and popular music. The findings revealed considerable correspondence between the respondents' personality characteristics and their media content preferences. Specifically, respondents scoring high on neuroticism—a personality type defined by traits such as anxiety, emotionality, and social isolation—expressed a strong preference for informative/news television programs and "downbeat" music while tending to avoid more lighthearted comedy and action/adventure fare. Those scoring high on psychoticism, on the other hand, evidenced significantly less interest in comedy offerings but displayed a strong preference for graphically violent horror movies.

Appreciation of contemporary rock music has also been shown to vary as a function of predominant personality characteristics. Robinson, Weaver, and Zillmann (1996), for instance, found that respondents scoring high on P enjoyed "hard" or "rebellious" rock music videos more than did their peers scoring low on P. The reverse pattern was evident for enjoyment of "soft" or "nonrebellious" rock music videos. Persons scoring high on P enjoyed nondefiant rock music less than persons scoring comparatively low on the personality type. In other words, the extent to which individuals viewed themselves as socially deviant and unwilling to live by society's rules and mores was positively related to their enjoyment of rebellious and defiant rock music.

Data from a recently completed investigation (Weaver, 1999a) further illustrate the utility of personality type dimensions in isolating unique patterns of media content preferences within an otherwise demographically homogeneous audience. Responses to a self-administered questionnaire were obtained from a sample of undergraduate volunteers. Collection of the data involved two steps. Initially respondents completed the EPQ-R, which, as noted previously, was then transformed into a categorical variable classifying the respondents into the three discrete E, N, and P personality type groups. In step two, approximately 6 weeks later, respondents completed an "Enjoyment of Music" questionnaire. The questionnaire detailed 13 genres of contemporary music, along with the names of three or four performers that, at the time, exemplified each genre. The genre "adult contemporary" was, for instance, linked with the artists Mariah Carey, Elton John, Take That, and Vanessa Williams. For each musical genre, respondents indicated whether they "loved it" or "hated it" on a rating scale. Principal components factor analysis of these ratings yielded a five-factor solution accounting for 67% of the variance. The five enjoyment-of-music factors were labeled Club music (defined by the "rhythm & blues," "rap," and "dance" genres), Rock music (defined by the "album rock," "modern rock," and "heavy metal" genres), Jazz music (defined by the "jazz," "contemporary jazz," and "reggae" genres), Classical music (defined by the "classical" and "new age" genres), and Popular music (defined by the "country" and "adult contemporary" genres).

The results of a respondent gender by personality type ANOVA computed for each music genre factor are detailed in Table 13.2. Concordant with the findings of Robinson, Weaver, and Zillmann (1996), the evidence at hand reveals that respondents in the P personality type group expressed considerably less enjoyment of Popular music than their E and N counterparts. Lower evaluations of Club

TABLE 13.2
Enjoyment of Music as a Function of Personality Type and Gender

Music genre	Respondent sex	Predominant personality type		
		Psychoticism	Extraversion	Neuroticism
Club	both	0.03b	0.20b	−0.32a
Rock	male	0.19ab	−0.19ab	0.50b
	female	−0.28a	0.13ab	−0.31a
Jazz	both	0.09	−0.06	−0.15
Classical	both	−0.08	−0.04	0.17
Popular	both	−0.49a	0.21b	0.22b
n		44	45	44

Note. Means, which were derived from standardized factor scores, with different superscripts differ at $p < 0.05$ by the Student-Newman-Keuls two-tailed t test.

music are also apparent for individuals in the N personality type group. Evidence that a genre of music typically incorporated into an overtly social activity such as public dancing would be disliked by those respondents most likely to avoid social interactions (cf. Weaver, 1998) appears quite harmonious with the essential thesis advanced in this work.

Further, an observed interaction between respondent gender and personality type in the enjoyment of the Rock music genre illustrates the limited utility of demarcating media content preferences within poorly articulated demographic strata. Both conventional wisdom and previous research (cf. Toney & Weaver, 1994) suggest that, all other factors being equal, respondent gender is a critical determinant of affective reactions to popular music. Typically, males show substantially stronger positive reactions toward rock music than females. Contrary to this generalization, however, the data displayed in Table 13.2 suggest that differences between male and female respondents in the enjoyment of rock music may be contingent on personality type. Indeed, the only clear discrepancy between the genders emerges within the N personality type, where males reported substantially more enjoyment of the Rock music genre than females.

CONCLUSIONS

Consistent with the arguments of others, the data at hand offer considerable support for the notion that "predispositions, group membership, personality patterns, and the like" (Klapper, 1960, p. 251) have a pervasive impact on the perception of the mass media and their contents. More importantly, the evidence at hand illustrates that careful reconsideration must be given to our traditional conceptualization of personality characteristics in mass communication research. At the very least, it appears that the intuitively determined amalgamations of unidimensional personality traits typical in earlier research might fruitfully be replaced by more extensive, integrated models of personality. In particular, the evidence detailed here suggests that adoption of an integrated model of personality in future research could move us much closer to fully understanding the hypothesized proximity between personality and media preferences.

Looking across the various findings reported in this chapter, distinctive profiles of perceptions of the mass media and their content begin to emerge for each personality type. The strong social orientation of individuals reporting extraversion as their predominant personality type appears, for example, to dominate their perceptions of the media. In particular, extraverts resolutely reject notions such as television viewing can provide them with a useful substitute for interpersonal companionship, and the TV remote control device is a handy tool for controlling others. At the same time, however, Es report clear preferences for musical genres (i.e., Popular and Club) that are typically prominent at social gatherings among young adults.

In stark contrast, the profile of media preferences revealed by individuals reporting neuroticism as their predominant personality type is distinguished by a general acceptance of the media, especially television. Perhaps because they suffer substantial anxiety, emotionality, and social isolation, Ns appear to strongly embrace television viewing as a means for passing time and obtaining companionship and stimulation. However, Ns also emerge as seemingly discriminating consumers who endorse the notion that the TV remote control device is a valuable tool for avoiding undesirable television content and express a dislike of styles of popular music normally associated with overtly social activities such as dance clubs.

Displaying a strong tendency toward social deviance and callousness, respondents reporting psychoticism as their predominant personality type appear indifferent toward television but endorse using the TV remote control device to annoy and tease others. Similarly, although they express disdain for "popular" music, Ps appear particularly attracted to media content typically considered to be at the outer limit of social norms (for more elaboration on this point, see chapter 10 by Hansen & Hansen, this volume).

This latter finding highlights an important consideration that must be incorporated in future research. Specifically, although H. Eysenck's three personality types appear to enjoy considerable reliability and validity across divergent cultural, ethnic, religious, and political strata, explication of which behaviors and what media content are socially deviant can vary significantly between cultures. A recent comparison of the movie preferences of American and German audiences as a function of personality type helps to illustrate this point (Weaver, Brosius, & Mundorf, 1993). As might be expected, vignettes of graphically violent films proved particularly appealing to high psychoticism scorers in both cultures. However, a culture by psychoticism interaction also emerged for vignettes of explicitly sexual films. Specifically, high psychoticism Americans expressed a significantly stronger preference for the sexual content than did their low psychoticism counterparts. The opposite pattern was evident for the German respondents. One explanation for this finding is that perceptions of the socially deviant and nonconforming nature of sexually explicit media content differ substantially between the two cultures. Media depictions of sexuality are readily available in Germany, and consequently may have been considered mundane and passé by German respondents. On the other hand, in America, where media content involving unfeigned sexual themes is atypical and often curtailed, the opportunity to consume such materials appears to have been particularly appealing to high psychoticism individuals.

Although the evidence detailed here is informative, some caveats must be acknowledged. There are, for instance, recent alternative conceptualizations of personality that offer well-integrated dispositional models (John, 1990). Prominent among these is the five-factor model advanced by McCrae and Costa (1987). Like its predecessors, the five-factor model incorporates both neuroticism and extraversion as predominant personality dimensions. On this foundation three other personality dimensions—openness, agreeableness, and conscientiousness—were added. Clearly, the potential explanatory utility of this more elaborate personality model must be considered in future research.

The fact that the findings summarized here involve only perceptions of the media and their contents is another limitation. We must be sensitive to the fact that self-reports of "how we feel" about an activity like media use may not provide the most reliable estimates of actual behavior (cf. Zillmann, 1985). With this in mind, direct behavioral assessments should offer considerable potential for future research into the impact of personality characteristics in the various stages of media selection, use, and consequence (cf. Bryant & Rockwell, 1993).

Finally, the potential mediating role of personality characteristics on individuals' attitudes, beliefs, and behaviors toward newer media technologies should not be overlooked. Indeed, while we can only speculate, it seems reasonable to expect that perceptions of the Internet, within each of the three personality types, might parallel those observed in this investigation. For individuals embracing the neuroticism personality type, the desirability of the Internet—with its essentially anonymous and socially safe, user-controlled window on the world—seems readily apparent. Activities such as online courses and chat rooms that minimize the need for direct social interaction with others could prove particularly attractive to N consumers. Conversely, individuals reporting extraversion as their predominant personality type might view the Internet as a potential problem because it can impede opportunities for social engagement. Unfortunately, exploration of these considerations must be left to future research.

REFERENCES

Allport, G. W. (1937). *Personality: A psychological interpretation*. New York: Holt.
Allport, G. W., & Odbert, H. S. (1936). Trait-names: A psycho-lexical study. *Psychological Monographs, 47*(No. 211).

Beville, H. M., Jr. (1985). *Audience ratings: Radio, television, cable*. Hillsdale, NJ: Lawrence Erlbaum Associates.

Blumer, H. (1969). *Symbolic interactionism*. Englewood Cliffs, NJ: Prentice-Hall.

Bryant, J. & Rockwell, S. C. (1993). Remote control devices in television program selection: Experimental evidence. In J. R. Walker & R. V. Bellamy, Jr. (Eds.), *The remote control in the new age of television* (pp. 73–85). Westport, CT: Praeger.

Cantril, H. (1940). *The invasion from Mars: A study of the psychology of panic*. Princeton, NJ: Princeton University Press.

Cattell, R. B. (1946). *Description and measurement of personality*. Yonkers-on-Hudson, NY: World.

Cattell, R. B. (1990). Advances in Cattellian personality theory. In L. A. Pervin (Ed.), *Handbook of personality and research* (pp. 101–110). New York: Guilford.

Conway, J. C., & Rubin, A. M. (1991). Psychological predictors of television viewing motivation. *Communication Research, 18,* 443–463.

Daly, J. A. (1987). Personality and interpersonal communication: Issues and directions. In J. C. McCroskey & J. A. Daly (Eds.), *Personality and interpersonal communication* (pp. 13–41). Newbury Park, CA: Sage.

Eastman, S. T., & Ferguson, D. A. (1987). *Broadcast/cable programming: Strategies and practices*. Belmont, CA: Wadsworth.

Eysenck, H. J. (1947). *Dimensions of personality*. New York: Praeger.

Eysenck, H. J. (1990). Biological dimensions of personality. In L. A. Pervin (Ed.), *Handbook of personality and research* (pp. 244–276). New York: Guilford.

Eysenck, H. J., & Eysenck, M. W. (1985). *Personality and individual differences: A natural science approach*. New York: Plenum Press.

Eysenck, S. G. B., Eysenck, H. J., & Barrett, P. (1985). A revised version of the psychoticism scale. *Personality and Individual Differences, 6,* 21–29.

Finn, S., & Gorr, M. B. (1988). Social isolation and social support as correlates of television viewing motivations. *Communication Research, 15,* 135–158.

Herzog, H. (1944). What do we really know about daytime serial listeners? In P. Lazarsfeld & F. Stanton (Eds.), *Radio research 1942–1943* (pp. 3–53). New York: Duell, Sloan, & Pearce.

Hovland, C., Janis, I., & Kelly, H. (1953). *Communication and persuasion*. New Haven, CT: Yale University Press.

John, O. P. (1990). The "big five" factor taxonomy: Dimensions of personality in the natural language and in questionnaires. In L. A. Pervin (Ed.), *Handbook of personality and research* (pp. 66–100). New York: Guilford.

Katz, E., Blumler, J., & Gurevitch, M. (1974). Utilization of mass communication by the individual. In J. Blumler & E. Katz (Eds.), *The uses of mass communications: Current perspectives* (pp. 19–32). Beverly Hills, CA: Sage.

Klapper, J. T. (1960). *The effects of mass communication*. Glencoe, IL: The Free Press.

Kubey, R., & Csikszentmihalyi, M. (1990). *Television and the quality of life: How viewing shapes everyday experience*. Hillsdale, NJ: Lawrence Erlbaum Associates.

Liebert, R. M., & Spiegler, M. D. (1994). *Personality: Strategies and issues* (7th ed.). Pacific Grove, CA: Brooks/Cole.

Marlowe, D., & Gergen, K. J. (1969). Personality and social interaction. In G. Lindzey & E. Aronson (Eds.), *The handbook of social psychology* (2nd ed., pp. 590–665). Reading, MA: Addison-Wesley.

McCrae, R. R., & Costa, P. T. (1985). Comparison of EPI and psychoticism scales with measures of the five-factor model of personality. *Personality and Individual Differences, 6,* 587–597.

McCrae, R. R., & Costa, P. T. (1987). Validation of the five-factor model of personality. *Journal of Personality and Social Psychology, 52,* 81–90.

McGuire, W. (1974). Psychological motives and communication gratification. In J. Blumler & E. Katz (Eds.), *The uses of mass communications: Current perspectives* (pp. 167–195). Beverly Hills, CA: Sage.

Mead, G. H. (1934). *Mind, self and society*. Chicago: University of Chicago Press.

Nolan, L. L., & Patterson, S. J. (1990). The active audience: Personality type as an indicator of TV program preference. *Journal of Social Behavior and Personality, 5,* 697–710.

Palmgreen, P. (1984). Uses and gratifications: A theoretical perspective. In R. N. Bostrom (Ed.), *Communication Yearbook 8* (pp. 20–55). Beverly Hills, CA: Sage.

Palmgreen, P., Wenner, L., & Rosengren, K. (1985). Uses and gratifications research: The past ten years. In K. Rosengren, L. Wenner, & P. Palmgreen (Eds.), *Media gratifications research: Current perspectives* (pp. 11–40). Beverly Hills, CA: Sage.

Perse, E. M., & Rubin, A. M. (1990). Chronic loneliness and television. *Journal of Broadcasting and Electronic Media, 34,* 37–53.

Richendoller, N. R., & Weaver, J. B. (1994). Exploring the links between personality and empathic response style. *Personality and Individual Differences, 17,* 303–311.

Robinson, J. P. (1981). Television and leisure time: A new scenario. *Journal of Communication, 31,* 120–130.

Robinson, T., Weaver, J., & Zillmann, D. (1996). Exploring the relation between personality characteristics and the appreciation of rock music. *Psychological Reports, 78,* 259–269.

Rosengren, K. E. (1974). Uses and gratifications: A paradigm outlined. In J. Blumer & E. Katz (Eds.), *The uses of mass communications: Current perspectives* (pp. 269–286). Beverly Hills, CA: Sage.

Rosengren, K. E., & Windahl, S. (1977). Mass media use: Causes and effects. *Communications: International Journal of Communication Research, 3,* 336–351.

Rubin, A. M. (1981). An examination of television viewing motives. *Communication Research, 8,* 141–165.

Rubin, A. M. (1983). Television uses and gratifications: The interactions of viewing patterns and motivations. *Journal of Broadcasting, 27,* 37–51.

Sparks, G. G., & Spirek, M. M. (1988). Individual differences in coping with stressful mass media: An activation-arousal view. *Human Communication Research, 15,* 195–216.

Stanford, S. W. (1984). Predicting favorite TV program gratifications from general orientations. *Communication Research, 11,* 519–536.

Stevenson, L., & Haberman, D. L. (1998). *Ten theories of human nature* (3rd. ed.). New York: Oxford University Press.

Tamborini, R., Stiff, J., & Zillmann, D. (1987). Preference for graphic horror featuring male versus female victimization: Personality and past film viewing experiences. *Human Communication Research, 13,* 529–552.

Toney, G., & Weaver, J. B. (1994). Effects of gender and gender-role self-perceptions on affective reactions to rock music videos. *Sex Roles, 30,* 567–583.

Weaver, J. B. (1991). Exploring the links between personality and media preferences. *Personality and Individual Differences, 12,* 1293–1299.

Weaver, J. B. (1998). Personality and self-perceptions about communication. In J. C. McCroskey, J. A. Daly, & M. M. Martin (Eds.), *Communication and personality: Trait perspectives* (pp. 95–117). Cresskill, NJ: Hampton Press.

Weaver, J. B. (1999a). *Personality and the enjoyment of popular music.* Unpublished manuscript, Virginia Polytechnic Institute and State University, Blacksburg.

Weaver, J. B. (1999b). *Individual differences in television viewing motives.* Unpublished manuscript, Virginia Polytechnic Institute and State University, Blacksburg.

Weaver, J. B., Brosius, H. B., & Mundorf, N. (1993). Personality and movie preferences: A comparison of American and German audiences. *Personality and Individual Differences, 14,* 307–315.

Weaver, J. B., Walker, J. R., McCord, L. L., & Bellamy, R. V. (1996). Exploring the links between personality and television remote control device use. *Personality and Individual Differences, 20,* 483–489.

Webster, J. G., & Wakshlag, J. J. (1983). A theory of television program choice. *Communication Research, 10,* 430–446.

Wober, J. M. (1986). The lenses of television and the prism of personality. In J. Bryant & D. Zillmann (Eds.), *Perspectives on media effects* (pp. 205–231). Hillsdale, NJ: Lawrence Erlbaum Associates.

Zillmann, D. (1985). The experimental exploration of gratifications from media entertainment. In K. Rosengren, L. Wenner, & P. Palmgreen (Eds.), *Media gratifications research: Current perspectives* (pp. 225–239). Beverly Hills, CA: Sage.

Zuckerman, M. (1991). *Psychobiology of personality.* Cambridge, England: Cambridge University Press.

Zuckerman, M., Kuhlman, D. M., & Camac, C. (1988). What lies beyond E and N? Factor analyses of scales believed to measure basic dimensions of personality. *Journal of Personality and Social Psychology, 54,* 96–107.

Zuckerman, M., & Litle, P. (1986). Personality and curiosity about morbid and sexual events. *Personality and Individual Differences, 7,* 49–56.

14
▼▼▼▼▼▼▼▼

The Aesthetics of Media Fare

Gerald C. Cupchik
Stephen Kemp
University of Toronto

EVERYDAY AND AESTHETIC STIMULI

A more complete but less lyrical version of this title would be "The aesthetics of media fare versus the pragmatics of media fare." The contrast between aesthetics and pragmatics applies equally to all messages of a visual, auditory, and written nature. Pragmatics is the theme underlying everyday cognition, which uses information to help achieve goals. Everyday messages are "monovalent" (Schmidt, 1982) in the sense that only single meanings are attributed to them. So when you read the newspaper or search the Internet for a review of a book or a movie, or information about your favorite sports team, you are searching for unambiguous facts. The entire organization of information on "the Net" is orchestrated to enable you to access this information quickly and efficiently. While messages might be packaged to look a little more "aesthetic," this only means they are made a little more visually salient in order to attract your attention.

Aesthetic activity is quite different because you are after a kind of experience and are involved in the process. It is intrinsically as opposed to extrinsically motivated; aesthetic activity is valued in and of itself (Berlyne, 1971, 1974). Aesthetic artifacts can also be distinguished from everyday information-oriented materials because they combine both subject matter and style. Subject matter is any kind of factually oriented (i.e., semantic) information about the physical or social world. Style has to do with the way that the physical/sensory qualities (i.e., syntactic information) of a message are organized and affect sensory experience. Moles (1958/1968) has argued that the material elements (i.e., dabs of color, or lines) of a painting are hierarchically organized. The pattern of organization (syntactic information) underlying the arrangement of colors, textures, lines, brushwork, composition, and so on, make up style. At another level, the organization of these material elements can denote objects in geometric space and are referential, thereby providing (semantic) information about subject matter. In a poem, style is embodied in rhyme and meter, whereas in a novel it has to do with the way the story is told. Each medium has its own special array of stylistic qualities, which can be manipulated by artists, authors, directors, and others involved at the creative end of the endeavor.

Research (Cupchik, Winston, & Herz, 1992) has shown that it is easier to discriminate subject matter (still-life versus portrait) than style (impressionist versus realist) and cognitive psychologists have provided a clear account as to why. In everyday life, we use the physical/sensory qualities of perception to identify useful objects and in the process these sensory qualities are discarded (Craik & Lockhart, 1972; Lockhart & Craik, 1990). The Russian Formalists (Shklovsky, 1917/1988) recognized this and argued that in order to have aesthetic experiences we have to "de-automatize" perception and arrest the everyday cognitive habit of focusing on object identification. Artistic creation and appreciation require slowing down the process of perception and reinvesting attention in the structure of physical/sensory qualities (Cupchik, 1992). Each medium has its own special structural qualities and viewers or readers must be patient in order to learn how to discriminate them.

This analysis implies that people in general should respond to subject matter more easily than style because the cognitive bias of everyday life disposes us to identify things. Research has in fact shown that untrained viewers approach artworks in different ways than do experienced viewers (Cupchik & Gebotys, 1988; Winston & Cupchik, 1992). When subjects were instructed to place triads of paintings or sculptures in a "meaningful" order, untrained viewers chose increasing representational accuracy as their criterion, while experienced viewers were more sensitive to stylistic differences (Cupchik & Gebotys, 1988). Similarly, untrained viewers preferred representational works, while trained viewers favored abstract pieces. Untrained viewers also favored works that were reminiscent of everyday life and evoked warm feelings, while experienced viewers preferred more challenging works that had powerful effects (Winston & Cupchik, 1992).

Thus far we have established that aesthetic artifacts in whatever medium combine subject matter and style and that it requires training to notice and critically evaluate stylistic qualities. Now, the word *aesthetics* is usually associated with a combination of beauty and the experience of pleasure. To perceive beauty is to take all the qualities embodied in the subject matter and style of a work and determine how well they balance; this is the classical principle of "uniformity amidst variety" (Hutcheson, 1725) better known as "unity-in-diversity." Accordingly, in a "beautiful" movie or television program, the acting, characters, plot, cinematography, and so on, are individually and collectively successful, thereby creating a harmonious experience. Similarly for a painting, subject matter, tone,

color, texture, line, and composition all work together to create powerful evocative effects. And when we read a short story, the characters, plot, language, images, and so on, entice us into a different world. One special quality of successful artworks, novels, films, and so on, is that they are "multileveled" (Kreitler &
Kreitler, 1972) or "polyvalent" (Schmidt, 1982) and "open" (Eco, 1962/1989) to
continuous interpretation. Each subsequent encounter with a successful work provides an occasion to notice something new, which becomes incorporated into our
more enhanced or deeper appreciation of it. Masterpieces provide this kind of
continuing stimulation. Thus, subjects viewing successful paintings and sculptures (possessing unity in diversity) found them to be more meaningful after a
second encounter (Cupchik, Spiegel, & Shereck, 1996).

This analysis provides a basis for arguing against any kind of comparison between media which seeks to establish that one is more aesthetically meaningful or
valuable than another. Each medium and genre embodies a blend of subject matter and style that can challenge or evoke pleasure. Beauty is therefore inherent in
the overall structure of the work and not in the medium itself. This means that
genres (e.g., opera or novels) and media (e.g., movies or television) cannot in and
of themselves be rank-ordered as more or less beautiful and pleasure giving. So
any analysis of media must incorporate the same principles that are applied to
other kinds of entertainment or cultural artifacts. What differs are the kinds of
subject matter and, in particular, stylistic qualities that are part of the medium.

HIGH AND LOW OR POPULAR CULTURE

However, there have been attempts at this attribution of superiority, as expressed
in the distinction between *High* and *Low* Culture. High Culture is usually associated with traditional museum art and prize-winning literature, whereas Low Culture is embodied in "Trash TV," (soap) operas, escapist films and novels, and so
on. According to Fishwick (1974), High or "elite" culture is "produced by talent-
ed individuals who follow rules . . . which both they and their audience know and
respect. This work is 'private' in that it implies a one-to-one relationship" (p. 2).
Fornas (1995) speculated that High Culture emerged when "the priestly, aristo-
cratic and bourgeois elites withdrew from the formerly communal folk culture
typified by the carnival. Then the bourgeois public sphere was dichotomized in
entertainment versus serious arts" (p. 145). Indeed, High Art artifacts possess
both "authenticity" and an "aura" of originality (Benjamin, 1967). This valuing
of originality led Greenberg (1946/1957) to associate High Art with the avant-
garde. "Retiring from public altogether, the avant-garde poet or artist sought to
maintain the high level of his art by both narrowing and raising it to the expression of an absolute in which all relativities and contradictions would be either resolved or beside the point: 'Art for art's sake' " (p. 99). It was Pascal, writing in
the 1700s, who argued against the hollowness of relaxation and amusement, as-

serting instead that people must learn to "stay quietly in their own chamber" (Lowenthal, 1950/1957, p. 48).

Van Peer (1997) cited the work of Gellner, an anthropologist, who argued that literacy (i.e., reading and writing) in High Culture, required self-discipline both in terms of mental concentration and bodily movements and posture. According to Goody (1986), writing makes it possible to codify ideas and values that will lay down standards of behavior. Thus, High Culture embodies a certain conservative ideological position emphasizing stability in our social system where "there are rules to which most citizens presumably adhere. These are rules for raising children and bringing up the young, for law-abiding conduct and work ethos, for service in the community and for not meddling with others' freedom" (Van Peer, 1997, p. 34).

Low Culture is associated with the lower classes, who are less literate, and is seen as part of a reaction against the demands of "civilized" society for rigor and responsibility. Lowenthal (1950/1957) traced the emergence of popular culture to Montaigne in the 16th century, who argued that people without faith would feel lonely in a postfeudal world. To address this loneliness he advocated diversion, which along with "escape, distraction, entertainment, and, last but not least, vicarious living" (Lowenthal, 1950/1957, p. 48) became a hallmark of the modern age. According to this reasoning, "What we call low culture takes its place within the diversity of such pleasurable activities, forming an antidote against the strains of our responsibilities. It is a reservoir of revitalization, and a rescue strategy for regaining a balance" (Van Peer, 1997, p. 34). A contrast is therefore drawn between the reality testing and challenge of High Culture and the indulgent pleasure of Low Culture.

Not surprisingly, the academic conservatives who favor High Art or Culture write about Popular Art in disparaging terms. Thus, Lowenthal (1950/1957) treated the phenomena of popular culture as "nothing but a manipulated reproduction of reality as it is; and in so doing, popular culture sanctions and glorifies whatever it finds worth echoing" (p. 49). He contrasted the "differences between popular culture and art, between spurious gratification and a genuine experience as a step to greater individual fulfilment. . . . In popular culture, men free themselves from mythical powers by discarding everything, even reverence for the Beautiful" (p. 51). Lowenthal tied popular culture to fascism in the first half of this century: "There is an interdependence between what the public wants and what the powers of control enforce upon the public in order to remain in power" (p. 55). It is here that Popular Culture spills over into Mass Culture and mass capitalism: "in all its media popular culture proves to have its own genuine characteristics: standardization, stereotypy, conservatism, mendacity, manipulated consumer goods" (p. 55).

Greenberg (1946/1957) reduced Popular Culture to kitsch, including "popular, commercial art and literature with their chromeotypes, magazine covers, illustrations, ads, slick and pulp fiction, comics, Tin Pan Alley music, tap dancing, Hollywood movies, etc., etc." (p. 102), and even the "*New Yorker*, which is fundamentally high-class kitsch for the luxury trade" (p. 103). And this is all "a product of the industrial revolution which urbanized the masses of western Europe and

America and established what is called universal literacy" (p. 102). So kitsch is ersatz culture, designed for people who are "insensible to the values of genuine culture" (p. 102); it is mechanical, operating by formulas, providing vicarious experiences and faked sensations.

Scholars who are interested in the British approach to cultural studies have "an appreciative non-judgmental attitude to ordinary tastes and pleasures" (McGuigan, 1992, p. 4). Of course Popular Culture has always been there in the "inherited oral wisdom" of folk cultures passed on in tales, songs, dances, games, and manners (Fishwick, 1974). Fishwick (1974) maintained that "Popular culture is *practice* and *event*-oriented—it leans . . . towards percept, not concept" (p. 6). This emphasis on experience makes it an "everything-all-at-once style" for which "Nothing is too old, too new, too obscure, too banal, too distant, too close" (p. 11). Popular Culture encompasses comic strips and comic books, advertisements, joke cycles, fads, radio and television programs, films, fashion, foods, popular fiction; what Malinowski termed the "imponderabilia" of everyday life (Berger, 1980, p. 16). It represents "an unflinching look at the real world today; a fascination with and acceptance of our mechanized, trivialized, urbanized environment; a mirror held up to life, full of motion and madness. It is rooted in new factors—physical and social mobility, mass production, abundance, anxiety" (p. 9). For the cultural populist, "the symbolic practices of ordinary people are more important analytically and politically than Culture with a capital C" (McGuigan, 1992).

Interestingly, Popular Culture has been related to post-modern discourse (Chaney, 1994). Popular Culture unfolds out of *modernism*, with its faith in progress, technology, and features of the urban world, such as advertising. For Chaney, the community engaged in Popular Culture feels excluded from High Culture and gives voice to these feelings of being marginal (as in many rebellious rock music videos). *Postmodernism* deals with appearances and involves an ongoing reflection on problems of representation, making use of this critical or ironic tone. In fact, "the privileged qualities of postmodernism—parody/pastiche, depthlessness, allegory, spectacular show, and an ironic celebration of artifice—have all been central to the submerged traditions of popular culture" (Chaney, 1994, p. 204). On a critical note, postmodernism loses its impact when its critique becomes overly intellectualized and arbitrary, becoming grounded in the mind of the critic while losing touch with the practices of everyday life.

Popular Culture inevitably becomes tied into Mass Culture, the beneficiary of modernist progress, which yielded the primary vehicles of mass communication, film, television and telecommunication. Marshall McLuhan's reputation was founded on his dictum, "the medium is the message," because television as a medium is different from print in its immediacy and simulation qualities. Alternatively, it can be said that "the medium is the messenger" because of its access to the masses and the immense choices that it offers. Of course those who are sensitive to political and economic issues will argue that this is precisely where culture interfaces with the social structure. In the period immediately following

World War II, social commenters such as Adorno (1950) and Lowenthal (1950/1957) were concerned about the ways that the masses could be responsive to exhortations by authoritarian leaders who provide an aesthetics of ritual to mask their subjugating intentions.

Benjamin (1967) has written about the effects that techniques of mass reproduction (e.g., the photo or lithograph) have on reactions to artworks. Conservative critics see the "contemporary masses" as accepting reproductions as replacements for the real thing (i.e., original artworks) because of a desire to bring objects closer (i.e., into their own home) in order to seek distraction. Chaney (1994) saw Benjamin as proposing that the pressures surrounding mechanical reproduction lead to a politicization of culture. In the postmodern period, Chaney replaced mechanical reproduction with *industries of mass distribution*; the political metaphor turns economic. The early popular interest in spectacular forms of entertainment (i.e., presumably in Greek and Roman times) is recreated because modern technology produces high quality "illusions of simulated reality" (p. 208) for the communication of information and entertainment. A crucial step in his argument is that the technology industry requires "capital investment in cultural production," "complex distribution networks," "enormous advertising budgets," and so on, which produce "pressures of agglomeration." The emergence of "global communication and entertainment corporations will effectively oligopalise mass culture" (p. 209), leading to a emphasis on consensualist values by showing people simulations of normality.

Zillmann and Gan (1998) pointed out that Adorno's (1950) view of music as a commodity ripe for exploitation led to an elitist rejection of whole genres like jazz or popular music, which could be standardized and foisted onto the masses. Instead, they adopted a more favorable view of the effects of mass production of artistic entertainment. Following Shils (1961), they maintained that industrial capabilities and teamwork would yield quality results and an ever increasing diversity of cultural products. According to the principles of *saturation marketing* (Epstein, 1994), the market success of groups with particular sounds leads to imitations and a saturated market that in turn encourages the development of a novel style. In this way, the profit motive actually stimulates creativity and innovation.

These contrasting views of massification can be reconciled. On the one hand, technological development facilitates both the creation and distribution of cultural artifacts. The shift from acoustic to electric guitar had a significant effect on the development of rock 'n' roll music. Similarly, electronic synthesizers make it possible to create new sounds that can be integrated with visual and virtual images. Culture progresses when these tools are used by local artists/musicians as part of their development. The distribution of these successful artifacts is facilitated by shifts from vinyl, to eight-track, cassette, CD, the Internet, and so on. Other artists/musicians who like what they see/hear may follow suit and a new genre or style emerges. As in all paradigm changes, innovation will take place when the implications of the style are used up.

On the other hand, when the distribution takes over, then companies seek to create taste groups in order to market their products. An unpleasant example of this process is embodied in the case where a company first decides on the little figures that will be marketed to children and only then creates the cartoon characters and story lines that give the figures life. Clearly, the cart (laden with advertising and product sales) comes before the creative horse. This is what Fornas meant when he argued that "subsuming work under capital increases its productive efficiency while making it instrumental, goal-oriented and technocratic, which produces problematic sides effects for human beings" (1995, p. 143).

RECONCILING THE NOTIONS OF HIGH, POPULAR, AND MASS CULTURE

It is best to begin by recognizing that "all dichotomies of high/low or art/popular culture are sociohistorical constructions" (Fornas, 1995, p. 145) and these distinctions can be blurred. With increased urbanization and an affirmation of the intellectual freedom of authors (e.g., the Goncourt brothers) and artists (e.g., Impressionist, Postimpressionist, Fauvist, and so on), High Culture incorporated elements of everyday life. For example, in a reaction against Academic painting, which favored classical and heroic motifs, French Realists like Courbet and Daumier introduced community and "low" life themes. The Impressionist painters who followed them created artworks that were originally seen as unfinished in style and trivial in theme; today they are "priceless."

" 'Serious' culture, the kind of culture which becomes canonised as 'art,' has always refreshed itself from the springs of popular culture, as the Russian formalists pointed out many years ago with their idea of 'the canonization of the junior branch' " (McGuigan, 1992, p. 3). Marshall McLuhan has underscored the tendency of High Culture to be permeated by "low-brow" culture, as reflected in the modernist work of James Joyce. On the other hand, beautiful works of art and crafts have been produced in poor and "primitive" societies around the world since the time of the cave dwellers of southern France. And even the most famous playwrights have been guilty of creating banal and sentimentalized plots of no great aesthetic merit. Thus, the complementary relations between High and Popular Culture must be acknowledged.

The distinction between High and Low Art can be profitably reconsidered to reveal complementary processes of creation and reception without recourse to social class analysis and the negative connotations implied by it. A neutral way to talk about a High work of art, literature, or television show for that matter, is to say that it must be understood in relation to works that preceded it. Thus, an original work extends or transforms a style that came before it. Being able to describe and explicate this transformation is a task for good critics, who can place a work in the context of what went before. In addition, original stylistic transformations do not reside in individual works of art (or literature), but rather are inferred from the shared qualities (i.e., family resemblance) underlying a set of works by a single artist (author) or by a group.

Now, the ability to discriminate an original development can apply both to the choice of subject matter, as in the mid-19th-century realistic/romanticized depiction of working-class families and urban settings, as well as to stylistic developments, a highly recognizable one being the emergence of impressionism. Artists (authors) who are part of the new wave are best able to locate original developments within the broad sweep of cultural progress. This skill at discriminating stylistic developments is comparable to learning to read a new visual or literary code. It is the code that is crucial and this should not be confused with literacy per se as in the sense of being able to read. This broader understanding of aesthetic literacy thus permits pre-scientific and illiterate cultures to contribute in a meaningful way to High Art and Culture.

While an appreciation of High Art and literature can be associated with an "effort after meaning" (Bartlett, 1932) or a need for interpretive challenge (Winston & Cupchik, 1992), responses to Low or Popular media forms can be related to a need for pleasure. In the latter case, the work is experienced and understood associatively in relation to ongoing events in the recipient's life. For this reason, music, film, literature, and so on, evoke emotional associations and extend beyond the work to the personal context. The focus of the recipient is not on the work itself in relation to what went before, but actually lies in the person's subjective experience. Challenge would only serve to confuse things, but more challenging rock music videos are more accurately recognized (Cupchik & Saltzman, 1999). Thus, music from the 1960s, which is so dear to the hearts of the aging professoriate, may seem remote to the undergraduates of today for whom music is frequently attached to videos as well as to their current experiences. Gans (1974) has similarly drawn a contrast between a focus on the creator of an artifact and its construction in High Culture and the products of lower culture, which are oriented to the recipient.

In the 20th century, the contrast between high and low culture has had an analog in approaches to literary criticism (Cupchik & Leonard, 1997). New Criticism assumed a correct interpretation of text and an objective reader. It sought to isolate the text; the intention of the author, the opinion of the reader, the time in which the text was written, the relationship to other texts, all were deemed irrelevant. By providing the literary critic with a claim to objectivity, the study of literature could assume equal standing to that of scientific knowledge (T. S. Eliot, 1932/1975). Thus, as in the case of science, there were rules to be learned, and then a strict application of these rules to a controlled field of evidence, secure from the "static" of such irrelevancies as opinion, emotion, politics, history, culture, and ideology. The vagaries of emotion, opinion, politics, history, and ideology, and well as psychological factors such as desire and the unconscious, were excluded.

In contemporary literary theory, the idea of the correct way to read a text has been replaced by a variety of critical approaches and New Criticism is now considered but one of them. The alternative reader-response approach focuses on the reader—not the text or the author—and locates the organizational structure that generates meaning or an interpretation as one occurring first within the reader, before being projected onto the text (Holland, 1975). At the same time, the text is presumed to set some limits on the capacity of the reader to project credible interpretations upon it. Iser notes that all texts have indeterminacies and gaps, and it is filling in these gaps where the act of interpretation takes place (Iser, 1978). Fish (1980) argues that the critic uses the interpretation of a given text as an occasion to communicate and interrogate the meaning-making conventions or interpretive strategies of a given community. In this way, history, ideology, and culture become a part of the equation as well, and suddenly the interpretation of an advertisement or a music video becomes as profound as a reading of Shakespeare. Cultural Studies enters the discussion by viewing all signifying texts as cultural artifacts and by insisting that the cultural context of the work must be taken into account with no distinction of High Culture from Low Culture (Leonard, 1993).

In summary, the notion of High Culture should not be attached to particular media, genres, or even styles, but rather to a challenging way of thinking about and understanding works as transformations of those that came before. A sophisticated analysis of developments in jazz or rock 'n' roll is comparable to similar analyses of opera, classical music, painting, and so on. Popular Culture, on the other hand, should be understood in the context of ongoing social and self processes that produce pleasure and arousal. These experiences and the factors that are responsible for them are very much restricted to the particular era within which they were developed. This analysis implies that one and the same aesthetic work can be understood either in relation to those that went before or in terms of the collective emotional experiences of pleasure and excitement that it evokes. It also implies that recipients can shift between challenge and pleasure orientations across episodes and even toward the same artifact.

REFLECTION AND REACTION

We have discussed High Culture in relation to originality and Popular Culture in relation to pleasure and excitement at particular times in history. But instead of originality, let us say we wanted to figure out the meaning of the piece and ask questions like "Why is it happening?" or "What's really going on here?" or simply "What does this piece mean?" The focus is on the stimulus end of the stimulus/response cycle; the stimulus is seen against the background of the response. These kinds of questions imply that somehow works of art, literature, and so on, are related to our social worlds, both reflecting them and informing us about them. When reflecting on the meaning of art, literary, and other works we must rely on our own experiences with the social world to help construe or imagine an-swers to these questions (Cupchik, 1995).

Reflection is a process whereby we bring to bear our own life experiences in the effort after meaning. Emotional stories (Cupchik, Oatley, & Vorderer, 1998) and even smells (Herz & Cupchik, 1995) evoke personal emotional memories. A criterion of *coherence* (Iser, 1978) is used to determine whether one's interpreta-tion handles all that is going on in the story, work of art, and so on. This process accommodates the idea that interpretive activity is open-ended and that works al-ways provide for additional interpretation (Cupchik, Spiegel, & Shereck, 1996). For this reason, reflection is part of a dynamic process and need never come to a complete end. People reread books (Cupchik, Leonard, Axelrad, & Kalin, 1998) and view films a second or third time to achieve even higher levels of integration.

But what happens when pleasure or excitement are the main reasons for en-tering aesthetic episodes? The focus is on the response against the stimulus back-ground in the stimulus/response cycle. In this case, if we want to achieve a par-ticular kind of pleasure or excitement, we go in search of stimuli embodying just the right quality that can manipulate the response. Thus, if we want to feel some kind of sentimental emotion, we find an appropriate romantic film and soap opera, or for the high-minded, a particular opera with just the right theme. And if we want a jolt of excitement, then a spy novel, rock concert or CD, or a porno-graphic film might do the trick. If a particular stimulus property alters (i.e., co-varies with) a particular dimension of emotional response, then we have a very behavioral kind of process going on. Now, behavioral processes in everyday life obey certain rules pertaining to principles such as stimulus generalization, habitu-ation, and so on, so the same rules should apply to reaction-driven aesthetic in-volvement. Works that bear a family resemblance to the one we like should sim-ilarly alter pleasure or arousal (stimulus generalization) and the repeated viewing of a work should diminish its evocative effects (habituation). It is important to re-member that if stimuli are chosen because of particular qualities, then the overall meaning of the work is not addressed.

In summary, if the meaning of the work is our focus, then past emotional ex-periences with similar characters or contexts should be brought to bear in the in-terpretive process as we swim through the multilayered stimulus. If the experi-ence of pleasure or excitement/calm is our goal, then particular kinds of stimuli are sought out and behavioral principles apply. There is therefore a trade-off be-tween rich interpretation and precise focus on affective dimensions of response. You can't have them both.

MATCHING AND MODULATION

The notions of *matching* and *modulation* have to do with the attachment and choice that people have regarding different forms of culture and entertainment. Matching takes place when a person prefers a work that expresses or mirrors his or her mood and emotional state. When a work "matches" the recipient's mood, it permits a feeling to emerge that is located within the self. This is the familiar process of catharsis that is central to psychodynamic theory and can be related to the notion of *projection* as expressed by the personality theorist Frank (1939) and the art historian Gombrich (1960). The work should be personally meaningful and the person should like it but does not have to be consciously aware of the hedonic tone of the piece. Modulation refers to a process whereby the person selects a work with the specific purpose of altering his or her mood or emotional state. When the person sets out to change his or her mood, the emotional tone of the work is important and the locus of the emotion is attributed explicitly to the piece and in fact can be compared with the state of the viewer.

Zillmann (2000; Bryant & Zillmann, 1984) has discussed *mood management*, the hedonistic premise of which sounds very much like a combination of the reactive model described here in conjunction with a mood modulation strategy. Accordingly, hedonistic motivation governs spontaneous entertainment choices; bad moods should be short-lived and their experiential intensity diminished, while good moods should be extended and their intensity enhanced. Bryant and Zillmann (1984) have shown, for example, that bored viewers and those under acute stress chose stimulating and unexciting programs, respectively. Similarly, high stress levels may lead to a preference for comedy viewing and decreased news consumption (Anderson, Collins, Schmitt, & Jacobvitz, 1996). Consistent with ideas underlying the reactive model, viewers who were apprehensive about crime avoided semantically relevant dramas that focused on violence (Wakshlag, Vial, & Tamborini, 1983).

Zillmann (2000) also cited data that is supportive of the reflective model in conjunction with mood matching. For example, O'Neil and Taylor (1989) found that acutely angry men became more involved in violent television programs if they believed that they would have a chance to eventually retaliate against the perpetrator of their anger; the violence of the show resonated with their anger. Under the theme of "misery loves company," Zillmann (2000) discussed the preference for love-bemoaning music. One aspect of Zillmann's theorizing that is relevant to the mood-matching model comes from his broad treatment of the empathy concept, encompassing the facilitative effects of motor mimicry, empathic reactions learned through stimulus-sensation linkages, and deliberate empathy in the form of perspective-taking mediated by focused cognitive efforts. The central part of this thesis concerns positive affective dispositions toward characters that foster empathic reactions and negative dispositions that inhibit them. This necessitates that authors and playwrights ensure that "respondents must be made to care about characters, either in a positive or in a negative way" (Zillmann, 1995, p. 48). Spectators can then respond to the characters as if they were friends or enemies from everyday life and accordingly invoke empathy or counter-empathy as a generalization of everyday experience. The match then works backwards with empathy for a positive character helping to modify the recipient's own emotional state.

More direct support for the dynamics underlying the matching concept comes from Scheff (1979), who has offered a theory of identification that links the concept of catharsis with that of aesthetic distance (Bullough, 1912). According to Scheff, a properly constructed drama enables spectators to come into contact with repressed emotions, but with sufficient distance that they are not overwhelmed. A "balance of attention" is created by the script, enabling spectators "to be both participants in, and observers of, the dramatic scenes" (p. 155). Playwrights and authors achieve this kind of "controlled identification" in part by making characters attractive embodiments of ideal values (e.g., intelligent, courageous), who are similar to members of the audience. Authors also use "awareness control," whereby the audience is "included in shared awareness with one or more of the characters, while one or more of the other characters are being excluded" (p. 157). Thus, when literary structure and meaningful emotions find each other under safe circumstances, catharsis occurs and the audience (and society) is better for it.

This brings up the whole issue of the viewer/reader's stance relative to aesthetic materials and events. First, the viewer/reader is expected to engage in a "suspension of disbelief," knowingly entering the imaginary world of aesthetic objects and events, and applying appropriate codes so as to understand the subject matter and style. Second, the recipient can personalize the event, searching for private memories that resonate to the narrative in the work. It is here that aesthetic distance enters into the process, with *overdistancing* (i.e., no personal relevance) leading to boredom and *underdistancing* (i.e., too personally relevant) leading to avoidance. Thus, in a study on responses to paintings that depicted solitary figures, "lonely" subjects found the works to be personally meaningful but focused on the style rather than the subject matter, which touched too closely on their own isolated lives (Cupchik & Wroblewski-Raya, 1998). Third, the recipient can adopt an ironic stance by appreciating the meaning embedded in layers of satire and purposeful use of symbolism. The recipient adopts the viewpoint of the artist/author with reference to the hidden meaning of the piece. In this manner, creative people who live under authoritarian regimes can circuitously engage in criticism of the government. Not surprisingly, Russian and Eastern European political humor achieved great heights.

SYNTHESIS

We have introduced a series of juxtapositions in this chapter that can be woven together into two coherent ways of relating to aesthetic and media stimulus events. High and Low Culture were divorced from individual artifacts, uncoupled from any notion of social class, and redefined in process terms. An orientation toward High Culture requires approaching artifacts intellectually and appreciating them in relation to ones that came before. The concern is not with this or that individual work, but rather with the qualities embodied in a series of works that represent transformations of earlier styles. This more objective orientation is related to New Criticism but it bears emphasizing that learning codes, visual or acoustic, should not be tied to literacy in a traditional sense. An orientation toward Popular Culture is more subjective, temporally defined, and involves personal associations, usually of an affective nature. For this reason, individual works can acquire evocative power because they resonate with a person's life experiences.

The contrast between reflective and reactive ways of approaching aesthetic and media events was understood in relation to the stimulus/response cycle. In the reflective approach, an emphasis is placed on an aesthetic stimulus against the background of the recipient's personal, emotional experiences in the lived world. The goal is to cover the unique meaning embedded in a single work of art, literature, film, and so on. Because the work is understood to be multilayered, the challenging interpretive process is open-ended and is facilitated by bringing to bear personal experiences with comparable themes. This helps the recipient construe possible meanings of the work. In the reactive approach, the stress is on the recipient's responses, addressing personal, affective needs by purposefully selecting aesthetic and media events that resolve desires for pleasure, stimulation, calm, and so on. This reactive process is distinctive because the work is examined in a more superficial way such that only the need-resolving qualities are focused on and behavioral principles, such as habituation, govern the stimulus–response relationship. An inverse relationship between richness of understanding (reflective process) versus precision of need satisfaction (reactive process) is very much in evidence here.

The matching versus modulation analysis concerns processes that shape preferences and the selection of artifacts and events. The matching process involves selecting works that express the recipient's mood and provide for the catharsis of pent-up emotion. This spontaneous activity involves an attachment to the perceived meaning of the work and can take place only when the work is not threatening. The liking of a particular work may not be accompanied by a conscious awareness of its mood. In contrast, the modulation process reflects an intentional attempt to change mood states by engaging a work that reduces states of tension or boredom. We would not expect the recipient to be in the mood embodied in the work. Thus, matching tends to be a spontaneous process, whereas modulation is engaged in purposively.

A clear link can be established between High Culture, reflection, and matching as modes of engaging media and aesthetic events. The High Culture work tends to be more multilayered and attracts a more reflective approach to speculate about its meaning. In doing so it engages the recipient at more levels of the personal and historical self. This apparent focus on the work provides a means for the individual to project personal meanings onto it in an unselfconscious manner and makes it possible to select works that match the recipient's mood. The High Culture-reflection-matching combination provides a route for the expression of emotion.

The alternative relationship involves Popular Culture, reaction, and modulation as modes of engagement. The Popular Culture work is salient and novel in the historical moment, thereby drawing attention. The salience of the work may be one-dimensional or easily analyzed so that recipients can readily understand it. In this way, bodily feelings of pleasure and excitement or calm can be experienced more easily than the deeper emotions evoked by complex works. When the features of a work are salient relative to the dimensions of bodily response, it is also easier to select works that modulate mood states. These kinds of contingencies make for a more superficial relationship between aesthetic appreciation and personal response. The Popular Culture-reaction-modulation combination facilitates the transformation of feelings.

In summary, this chapter has attempted its own version of unity-in-diversity based on the notion that different psychological theories can be seen as appropriate for different circumstances. One line of theorizing touches on the problem of finding meaning both in works of art, literature, media, and so on, and in one's own life. It is argued here that the two ways of finding meaning are intimately related in the aesthetic context. A second line of theorizing is more sensitive to bodily states and desires, which can be accommodated by different kinds of aesthetic and media stimuli. Not surprisingly, the principles of behaviorism seem to apply here.

And still we are left with a tantalizing paradox. Although the aesthetic attitude of the revolutionary artist may focus on the development of original style, the door is open for the seemingly accidental selection of subject matter. How convenient that sensual desires might be sublimated by the depiction of nudes in the Baroque or Rococo styles. Conversely, when attention is paid to the accurate rendering of the subject (a figure) in a sculpture, emotion might unconsciously and inadvertently leak out when the artist powerfully squeezes the soft clay. The complementary relations between these two constellations, High Culture-reflection-matching and Popular Culture-reaction-modulation, remain to be explored.

REFERENCES

Adorno, T. (1950). A social critique of radio music. In B. Berelson and M. Jarowitz (Eds.), *Reader in public opinion and communication* (pp. 309–316). Glencoe, IL: Free Press.

Anderson, D. R., Collins, P. A., Schmitt, K. L,. & Jacobvitz, R. S. (1996). Stressful life events and television viewing. *Communication Research, 23*, 243–260.

Bartlett, F. C. (1932). *Remembering: A study in experimental and social psychology*. Cambridge, England: Cambridge University Press.

Benjamin, W. (1967). The work of art in the age of mechanical reproduction. In H. Arendt (Ed.), *Illuminations* (pp. 217–251). New York: Schocken Books. (transl. by Harry Zohn)

Berger, A. A. (1980). *Television as an instrument of terror: Essays on media, popular culture, and everyday life*. New Brunswick, NJ: Transactions Books.

Berlyne, D. E. (1971). *Aesthetics and psychobiology*. New York: Appleton-Century-Crofts.

Berlyne, D. E. (1974). *The new experimental aesthetics: Steps toward an objective psychology of aesthetic appreciation*. Washington, DC: Hemisphere.

Bryant, J., & Zillmann, D. (1984). Using television to alleviate boredom and stress: Selective exposure as a function of induced excitational states. *Journal of Broadcasting, 28*(1), 1–20.

Bullough, E. (1912). 'Psychical distance' as a factor in art and as an aesthetic principle. *British Journal of Psychology, 5*, 87–98.

Chaney, D. (1994). *The cultural turn: Scene-setting essays on contemporary social history.* London: Routledge.

Craik, F. I. M., & Lockhart, R. S. (1972). Levels of processing: A framework for memory research. *Journal of Verbal Learning and Verbal Behavior, 2,* 671–684.

Cupchik, G. C. (1992). From perception to production: A multilevel analysis of the aesthetic process. In G. C. Cupchik and J. Laszlo (Eds.) *Emerging visions of the aesthetic process* (pp. 83–99). New York: Cambridge University Press.

Cupchik, G. C. (1995). Emotion in aesthetics: Reactive and reflective models. *Poetics, 23,* 177–188.

Cupchik, G. C., & Gebotys, R. J. (1988). The search for meaning in art: Interpretive styles and judgments of quality. *Visual Arts Research, 14,* 38–50.

Cupchik, G. C., & Leonard, G. (1997). The two "I's" of the aesthetic process. In L. Dorfman, C. Martindale, D. Leontiev, G. C. Cupchik, V. Petrov, & P. Machotka (Eds.), *Emotion, creativity, and art* (pp. 81–100). Perm, Russia: Perm Institute of Culture.

Cupchik, G. C., Leonard, G., Axelrad, E., & Kalin, J. (1998). The landscape of emotion in literary reception: Generating and receiving interpretations of James Joyce. *Cognition and Emotion, 12*(6), 825–847.

Cupchik, G. C., Oatley, K., & Vorderer, P. (1998). Emotional effects of reading excerpts from short stories by James Joyce. *Poetics, 25,* 363–377.

Cupchik, G. C., & Saltzman, M. (1999). Recognition memory for serious and light rock music videos. *Empirical Studies of the Arts, 17*(1), 59–72.

Cupchik, G. C., Spiegel, S., & Shereck, L. (1996). Unity in the diversity of aesthetic response. *Visual Arts Research, 22,* 1–10.

Cupchik, G. C., Winston, A. S., & Herz, R. S. (1992). Judgments of similarity and difference between paintings. *Visual Arts Research, 18,* 36–49.

Cupchik, G. C., & Wroblewski-Raya, V. (1998). Loneliness as a theme in painting. *Visual Arts Research, 24*(1), 65–71.

Eco, U. (1989). *The open work.* Cambridge, MA: Harvard University Press. (original work published 1962)

Eliot, T. S. (1975). Tradition and the individual talent. In F. Kermode (Ed.), *Selected Prose* (pp. 37–44). London: Faber and Faber. (original work published 1932)

Epstein, J. S. (1994). Misplaced childhood: An introduction to the sociology of youth and their music. In J. S. Epstein (Ed.), *Adolescents and their music: If it's too loud, you're too old* (pp. xiii–xxxiv). New York: Garland.

Fish, S. (1980). *Is there a text in this class? The authority of interpretive communities.* Cambridge, MA: Harvard University Press.

Fishwick, M. (1974). *Parameters of popular culture.* Bowling Green, KY: Bowling Green University Press.

Fornas, J. (1995). *Cultural theory and late modernity.* London: Sage.

Frank, L. K. (1939). Projective methods for the study of personality. *The Journal of Psychology, 8,* 389–413.

Gans, H. J. (1974). *Popular culture and high culture: An analysis and evaluation of taste.* New York: Basic Books.

Gombrich, E. H. (1960). *Art and illusion: A study in the psychology of pictorial representation.* Princeton, NJ: Princeton University Press.

Goody, J. (1986). *The logic of writing and the organization of society.* Cambridge, England: Cambridge University Press.

Greenberg, C. (1957). Avant-garde and kitsch. In B. Rosenberg and D. W. White (Eds.), *Mass culture: The popular arts in America* (pp. 98–110). New York: The Free Press of Glencoe. (original work published 1946)

Herz, R. S., & Cupchik, G. C. (1995). The emotional distinctivenss of odor-evoked memories. *Chemical Senses, 20,* 517–528.

Holland, N. (1975). *Five readers reading.* New Haven, CT: Yale University Press.

Hutcheson, F. (1725). *An inquiry into the original of our ideas of beauty and virtue.* London: D. Midwinter and others.

Iser, W. (1978). *The act of reading.* Baltimore, MD: Johns Hopkins University Press.

Kreitler, H., & Kreitler, S. (1972). *The psychology of the arts.* Durham, NC: Duke University Press.

Leonard, G. (1993). Joyce and advertising. *James Joyce Quarterly, 30.4/31.1,* 573–592.

Lockhart, R. S., & Craik, F. I. M. (1990). Levels of processing: a retrospective commentary on a framework for memory research. *Canadian Journal of Psychology, 44,* 87–112.

Lowenthal, L. (1957). Historical perspectives of popular culture. In B. Rosenberg and D. W. White (Eds.). *Mass culture: The popular arts in America* (pp. 46–58). New York: The Free Press of Glencoe. (original work published 1950)

McGuigan, J. (1992). *Cultural populism.* New York: Routledge.

Moles, A. (1968). *Information theory and esthetic perception* (J. E. Cohen, Trans.). Urbana: University of Illinois Press. (original work published 1958)

O'Neil, E. C., & Taylor, S. L. (1989). Status of the provoker, opportunity to retaliate, and interest in video violence. *Aggressive Behavior, 15,* 171–180.

Scheff, T. J. (1979). *Catharsis in healing, ritual, and drama.* Berkeley, CA: University of California Press.

Schmidt, J. S. (1982). *Foundations for the empirical study of literature.* Hamburg, Germany: Helmut Buske Verlag.

Shils, E. (1961). Mass society and its culture. In N. Jacobs (Ed.), *Culture for the millions? Mass media in modern society* (pp. 1–27). Princeton, NJ: Van Nostrand.

Shklovsky, V. (1988). Art as technique. In D. Lodge (Ed.), *Modern criticism and theory* (pp. 16–30). New York: Longman. (Original work published 1917)

Van Peer, W. (1997). "High"/"low" cultural products and their social functions. *Empirical Studies of the Arts, 15*(1), 29–39.

Wakshlag, J., Vial, V., & Tamborini, R. (1983). Selecting crime drama and apprehension about crime. *Human Communication Research, 10,* 227–242.

Winston, A. S., & Cupchik, G. C. (1992). The evaluation of high art and popular art by naive and experienced viewers. *Visual Arts Research, 18,* 1–14.

Zillmann, D. (2000). Mood management in the context of selective exposure theory. In M. E. Roloff (Ed.), *Communication yearbook 23,* pp. 103–123.

Zillmann, D. (1995). Mechanisms of emotional involvement with drama. *Poetics, 23,* 33–51.

Zillmann, D., & Bryant, J. (1994). Entertainment as media effect. In J. Bryant & D. Zillmann (Eds.), *Media effects: Advances in theory and research* (pp. 437–461). Hillsdale, NJ: Lawrence Erlbaum Associates.

Zillmann, D., & Gan, S. L. (1998). Musical taste in adolescence. In D. J. Hargreaves & A. C. North (Eds.), *The social psychology of music* (pp. 161–187). Oxford, England: Oxford University Press.

Author Index

Subject Index